Social Anthropology

Robert Redfield

Social Anthropology
Robert Redfield

edited by
Clifford Wilcox

With an introduction by the editor

Transaction Publishers
New Brunswick (U.S.A.) and London (U.K.)

> GN21.R33 A3 2008
> 0134112408l5
> Redfield, Robert,
>
> Social anthropology
>
> c2008.
>
> 2008 11 13

Copyright © 2008 by Transaction Publishers, New Brunswick, New Jersey.

All rights reserved under International and Pan-American Copyright Conventions. No part of this book may be reproduced or transmitted in any form or by any means, electronic or mechanical, including photocopy, recording, or any information storage and retrieval system, without prior permission in writing from the publisher. All inquiries should be addressed to Transaction Publishers, Rutgers—The State University of New Jersey, 35 Berrue Circle, Piscataway, New Jersey 08854-8042. www.transactionpub.com

This book is printed on acid-free paper that meets the American National Standard for Permanence of Paper for Printed Library Materials.

Library of Congress Catalog Number: 2007045402
ISBN: 978-1-4128-0694-7
Printed in the United States of America

Library of Congress Cataloging-in-Publication Data

Redfield, Robert, 1897-1958.
    Social anthropology / Robert Redfield ; Clifford Wilcox, editor ; with an introduction by the editor.
        p. cm.
    Includes bibliographical references and index.
    ISBN 978-1-4128-0694-7
    1. Redfield, Robert, 1897-1958. 2. Anthropologists—United States—Biography. 3. Anthropologists—Mexico—Biography. 4. Ethnology—Mexico. 5. Mexico—Social life and customs. I. Wilcox, Clifford, 1956- II. Title.

GN21.R33A3 2008
301.092—dc22   2007045402
[B]

To Michelle, for her unfailing belief in me

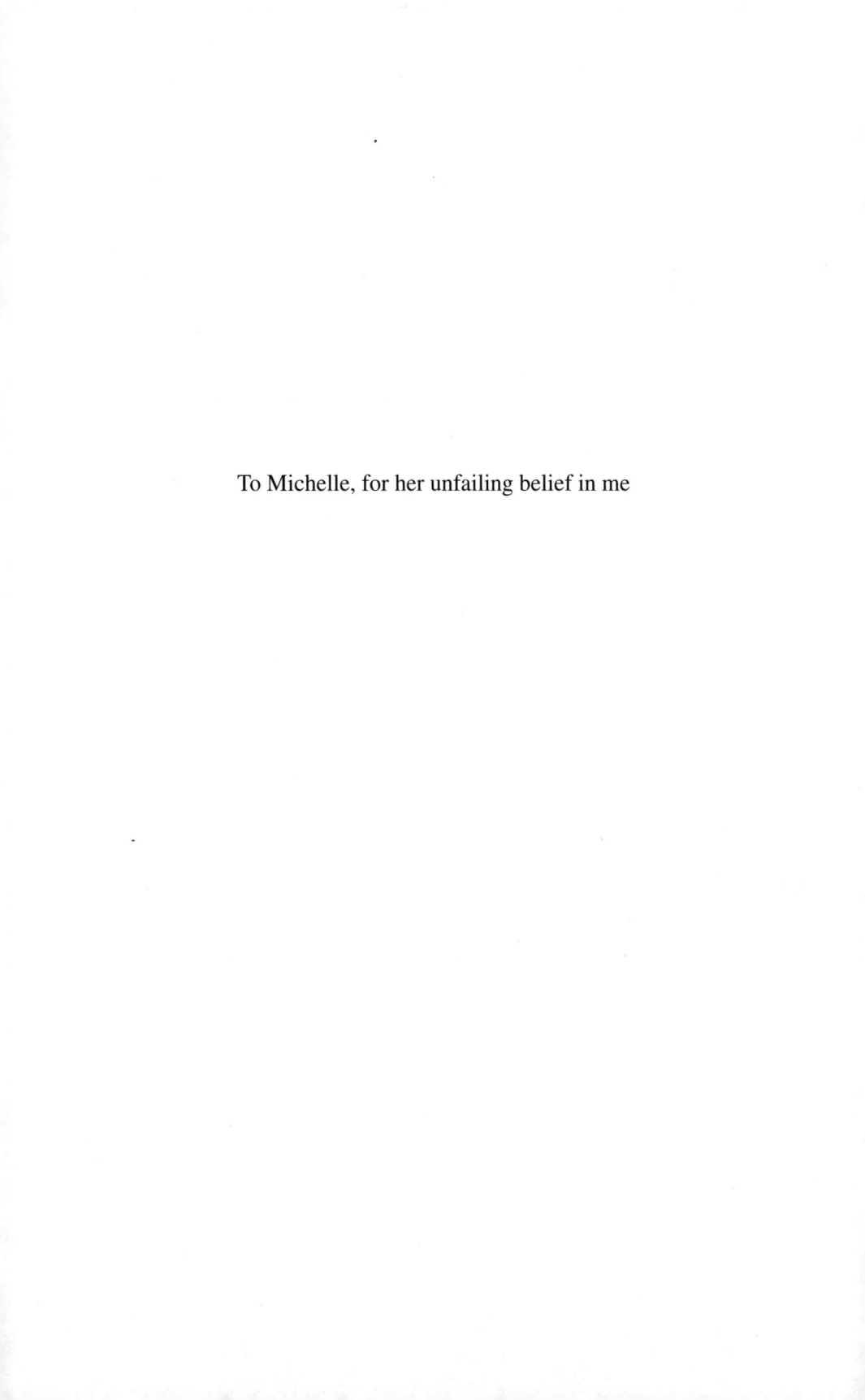

Contents

Acknowledgments ix

Introduction by Clifford Wilcox xiii

PART I MODERNIZATION

1. Anthropology, A Natural Science? 3

2. Among the Middle Americans 13

3. A Note on Method 17

4. The Mexican Folk 25

5. Sociological Investigation in Yucatan 35

6. Robert E. Park to Robert Redfield, 23 January 1932 39

7. Culture Changes in Yucatan 43

8. The Folk Culture and Civilization 57

9. The Folk Society and Culture 85

10. The Folk Society 97

PART II   PEASANTS

11. The Intermediate Community — 123

12. Introduction to *St. Denis: A French Canadian Parish* — 129

13. Later Histories of the Folk Society — 135

14. Peasantry: Part Societies — 157

PART III   COMPARATIVE STUDY OF CIVILIZATIONS

15. The Villager's View of Life — 177

16. The Primitive World View — 195

17. The Social Organization of Tradition — 207

18. The Cultural Role of Cities — 227

19. Civilizations as Cultural Structures? — 253

Selected Bibliography — 265

Index — 271

Acknowledgments

In the process of preparing this text, I have been assisted by numerous individuals in a variety of different ways. I have profited greatly by the careful and critical readings that Richard Cándida Smith and John S. Gilkeson, Jr. provided for both the introductory essay and several related preliminary papers. I am most grateful for their astute criticism and commentary. I also want to acknowledge my wife, Michelle Azimov, who has repeatedly made time where none existed in order to read chapters and sections and provide me the ear and critical perspective of the educated general reader.

In addition, I want to acknowledge the kind assistance provided to me by Robert Redfield's literary heirs, James M. Redfield, Lisa Redfield Peattie, and Joanna Redfield Gutmann. They have encouraged and assisted me from my earliest efforts in researching and writing on the development and influence of Redfield's ideas. And for this volume, they each waived royalty rights associated with republication of his essays. For this gesture, I want to express my sincere appreciation. I also want to express appreciation for the kind assistance I received in relation to republication of Redfield's works from Perry Cartwright of the University of Chicago Press and Stephanie Munson of Cornell University Press.

Finally, I want to acknowledge the support and interest in this project provided by Irving Louis Horowitz, chairman of Transaction Publishers. His commitment over the course of several decades to publishing both new and classic works in social science has greatly enriched the academic reading public. His support, coupled with the assistance of the editorial staff at Transaction Publishers, has made preparation of this book a pleasure.

* * *

Permission granted by copyright holders for the following pieces is gratefully acknowledged:

"Anthropology, A Natural Science," reprinted from *Social Forces* 4 (June 1926): 715-721; reprinted by permission of the University of North Carolina Press. "Among the Middle Americans," reprinted from *University of Chicago Magazine* 20 (March 1928): 242-247; reprinted by permission of the University of Chicago Magazine. "A Plan for the Study of Tepoztlán, Morelos," reprinted from "A Plan for the Study of Tepoztlán, Morelos," Ph.D. diss., University of Chicago, 1928), 1-10; reprinted by permission of James M. Redfield; "The Mexican Folk," reprinted from *Tepoztlán, A Mexican Village: A Study of Folk Life* (Chicago: University of Chicago Press, 1930), 1-14; reprinted by permission of the University of Chicago Press. "Sociological Investigation in Yucatan," reprinted from *Carnegie Institution of Washington, Year Book* 30 (Washington, D.C.: Carnegie Institution of Washington, 1931), 122-24; reprinted by permission of the Carnegie Institution of Washington. Robert E. Park to Robert Redfield, 23 January 1932; reprinted with permission of James M. Redfield and the Special Collections Research Center, University of Chicago Library. "Culture Changes in Yucatan," reprinted from *American Anthropologist* 36 (January-March 1934): 57-69; reprinted by permission of the University of California Press. "The Folk Culture and Civilization," reprinted from *The Folk Culture of Yucatan* (University of Chicago Press, 1941), 338-369; reprinted by permission of the University of Chicago Press. "The Folk Society and Culture," reprinted from *American Journal of Sociology* 45 (March 1940): 731-742; reprinted by permission of the University of Chicago Press. "The Folk Society," reprinted from the *American Journal of Sociology* 52 (January 1947): 293-308; reprinted by permission of the University of Chicago Press. "The Intermediate Community," reprinted from *Tepoztlán, A Mexican Village: A Study of Folk Life* (University of Chicago Press, 1930), 217-223; reprinted by permission of the University of Chicago Press. Introduction to *St. Denis: A French Canadian Parish* by Horace Miner (University of Chicago Press, 1939), xiii-xix; reprinted by permission of the University of Chicago Press. "Later Histories of the Folk Society," reprinted from *The Primitive World and Its Transformations* (Cornell University Press, 1953), 26-53; reprinted by permission of Cornell University Press. "Peasantry: Part Societies," reprinted from *Peasant Society and Culture: An Anthropological Approach to Civilization* (University of Chicago Press, 1956), 23-39; reprinted by permission of the University of Chicago Press. "The Villager's View of Life," reprinted from *The Folk Culture of Yucatan* (University of Chicago Press, 1941), 110-131; reprinted by permission of the University of Chicago Press. "The Primitive World View," reprinted from *Proceedings of the American Philosophical Society* XCIV (1952): 30-36; reprinted by permission of the American Philosophical Society. "The Social Organization of Tradition," reprinted from *Peasant Society and Culture: An Anthropological Approach to Civilization* (University of Chicago Press, 1956), 40-59; reprinted by permission of the University of Chicago Press. "The Cultural Role of Cities," reprinted from *Economic Development and Cultural Change* 3 (October 1954): 53-73; reprinted by permission of the University of Chicago Press. "Civilizations as Cultural Structures," reprinted from *The Papers of Robert Redfield: Human Nature and the Study of Society*, vol. 1, ed. Margaret Park Redfield (University of Chicago Press, 1962), 392-401; reprinted by permission of the University of Chicago Press.

Introduction

The 1920s proved to be a remarkable decade for American anthropology. The field, which had emerged only recently as a university discipline, produced a cohort of students who would not only profoundly shape the field itself, but also exert influence as public intellectuals for decades to come. Among these noteworthy students of the 1920s were Margaret Mead, Ruth Benedict, Melville Herskovits, and Robert Redfield. Mead, Benedict, and Herskovits all studied with Franz Boas, and each of them stands as a distinguished interpreter of Boas and extender of his legacy.[1] Redfield stands as distinct in this group, however, as not being a student of Boas. Indeed, from his early career as a graduate student, Redfield defined himself in opposition to some of Boas's central principles. While he clearly accepted the basic tenets of Boasian anthropology, in particular the strictures against racist interpretations popular through much of the nineteenth century, Redfield argued that Boas's efforts to rid anthropology of all evolutionary notions had gone too far. Certainly much of the evolutionary thinking common to nineteenth-century anthropology reflected shameless racist ideologies, Redfield admitted, but evolutionary thinking in and of itself was not necessarily racist and could be used to bring needed theoretical scope to the emerging discipline, especially in relation to the study of social change. Redfield devoted his own studies from his earliest graduate work through his entire career toward exploring the processes of social transformation, particularly the transformation from less developed to complex societies, and as such served as one of the primary formulators of American social anthropology.[2]

Redfield's work gained wide attention and stimulated much discussion not only while he was alive, but also for almost two decades following his death. Reading his work provides insight into many of the primary debates that shaped American anthropology during the mid-twentieth century, the period of greatest growth and transformation for the discipline. More important, though, reading Redfield's work has relevance for us today. His work provides a powerful example of the value and proper conduct of social science. His writings demonstrate clear engagement with relevant social issues yet reflect necessary distance and objectivity. He shows by example that social science has a moral dimension and, when done properly, has the potential to elevate practitioners and readers in the same manner as humanistic scholarship. His eloquent explorations of the nature and consequences of modernity, moreover, stand as important contributions to a long and continuing discussion.

Finally, both his scholarship and institutional achievements in comparative civilizations studies represent a signal accomplishment in the effort to define a cosmopolitan outlook within American scholarship and society. Redfield spoke often of the "dialogue of civilizations," and as such held fast to the notion that members of the great civilizations had much to teach each other and, indeed, needed to reach out and communicate for the very survival of the planet. He expressed skepticism over official policies that fostered xenophobic attitudes among Americans as the Cold War heated up in the 1950s, and his writings suggest that he would have little tolerance for today's pessimistic "clash of civilizations" notion. His work demonstrates, instead, the power of connections between cultures and civilizations and thus offers a valuable corrective in today's discourse over the interactions among and destinies of the world's major civilizations.

Redfield's Ideas and Influence: An Overview

Robert Redfield (1897-1958) earned his doctorate in sociology and anthropology at the University of Chicago in 1928. From the inception of the university in 1892 through the 1920s, anthropology and sociology constituted a single department. Although this arrangement resulted in part merely from administrative convenience, it exercised important intellectual consequences, especially upon Redfield. Throughout the 1920s, students could choose to concentrate in one field or another, but all were required to take several courses in common. Redfield, more than his colleagues, chose to pursue both fields with equal intensity. He formally identified himself as an anthropologist, but he developed a cross-disciplinary methodology through his training at Chicago that resulted in his adopting a pronounced sociological approach to anthropology.

Two primary factors shaped Redfield's intellectual development: (1) the deep-seated critique of civilization that emerged among European and American intellectuals following World War I and (2) his father-in-law, University of Chicago sociologist Robert E. Park. Throughout the

Victorian era and up to the outbreak of war in 1914, Western intellectuals thought of themselves in highly self-congratulatory terms and widely regarded Western civilization to represent the apex of achievement in refinement and sophistication. Yet the violence and raw national hatreds unleashed by the war shattered this easy confidence, and writers and intellectuals throughout the West began to question the nature not only of Western civilization, but of civilization itself, particularly the equation of civilization with progress. Over the course of the 1920s, such writers as F. Scott Fitzgerald, Oswald Spengler, T. S. Eliot, and Edward Sapir wrote withering critiques of Western Civilization. Redfield, who had spent several months in the ambulance corps in France during World War I and had been frankly horrified by what he had seen in the war, came of age intellectually reading the postwar novelists and poets, and their critical view of the effects of civilization on culture held a powerful sway over his thinking for years to come.[3]

The second powerful influence shaping Redfield's thinking stemmed from his close relationship with his father-in-law Robert E. Park. It was Park who had encouraged him to return to the university to pursue a Ph.D. in social science after he had already earned a law degree. And it was Park who through frequent conversations with Redfield, both verbal and written, helped Redfield shape his intellectual agenda for the first fifteen years of his career. Park was one of the principal theorists of the first generation of American sociologists and stands as one of the major architects of what came to be known as the "Chicago School" of sociology. His formal academic training was in philosophy; he first earned a B.A. under John Dewey at the University of Michigan, then an M.A. under William James at Harvard, and finally, a Ph.D. in Germany, studying first with Georg Simmel at Berlin and finishing under Wilhelm Windelband at Heidelberg. Park derived from his philosophical studies a keen interest in the structure of knowledge. He was anxious to define the relationships between the various new disciplines that had emerged in American higher education during the late nineteenth century and wanted, in particular, to formalize the position of sociology as the premier field in the new social sciences. Park labored vigorously to distance academic sociology from its former association with social work and so-called "uplift efforts." From Windelband, Park derived the notion that the human sciences could be divided into two distinct branches, the idiographic, characterized by a focus on historical and cultural particulars, and the nomothetic, which focused on elaboration of causal law-like explanations.[4]

Redfield's agenda can be seen as an attempt to push in the same nomothetic direction that Park had defined for sociology. In particular, he was interested in using anthropology to study a single issue, the process of social change, or as he termed it, the process of transformation from culture to civilization. The empirical study of social change constituted a primary focus of attention for Chicago sociologists during the early decades of the twentieth century, but few anthropologists had made it the object of systematic research. Redfield believed, however, that anthropologists could contribute much to the study of social change, especially through their ethnographic methods of community study. He committed himself, therefore, to reorienting anthropological methods to study phenomena previously considered almost exclusively by sociologists. His efforts in cross-pollinating anthropology with sociology proved foundational for the development of American social anthropology.

In order to understand Redfield's interest in the empirical study of social change, it is necessary to examine this issue within the larger context of the development of Chicago sociology during the first few decades of the twentieth century. Consideration of social change itself, of course, was not unique to the Chicago sociologists. This preoccupation had been central in the works of virtually all nineteenth-century sociologists. These earlier thinkers had considered social change, however, on a largely theoretical level. The grand theories of development advanced by such sociologists as Herbert Spencer, Ferdinand Tönnies, and Emile Durkheim rested upon a mixture of historical analysis and conjecture rather than empirical research. The Chicago sociologists, especially the generation of W. I. Thomas and Robert E. Park, recognized that despite many earlier claims to scientific status, sociology had by the early twentieth century still not become a scientific discipline. Thomas, Park, and their associates dedicated themselves accordingly to transforming American sociology from a theoretical exercise to an empirical science.[5]

Between 1915 and 1925, Thomas, Park, and their colleague Ernest Burgess developed an empirical process for studying the process of social change that consisted of close characterization of a group or community within the city of Chicago that was undergoing rapid change. Usually, this meant studying a group of recent immigrants to the city. Redfield, guided largely by Park, suggested that an alternative, possibly superior, approach would be to study a small community lying just on the border of industrial civilization and to observe the changes ongoing in such a society. Redfield had traveled in Mexico before enrolling in graduate school, and he had been struck by the level of changes sweeping through post-revolutionary Mexico. Accordingly, he proposed that for his dissertation research he study a Mexican village, one that lay close within the influence of industrial civilization, to try to develop a deeper understanding of the general process of social change.[6]

Anthropology was best suited for study of such traditional villages, Redfield argued, through its intimate ethnographic methods of community study. Yet he announced in the introduction to his dissertation that he did not intend to conduct a conventional ethnographic study. Instead, his would be a study that used anthropological technique to gather data, but a sociological framework in which to interpret the data. He attempted here, especially, to distinguish his work from that of Franz Boas and his students. Boas had used community studies, he argued, merely as a means of documenting dying cultures and resisted attempts, furthermore, to draw broader generalizations from case studies. Redfield advocated that community studies be undertaken, instead, specifically for the purpose of developing general or nomothetic explanations of social and historical processes.[7]

Redfield conducted fieldwork for his dissertation from November 1926 to July 1927. Accompanied by his wife and two small children, he lived in the town of Tepoztlán, Mexico and conducted an ethnographic survey of the village, taking specific note of how Tepoztlán was losing the characteristics of a traditional village and becoming more like a modern town. After returning to the United States, he spent the next year writing up his results, submitting his completed account in 1928 as his dissertation. Upon completion of his dissertation, he accepted a position as an assistant professor of anthropology at the University of Chicago, where he was to remain his entire career. He published his study of Tepoztlán in 1930, unmodified except for the introduction as *Tepoztlán, A Mexican Village: A Study of Folk Life*.[8]

Tepoztlán was well received by both popular and scholarly critics, and it served to gain Redfield national renown as one of the most promising of the second generation of academic American anthropologists. He displayed striking originality in his account of this small village that lay 45 miles outside the metropolis of Mexico City. Contrary to other anthropologists of the period, his work did not portray village life in a timeless state, in what has come to be known as the "ethnographic present." Other anthropologists wrote about primitive villagers, Redfield observed, as if they existed outside of time. He wanted, on the contrary, to write these people back into time, indeed to show that their seemingly static way of life was being subtly transformed by forces from without. Tepoztecans, in his depiction, were an "intermediate" or "folk" people caught in the middle of the "general type of change whereby primitive man becomes civilized man, the rustic becomes the urbanite."

A haunting sense of transition pervades his text. His chapters form a series of vignettes, each describing a particular aspect of village life. He begins each chapter as if the life he is describing were timeless. Yet he concludes almost every chapter with the suggestion that the system or pattern just described is on the cusp of change. Early in the text, he proposes that Tepoztecans can be divided into two types: *tontos*, or "ignorant" ones who represent the majority of the people, and *correctos*, or the few self-conscious members of the intelligentsia. The distinction between these two social psychological types, one inward-looking and tradition-bound, the other outward-looking and directed toward modernity, anticipated Robert Merton's later distinction between "locals" and "cosmopolitans." Redfield alluded to the spreading influence of the secularizing, rationalizing *correctos* whenever he spoke of the creeping change apparent in the village. And in the final two chapters, "The Folk in the City World" and "The Intermediate Community," he explicitly developed his characterization of the Tepoztecans as transitional people, marginal figures caught between tradition and modernity.[9]

Yet, despite Redfield's extensive discussion in *Tepoztlán* of the process of social change, his study failed to deliver on its promise of providing fundamental processual generalizations. His study operated, in sum, largely on the descriptive rather than analytical level. Following completion of *Tepoztlán*, Redfield launched a much more ambitious comparative study of several Mexican villages and towns that he hoped would provide data to support broad generalizations about the process of modernization. With generous funding obtained from the Carnegie Institution of Washington, Redfield and a small team of investigators initiated in 1932 a set of four community studies on the Yucatan peninsula. Specifically, the project consisted of the comparative study of a tribal village (Tusik), peasant village (Chan Kom), small town (Dzitas), and city (Mérida). Mérida is the only city in Yucatan, and it is located in the upper northwest portion of the peninsula; Dzitas, Chan Kom, and Tusik lie in an arc extending progressively southward from Mérida. Redfield's design for this study represented an attempt to use controlled community studies to examine the processes involved in transformation of tribal villages into towns and towns into cities.

Ideally, a study of this process would be conducted through observation of a single village over an extended period of time. Because transformation of a village into a town or town into a city requires decades or centuries, this experiment realistically defies completion. Redfield attempted to get around this time limitation, however, by manipulating experimental variables to simulate the effect of passing time. He had made the simple observation that as one travels southward out of Mérida toward the rainforest, located along the southeast coast of the peninsula, each town or village appears progressively more primitive. Driving from the modern city of Mérida down to the primitive village of Tusik in the rainforest produced the effect, therefore, of passing through discrete cultural zones, of driving backwards into time. By allowing space or distance from Mérida to substitute for the passage of time, Redfield attempted to create the illusion that he was actually observing the transformation of a single village into a town and then city. His four community studies would represent, in short, a series of still sociological photographs that depicted intermediate stages in the process of a single transformation.[10]

The Yucatan studies occupied Redfield and his team of investigators for over a decade. He initiated the project in 1930 and did not release the final book presenting his results and interpretations, *The Folk Culture of Yucatan*, until 1941. Redfield found that distance from Mérida did appear to act in a general sense as an independent or causal variable in regards to social characteristics of the surrounding towns and villages. The closer a settlement was to Mérida, the greater was the observed level of social disorganization, secularization, and individualization (Redfield's equivalent of anomie). In presenting his conclusions, Redfield also offered a caveat. He clearly stated that he did not consider his study equivalent to historical inquiry. The substitution of space for time was but a crude approximation of historical process and was intended to yield insight into knowledge of sociological processes rather than historical occurrences.[11]

The Folk Culture of Yucatan far exceeded Redfield's earlier Tepoztlán study in scope and sophistication. And while it fell short of delivering the general nomothetic description of change that he had aimed for, it provided the basis for Redfield's most far-reaching and influential construct describing social change. Redfield had initially approached both his Tepoztlán and Yucatan studies with the conception that the transition from so-called primitive to urban society could be conceived as a dichotomy. This dichotomous conception had been advanced by such late nineteenth-century thinkers as Ferdinand Tönnies and Emile Durkheim and had held currency with social scientists into the 1920s. Through his Yucatan work, though, Redfield came to regard the dichotomous view of change as inadequate. The transition from primitive to urban society could be conceived, he advanced, not merely as a dichotomy, Gemeinschaft to Gesellschaft for example, but as a continuum. He concluded from his analysis of the social transformation from village to town to city in Yucatan that change proceeded along three axes: organization-disorganization, piety-secularization, and community-individualization. Any society, he argued, could be seen as lying along various points of these three axes. Redfield elaborated on this notion in subsequent publications following *The Folk Culture of Yucatan*, and the concept came to be known as the "folk-urban continuum." This concept exercised profound influence, especially among sociologists in the 1940s to 1950s, in the discussion of social and cultural change.[12]

Redfield's work influenced not only social theorists, but also it served as a springboard for an entire generation of field research. His folk-urban typology, in particular, proved valuable to anthropologists and sociologists interested in conducting empirical research on social transformation. Although American social scientists had advanced numerous similar constructs during the early to mid-twentieth century, Redfield's folk-urban construct proved to be one of the most influential. Two explanations can be offered for the extent of this influence. First, Redfield was the first to use a typological scheme as a framework for on-the-ground anthropological research. Specifically, his Yucatan study gained wide attention because it demonstrated the power of a typological scheme for generating testable hypotheses. Redfield's empirical framework provided the basis for numerous studies undertaken to challenge his conclusions. His model essentially set the terms of the debate and pattern of study for the next thirty years for those who agreed and disagreed with him over the nature and dynamics of social change in peasant societies and cultures. A second reason for the extent of Redfield's influence derived from the leverage it provided anthropologists of the period for expanding their studies beyond remote isolated villages. Redfield's folk-urban construct provided a model that related village studies to the larger sociocultural matrix in which they were imbedded. His theoretical work thus offered mid-century social scientists a valuable methodology for framing and contextualizing ethnographic community studies.[13]

Following publication of *The Folk Culture of Yucatan*, Redfield shifted his attention away from field research and writing. University of

Chicago president Robert Hutchins had appointed Redfield in 1934 to be chairman of the Social Sciences Division at Chicago, and from the late 1930s through the 1940s, Redfield shouldered an increasingly demanding administrative load that left him little time for research and writing. This fallow period proved to be a critical turning point in his intellectual development. Chicago initiated several far-reaching curricular reform measures during the late 1930s and early to mid-1940s, and Redfield took an active role in those concerning the social sciences. His participation in these reform efforts profoundly affected his thinking and stimulated him to reassess many of his earlier positions. Most notably, he rethought his ideas about history, and he broadened his focus beyond analyses of villages and cities to consideration of civilizations, particularly the origins and growth of the major civilizations.[14]

Redfield was not alone during the 1930s and 1940s in turning toward exploration of the nature and dynamics of civilization. In 1923, Oswald Spengler had published *The Decline of the West*.[15] This book had gained wide popularity on both sides of the Atlantic, finding readers among scholars and the lay public. Through this work, Spengler almost single-handedly initiated a new field of inquiry—comparative civilization studies. Numerous European and American thinkers, including Pitirim Sorokin, A. L. Kroeber, F. S. C. Northrop, and particularly Arnold J. Toynbee, had followed Spengler in exploring the dynamics of world civilizations. In addition, from the early 1940s forward, a group of historians and archaeologists associated with the University of Chicago's Oriental Institute had launched an innovative series of investigations into ancient Mesopotamia. These scholars, among whom were Henri Frankfort, Thorkild Jacobsen, Robert Braidwood, and John Wilson, conceived their studies more broadly than the mere historical consideration of the ancient Near East and addressed themselves to larger questions regarding the origins and dynamics of all civilizations. Redfield saw a parallel interest with his colleagues at the Oriental Institute and associated closely with them through the late 1940s and 1950s.[16]

From Spengler through Toynbee, students of comparative civilizations focused almost exclusively on high culture. Yet in the early 1950s, Redfield challenged this elite conception of civilization. Civilizations embraced both high and low culture, he argued, and could not be characterized adequately without dealing with both cultural levels. This notion represented a radically new conception of civilization. Redfield recognized that civilizations conceived as such dialectical systems—the historic product of interaction between elite and non-elite cultures—could only be studied through a distinct methodology. He dedicated himself over the 1950s to developing such a methodology—a way, in short for studying civilizations "from the bottom up." He advanced two distinct approaches for studying non-elite cultures within civilizations: (1) the analysis of world views, especially of peasants, and (2) analysis of the composite system of what he called the "great and little traditions" of belief within civilizations.

The world view of a people, in Redfield's definition, encompassed the totality of ideas that people within a culture shared about the self, human society, and the natural and spiritual worlds. Most important, world view offered an insider's view; it constituted a deliberate attempt by an observer to construct a representation of how individuals within a culture conceptualize the world upon which they looked out. Redfield had begun to develop his notion of world view in the late 1930s, as he conducted his comparative studies of Yucatan communities. When he and his co-investigator Alfonso Villa Rojas had described the intellectual and spiritual dimensions of life for the Maya villager in *Chan Kom: A Maya Village* (1934), the first text in their Yucatan studies, they had presented the villagers' views of nature and the gods in separate chapters.[17] This approach corresponded with standard ethnographic practice during the 1930s. But in *The Folk Culture of Yucatan* (1941), Redfield broke with this conventional approach, because he had come to regard accounts that separated various dimensions of the villagers' inner worlds, such as his earlier Chan Kom, as distortions. He had come to believe that anthropologists needed to present the body of beliefs about the self, nature, and the gods held by members of a folk culture as an integrated system and not merely a collection of disjointed ideas. In his chapter "The Villager's View of Life" in *The Folk Culture of Yucatan*, Redfield presented an initial conception for such an integrated view.[18]

In the early 1950s, after Redfield received a substantial grant from the Ford Foundation to develop a program at Chicago in comparative civilization studies, he advanced a theoretical conceptualization of world view studies and began to urge others to pursue such investigations. Redfield's major contribution was to construct a formal definition of the notion of world view. He advanced this definition of world view first in an article in the *Proceedings of the American Philosophical Society* and the following year in a book, *The Primitive World and Its Transformations* (1953).[19] Here he proposed that all cultures held a distinct world view that could be used as a category of cross-cultural comparison. He defined world view as the "way a man, in a particular society, sees himself in relation to all else. ... It is that organization of ideas which answers to a man the questions: Where am I? Among what do I move? What are my relations to these things?" Redfield recognized that several similar classificatory models existed, such as the study of a people's ideal pattern, ethos, and national character, and he took pains to distinguish world view from these other constructs. The notion of national character, he acknowledged, was especially close to that of world view. The two constructs differed markedly, however, in orientation of viewpoint. "While 'national character' refers to the way [a] people look to the outsider looking in on them, 'world view' refers to the way the world looks to that people looking out."[20]

To use the concept of world view, Redfield continued, "is to assume certain human universals." Most important, it implied that in every society, each member was conscious of a self. Persons within all societies distinguished themselves from all else. The self stood therefore as the "axis of world view."[21] Redfield drew upon the ideas of George Herbert Mead to develop his conception of how persons within different societies drew distinctions between self and others. The world view of all peoples also allowed for some way to discriminate between the human and not human—in short, world views invariably implied some notion of human nature. Finally, every world view embraced a distinction between "God" and "nature." The world view of a people—the ideas system of the average person not the product of reflective intellectuals—thus represented, Redfield proposed, a distinctive quality of a people that could be used to characterize individual cultures and, possibly, civilizations.[22]

Redfield extended his thinking regarding the role of anthropology in the study of civilization through development of his "great and little traditions" construct. Through a series of articles written in the early 1950s and, most completely, in his last brief book *Peasant Society and Culture: An Anthropological Approach to Civilization* (1956),[23] he argued that two levels of culture run through complex civilizations, the "great tradition of the reflective few" and the "little tradition of the unreflective many." These dual traditions exerted mutual influence in defining any of the major civilizations. Yet the same mode of study could not be used to study both traditions; the same scholars could not attempt both studies. Redfield proposed that comparative civilization studies could best proceed with a division of scholarly labor.[24]

He suggested that the humanists, who were trained in philosophy, philology, history, and literary analysis, continue with their analyses of written texts of the urban elite. Humanist scholars, however, had previously overlooked the traditional oral cultures, the little traditions of the masses that lived in the myriad of rural villages embraced within major civilizations. Redfield argued that anthropologists were best prepared to study these little traditions and urged them to slip into the "back entrances" of civilizations to study the peasant societies and rural villages. Not only would the composite view of high and low cultures produce richer characterizations, but also Redfield argued this composite view was essential to understanding civilizational dynamics. For in Redfield's conception, the great and little traditions are intertwined and bound together in a process of mutual transformation. The ideas of the non-elite commoners are progressively transformed through conscious reflection by the literary few into the hierarchical canons of the great tradition. Yet this process is not a unidirectional system. The little tradition also constantly reforms and reshapes elements of the codified great tradition. Thus Redfield's model suggested that idea systems changed through dialectical exchange between two levels of thought that mutually coexisted within a civilization.[25]

Redfield's thinking regarding world view studies and dual exploration of great and little traditions exerted a powerful influence among mid-twentieth-century students of comparative civilization. Not only did he firmly establish the role of anthropologists in civilization studies, but also he provided a conceptual framework that facilitated discussion of the operation of symbolic and ideological transformations within civilizations. Redfield's contributions to comparative civilizations studies complemented his previous work on the analysis of social change in peasant villages, specifically his elaboration of the folk-urban continuum based upon his Tepoztlán and Yucatan studies. Indeed, Redfield's primary contribution to the study of social transformation from the village to civilization level consisted of the development of a vocabulary for a generation of American social scientists for discussion of social process or change. During the first half of the twentieth century, American social theorists had largely ignored macrosociological issues and had focused primarily on the micro level—on social interactions within neighborhoods and cities. Few theories existed in the late 1940s and early 1950s that could provide terms useful for discussion of social dynamics on a grand scale and, particularly, could serve to undergird structured field research. Redfield not only provided a conceptual apparatus for discussion of social change, but also he greatly stimulated broad processual studies through his own fieldwork and frameworks of analysis, and his theoretical and empirical work set the terms of debate among anthropologist and sociologists studying social change from the 1940s through early 1960s. His theoretical work was largely eclipsed by the mid-1960s through the explosion of Weberian- and Parsonian-based social theory. Nevertheless, Redfield's combination of theoretical notions and empirical studies continued to provoke discussion and controversies among social scientists into the 1970s.[26]

Selected Writings

Over the course of his career, Redfield demonstrated a remarkable sense of focus. A single overarching theme unites almost all his work in social anthropology: the study of social change. This work can be seen as falling into three related sub-categories: (1) modernization; (2) peasants; and (3) comparative study of civilizations.

Modernization

Redfield's interest in modernization appeared early and can be seen in works published when he was still a graduate student; this interest persisted across the course of his entire career. In his first published paper, "Anthropology, A Natural Science?" (1926), he expressed a theme that would distinguish his work from the 1920s through early 1940s, namely his interest in seeing anthropology aspire to construction of predictive models. In conceptualizing his first major research project, his dissertation research on the village of Tepoztlán, he grounded his work on the notion that clear patterns of social change could be elucidated through empirical study of peoples who lived on the borders of civilization and were thus subjected to powerful forces of transformation. His article "Among the Middle Americans" (1926) reflected his optimism that his Tepoztlán study would yield not mere description but predictive generalizations about social process.[27]

He clearly articulated his methodological assumptions in the introduction to his Ph.D. dissertation "A Plan for the Study of Tepoztlán, Morelos" (1928). In this introduction, he boldly announced his intention to use empirical study to derive general principles of social evolution. He understood that by taking on the study of evolution through anthropological investigation he was challenging disciplinary strictures laid down by no less than Franz Boas. Boas had originally expected the historically-grounded studies executed by his many students to yield larger generalizations about social process and dynamics in traditional cultures. Yet these studies, Redfield averred, had long since lapsed into mere antiquarianism. And with the bravado of a graduate student just launching his intellectual project, Redfield charged that studies pursued in the traditional Boasian mode had lost that scientific impulse that once inspired them and claimed that the "scientific impulse [had come] to rest in history, in the unveiling of another thread of the past." Anthropology, in Redfield's vision, was capable of continuing both its conventional work of "preserving the record, depictively, of dying cultures" as well as formulating law-like generalizations, which his study would attempt to do by analyzing social change "as it happens."[28]

Redfield softened his claims somewhat in the published version of his dissertation, *Tepoztlán, A Mexican Village, A Study of Folk Life* (1930). While most of his text was unchanged, he removed the overt challenges to Franz Boas from the introduction. Nevertheless, he clearly maintained his stated interest in the empirical study of social change. Describing the reaction of villagers, such as the Tepoztecans in his study, to encroaching change, he anticipated the formulations of mid-century modernization theorists, stating "modern industrial civilization appears to reach the marginal peoples as a sort of complex: those that survive the effect tend to react, it would seem, in ways different yet often comparable."[29]

Redfield greatly extended his ideas about modernization through his 1930s Yucatan community studies. At the outset of his study, he outlined his initial assumptions and methodology in "Sociological Investigation in Yucatan" (1931), which was published in the *Carnegie Institution of Washington Year Book*, the annual proceedings of the organization funding his research.[30] In a remarkable letter from his father-in-law Robert E. Park, who was on leave from the University of Chicago teaching at the University of Hawaii when Redfield's article appeared, we can see Park's reactions to Redfield's plans for his Yucatan study.[31] Obviously very engaged in his son-in-law's work, Park suggested that Redfield attempt to ground his research on a more typological base and suggested a schema that eventually Redfield developed into his folk-urban continuum construct. Redfield willingly incorporated Park's suggestions into his work and in an article he published midway through his Yucatan study, "Culture Changes in Yucatan" (1934), he provided a detailed explication of his theoretical and empirical approach for his study.[32] This article is particularly noteworthy in that it reflects Redfield at his most optimistic and ambitious regarding his aims for his Yucatan studies. Redfield summarized the conclusions to his Yucatan work in "The Folk Culture and Civilization," the final chapter to *The Folk Culture of Yucatan* (1941).[33] In the articles, "The Folk Society and Culture" (1940) and "The Folk Society" (1947), Redfield advanced two important extensions to the ideas that emerged from his Yucatan studies. In these articles, he elaborated upon his notion of folk culture, which he presented as the antithesis of urban culture as described by his Chicago colleague Louis Wirth. Finally, Redfield offered in "The Folk Society" his most succinct explanation of his notion of the folk-urban continuum.[34]

Peasants

Redfield's ideas regarding peasants emerged directly from his work on modernization. Virtually all his ethnographic studies focused on what he called "intermediate peoples," or peasants, who lived caught between traditional remote villages and urban civilization. Over the course of his career, he invested much effort in trying to define the nature of peasant society and culture, particularly its dual role as subject and actor in the transformation of villages into towns and cities. He initially articulated his conception of these intermediate peoples, which he first termed "folk" in the introduction to and final chapter of *Tepoztlán*. He refined his notion of folk in the *Folk Culture of Yucatan*. In both *Tepoztlán* and the *Folk Culture of Yucatan*, his conception of folk society was primarily defined in cultural terms.[35] Redfield continued to work with his notion of the folk as intermediate peoples over the course of the 1930s, though, and by the end of the decade, he had begun to shift his attention from cultural to structural aspects of folk society. He first expressed this shift in perspective in the introduction he wrote to his student Horace Miner's book, *St. Denis: A French Canadian Parish* (1939). In this essay, Redfield used the term peasants where he had previously used folk, and he spoke more precisely about the societal role played by peasants. He observed that the study of peasants held value for both anthropology and sociology, claiming that "to study the peasant peoples is to ... draw into a single field of investigation all the societies of the earth from the simplest to the most complex." He emphasized, furthermore, that study of peasant peoples, who "form[ed] a middle term in the equation of culture and civilization" would enable social scientists to cross disciplinary boundaries, an essential move if true progress were to be made in developing a "science of society and culture."[36]

While during the 1920s and 1930s, Redfield was one of only a few social scientists focusing on study of peasant societies, the 1940s saw a surge of interest in study of peasants by scholars from a variety of disciplines. Redfield devoted most of his time during this decade to his administrative duties at Chicago. But he returned to active research and writing at the close of the decade, and from the late 1940s through the mid-1950s, he constructed his most mature formulations regarding peasants. In *The Primitive World and Its Transformations* (1953), particularly in his chapter "Later Histories of the Folk Society," he examined the origins of peasant societies and offered a strongly historical interpretation that differed markedly from his previous structural conceptions. He also focused more on political and economic dimensions of peasant societies than he had in his earlier works.[37] Redfield provided his most sophisticated treatment of peasants, however, in *Peasant Society and Culture: An Anthropological Approach to Civilization* (1956). In this brief text, Redfield first advanced a historical summary of the process by which social scientists came to focus on study of peasant peoples. His chapter "Peasantry: Part Societies" provided not only an extended definition of the social and historical roles of peasants, but also a highly nuanced discussion of how Redfield's ideas were situated in the context of the burgeoning mid-century dialogue over peasant studies. This text proved to be a foundational text for peasant studies, which became a central sub-discipline within anthropology during the second half of the twentieth century.[38]

Comparative Study of Civilizations

Closely related to Redfield's work on peasants are his writings on comparative civilizations studies. His most important contributions to this field include his work on world view studies, community studies, and development of his Great and Little Traditions construct. The clear starting point in Redfield's writings on world view is his own characterization of the world view of the Yucatecan villager that he published as "The Villager's View of Life" in *The Folk Culture of Yucatan*. Here Redfield described the "pattern of meanings and standards" that enabled villagers to locate themselves physically in the universe as well as socially among themselves and other peoples and to construct a moral order to guide their conduct. He also offered an insightful portrayal of the relationship of the villagers to nature and the natural resources upon which their lives were entirely dependent.[39] Redfield complemented his example of a world view portrait through his theoretical description of the value of and methodology for world view studies in an article "The Primitive World View," published in the *Proceedings of the American Philosophical Society* and later in expanded form as the second chapter of *The Primitive World*. In this article Redfield articulated fundamental axes of comparison for world views of different peoples and demonstrated how comparative world view studies could contribute to the larger effort to characterize entire civilizations.

Probably most influential of all Redfield's contributions to comparative civilizations studies, though, was his Great and Little Traditions construct. He articulated his most succinct expression of this construct in "The Social Organization of Tradition," published in *Peasant Society and Culture*.[40] Redfield demonstrated the power of this notion, moreover, using it as the primary analytical lens in the article he co-wrote with his Chicago colleague Milton Singer, "The Cultural Role of Cities" (1953). In this paper, Redfield and Singer analyzed the role of cities in the "formation, maintenance, spread, decline, and transformation of civilizations." They posited two distinct cultural roles played by cities, which they referred to as "orthogenetic" and "heterogenetic" roles. Using these two polar types, they explored the roles of the intelligentsia in cities characterized by the focused elaboration and extension of canonical great traditions, such as Mecca, Delhi, and Kyoto, versus the roles of intellectuals in cities of commerce and secular learning, such as London, New York, and Tokyo, which became the loci of differing traditions, "center[s] of heresy, heterodoxy, and dissent, of interruptions and destruction of ancient tradition, of rootlessness and anomy." The structural and cultural vocabulary that Redfield and Singer advanced for discussing change processes in world cities proved highly influential both in the development of urban anthropology as well as comparative civilizations studies from the 1950s through 1970s.[41]

Redfield's final work, unfinished before his death in 1958, was to be a brief book on the theory and methodology of comparative civilizations studies. He completed the first three chapters for this book, and they provide a formalized statement of his thinking regarding civilizations and a description of comparative methodology anthropologists could use to study the little traditions within major civilizations. In the first two chapters, "Civilizations as Things Thought About" and "Civilizations as Societal Structures? The Development of Community Studies," Redfield provided a working definition of civilization and elaborated on ideas he had advanced earlier in *Peasant Society and Culture* regarding the necessity of studying civilizations "from the bottom up," i.e. through the lens of village studies. He emphasized particularly the need to situate village studies within a civilizational context. In the third chapter, "Civilizations as Cultural Studies," which is included here, Redfield extended ideas he had presented earlier on the role that world view studies and his Great and Little Traditions construct could play in conducting comparative civilizations studies. Unfortunately, his death in 1958 cut short his work on this final book. Yet the preliminary chapters that he did complete represent the culminating thoughts of an entire career spent thinking about the mechanisms and patterns of cultural change conceived both at the level of traditional villages or communities and the grand civilizations in which such communities are enmeshed.[42]

Redfield's writings not only exerted a powerful influence over the course of his career, but also they continued to prove influential well through the 1970s, almost two decades following his death. Not only did he provide many of the methodologies and theoretical terminologies for study of peasants and non-elite members of civilizations, but also his work stimulated multiple studies and restudies, many of which were aimed at contradicting his conclusions. Reading Redfield today provides insight into the debates that animated mid-twentieth-century anthropology and sociology. Even more important, Redfield's writings provide us an outstanding example of what social science can achieve. In his work we see the pursuit of an intellectual agenda for development of a conceptual vocabulary to describe the process of social change in general terms coupled with a moral agenda for understanding the dimensions and consequences of this change both for the its subjects and agents.

Notes

1. On Franz Boas's shaping influence in American anthropology during the first three decades of the twentieth century, see George W. Stocking, Jr., "Introduction: The Basic Assumptions of Boasian Anthropology," in *The Shaping of American Anthropology, 1883-1911*, edited by George W. Stocking, Jr. (New York: Basic Books, 1974), 1-20 and Marvin Harris, *The Rise of Anthropological Theory: A History of Theories of Culture* (New York: Thomas Y. Crowell Company, 1968), 250-289.
2. For an expanded discussion of Redfield's challenge to Boas, see Clifford Wilcox, *Robert Redfield and the Development of American Anthropology* (Lanham, Md.: Lexington Books, 2004), 1-3; this essay overall draws heavily upon my treatment of Redfield in this text.
3. Warren Susman provides an insightful discussion of the culture-civilization discourse in "Culture and Civilization: The Nineteen-Twenties," in *Culture as History: The Transformation of American Society in the Twentieth Century* (New

Introduction   xxxi

York: Pantheon), 105-121 and "The Culture of the Thirties," ibid., 150-183. On the influence of this discourse on Redfield, see George W. Stocking, Jr., "The Ethnographic Sensibility of the 1920s and the Dualism of the Anthropological Tradition," in *The Ethnographer's Magic and Other Essays in the History of Anthropology* (Madison: University of Wisconsin Press, 1992) and Wilcox, *Robert Redfield*, 15-32.

4. On the intellectual development of Robert E. Park see Fred H. Matthews, *Quest for an American Sociology: Robert E. Park and the Chicago School* (Montreal and London: McGill-Queen's University Press, 1977), 4-56.
5. For a discussion of the rise and influence of the "Chicago School" of sociology, see Matthews, *Robert E. Park and the Chicago School*, 121-156; John Madge, *The Origins of Scientific Sociology* (New York: Free Press of Glencoe, 1962), 52-125; and Martin Bulmer, *The Chicago School of Sociology: Institutionalization, Diversity, and the Rise of Sociological Research* (Chicago: University of Chicago Press, 1984), 28-128.
6. On the specific influence of Robert Park and the Chicago School of Sociology on Redfield, see Wilcox, *Robert Redfield*, 21-32.
7. Robert Redfield, "A Plan for the Study of Tepoztlán, Morelos," (Ph.D. diss., University of Chicago, 1928), 1-10.
8. Robert Redfield, *Tepoztlán, A Mexican Village: A Study of Folk Life* (Chicago: University of Chicago Press, 1930); Wilcox, *Robert Redfield*, 30-32.
9. Redfield, *Tepoztlán*, 205-223; on the reception of *Tepoztlán*, see Wilcox, *Robert Redfield*, 41-49.
10. On the background and conceptualization of Redfield's Yucatan studies, see Wilcox, *Robert Redfield*, 49-54.
11. Robert Redfield, *The Folk Culture of Yucatan* (Chicago: University of Chicago Press, 1941).
12. Redfield, *Folk Culture of Yucatan*, 338-369.
13. On the influence of T*he Folk Culture of Yucatan* and the folk-urban continuum, see Wilcox, *Robert Redfield*, 58-70.
14. Redfield's "fallow period" during the 1940s included both extensive administrative work at Chicago and national-level work as a public intellectual in the interest of such causes as atomic weapons control, racial desegregation in schooling, and advocacy for a world constitution. Wilcox, *Robert Redfield*, 77-86.
15. Oswald Spengler, *The Decline of the West*, trans. Charles Francis Atkinson, 2 vols. (New York: Alfred A. Knopf, 1926).
16. On the Chicago civilizations dialogue of the late-1940s and 1950s, see Wilcox, *Robert Redfield*, 114-118.
17. Redfield, Robert, and Alfonso Villa Rojas. *Chan Kom: A Maya Village*. Washington, D.C.: Carnegie Institution of Washington, 1934; reprint (Chicago: University of Chicago Press, 1962).
18. Redfield, *Folk Culture of Yucatan*, 110-131.
19. Robert Redfield, "The Primitive World View," *Proceedings of the American Philosophical Society* 96 (February 1952): 30-36; *The Primitive World and Its Transformations* (Ithaca, N.Y.: Cornell University Press, 1953), 84-110.
20. Redfield, "Primitive World View," 30.
21. Ibid.
22. Redfield, "The Primitive World and Its Transformation," 90-99.
23. Robert Redfield, *Peasant Society and Culture: An Anthropological Approach to Civilization*, (Chicago: University of Chicago Press, 1956), 40-59.
24. Ibid., 41-42.
25. Ibid., 46-50.

26. Wilcox, *Robert Redfield*, 63-70, 182-185.
27. Robert Redfield, "Anthropology, A Natural Science?" *Social Forces* 4 (June 1926): 715-721; "Among the Middle Americans," *University of Chicago Magazine* 20 (March 1928): 242-247.
28. Redfield, A Plan for the Study of Tepoztlán, Morelos," 3-7.
29. Redfield, *Tepoztlán*, 1-14.
30. Robert Redfield, "Sociological Investigation in Yucatan," *Carnegie Institution of Washington Year Book* 30 (Washington, D. C.: Carnegie Institution of Washington, 1931), 122-124.
31. Robert E. Park to Robert Redfield, 23 January 1932, box 1, folder 8, Robert Redfield Papers, Special Collections, Joseph Regenstein Library, University of Chicago, Chicago.
32. Robert Redfield, "Culture Changes in Yucatan." *American Anthropologist* 36 (January-March 1934): 57-69.
33. Redfield, *Folk Culture of Yucatan*, 338-369.
34. Robert Redfield, "The Folk Society and Culture," *American Journal of Sociology* 45 (March 1940): 731-742; "The Folk Society." *American Journal of Sociology* 52 (January 1947): 293-308. The most famous explication of urban culture by Louis Wirth is found in his "Urbanism as a Way of Life." *American Journal of Sociology* 44 (July 1938): 1-24.
35. Redfield, *Tepoztlán*, 1-14; *Folk Culture of Yucatan*, 338-369.
36. Robert Redfield, introduction *St. Denis: A French-Canadian Parish* by Horace Miner (Chicago: University of Chicago Press, 1939; reprint Phoenix Books, 1963), xiii-xix.
37. Redfield, "Later Histories of the Folk Society," chapter in *Primitive World*, 26-53.
38. Redfield, "Peasantry: Part Societies," chapter in *Peasant Society and Culture*, 23-39.
39. Redfield, "The Villager's View of Life," chapter in *Folk Culture of Yucatan*, 110-131.
40. Robert Redfield, "The Social Organization of Tradition," chapter in *Peasant Society and Culture*, 40-59.
41. Robert Redfield and Milton Singer, "The Cultural Role of Cities." *Economic Development and Cultural Change* 3 (October 1954): 53-73.
42. Robert Redfield, "Civilizations as Things Thought About," "Civilizations as Societal Structures? The Development of Community Studies," and "Civilizations as Cultural Structures," chapters in *The Papers of Robert Redfield: Human Nature and the Study of Society,* vol. 1, ed. Margaret Park Redfield, (Chicago: University of Chicago, 1962), 364-401.

Part I

Modernization

1

Anthropology, A Natural Science?

Redfield published "Anthropology, A Natural Science?" while still in graduate school. Largely influenced by his father-in-law Robert E. Park, Redfield expressed here conceptions of both anthropology and sociology that would inform his work over the course of most of his career. Redfield argued that while during the 19th century anthropology had proceeded according to the methods of natural science, the discipline had shifted toward a historical approach in the early 20th century. Redfield attributed this shift primarily to the influence of Franz Boas, who had opposed the generalizing or scientific approach of the nineteenth century because it was so closely associated with racist social evolutionary notions. Redfield suggested, however, that as of the first decades of the 20th century, a resurgent scientific trend could be discerned within anthropology and that the discipline now stood at a crossroads between the historical and scientific approaches. He concluded by arguing, as had Robert E. Park, that anthropology could advance scientifically most effectively by aligning itself with sociology, the lead organizing social science. Essentially, anthropology could by most productive, he proposed by harnessing its on-the-ground empirical techniques to gather facts and data that could then by useful to the generalizing efforts of sociology. This article provides a clear statement of the generalizing law-seeking approach that would guide Redfield's work in social anthropology over the course of his entire career.

Science, broadly speaking is the systematic investigation of observed phenomena. It is recognized that this investigation may be directed towards one of two distinct and opposable ends. It may be the aim of such investigation to discover and set out specific sequences, temporal or spatial, of objects and events. History and geography are scientific disciplines of this sort. They are sometimes called descriptive sciences. In fact all sciences are descriptive, but the events or objects of the historical-geographical sciences are described as they are encountered in time or space, and each datum is unique and not subject to verification.

The term natural science, on the other hand, is often reserved for scientific investigation that seeks to classify data and to reduce a wide range of observed phenomena to a brief statement or formula. This formula is termed a natural law. It is, of course, not a law at all: it compels nothing.

First published in *Social Forces* 4 (June 1926): 715-721.

It is merely a shorthand description of phenomena observed to recur.[1] It is the processual counterpart of the generic concept. It is tested pragmatically, not by any standard of absolute truth.[2] Physics and chemistry are sciences of this sort.

Among recent general sociological books, this distinction is explicitly set forth in Park and Burgess, *Introduction to the Science of Sociology*, pp. 12-24, and is recognized in C. M. Case, *Outlines of Introductory Sociology*, xvi-xvii.

But while the facts of history and of natural science are of distinct characters, history and natural science do not remain distinct, but in certain regions of inquiry the one tends to become the other. Geography, in its established phase, is a purely descriptive (i.e., depictive) science, but nevertheless it is forever tending to reduce its data to types and is thus forever passing over into natural science.[3] Even the historians do not in every case confine themselves to events. In becoming a "comparative historian," Professor F. J. Teggart has sought to "do for human history what biologists are engaged in doing for the history of the forms of life."[4] So he calls his book *The Processes of History*. History, to him, is to become a natural science, i.e., sociology.

From the point of view of this distinction, it is interesting to consider the methods of anthropology. Unlike sociology, anthropology has no roots in philosophy. It arose out of a scientific interest in primitive and prehistoric man. Anthropological science thus grew up around a body of materials and not around a defined method. For this reason its relation to history and to natural science did not at once become clear. Its interest in this connection lies in the fact that anthropological method has been both that of history and that of a natural science. Certain of its workers and certain of its schools have inclined to one of the two methods, while others have inclined to the other. In a paper defining the field and principles of anthropology, Boas simultaneously embraced both methods.

> In this sense, anthropology is the science that endeavors to reconstruct the early history of mankind, and that tries, whenever possible to express in the form of laws ever-recurring modes of historical happenings.[5]

The natural science method was once *the* anthropological method. In the early days, when anthropologists wrote under the dominance of the evolutionary viewpoint, before Boas had appeared to reduce their hypothetical schemes to unsound conjectures, anthropologists employed the comparative method, and were thereby natural historians or natural scientists. Tylor, for example, declared that to many educated minds (but not to Tylor):

there seems something presumptuous and repulsive in the view that the history of mankind is part and parcel of the history of nature, that our thoughts, wills and actions accord with laws as definite as those which govern the motion of waves, the combination of acids and bases, and the growth of plants and animals.[6]

Although Tylor did not entirely overlook the fact that the culture of any group has been largely determined by the experiences of that group, his interest lay in reducing human behavior to types.

> In studying both the recurrence of special habits or ideas in several districts and their prevalence within each district, there come before us ever-reiterated proofs of regular causation, producing the phenomena of human life, and of laws of maintenance and diffusion according to which these phenomena settle into permanent standard conditions of society at definite stages of culture.[7]

Tylor and his contemporaries, sought to reduce cultural data to classes, and to tell the history of the development of such classes. So, for example, as has been pointed out by Park and Burgess, Westermarck's *History of Human Marriage* is, more exactly, a natural history of human marriage. Westermarck calls his method "comparative sociology":

> Its ultimate object is, of course, the same as that of every other science, namely, to explain the facts with which it is concerned, to give an answer to the question, why?[8]

This interest in a search for fundamental social laws was halted when the assumptions of the evolutionistic anthropologists were pointed out and their central fallacy made clear. As early as 1896 Franz Boas[9] showed that this fallacy lay in the false assumption that the same phenomena are always due to the same causes, and in the conclusion therefrom that there is one uniform pattern of cultural evolution applicable to all groups. In a paper in which he made this criticism of the comparative method, as then practiced, Boas announced the program for future anthropological investigation—a program which was to be faithfully followed by American anthropologists for a generation.[10]

> The immediate results of the historical method are, therefore, histories of the cultures of diverse tribes which have been the subject of study. I fully agree with those anthropologists who claim that this is not the ultimate aim of our science, because the general laws, although implied in such description, cannot be clearly formulated nor their relative value appreciated with a thorough comparison of the manner in which they assert themselves in different cultures. But I insist that the application of this method is the indispensable condition of sound progress. The psychological problem is contained in the results of the historical inquiry. When we have cleared up the history of a single culture and understand the effects of environment and the psychological conditions that are reflected in it we have made a step forward, as we can then investigate in how far the same causes or other causes were at work in the development of other cultures. Thus by comparing histories of growth general laws may be found. This method is much safer than the comparative method, as it is usu-

ally practiced, because instead of a hypothesis on the mode of development actual history forms the basis of our deductions.

Similar reactions to evolutionistic anthropology took place in England and in Germany, and anthropology became a historical science. During the first quarter of this century anthropologists have been engaged largely in determining the distribution of specific traits of specific peoples, and in offering hypotheses as to the histories of specific groups without written records. They have been dealing with events. In Kroeber's *Anthropology* he states that "anthropology has been occupied with trying to generalize the findings of history,"[11] but in fact the pages which follow this statement generalize very little upon history; they are history. The historical method employed by recent American anthropologists has been clearly formulated by Kroeber:

> It is historical in the sense that it insists on first depicting things as they are and then inferring generalization secondarily if at all, instead of plunging at once into a search for principles. It may not seem historical in the literal conventional sense because the ethnologist's data are not presented to him chronologically. He is therefore compelled to establish his time sequences. This he does by comparisons, especially by taking the fullest possible cognizance of all space factors—geography, diffusions, distributions. As soon, however, as he has reconstructed his time sequences as well as he may, he follows the methods of the orthodox historian. He describes, giving his product depth through consideration of environmental and especially of psychological factors; but he describes only. It is each unique event that holds his interest, not the common likeness that may seem to run through events but which he finds, as he remains objective, to dilute thinner in proportion as he scrutinizes more accurately and finally to melt into intangibilities. ...
>
> In essence, then, modern ethnology says that so and so happened, and may tell why it happened thus in that particular case. It does not tell, and it does not try to tell why things happen in society as such.[12]

At the same time Kroeber kept in mind a more remote end of cultural anthropology in natural science:

> As long as we continue offering the world only reconstruction of specific detail, and consistently show a negativistic attitude toward broader conclusions, the world will find very little of profit in ethnology. People do want to know why.[13]

In general, recent American anthropologists have been practical field workers who have had little occasion to stop and reflect upon their methods and distinguish the historical interest from that of natural science. Of those who have appreciated that there is here a fundamental difference in the logical character of facts, Kroeber has made the clearest statements. He did not, however, make the sharp distinction immediately. His "Eighteen Professions," published in 1915, is an affirmation by an anthropologist that his method is historical. Kroeber felt the fundamental difference between the method of history and the method of natural science, but in this paper he assumed that cultural phenomena were incapable of treatment by a natural science. He called all natural science "biology."

"Anthropology today includes two studies which fundamental differences of aim and method render irreconcilable. One of these branches is biological and psychological; the other, social or historical. ... In what follows, historical anthropology, history and sociology are referred to as history. Physical anthropology and psychology are included in biology." He concludes: "In fine, the determinations and methods of biological, psychological or natural science do not exist for history, are disregarded by consistent biological practice. Most biologists have implicitly followed their aspect of this doctrine, but their subsequent success has tempted many historians, especially sociologists, anthropologists and theorists, to imitate them instead of pursuing their proper complementary method.[14]

But in a later paper,[15] Kroeber made a clear distinction between the historical-geographical and the natural science methods. "Data may be viewed directly as they present themselves or we can seek to pass through them to the processes involved." In the realm of the "superorganic," "culture history" is a "depiction of phenomena," while "social psychology" is "formulation of processes." In this paper Kroeber acknowledges the possibility of a natural science of the superorganic, and sociology is no longer included with history: "There is no a priori reason visible, accordingly, why a science of cultural mechanics or social psychology, or sociology, is impossible" (p. 640). Such a sociology must, he says, consistently view "social phenomena and forces as cultural, and not as aggregations and products of psychic phenomena and forces" (p. 650).

Now the interesting fact is that though modern anthropology is primarily history, it does tend in various regions of inquiry to become this "social psychology" or "sociology" of which Kroeber speaks. It does occasionally "pass through data to the processes involved." Physical anthropology, of course, has long since advanced beyond a mere taxonomic classification of biological types of the human species, and frequently directs its attention to the processes whereby somatological change takes place. Primitive linguistics early sought out types and processes. Archaeology remains closest to history.[16] It is the ethnologist who deals with the phenomena of the superorganic.[17] At first the method of the ethnologist was simply depictive. Ethnology came to be distinguished from ethnography, the latter term meaning descriptive (depictive) ethnology, only when ethnology came to be something besides mere description. Ethnologists do reduce their data to types, and they do arrive at formulations of processes.

An example of how descriptions of processes are almost inevitable in considering ethnological problems could be found in almost all modern ethnological writing, but we may take as an example a paper by Edward Sapir entitled "Time Perspective in Aboriginal American Culture: A Study in Method."[18] In it, Dr. Sapir is unequivocal in his view that modern anthropology is a purely historical science:

> Cultural anthropology is more and more rapidly getting to realize itself a strictly historical science. Its data can not be understood, either in themselves or in relation to one another, except as the endpoints of specific sequences of events reaching back into the remote past. Some of us may be more interested in the psychological laws of human development that we believe ourselves capable of extracting from the raw materials of ethnology and archaeology, than in the establishment of definitive historical facts and relationships that would tend to make this material intelligible, but it is not at all clear that the formulations of such laws is any more the business of the anthropologist than of the historian in the customarily narrow sense of the word.... Granting that the labours of the folk-psychologists are justifiable in themselves, the main point remains that so-called primitive culture consists throughout the phenomena that, so far as the ethnologist is concerned, must be worked out historically, that is, in terms of actual happenings, however inferred, that are conceived to have a specific sequence, a specific localization, and specific relations among themselves.

Sapir presents an exhaustive outline of means whereby the relative priority of cultural elements in defined cultures may be determined. Such, for example, are "principles of necessary presupposition," "relative firmness of association," cultural elaboration and specialization," etc. But this leads him to express in general formulae the recurrence of phenomena which may be relied on to establish such a chronology, and the refinement of such formulae leads to the statement of natural "laws." Thus, in inquiring into the limitations upon the information to be obtained from the interpretation of the geographic distribution of culture traits, he is led to make this statement:

> A culture element is transmitted with maximum ease when it is conceptually readily detachable from its cultural setting, is not hedged about in practice by religious or other restraints, is without difficulty assimilable to the borrowing culture, and travels from one tribe to another living in friendly, or at least intimate, relations with it, particularly when these tribes are bound to each other by ties of intermarriage and linguistic affinity and are situated on an important trade route.

Here the ethnologist has stated a "natural law," the description of processes originating as sort of by-product of the historical account. The descriptive formulation just quoted is made not as an end, but as a means of finding out what happened in a certain place at a certain time. The processes of diffusion are defined as a guide to the historical investigator. But there is a tendency, with certain ethnologists, for these processes to become a scientific end in themselves, and at this point ethnology has become a natural science. The process of diffusion is the process most extensively treated by ethnologists, but a wider and wider field of explanatory science tends to be developed by them. This tendency is clearly marked in Clark Wissler's *Man and Culture*.[19] This is in very large measure an attempt to formulate cultural processes. Particularly in the chapter, "The Rationalization of Culture Processes," does Wissler anticipate an explanatory science of cultural phenomena, which shall have for its end *control*.[20]

Another ethnologist whose interest was in large measure that of a natural scientist is W. H. R. Rivers. It is particularly interesting to note this fact in view of the attempts of the extreme diffusionists to identify his work completely with their own. Elliott Smith and W. J. Perry are simply historians (perhaps some of their American critics would prefer to say mythologists!); they conceive it their task to tell the story of the migration of culture elements from the supposed Egyptian center. Rivers had a broader interest. In an early paper,[21] Rivers is ostensibly inquiring into the problem of what folkways are more easily borrowed, as a means to the "analysis of cultures," that is the determination of historical sequences in certain defined areas. But in reading the paper there is always a feeling that Rivers is interested in these matters of process in themselves.

Writing nine years later, in his *Social Organization*, Rivers discusses this aspect of ethnology without reference to an ultimate historical purpose. He begins by saying:

> I am one of those who believe that the ultimate aim of all studies of mankind, whether historical or scientific, is to reach explanations in terms of the ideas, beliefs, sentiments and instinctive tendencies by which the conduct of man, both individual and collective, is determined.[22]

He then proceeds to study social organization "as a process," and from his data deduces general formulae descriptive of recurrent phenomena in the field of social organization. As his *Social Organization* is a description of the processes whereby forms of social grouping come into being, so his *Medicine, Magic, and Religion* is essentially a natural history of curative practices, describing the process of their change from irrational to rational behavior. Rivers studies, by comparative ethnology, ways of behavior, stimulated by the crisis of disease, i.e., ways of curing the disease; this part of the book is a description of the process whereby merely expressive behavior gives way to a rational therapeutic treatment.

Anthropology, therefore, although in large measure a historical science, ever and again tends to become a natural science. To what extent its contribution to a nomothetic science of human behavior will remain independent, or will become merged with other disciplines having this method and interest, remains uncertain. It is probable that for some time its important contribution will remain the collection of a wide variety of invaluable data. Upon these data sociologists and social psychologists are in a large degree dependent.

Notes

1. Karl Pearson, *The Grammar of Science*, 77. A. D. Ritchie, *The Scientific Method*, 55. Hobson, *The Domain of Natural Science*, 26. L.L. Bernard, "Scientific Method and Social Progress," *American Journal of Sociology* (July 1925).
2. Vaihinger, *The Philosophy of "As If,"* 215.
3. As, for example, Jean Brunhes, *Human Geography*.
4. F. J. Teggart, *The Processes of History*, 1918.
5. Franz Boas, *Anthropology*, 8.
6. Edward B. Tylor, *Primitive Culture*, 7th ed., 1914, 2.
7. Ibid., 13.
8. Edward Westermarck, *The History of Human Marriage*, 5th ed., Vol. I, p. 2.
9. Franz Boas, "The Limitations of the Comparative Method of Anthropology," *Science*, N.S., Vol. IV, No. 103, p. 904.
10. Boas, op. cit., 907.
11. A. L. Kroeber, *Anthropology*, 5.
12. A. L. Kroeber, Review of Lowie's *Primitive Society*, *American Anthropologist*, N.S., Vol. 2, 1910, 377, 380. The identification of ethnology with history is likewise made by Lowie (*Culture and Ethnology*, 82-83): "A given culture is, in a measure at least, a unique phenomenon. In so far as this is true it must defy generalized treatment, and the explanation of a cultural phenomenon will consist in referring it back to the particular circumstances that preceded it. In other words, the explanation will consist in a recital of its past history. ..." So, too, a historian: "It seems, then, that while there is a clear-cut distinction to be made between the subject matter of anthropology and that of history, and while there is a wide difference to be noticed in the literary form assumed by the typical statement of results in the one study and the other, the fundamental methodological portion of the two is identical." F. J. Teggart, Anthropology and History," *Journal of Philosophy, Psychology, and Scientific Method* 19 (1919): 693.
13. Kroeber, op. cit., 380.
14. A.L. Kroeber, "Eighteen Professions," *American Anthropologist*, N.S. Vol. 17, 1915, 283-288.
15. A. L. Kroeber, "The Possibility of a Social Psychology," *American Journal of Sociology*, Vol. 23, 1917, 633-650.
16. Yet even here the work of Jane Harrison (although she is not an anthropologist), is case where archaeological materials are treated essentially by the method of natural science. The aim there is to describe the myth and religion of an extinct people

so far as may be determined from archaeological evidence, as types of behavior occasioned by certain fundamental human motives. (Jane Harrison, *Prolegomena to the Study of Greek Religion* [Cambridge, England, 1908]; *Themis, A Study of the Social Origins of Greek Religions* [Cambridge, England, 1912]; *Mythology* [Boston, 1914]).

17. "Culture is, indeed, the sole and exclusive subject matter of ethnology." Robert M. Lowie, *Culture and Ethnology*, 5.
18. Canada Dept. of Mines, Memoir 90, Ottawa, 1916.
19. Thomas Y. Crowell Co., New York, 1923.
20. "So conceiving culture to be the expression of the most distinctive phase of man's original nature, anthropology seeks to comprehend and formulate the modes and conditions of this expression in just the same way as we now deal with other phenomena." (Wissler, *Man and Culture*, 327).
21. W. H. R. Rivers, "The Ethnological Analysis of Culture," *Nature*, 1911, 358-60.
22. Rivers, *Social Organization*, 3.

2

Among the Middle Americans

Shortly after returning from conducting the fieldwork for his dissertation in Tepoztlán, Mexico, Redfield described his experiences in an article published in the University of Chicago Magazine. He wrote this article for the general reader, and in many ways it was a typical human interest story, particularly in the manner in which he depicted the integration of his family into the community of Tepoztlán. Redfield had conducted his fieldwork accompanied by his wife and two small children, a daughter age three and a son five months old, and he found that the baby and toddler proved to be marvelous bridges to the native Tepoztecans. Redfield's wife, Greta, served as a co-investigator in conducting fieldwork, and she developed strong relationships with the women of Tepoztlán through shared child-rearing concerns. Yet Redfield offered more in this story than mere humorous observations and traveler's anecdotes. Instead, he continued the line of thought first advanced in his 1926 Social Forces article, particularly in regards to defining an expanded and reenergized conceptualization of the role of anthropology among the social sciences. Anthropology faced a juncture, he argued, in which it could rise above mere antiquarianism and, if pushed, align itself with contemporary sociologists in "scientific" study of peoples undergoing rapid change, especially those traditional peoples actively emigrating to large American cities. The scientific studies Redfield referred to were those then being conducted by the sociologists of the "Chicago School," and he clearly indicated that he saw his work falling within this tradition. And while it would progressively decline in his work over the course of his career, Redfield expressed here a pronounced instrumentalist "social engineering" conception for his Tepoztlán study and the role of anthropology in general.

Not all Indians live on reservations and not all ethnological fieldwork is done in order to rescue the remnants of dying civilizations. Ethnologists have been busy making such rescues; and hard and even heroic work it has sometimes been to record primitive customs that are rapidly going down beneath the wheels of modern civilization. But they have done this work so well that now they feel able to take a broader view of their responsibilities and even to find time to be interested in the present and future of peoples, and not simply in their past.

The anthropologists of the University of Chicago are among those who are developing plans for the study of contemporary peoples.

First published in the *University of Chicago Magazine* 20 (March 1928): 242-247.

They hope that they may collaborate with the sociologists in scientific studies of foreign populations who do now and who promise even more to present practical problems to the people of the United States. Following capital, we go abroad to meet these people in their own homes, and pursuing employment and a higher standard of living, they come into our country; and in both cases problems arise, of politics, of administration, of immigration, of social welfare.

The Mexicans, perhaps above all other peoples, present to us plenty of problems of both sorts. Our foreign affairs are in no small measure Mexican, and the immigrants we now admit are largely Mexican. Moreover the Mexicans constitute a whole series of ethnological and sociological problems to themselves, because of the cultural gulf between the small educated class and the great majority of ignorant peons. This uneducated majority is largely Indian in blood, and its representatives preserve many ancient customs. But they are not a primitive, tribal people, like those First Americans, now largely on reservations in this country. Neither are they as sophisticated as those later Americans of Chicago and elsewhere. They are a mixture, already centuries old, of colonial Spanish elements and of ancient Indian elements. They are an intermediate kind of people, illiterate rather than pre-literate. They are Middle Americans culturally as well as geographically.

A noteworthy beginning in the study of the peasant peoples of Mexico was made by Dr. Manuel Gamio, the distinguished one-time director of anthropology with the Mexican National Government. It was Dr. Gamio, whose invaluable advice was sought and generously given when our expedition was made possible by a fellowship granted by the Social Science Research Council. Dr. Gamio suggested the site for the work: Tepoztlán, a village of the ancient Tlahuicas, a tribe closely allied to the Aztecs. This village, typical of the Middle Americans, is situated in the State of Morelos, some sixty miles south of Mexico City. The community is on no principal line of travel; economically it does no more than support itself; therefore the contacts with the city, although frequent and going back four hundred years, introduce no more than a dilution of modern city ways into a peasant village.

In November of 1926 our party entered and took up quarters in Tepoztlán. It was a family party; for the other members of the expedition were Mrs. Redfield and our two children, one five months old and the other not yet three years. Mrs. Redfield's mother, Mrs. Park, wife of Professor Robert E. Park, also accompanied us and remained the first four weeks.

We entered Tepoztlán on horseback, for all communication with the village is by narrow mountain trails. No wheel ever turns in the streets of Tepoztlán. On exploratory visits I had found a suitable house. It had only one room, and in this five of us slept, cooked, ate and did fieldwork in ethnology. But the room was large, and it commanded an extraordinarily beautiful view of the mountain-walled subtropical valley. Food was excellent; we brought some down from Mexico City, and we made good use of the local fruits. There were milk cows; so the baby throve.

As junior ethnologist, the baby more than earned his keep. All people are interested in babies. Certainly Mexican Indians are; and they came around in numbers to see him fed orange juice—which, they said, would keep his teeth from coming out—and to advise us of the dangers of allowing him to sleep out of doors where sickness might fall on him from the trees. But this sort of comparative child-care was just what we wanted to stimulate, and soon we had many friends and were collecting much of the information we wanted. Indeed our principal loss was of privacy and sleep.

Mrs. Redfield made a study of native cookery, both festal and secular, including a collection of folk-recipes. She also collected the data on birth customs, and postnatal care. (She tells me that after the baby comes the mother crawls into the sweat-house together with the midwife and any women who may be assisting in caring for the child, there to be steamed together, and that afterwards you pay the midwife with a bottle of wine and some cigarettes.)

It was much to be regretted that after about three months we found it advisable to bring Mrs. Redfield and the children back to Mexico City. All three were flourishing in Tepoztlán, but increasing insecurity in the region became a pointed suggestion when a band of rebels entered the town one night and put up a brief battle with the townspeople. Observing the proverbial discretion, we tested our valor by leaving our more conspicuous house and passing along the shadowed side of the moonlit road into the house of Señor Jesus Conde. We emerged when the clamor passed to stop some of the riderless horses and pick up a few of the wounded.

This man, Señor Conde, although, like almost all the rest, a full-blooded Indian, is a man of education, and one of those few Tepoztecans who feel the cultural backwardness of the community and wish to modernize it. The rise of self-consciousness in these retarded people and its effect upon the development of classes and personalities was a matter in which we were much interested and from Señor Conde we obtained much relevant material. He also assisted me in the study of Nahuatl, with which a small beginning was made. The Tepoztecans are essentially bilingual, speaking the native Indian language as well as Spanish.

In spite of the loss of Mrs. Redfield's assistance, the results of the season's work, which continued until the following July, although largely exploratory, are most satisfying. The fieldwork of the entire period—some eight months—was done in this one village, and a good understanding of its possibilities for more intensive study was obtained. A good representative collection of local songs was one result. These are in the main orally transmitted, and of very local provenience. Some are traditional and religious, and others are of the ballad type. Many of these latter deal with the exploits of Emiliano Zapata, the notorious rebel leader of the Indians of Morelos; about his famous figure many legends cling. Many of the Tepoztecans were his men; and with one of these I became very intimate. We also obtained much information on the treatment of disease, and made a collection of remedial plants. Scores of fiestas were observed, and a good introductory description worked out of the social and religious organization. I am much encouraged in the feeling that a technique for the study of these intermediate folk peoples can be developed which will warrant intensive work by many ethnologists.

The entire personnel of this exploratory expedition suffer from occasional nostalgia for the charming people and the lovely valley where the work was done. It is to be hoped that the very recent news, contained in a letter from Señor Conde, that a local group in Tepoztlán have begun a rebellion against the Federal Government, is to be construed as no more than a minor disturbance of a life delightful as it is remote, and scientifically provocative as it is delightful.

3
A Note on Method

> *In the introduction to his dissertation, Redfield advanced the most sharply articulated version of his vision for a revised approach to anthropology. He positioned his work clearly against that of Franz Boas, the father of American professional anthropology. While Boas deserved all due respect for establishing the field as an academic discipline and raising up a full generation of graduate students and practitioners, Redfield argued, Boas had also exercised a stultifying effect on the discipline. In his efforts to oppose the social evolutionary notions so prevalent in 19th-century anthropology because of their racist underpinnings, Boas had gone too far, Redfield charged, and had quashed the theoretical and developmental impulse within the discipline. Anthropologists could engage in social evolutionary conceptions, Redfield proposed, provided they took care to avoid the contamination of racist assumptions. Redfield advanced his own study as an example of an inquiry that sought to go beyond the mere antiquarianism that Boasian historical studies had become by the 1920s, and rise instead to the level of social anthropology, an empirical discipline informed by generalizing theoretical assumptions.*

In 1905 Franz Boas, generally regarded as the founder of American anthropology, declared that

> anthropology is the science that endeavors to reconstruct the early history of mankind, and that tries, wherever possible, to express in the form of laws ever-recurring modes of historical happenings.[1]

In this single sentence he simultaneously embraced for anthropology the method of history and the method of explanatory science. At their extremes these two methods, these two interests, are in logical character quite opposed. The one, like art, communicates concrete and unique experiences; the other makes general statements of phenomenal recurrences and has for its goal prediction. An account of the varying predominance of the one or the other is a history of the anthropological method.

The first important anthropological school, the "evolutionistic" school of the second half of the nineteenth century, sought the laws of social change.

First published in "*A Plan for the Study of Tepoztlán, Morelos*," (Ph.D. diss., University of Chicago, 1928), 1-10.

> In studying both the recurrence of special habits or ideas in several districts and their prevalence within each district, there come before us ever-reiterated proofs of regular causation, producing the phenomena of human life, and of laws of maintenance and diffusion according to which these phenomena settle into permanent standard conditions of society at definite stages of culture.[2]

But with Tylor and his contemporaries the two methods approached each other in the intermediate field of natural history. To them the history of an institution, even of a society, was representative of a type; and they were interested in defining that type. These types of institutional change were the "stages of culture" which aroused the students who followed them to critical protest. The fundamental assumption, that all groups must, in their nature, develop according to one pattern, was exposed as a mere assumption, an assumption which could not stand for a minute when once specific sequences were actually worked out.

To Boas[3] and to others[4] the resort to special investigations into unique series, geographical or historical, was a mere detour, a necessary prerequisite to a really sound explanatory science. Generalizations of social change were possible, if properly purged of the evolutionistic assumption. They would be "uniformities independent of the time factor."[5] But with some who made careful geographical and historical studies[6] of particular primitive peoples the scientific impulse came to rest in history, in the unraveling of another thread in the web of the past. And indeed archaeologists and ethnologists together, by many detailed researches into the pre-literary period, have helped to make possible the "New History" of today. Archaeology[7] almost entirely, and ethnology very largely,[8] remain history. As "culture history" they link historical astronomy and historical geology with history proper.[9]

Nevertheless the return to an interest in processual generalizations in the field of social anthropology, and the reemployment of what is essentially the comparative method, has in recent years been clearly marked. After all, no more than a shift of emphasis is needed to turn the investigator from the field of history to that of normalistic science. In devising techniques for determining the relative priority of cultural elements where there are no written records, social anthropologists have made general formulations as to the nature of social changes as, for example, general statements as to the relative case of diffusion of different types of culture. Such generalizations may be merely incidental to an interest fundamentally historical,[10] or they may become the scientific end in themselves. This they have become in the case of Wissler, who is now largely engaged with inquiries into the diffusion process, not in order to write history, but in order to achieve control of contemporary and future change.[11] Kroeber's more ultimate aim is at least in part that cultural anthropology shall cultivate "pure science,"[12] and the interest in culture process as distinct from culture history is unequivocal in Malinowski.[13]

Anthropology in general, and ethnology in particular, grew up around a body of data, and only in the adolescence of the science has its new self-consciousness made clear its methodological affiliations with other disciplines.[14] As the explanatory interest, with its aim prediction, detaches itself from historiography, the restriction in materials to the cultures of primitive peoples is increasingly felt to be artificial and unnecessary. As soon as one is interested in parallels, one turns to the materials of one's own culture for more examples with which to test a tentative generalization. And in fact Wissler's *Man and Culture* draws a considerable part of its illustrations from modern and Western civilization; even in Lowie's *Primitive Religion*[15] primitive behavior is illuminated by illustrations from civilized behavior; while in Kroeber's recent inquiry into cyclical recurrences in cultural phenomena[16] the beginning is made not with ethnological materials but with data from modern history, with dress fashions in the nineteenth century and with the shapes of medieval and of modern spoons.

At the time it comes to be felt that the inevitable limitations imposed by archaeological and even ethnological research regrettably restrict the class of data that fall within the purview of social anthropology. The social anthropologist ordinarily begins by working out specific historical sequences involving culture traits of primitive peoples. The events reconstructed have passed, and their only record is the artifact and the objectively described traits, with their distributions. The mere account of the diffusion of exteriorly similar traits is felt to be only a small part of the real story. The "psychological approach," hailed as the fruitful trend of cultural anthropology,[17] involves apparently two related ideas: the possible reduction of human behavior to types,[18] and the enlargement of the conceptual scheme to provide for such phenomena as the attitude of the group practicing a cultural trait toward that trait, toward themselves and toward other cultures. Much the same is implicit in Malinowski's "functional anthropology." Malinowski seeks general characteristics of human behavior,[19] and for him the "meaning" of a culture trait is everything; i.e., he regards customs as so many types of social control.[20]

If, therefore, the interest is in studying social processes for their own sake, it would seem a more direct procedure to study such processes as they occur, rather than to content oneself with comparing the historical sequences so laboriously determined by historical methods. In sequences of the latter sort only a small part of all the facts can ever be recaptured when the groups described are peoples without writing. If one is interested in studying what happens rather than what happened, ones moves more directly if ones studies it as it happens. Now that the power and personnel of anthropology has grown, it can undertake such investigations and still continue its work of preserving the record, depictively, of dying cultures.

The accustomed field of ethnological activity—the less sophisticated peoples—and the single important processual concept employed by ethnologists—diffusion—define in advance, in terms of both data and of method, the type of social change which ethnologists can most hopefully study. The most extensive group of diffusional changes now taking place are those resulting from the contact of modern Western civilization upon the peoples peripheral to that center of influence. Upon the frontiers of that change go on a series of diffusions, of acculturations, which can be studied as current processes. Modern industrial civilization appears to reach the marginal peoples as a sort of complex: those that survive the effect tend to react, it would seem, in ways different yet often comparable. Perhaps tractors, newspapers, linguistic revivals, technical manuals of craftsmanship and a strong emotional attitude toward foreigners—an ambivalent attitude, at once compounded of admiration and contempt—together constitute one of those uniformities independent of the time factor.

What excuse can be offered for setting down these remarks by way of preface to a dissertation embodying ethnographic notes made in a Mexican village during 1926-27? The chapters that follow do not record a detailed study of contemporary change, such as the preceding pages indicate might be made by ethnologists. The purpose of the field investigation was primarily ethnographic: to describe the round of life in a typical Mexican village community. Impetus to the project was given by the current practical interest in Mexican immigrants in the United States. A description of culture traits characterizing such immigrants would constitute, it was supposed, a description of the mental content and form which they would bring with them, and so indicate the amount of adjustment they would have to undergo in accommodating themselves to the new milieu.

The following pages are, generally speaking, ethnography. But ethnography is not photography; any ethnographic description is more than depiction and involves a selection of elements which will vary with the interests, temperament and experience of the ethnographer. And the selection that has been made here was determined by the interest of the present ethnographer in the possibility of studying, in the field, the social changes following upon contact of modern industrial civilization with the marginal peoples. He has not conceived his task to be the rescue of survivals from aboriginal culture. He has attempted to collect, for example, not those folksongs which most closely preserve pre-Columbian characteristics but those which are today vivid and meaningful in the lives of the contemporary folk. That those songs are almost entirely European in character is irrelevant.

Not only has he turned his attention only to those cultural forms which are today productive, which are today close-knit strands in the web of social life for the community under consideration, but he has welcomed any opportunities to suggest the trend of future change. The reorganization of the culture here considered under the slowly growing influence of the city and city civilization is a process—a diffusion process—which ought and will be studied. It is, the writer assumes, an example, within convenient limits, of the general type of change whereby primitive man becomes civilized man, the rustic becomes the urbanite.

The pages that follow do not, however, make such a study. No more do they present a complete description of the life of the village where the work was done. The notes are far too fragmentary for that; an adequate ethnographic report cannot be made in eight months—eight years is not too long. These chapters are only a sketch, a skeleton, of the life of the village, but a sketch of the culture not primarily as it looks backward to its historical antecedents but as it looks forward to the modern life it is very slowly approaching. Because the report which follows deliberately seeks out the frontier of social change in this particular Mexican village, and attempts to set down some of the respects in which the older culture is changing, it may be regarded as a "plan" for an actual study of contemporary change. Because of this interest, the writer has not hesitated to depart from the usual chapter classification of ethnographic reports, and to group his materials in categories that seem to him more closely to represent groupings that would be serviceable in such a study.

The tenor of the foregoing remarks is that this report seeks to call the attention of ethnologists to the study of contemporary diffusional change, and to the largely unoccupied scientific field of the peasant peoples as distinguished from the primitive or tribal peoples. The community described in the succeeding pages is not a primitive tribe that has not yet met the impact of Western civilization. Nor is it such a simple society that has met this impact and is now in resulting disorganization. For three centuries or more this community has been in a state of substantial equilibrium, accommodated to the European culture which conquered it, but which, in its later urban manifestations, still remains outside it. The people of this village are, it would seem, a peasant people, a "folk" people in the narrower sense of that word, whose lives are defined in large part in terms of that larger, outside modern civilization within which they are enclaved. To suggest means whereby the nature of this intermediate type of culture might be defined would seem to be worthwhile.

Notes

1. [Editor's Note: Redfield's text contains a typographical error—the document he cites by Franz Boas appeared in 1908 not 1905.] Franz Boas, *Anthropology: A Lecture Delivered at Columbia University, December 18, 1907* (New York: Columbia University Press, 1908), 8.
2. Edward B. Tylor, *Primitive Culture*, 7th ed. (New York: Brentanos, 1924), 2. So too, Westermarck's "comparative sociology" has for its object "to explain the facts with which it is concerned, to give an answer to the question, why?" *The History of Human Marriage*, 5th ed., vol. 1 (London: Macmillan, 1921), 2.
3. "The immediate results of the historical method are, therefore, histories of the cultures of diverse tribes which have been the subject of study. I fully agree with those anthropologists who claim that this is not the ultimate aim of our science, because the general laws, although implied in such a description, cannot be clearly formulated nor their relative value appreciated without a thorough comparison of the manner in which they assert themselves in different cultures." Franz Boas, "The Limitations of Comparative Method of Anthropology, *Science*, n.s. 4 (18 December 1896): 904.
4. "As long as we continue offering the world only reconstructions of specific detail, and consistently show a negativistic attitude toward broader conclusions, the world will find very little profit in ethnology. People do want to know why." A. L. Kroeber, review of *Primitive Society* by Robert Lowie in *American Anthropologist*, n.s. 22 (1920): 377-381.
5. R. H. Lowie, *Primitive Society* (New York: Boni and Liveright, 1920), 436.
6. As for example the careful historical studies of Berthold Laufer.
7. Only in the work of Jane Harrison (*Prolegomena to the Study of Greek Religions*; *Themis, A Study of the Social Origins of Greek Religions*; *Mythology*) do we find archaeological materials employed with the method of natural science.
8. In Kroeber's *Anthropology* the assertion is made that "anthropology has been occupied with trying to generalize the findings of history." But in fact most of that book *is* history: the history of European and Oriental and other cultures. [A. L. Kroeber, *Anthropology* (New York: Harcourt Brace and Company, 1923)].
9. The immediately preceding link is race history. The field of physical anthropology tends to divide into an interest in historical hypotheses as to the origins and movement of racial groups, and into human biology—inquiries into the laws and mechanisms of somatological change.

A Note on Method 23

10. As are the elaborate and ingenious general formulae describing the diffusion process in E. Sapir's "Time Perspective in Aboriginal American Culture: A Study in Method." "A culture element is transmitted with maximum ease when (i.e., whenever) it is conceptually readily detachable from its cultural setting, is not hedged about in practice by religious or other restraints," etc.
11. *Man and Culture*, especially the chapter on "The Nationalization of the Culture Process." Also *The Relation of Nature to Man in Aboriginal America*.
12. Address delivered before the Social Science Research Council at Hanover, New Hampshire, August 25, 1927, under the title "Study of Cultural Phenomena" (unpublished).
13. "Whatever might be the value of an interest in origins of culture, it is obvious that unless these data bear in one way or another upon modern conditions, the purely antiquarian anthropology cannot be of any great utility, and so far very little effort has been devoted to make evolutionary anthropology bear upon the actual problems of modern life.

    "Again, the diffusionist writings, the reconstructions of past history of the various primitive races, is of no obvious or direct importance in modern questions. Whether mother-right has moved on the American continent from southeast to northwest, or whether moccasins were first discovered among the Algonquins of the northeast and gradually moved toward Mexico, this important historical fact has a theoretical significance perhaps, but it cannot very well be used by the social student in discussing prohibition, the Negro problem, the question of divorce, of sexual morality, and so on."

    "The recognition that social process is submitted to definite rules exactly as natural process is subject to the laws of physics, chemistry, and biology, finds a very tenacious opposition in the science of society." Address under the title "Anthropology as a Social Science," before the Social Science Research Council at Hanover, N.H., August 19, 1926 (unpublished).
14. A. L. Kroeber, "The Possibility of a Social Psychology," *American Journal of Sociology* 23 (1917): 633-650; A. R. Radcliffe-Brown, "The Methods of Ethnology and Social Anthropology," *South African Journal of Science* 20 (October 923): 134-147.
15. New York: Boni and Liveright, 1924.
16. Address before the Social Science Research Council, August 10, 1927 (unpublished). See also Kroeber's "On the Principle Order in Civilization Exemplified by Changes of Fashion," *American Anthropologist*, n.s. 21 (191): 235-263.
17. A. A. Goldenweiser, "Cultural Anthropology" in the *Making and Prospects of the Social Sciences*, ed. Harry Elmer Barnes (New York: Alfred A. Knopf), 210-254.
18. "[A]n analysis ... of certain general and characteristic but not universal phenomena." Ibid., 251.
19. For example, in discussing magic, he says: "The type of belief met in magic is always an affirmation of man's power to deal with the situation by a rite or a spell. This belief simply repeats in a standardized manner what hope all the time has whispered within the individual's own mind. Again, the rite repeats in a fixed, definite form what the natural expression of emotion already contains, only, as a rite, it is carried out with a purpose and with the conviction that it is a means to an end.

    "When we compare the forms of the fixed magic ritual they are remarkably akin to the response of upset equilibrium occurring under similar conditions. Black magic, which corresponds to the sentiment of hate, and which replaces the outbursts of impotent rage, contains in its most typical ritual of stabbing, pointing the bone, mimic destruction, in the text of its formulae, a reproduction of the various gestures, words, and types of behavior which we can watch in the natural vent of emotions." Article on "Anthropology," *Encyclopedia Britannica*, 13th edition, p. 136.

20. "The functional view of culture insists therefore upon the principle that in every type of civilization, every system, material object, idea and belief fulfills some vital function; has some task to accomplish, represents an indispensable part within a working whole." Ibid., 133.

4

The Mexican Folk

In revising his dissertation for publication, Redfield devoted special attention to the introduction. Specifically, he removed the sharp critique of Franz Boas and his influence within American anthropology and indeed only briefly addressed concerns so forcefully stated previously regarding the antiquarian nature of most American anthropology during the first twenty-five years of the twentieth century. Rather, he focused his introduction on defining a type of peoples, the "folk," who occupied an intermediate rung on the ladder between traditional and modern. In trying to advance this new term, Redfield was attempting to move beyond social developmental depictions that connoted inferiority or were in any sense condescending. He intended the term "folk" to have general applicability and to describe intermediate peoples caught between tradition and modernity both in remote Mexican villages, such as Tepoztlán, as well as villages and towns within other cultures across the world. This effort at defining intermediate peoples in a generic and value neutral way proved to be a long-time concern for Redfield, one in which he pursued with increasing specificity over his career.

The terms "folk lore," "folk song," and even "folk ways" have a meaning in considering Mexico which they lack in connection with a country such as ours. The ways of the folk, largely unwritten and unremarked, constitute the real Mexico. "In few countries," says Gruening, "is political history less significant than in Mexico, yet its historiographies are preeminently political."[1] The formal institution, the explicit statement of program or policy, the bulk of contemporary documents, lie remote from the ways of the masses and record their history almost not at all. The world of the cultivated classes, who alone are articulate and who alone communicate freely with us, is a world apart from that of the folk. To learn and to set down the ways of the folk, one must encounter them directly and intimately; they are not otherwise to be found. Ethnology is the form which any careful study of contemporary history tends to take in Mexico.

First published in *Tepoztlán, A Mexican Village: A Study of Folk Life* (Chicago: University of Chicago Press, 1930), 1-14.

I

What is the "folk"? If its meaning be reached backward from the terms which begin this page, it is a group which has folk lore and folk songs. For such material the collector goes to the primitive tribes or to the simpler peasant peoples enclaved within the borders of civilized nations. These are "folk" peoples. What characteristics distinguish them? Such peoples enjoy a common stock of tradition; they are the carriers of a culture. This culture preserves its continuity from generation to generation without depending upon the printed page. Moreover, such a culture is local; the folk has a habitat. Wandering folk, as, for example, the gypsy, do occur, but then special factors of social isolation cause them to preserve their folk character among a people who are not folk. Within the folk group there is relatively small diversity of intellectual interest; attitudes and interests are much the same from individual to individual, although, presumably, there is the same range of inherent temperament as in any other group of the same size. And finally, the folk peoples are country peoples. If folk lore is encountered in the cities it is never in a robust condition, but always diminishing, always a vestige.

There are plenty of such folk peoples in Mexico. Some, like the Lacandones and (until perhaps recently) the Tarahumares, are as truly primitive, as truly preliterate, as a Melanesian tribe. More, however, have long since reached an adjustment with Western civilization, as represented by the upper and governing classes; and now the complex of their culture is interwoven with the modern social and economic order. They use money, wear commercial textiles, perhaps know how to read and write, and employ at least the terminology and some of the ritual forms of Catholic Christianity. They are much like isolated, illiterate peasant peoples everywhere. The former class of peoples has been regarded as the subject of ethnology (*Völkerkunde*); the second of what has conventionally been distinguished as "folk lore" (*Volkskunde*). Both sorts of groups are folk peoples.

But the series of culture types to be found in Mexico does not end with these simple societies. Mexico is in no small part modern; every year it becomes more so. In the more sophisticated villages of the north, in the middle classes in the cities everywhere, are to be found a people much like the masses in our own country. They not only can read, but they do read. The folk hear rumor; these people read news. Through the newspaper and its closely related organs of information and popular interest, the popular magazine and the moving picture, these latter people come to share in interests which are not local but are even international. Communication by way of oral tradition with the preceding generations has with such people come to play a smaller part in determining the patterns of their thinking; they are communicating with contemporaries like themselves in other cities and in other lands; and through printing and pictures they draw upon the accumulated experience of groups geographically and historically remote. They are ceasing, or have already ceased, to be a folk people.

Apparently there are people in Mexico who are folk peoples, with folk lore and folk songs and folk ways which are often indigenous and local to the particular community, but there are also people, largely in the towns, who are no more a folk people than are the citizens of Grand Rapids or Bridgeport. And apparently the "modernization" of Mexico is the gain of this second kind of people at the expense of the first. Yet in spite of this change, the bulk of the Mexican population are folk. With us it is the other way. The southern Negro is our one principal folk. He has a local tradition orally transmitted; he makes folk songs. Except for him we have to search for folk peoples in the United States. In the mountains of the South and Southeast we have a sort of vestigial folk. And here and there, in such occupations as involve long periods of isolation and a relative independence of the printed page—as, for example, among lumbermen or cowboys—a sort of quasi-folk develop, who write anonymous folk songs and sometimes build up, around campfires, folk sagas of the Paul Bunyan variety.

II

How are we to define the difference between the Mexican masses and our own? What are some of the characteristics of the folk that set them off from "the common people" who are not folk? It may be suggested that the difference is made clear in the distinction between folk song and popular song, folk tale and popular literature. It is, at the extremes, the difference between the animal tales or witch stories of tribal Indian or simple peasant, and the American magazines of the "true confessions" type. Or it is the difference between the traditional chant to accompany Indian or African ritual, or the equally traditional folk song of Mexican *peón* or Romanian peasant, and "Singin' in the Rain" or "You've Never Been Blue."

It perhaps needs to be pointed out that these two sorts of songs, two sorts of literatures, are alike at all. But alike they certainly are. They belong together when contrasted with the sophisticated art and literature of the more self-conscious intelligentsia. They are quite different, and different in the same way, from Proust or Stravinsky. They are both, folk song and popular song, written because they will be sung; they are both, folk tale and popular story, composed because they will be heard or read. The sophisticated art is formed in conformity with self-conscious canons of taste. It is composed not to be read by everybody, but to be appreciated by the few. It is written not in the widespread and easy images of the folk, but in more deliberately constructed forms. It has a horror, for example, of *clichés*.

This is the difference which Sumner[2] speaks of when he distinguishes the "masses" from the "classes." The "classes" are the minority of sophisticated people who at least in literate society tend to occupy a mental world apart from that of the masses. The "masses," on the other hand, include both "folk" peoples and the common people of civilized and completely literate countries. For this second kind of "masses" there appears to be no name available,[3] and inventing new terms is of doubtful wisdom. Completing the proportion: "folk" is to "folk song" as "popular song" is to x—one might suggest *populus*, or better, *demos*.

The differences between folk song and popular song, or folk tale and popular literature, afford an approach to the difference between "folk" and demos. The popular song is obviously more sophisticated. It is written deliberately, for sale. The folk song is more "artless." The popular song has an author; the folk song easily loses its composer. The question of communal composition does not arise in the realm of popular literature as distinguished from folk literature. The popular song or story is written in order that it may be sold; the composer earns a living out of it, or hopes to. And finally, there is the obvious and important difference between a composition that depends upon writing and one that needs only singing or speaking and hearing. And from this difference flow a number of significant corollaries. The folk song is much more local; it is commonly expressed in local terms; it has local allusions. The popular song refers to a much wider community of experience. The popular song, being written, is standardized; of it one does not collect "versions." Popular songs that develop versions are passing into folk songs. But the *Saturday Evening Post* appears in almost three million identical versions every Thursday. And the popular song, the popular story, exist in the world of fashion and fad. Among the folk, where communication is much slower, there is much less fashion; at least, in folk literature, there are probably no "rages." The "rage" is a trait of the *demos*.

If we turn to the songs and to the literature which are current in Mexico, we find examples of all three sorts: sophisticated, popular, and folk. That type of song and story which has widest currency, however, is in many respects transitional between folk literature and popular literature, folk song and popular song. The more primitive village peoples still sing the ancient traditional songs and tell the old traditional tales. The peoples of the towns and cities, at least the middle and upper classes there, sing sentimental songs, which are locally Mexican, and even the jazz ditties of ephemeral favor in New York or London. But in between lies a great mass of transitional literature, a sort of "folk-popular" literature, which expresses the fact that in Mexico we have a collection of folk peoples who are becoming *demos*.

This intermediate literature is best known from its outstanding form, the ballad known as *corrido*.[4] The *corrido* is in first instance orally transmitted. The composer, a singer of local prestige, communicates it to the circle of listeners; it tends immediately to become anonymous. But it is not wholly independent of writing. In the rural districts it may be set down in private copy-books, and in the cities it sometimes circulates on cheap printed leaflets—just as did the "broadside ballad" of Elizabethan England.

The subject matter of this popular literature is always what interests the Mexican masses: war, crime, catastrophe, and especially popular heroes and popular scapegoats. And in its constantly shifting content, as the old *corridos* die and the new *corridos* are composed, it constitutes a sort of collective diary of the Mexican masses. At its lower margin, in the more traditional songs that persist in local communities for generations, this literature merges with the typical folk literature of primitive peoples. Its upper margin, the news ballad of crime or passion, passes into the lower margin of our own popular literature—the doggerel verses about Floyd Collins or the Hall-Mills case now circulated on mail-order phonograph records.

The essential difference between the *corrido* and the folk song of a truly primitive people appears to lie in the tendency of the *corrido* to enter into the realm of news, public opinion, and even propaganda. The *corrido* is a news organ. It informs what comes to be a public of the events which concern it, and especially of the excitements which nourish its interest. It tends, one would venture, to become a mechanism for conflicting local attitudes. A man sung as a bandit in one community may be sung as a redeemer in another; the circulation of these songs tends to define his position in more generally accepted terms. In this relation of the *corrido* to a discussion which is more impersonal than the intimate interchange of ideas in a completely self-sufficient folk community, the *corrido* is related to that rise of nationalistic feeling which begins to give to the changes which are going on in Mexico a special, and at the same time a characteristic, form.

III

The change which is obviously going on in Mexico can be described, it may be, in terms more fundamental than "the spread of education" or "economic development," although these are of course important aspects of that change. To the social anthropologist the change is that which is represented by the gain of popular literature at the expense of folk literature. It is a change in type of culture. It may furthermore be provisionally assumed that this change has elements in common with others which are taking place in countries similarly placed with respect to the widening influence of modern Western industrial civilization. Mexico is but one of the peoples on that frontier of contact. Modern industrial civilization appears, offhand, to reach these marginal peoples as a sort of complex; those peoples that survive tend to react, it would seem, in ways different yet often comparable. Perhaps tractors, newspapers, linguistic revivals, technical manuals of craftsmanship, and a strong emotional attitude toward foreigners, compounded at once of admiration and contempt, represent recurrent elements in a describable process.

There is a growing disposition on the part of cultural anthropologists to study social processes as such, rather than to rest content with the mere description of cultures or the solution of specific historical sequences. In large part ethnologists remain geographers and historians; they describe what is or was in that particular place, and tell how it got there. With many the scientific interest comes to rest in history, in the unraveling of another thread in the web of the past. Archaeologists and ethnologists together, by many detailed researches into the preliterary periods, have helped to make possible the "new history" of today.

Nevertheless the return to an interest in processual generalizations in the field of social anthropology, and the re-employment of what is essentially the comparative method, has in recent years been clearly marked. Anthropologists once more seek generalizations upon social change. With some, as with Wissler,[5] inquiries into the diffusion process have been made, not in order to sharpen tools for historical research, but in order to achieve control of contemporary and future change. Kroeber's more ultimate aim is at least in part that cultural anthropology shall cultivate "pure science,"[6] and the interest in culture process as distinct from culture history[7] is unequivocal in Malinowski.[8]

If the interest of the student lies in an investigation of social processes in general terms, it would seem a more direct procedure to study such processes as they actually occur, rather than to content one's self with comparing the historical sequences so laboriously determined by historical methods of the ethnologist, who works without the direct sources of written records. In sequences of the latter sort only a small part of all the facts can ever be recaptured. If one is interested in studying what happens rather than what happened, one moves more directly if one studies it as it happens. Now that the power and personnel of anthropology has grown, it can undertake such investigations and still continue its work of preserving the record of the dying cultures.

That it is still possible to study the more isolated groups of Mexico in order to learn something about the pre-Columbian cultures, and about the changes which they underwent when they came in contact with the Spaniards, is not to be denied. Such a study would be a study of a dead culture and of a past change. It is merely to be pointed out that such was not the interest which took the writer to Mexico. To learn as much as can be learned as to the history of the present culture of Tepoztlán is a part of any thorough study of that culture. But the interest in the following pages lies more particularly with the current changes. The task was not conceived to be the rescue of survivals from aboriginal culture. There was no attempt to collect, for example, folk songs persisting in the memory of any individual which might most closely preserve pre-Columbian characteristics, but rather to study those songs which are today vivid and meaningful in the lives of the contemporary folk. That these songs are almost entirely European in character is interesting, but in no way limits their importance.

The Mexican folk are not necessarily Indian. The folk culture is a fusion of Indian and Spanish elements. The acculturation which gave rise to this mixed culture took place three hundred years ago, largely within the first few generations after the Conquest. The analysis of the Mexican folk culture into Spanish and Indian elements is one problem—a historical problem. The description of changes occurring in that folk culture due to spread of city ways is another problem—a study of a contemporary change.

The disorganization and perhaps the reorganization of the culture here considered under the slowly growing influence of the city is a process—a diffusion process—which can and will be studied. It is, the writer assumes, an example, within convenient limits, of the general type of change whereby primitive man becomes civilized man, the rustic becomes the urbanite.

Notes

1. Ernest Gruening, *Mexico and Its Heritage* (New York: Century Co., 1928), p. x.
2. "It is a question of the first importance for the historian whether the mores of the historical classes of which he finds evidence in documentary remains penetrated the masses or not. The masses are the real bearers of the mores of the society. They carry tradition. The folkways are their ways. They accept influence or leadership and they imitate, but they do so as they see fit, being controlled by their notions and tastes previously acquired. They may accept standards of character and action from the classes, or from foreigners, or from literature, or from a new religion, but whatever they take up they assimilate and make it a part of their own mores, which they then transmit by tradition, defend in its integrity, and refuse to discard again. Consequently the writings of the literary class may not represent the faiths, notions, tastes, standards, etc., of the masses at all. The literature of the first Christian centuries shows us scarcely anything of the mores of the time, as they existed in the faith and practice of the masses. Every group takes out of a new religion which is offered to it just what it can assimilate with its own traditional mores. Christianity was a very different thing amongst Jews, Egyptians, Greeks, Germans and Slavs. It would be a great mistake to suppose that any people ever accepted and held philosophical or religious teaching as it was offered to them, and as we find it recorded in the books of the teachers. The mores of the masses admit of no such sudden and massive modification by doctrinal teaching. The process of assimilation is slow, and is attended by modifying influences at every stage" *(Folkways,* p. 46).

    Sumner did not distinguish between the folk, a country people among whom culture is built up, and the urban proletariat, among whom it tends to breakdown.
3. "Proletariat" appears to be a related term.
4. "The commonest form of musical expression is the *corrido,* literally, 'current happening.' Any event that touches the people immediately finds its way into this form of ballad. Its words are printed on a gaudy sheet of paper, usually green or pink, embellished often by a lurid wood cut. The verse is doggerel and the music a 'catchy' refrain. But the *corridos* are a valuable index to popular thought. During the Revolution Zapata outranked all other figures in the variety and number of *corridos* about him. Villa, pictured as 'muy hombre,' the hero of gigantic exploits, came next. Carranza did not figure in *corridos*—he made no appeal to popular imagination. 'The arm of Obregon'—the arm lost on the field of battle—did. Heroic, tragic, gruesome, pathetic themes prevail. Deeds of

valor, floods, earthquakes, famines, calamities generally, which affect the people, are instantly sung. The writer usually begins by announcing the subject of his verse—as if addressing an audience, and in concluding often takes leave of it. He is a modern troubadour—but instead of offering his vocal wares to the mighty, as of old, the people are his patrons, for the *corridos* are sold for a centavo or two in the markets.

"An essential quality of the *corridos* is their ingenuousness: The writer is wholly frank. He tells not only of his hero's prowess, but of his weaknesses—his drunkenness, his offenses against law and order, his fickleness to his sweethearts as well as their faithlessness. And just as he views the hero of his theme without illusion he applies similar measurements to the great and near-great of his country—the generals and politicians" (Gruening, *Mexico and Its Heritage*, pp. 647-48).

5. *Man and Culture,* especially the chapter on "The Rationalization of the Culture Process"; also *The Relation of Nature to Man in Aboriginal America.*
6. Address delivered before the Social Science Research Council, at Hanover, N.H., August 25, 1927, under the title "Study of Cultural Phenomena" (unpublished).
7. The logic of this distinction is presented in A. L. Kroeber's "The Possibility of a Social Psychology." Radcliffe-Brown (art., "The Methods of Ethnology and Social Anthropology") makes the distinction quite clear, suggests a number of significant implications, and proposes the term "ethnology" for the historical discipline and "social anthropology" for the interest in arriving at natural laws of social change.
8. "Whatever might be the value of an interest in origins of culture, it is obvious that unless these data bear in one way or another upon modern conditions, the purely antiquarian anthropology cannot be of great utility, and so far very little effort has been devoted to make evolutionary anthropology bear upon the actual problems of modern life.

"Again, the diffusionist writings, the reconstructions of past history of the various primitive races, is of no obvious or direct importance in modern questions. Whether mother-right has moved on the American continent from southeast to northwest, or whether moccasins were first discovered among the Algonquins of the northeast and gradually moved towards Mexico, this important historical fact has a theoretical significance perhaps, but it cannot very well be used by the social student in discussing prohibition, the Negro problem, the question of divorce, of sexual morality, and so on.

"The recognition that social process is submitted to definite rules exactly as natural process is subject to the laws of physics, chemistry and biology, finds a very tenacious opposition in the science of society" (address under the title "Anthropology as a Social Science" before the Social Science Research Council at Hanover, N.H., August 10, 1926 [unpublished]).

5

Sociological Investigation in Yucatan

At the close of Tepoztlán, *Redfield acknowledged that his study was only a beginning and that it had not actually delivered on his boldest expectation of elucidating the principles of social change through study of change "as it happens." A fundamental limitation of his study had been its lack of a comparative dimension. He had successfully observed and mapped changes within Tepoztecan society but without one or more external entities to compare these changes against, his observations did not easily lend themselves to generalizations. Following his study of Tepoztlán, Redfield conceived of a broader investigation grounded on a comparative basis. The Carnegie Institution of Washington had sponsored a broad-ranging set of historical and archeological investigations in the nearby Yucatan peninsula, and Redfield successfully obtained support from this organization to pursue complementary anthropological studies on the peninsula. Redfield conceived of a series of community studies focusing on four towns and villages of varying degrees of size, complexity, and sophistication that he could use to study the fundamental processes of social change and transformation. The Carnegie Institution of Washington provided Redfield funding for this investigation for the full decade of the 1930s. This summary of his design, published as his first annual status report, provides a clear description of his initial goals and efforts at defining a comparative methodology for anthropological study.*

There is a marked disposition among social anthropologists to make their work a contribution to the understanding and control of life; probably it does no harm to be a little presumptuous. At any rate, few students of the simpler peoples want their work to result in merely a miscellany of curious information, and many quite definitely strive to derive from it some general knowledge of human ways. No behavior in nature so challenges the usefulness of the scientific method as does human behavior. Some of us are disposed to accept that challenge, and to turn our scientific interest toward the "what happens, and why" in the ways of men.

If we are interested in what happens, it seems best to study it while it happens. It is true that we want to know the history of the people we are studying, because that helps us to learn what experiences have brought about their present characteristic behavior. But the history of non-liter-

First published in *Carnegie Institution of Washington, Year Book* 30 (Washington, D.C.: Carnegie Institution of Washington, 1931), 122-124.

ate peoples is poor in intimate materials. Many more facts are knowable about changes that go on before one's eyes.

There is reason to suppose that such changes may be more easily understood in simpler societies where the factors in the situation are relatively few. This gives the student of the folk peoples an advantage. In Yucatan, we believe, for several reasons this advantage can be pressed. The essentially insular character of Yucatan defines the field of study. The history of the Maya and of the contact of Indian and Spanish civilization is being intensively studied by competent specialists. There exist within a small area communities exhibiting a range of civilization from the primitive tribe to the urban aggregate. And finally, many of these communities, under the influence of modern industrial civilization, are undergoing striking changes.

With this viewpoint and these hopes, we have begun the study of selected communities that lie along this range of civilization. We are seeking to make the studies of the separate communities comparable with one another, and we are trying to describe changes that are going on. The entire resulting description should have a dynamic character; it ought to sketch out a process—the process of becoming civilized.

This year Alfonso Villa and I pursued a study of Chan Kom, a village lying about twelve miles south of Chichen Itzá. Circumstances there were extremely favorable, due to the goodwill gained in the neighborhood by Miss MacKay of the Chichen Itzá staff and to Villa's two years of selfless service in the village as a teacher. We were therefore able to study the community with the friendly cooperation of its inhabitants. Materials were collected representing the entire round of life of the people. Included are detailed materials on the utilization of the land and the expenditure and division of labor and considerable information on both Christian and pagan elements in the religious belief and practice.

We tried, furthermore, to report not merely the abstract patterns of custom, but also the living community which is the carrier of those customs, and the changes which both customs and community are undergoing. The particular interest of Chan Kom in connection with the larger project lies in the fact that Chan Kom stands right on the frontier of changes now going on among the Maya. The people are still a homogeneous folk people, dependent upon oral tradition and largely isolated from the world. Yet they are deliberately seeking to relate themselves to the more modern civilization of the towns, encouraging education, sanitary reforms and rational horticulture. In organizing a cattle cooperative to care for cattle offered by the Socialist government of the State, the villagers arranged to have the shaman perform the ceremony of blood-sacrifice to exorcise the evil spirits from the new herds. Chan Kom looks both forward and back.

This Chan Kom study is to be kept unfinished, for the full significance we would like it to have will be realized only if it fits into the series of similar studies forming a description of culture and civilization in Yucatan. A part of my time was therefore spent this year in preparing for these other studies. We wish to include some study of Mérida, for only there is the full participation influence of modern industrial civilization realized. Therefore I made acquaintance with that city and, with Mrs. Redfield's help, investigated the sources of materials there available and collected documentary and statistical data. We made some study of the newspaper and other published materials, obtained data on the distribution of civilization within the urban area, and learned something of the location and nature of the sub-communities in the city. In January 1932, Dr. Asael T. Hansen is to begin field work on the project; he will carry forward the study of Mérida by investigating one sub-community and will probably do the same for a village of peons near Mérida. We plan to include in later years one of the *mestizo* towns where the simple folk culture tends to acquire some of the complexities of civilization.

Dr. Hansen's study will represent one step up from Chan Kom. One step down is represented by Indian villages in Quintana Roo. Villa and I visited the northernmost villages of this area in April 1931, and have laid plans to begin work in them in November or December of this year. The Quintana Roo Maya have customs much like those we find in Chan Kom, although retaining more archaic features, but the temper of the communities is entirely different. Most of the people do not welcome modernization, and many of the villages are definitely hostile to it. These Maya face not the future, but the past. Their social milieu is not one of settled townspeople much like themselves, as in Yucatan, but of traveling traders and migratory *chicleros*. They retain, therefore, their own intervillage organization: a sort of theocratic-military federation under the dominance of oracular shamans and chieftains grown wealthy as chicle contractors. Here the Chan Kom study should find contrast; here Villa is to begin work next fall. Still later, we may step down again and study a still more primitive community farther south or southwest in the Maya area.

6

Robert E. Park to Robert Redfield, 23 January 1932

The primary intellectual influence of Redfield's life was his father-in-law, Chicago sociologist Robert E. Park. Park had encouraged Redfield to pursue a career in social science, and from the time Redfield was in graduate school through his early years as a professor, Park exerted a profound influence on Redfield's thinking. Much of their interaction took place through letters, in which they often discussed social scientific topics. The letter reprinted here reflects Park's response to his reading of "Sociological Investigation in Yucatan." At the time of the paper's publication, Park was in Honolulu teaching at the University of Hawaii. Park responded enthusiastically to Redfield's description of his Yucatan study and offered Redfield several ideas which were to exercise profound influence upon his thinking and practice. Most important, Park urged Redfield to ground his study more theoretically, drawing especially upon the conceptualization Park had used in his own writings in which he conceived social change as a dynamic in which family-based societies (tribes) eventually gave way to territory-based societies (states). Park urged Redfield not only to seek to use this analytic framework in his Yucatan research, but also as an organizing principle for the basic ethnology course he had begun to teach at the University of Chicago. Park's suggestions resonated strongly with Redfield, and they exercised a shaping influence in his work over his entire career. Park's notions clearly underlie Redfield's later formulation of his Folk-Urban Continuum, and the ethnology course Redfield organized along Park's suggested lines became Redfield's trademark course "The Folk Society." Redfield recognized the profound influence of this letter upon his thinking and, while organizing his papers late in his life, penciled "of historical interest" at the top of the first page.

University of Honolulu [*sic*]
Jan. 23, 1932

My Dear Bob:

In spite of the excellent news service between Chicago and these islands it has not until very recently transpired that the illness which has confined you so long to the house is pneumonia—in a mild form. Well, pneumonia, in any form, is a serious matter as I know from experience. You had best not hurry to get back into the harness again. I advise you to

---

Unpublished letter: Robert E. Park to Robert Redfield, 23 January 1932, box 1, folder 8, Robert Redfield Papers, Special Collections, Joseph Regenstein Library, University of Chicago, Chicago.

take whatever rest is coming to you and use it, as you seem to be doing, to reflect on the work you have ahead of you. I am doing a good deal of loafing myself and feel better for it.

I read with very real interest your paper or report on your work in Yucatan made in Washington and thought you made a most intelligent and persuasive statement of the matter. I am going to show this paper to Peter Buck, the Mauri anthropologist, who is much interested in what he characterizes as the Chicago point of view. By that he means the proposal to study the transition from a tribal to a national and international type of culture, as it takes place, has taken place and is taking place, wherever the remnants of any tribal culture still persists.

My own notion now is to think of this transition as a change from a familial form of society, based on kinship relations, and a territorial form of society, based on economic competition and cooperation. This seems to be merely repeating what I have said before, and it is only that now my conception of the differences between the two types of social organization and cultural traits which are associated with each is less hazy than it was.

In order to make knowledge in this field more precise and in order to make studies in this field more systematic it seems to me important to define our working concepts, i.e. the tribe and the state, with logical precision. Thus conceived, whatever the tribe and the state are now or have been, historically, they become ideal concepts, to which perhaps nothing real actually conforms, but to which every type of society tends to conform. Such a procedure will probably be abhorrent to most social anthropologists but I believe it will be useful to any one who wants to think clearly in this field. Furthermore I conceive these terms not as doctrines, but as working hypotheses and as such they might be accepted with a certain amount of tolerance even by the historical school of anthropology and sociology.

To you and others who are seeking to study and make intelligible the processes by which a society makes a transition from one fundamental type of social organization to another they seem to me almost indispensable.

As in the case of the study of familial society or society founded on the kinship group the important thing is marriage customs; the manner in which tradition arises and is transmitted; the sources of authority and of obligation; the manner in which solidarity is created and morale maintained through religious ceremonies and festivals; the organization of age and sex groups within the tribe. So in the study of territorial society the most important things to note and investigate are the forms in which trade and barter arise; the gradual rise of a society without common mores or religious conceptions, but based on competitive cooperation. Political organization, in the sense in which Teggart uses that term, arises first to regulate and control the forces of society that arise when men come together or are brought together because they are useful to one another.

It is in such a society that the conception of freedom, of justice, fair play, toleration, public opinion, law as something different from custom, and all the other notions characteristic of modern life and modern society seem to have arisen.

What I am coming to is this, namely, it might be well, if you have not yet done so, to consider the possibility of studying Mérida and the backcountry where tribal society still exists, with respect to trade. What form does trade take out in the hinterland? Trade can hardly be said to exist within the limits of the tribe; what form does that larger society, within which trade does take place, assume as trade relations arise and extend to ever wider regions?

Such a study would not be primarily for the purpose of finding out to what extent trade and barter was bringing in new forms of culture and how it was changing the traditional forms of life. It would be designed rather to discover the character of the new society that was coming into existence as a result of trade. Primitive communism, under these circumstances, must be giving way to some more individualistic form of society. Old ideas of property based on the familial form of society would naturally, under these circumstances, give way to forms of property that are defined by the state and by statute law. New forms of crime and disorder, personal and social, must be taking place. The socialism and communism which you have in Mérida and which seem to have assumed a more or less sectarian and doctrinaire form there, are the repercussions and the reactions against this growing individualism and its consequences.

The concept of social organization as the anthropologists conceive it, includes little more than organization of the family. If now trade and the type of social relations that rest upon trade are included under the term social organization, it gains an extension which includes not merely the kinship group but the state or territorial society. The very extension of the term suggests the contrast between the communism of the kinship society and the individualism of the territorial society as something fundamental.

Lind's introductory course in sociology at the University of Hawaii is now organized around these two concepts of familial and territorial society. You have already considerable materials more or less organized around the conception of the kinship group. Why not now begin gathering materials around the conception of a territorially organized society, such as you have in Yucatan and the other Mexican states?

In this way you could make your studies in Yucatan contribute to your introductory course in Ethnology and you could make this introductory course, if extended to the study of the primitive state and political society, valuable to your investigations in Yucatan.

The study of trade, involving as it does the division of labor, connects up with the study of the material civilization. The study of the external relations of cultural groups occupying contiguous territory, involves the study of all those aspects that are not likely to fit into the conception of familial society. Trade, migration, conquest, the extension of political power over peoples of different cultures have created the forms of society in which we now live. The multiplication of the commodities that enter into commerce; the rise of a money and credit economy; definition and transfer of individual as against communal rights in the land; the introduction of the conception of legally defined responsibility as contrasted to personal and moral obligation; the conception of education as a rational rather than ritualistic procedure—all these are elements in the new organization of society that probably exists in Mérida but not in the community outside.

Well, these represent some of my reflections upon the contents of your letter. I give them to you for what they are worth. ...

Cordially,
(Robert E. Park)

7

Culture Changes in Yucatan

Redfield wrote this article midway through conducting his Yucatan study. He and his assistants had intensively studied three of the four communities that would be included in the full study. The initial data seemed to support fully Redfield's basic hypotheses, and it appeared that his methodology for studying the collection of communities in the Yucatan would deliver results which provided empirical evidence confirming his theoretical model of social change. This article reflects the optimism associated with the early to middle phases of his grand comparative study before his own research, and particularly that of his colleague Sol Tax's, raised empirical findings that did not seem to square with certain aspects of Redfield's theoretical model. As such, this article provides an excellent view into the study conceived in its most optimistic and idealistic terms.

I

In studying any culture known to be derived historically from two markedly different sources—as for example any of the cultures of the present Indian-Spanish populations of Mexico and Central America—one's interest is inevitably engaged in an attempt to analyze the culture into its two principal historical components. The investigator seeks to assign each element of present-day custom to a Spanish or to an Indian origin. This familiar problem has attracted Dr. Asael Hansen, Mrs. Hansen, Mr. Alfonso Villa, Mrs. Redfield, and myself in the course of ethnological work which we are now carrying on among the Maya of Yucatan on behalf of the Carnegie Institution of Washington. Of course it turns out that some elements of the contemporary Yucatecan culture are easily to be identified with Spanish or with Indian influence, while others are refractory to this historical analysis.

Where elements of culture are definitely known from Europe, and where they are also not characteristic of American Indian cultures, they are without difficulty regarded as importations from Spain. In Yucatan such elements, to mention only examples, are oranges, ordinary domestic fowl, cattle, rice, saffron and other Old World condiments, trousers, the seven-day week, the novena, crossing one's self, the idea of incubus

First published in *American Anthropologist* 36 (January-March 1934): 57-69.

and succubus, and possibly also the ghoul and the witch's familiar, the notion of the evil eye, purgatory, and probably judgment of the soul after death. Other traits are not known to characterize sixteenth-century Europe and are either actually reported for the ancient Maya by the first white invaders or else are known to be characteristic of other American Indian cultures. In Yucatan such elements, which must of course be regarded as indigenous and pre-Columbian, are most of the agricultural techniques centering about maize; the fire drill; the loincloth and the sandal; the hammock (although its use may not have become general in Yucatan until after the Conquest); the notion that eclipses are caused by an animal that is devouring the sun or the moon and that, should the luminary fail to reappear, the household furnishings would revolt against their masters and devour them; the idea of four cardinal directions associated with rain-, sky-, and maize-deities and with colors; multiple rain-gods, associated with clouds, the east, lightning and thunder, the cenotes, gourd-rattles and calabashes, and objects of special cult involving ritual breads and oriented altars; the ritual breads themselves, made of maize and squash seed and baked in an earth oven; bee-deities, the objects of a special cult; deer-gods (who bear almost the same name as the patrons of hunters mentioned by Landa[1]); bark-beer as a ceremonial drink; offerings of turkeys, ritually killed, especially as offered at regular four-year intervals; and divination by casting grains of corn.

Other elements, as for example many techniques of house construction, are equally safely, though more circumstantially, assigned to an Indian origin. These elements are not affirmatively recorded for the ancient Maya; but they are harmonious with Indian cultures and are difficult to imagine in a European setting. Such a trait is the ceremony whereby at an age of three or four months certain objects connected with the future activities of the child are placed in the child's hand and it is for the first time set astride the hip. A ritual not very different is reported for the ancient Aztecs.

Other traits, however, do not readily yield to this sorting-process into one of two pigeonholes. Many elements in the culture of present-day Yucatan have both ancient Indian and European parallels and could be attributed to either source, or to both. Shall we say that the custom of making religious pilgrimages to distant shrines is an Indian or a European custom in Yucatan today, when the historians tell us that both Indian and Europeans have long made such pilgrimages? Are the patron santos of present-day Maya villages the descendants of the local saints of the Mediterranean world, or are they translations of pagan patron gods?

We can probably say that they are both, but that is about all we can say, lacking information as to just what was in the minds of the sixteenth-century Maya before and during the period of Catholization. The number thirteen, which plays an important part in the present-day Maya rituals, is almost surely derived from indigenous culture, just as three and seven, which go together in the Catholic prayer context, are probably European. But what of nine, which now is a magical and sacred number in a wide variety of ritual contexts? We can only point out that the ancient Maya had nine gods of the underworld as they had thirteen sky-gods and also that the Catholic novena was introduced by the missionaries and is still generally practiced.

I have been interested in the first-fruit ceremony performed throughout Yucatan when the maize is ripe. In the remoter villages this ceremony involves the offering in the cornfield of thirteen ears of maize to pagan gods while Maya prayers are recited by a shaman-priest. But, as the observer moves nearer and nearer the city, this ceremony takes on, little by little, more and more of the elements of a medieval harvest home until at last it does not look at all Indian; the account of it reads like a page from Chamber's Book of Days. At what point does this ceremony cease to be Indian in origin and become Spanish?

Or consider the custom of bleeding for illness. This treatment, accompanied by cupping, is performed in Yucatan much as an old-time European barber would do it; and no doubt the Spanish conquerors were familiar with it. But the shaman-priest who bleeds his patients in the villages often uses a rattlesnake's fang as his instrument, and, when he prescribes blood letting to his patient because the sick man's ailment has been caused by his failure to offer the maize-gods the ritual they expect, it begins to suggest the penance by bloodshed of the ancient Maya.

With respect to the historical origins of some of the most fundamental complexes of contemporary Maya practice and belief, I find myself unable to make any statement. Among such I may mention the basic twofold category of "hot" and "cold" into which are divided foods, medicine, lands, and people; the ceremonial planting of a ceiba pole to which the bulls are tied in the festal bullfight; the dance with a decorated pig's head and a decorated pole; and the far-reaching and important concept of evil winds, named, specialized and semipersonified, that are thought to cause most illnesses. Many of these special problems are, however, capable of solution. One needs a familiarity with Spanish folk cultures and a thorough study of early sources on Maya culture at the time of the Conquest.

The student experienced in Indian but not in European cultures tends to attribute to Indian origins elements of culture that are actually at least in part Spanish. Sometimes the reasons are apparently very good. The Maya today predict the weather for the coming year by observing the weather on each of the first twelve days of January, then check this observation by reading the next twelve days as corresponding to the months in reverse order, and further check it by dividing the last six days into halves, and the last day into hours. This custom—first reported, I believe by Starr—has been regarded by writers on the Maya as aboriginal, probably because it was known only from the Maya area and because Landa says the priests, in the second month of the Maya year, opened their books and read the prognostications of that year. But the identical custom, under a Spanish name, has turned up in regions far from Maya influence and where Indian influence of any sort is small or non-existent—in Santo Domingo, in Venezuela, and in Costa Rica. So the likelihood that the custom is native to the Maya is much reduced. In historical inquiries of this sort, often a very small change in facts will bring about a diametric reversal of conclusion.

These remarks will serve to suggest some of the reasons why those of us who are studying the contemporary Maya of Yucatan are disposed to turn from this problem of historical analysis to a problem of another sort, which I will soon state. In the first place these historical problems, as has just been indicated, are incapable of solution from a consideration of the contemporary Maya culture alone, but wait upon study of sources as to the pre-Columbian Maya and upon knowledge of Indian and European folk cultures. In the second place, some cannot be solved at all; or rather, the question, Indian or Spanish? cannot be asked in these cases; for some customs are probably both Indian and Spanish. In fact, some are probably neither Indian nor Spanish, in the sense that neither sixteenth-century culture exhibited the custom now characterizing the present-day peoples. Thus there is today an important belief, many years ago described by Brinton, in the supernatural character of the clay images, incense-burners, and other pottery artifacts made by the ancients and encountered by the present-day people. These beings, the alux, are regarded as mischievous spirits and are propitiated in certain ceremonies. Although it is conceivable that European ideas of fairies and goblins have influenced the development of this complex of ideas and practices, it is also quite possible that this is a parallel development, or degeneration, of god to goblin, that has taken place in Yucatan with the systematic destruction of the pagan religion by the priests.

Indeed, ultimately, no Yucatecan culture element, whether originating in Europe or in America, turns out to be the same today as it was in 1519. We may say that the rain-gods, bearing the same name (*chaacs*) and many of the same attributes, are the same rain-gods of the ancients. But today they are captained by Saint Michael, they ride on horseback, and so riding are plainly confused with the horsemen of the apocalypse. We may observe the shaman-priest, sacrificing a turkey which is held by wings and feet by four men designated, under the name "*Chaacs*" so to act, and recall how closely this picture conforms with Landa's account of the mode of human sacrifice performed by the Mayas of his time. But we cannot say that the connotations of meaning of the present-day act correspond at all closely with what went on in the minds of the actors in the ancient drama.

The present-day culture is a closely integrated body of elements derived from Spanish and from Indian sources and all entirely remade and redefined in terms of one another. Nothing is entirely Indian, nothing is entirely Spanish. The ritual offering to the rain- and maize-gods incorporates the forms of a Catholic communion, but the chalice is a calabash and the sacramental wine is the bark-beer of the ancients. The books of Chilam Balam tell us that anciently there was an important cult centering around the *plumeria* flower (*nicte*), but today that flower, instead of being used in the rituals predominately pagan, as we might expect, is the appropriate adornment of Catholic altars and the suitable offering to the saints.

And in the third place—to return to the considerations which check the historical analyst—these problems, even if solved, do not easily lead into larger problems. If we are to distinguish science from history in that the former seeks always to reduce phenomena to general categories of wider and wider scope, then these problems do not readily lend themselves to science. We may be able to assign the day-count which I just cited to the Spanish heritage, but having done so we are not in a position to compare this fact with another like it and erect a generalization on that base. Facts of this sort tend to remain discrete and non-comparable; the scholarly effort comes to rest when the assignment to the one heritage or the other has been made. To use these facts in making generalizations we would have to know a great deal, probably more than we can ever know, as to what—for example—happened when the weather-prognostication custom was imported to the ancient Mayas, and as to what their culture at the time was like.

II

The type of historical analysis which I have just been illustrating, if it can be taken as the sum of its details, amounts to a study of an instance of acculturation: the cross-modification and fusion of Indian and Spanish cultures. But as such it is a study of a series of events four hundred years after their occurrence, of events that took place in a period forever beyond direct observation and poorly documented by historians. The ancient Maya culture is known only very sketchily; the recovery of sixteenth- and seventeenth-century Spanish culture is a special problem; and just what took place when the two met is to be known only in so far as written records, as yet not collected, reveal it to us, or as a series of dubious historical inferences from consideration of the culture of the present time.

In view of these difficulties it is natural that an interest in culture changes should find lodgment, in Yucatan, in changes nearer at hand and more subject to direct observation. My associates and I have found such a problem in the study of the changes taking place in the Yucatecan folk culture—this integrated and unified mode of life which has been made of both Indian and Spanish elements and which characterizes the hinterland villages and the peninsula and Yucatan today. Beginning with this culture as a point of departure, we find it unnecessary to commit ourselves to assertions as to the precise ways in which Spanish and Indian elements contributed to make it up; our concern is with what has recently taken place in this culture and is currently taking place in it under influences exerted by increasing mobility and communication. The culture changes of the peninsula have, of course, always taken place as a result of contact and communication, but thus broadly stated they are not changes that ceased when the Spanish influences diminished or that were most marked in the sixteenth century; on the contrary they become increasingly effective with the spread of what we call "civilization"—that is, schools, roads, and economic exploitation. These changes are happening under one's eyes.

The procedure which we have adopted to study these changes is the simultaneous comparative observation of several Yucatecan communities that have been affected by modern influences in varying degrees. We have selected three or four communities and ranged them in the order represented by the degrees to which these modern influences have impinged upon them. This we are able to do with assurance, because of the simplicity of the situation in the peninsula with reference to contact and communication. The peninsula is a single geographic region: a forested limestone plain. The rainfall increases as one goes southeastward until it is so great that human habitation is difficult. Mérida, the capital city, is located in the northwest corner of the peninsula. This is the center of contact and of influences political, social, and cultural. From this point the roads and railroads move outward, becoming, in the southeast, trails through the bush. These trails, as one continues to move southeastward, become less frequent and less traveled, until one reaches the isolation of central Quintana Roo, where the Indians are visited only by the *chiclero* and the occasional traveling merchant.

We have begun studies in three communities. Mentioned in this same order of increasing remoteness, there are: first, the city of Mérida itself; second, a community on the southeasternmost branch of the railroad, and third, a village some thirty miles in the bush to the south of the second community. This last community, which I shall speak of as "the village,' is inhabited by persons of nearly pure Maya blood and with Maya surnames; there has been a school in the community for a dozen years; it is not yet, but is likely soon to be, in communication by wagon road with the rest of Yucatan. The second community, which I shall refer to as "the town," includes many persons with much white blood; about half the inhabitants bear the Spanish surnames and speak Spanish along with Maya; the community has had a school for many generations; and it is the seat of a central municipal government, a judicial district, a federal school district, and a newspaper correspondent. We hope also to add a fourth, and most isolated, community: a village of the still tribally organized Indians of Quintana Roo. Mr. Villa has made four or five trips among these villages, but the work done there is still insufficient to permit me to include this fourth type of community in the summary comparison which I am about to make.

This comparison is underlain by a fundamental assumption: that by means of it we shall be able to outline a process of culture change, that we shall be able to indicate what is taking place in the folk culture under influences from the city and from the world outside of Yucatan. It will readily occur to one that this problem could be studied in at least two other ways. One might select a single community and observe what happened to it over a period of time during which it was exposed to these influences. But obviously this procedure would require a number of years. Or one might again take a single community and make two (or more) studies of its culture: one, of its contemporary mode of life, and another, of its mode of life a generation or two ago, as reported to the investigator from the memory of the older inhabitants. These two cultures could then be compared. We have in fact made some use of this latter procedure. For reasons which I shall try to make apparent, it is not necessary for us to assume that the life of the village we are studying represents an earlier stage in the development of what we now find in the town, and indeed this is not in detail the case; but as a matter of fact we have frequently found the older people in the town recalling from their childhood customs and features of social organization which are today characteristic of the village. That is to say, one can go back either in time or in space, one can delve into memory or retreat into the bush, and reach the same set of facts. One example will illustrate this. Today in the city a young man, even of a lower-class family, selects his own wife and himself makes request of the girl's father for permission to marry her.[2] It is remembered, however, that the boy's father and mother used to make this formal request. In the town the latter practice is general, although the actual selection of partners is made by the young people themselves. The older people look back, with some regret, to the days when older people arranged the marriages, selecting husbands for their daughters and wives for their sons. Coming to the village, we find that there marriages are in fact parentally arranged and controlled, the girl having nothing to say in the matter, and the boy very little. The coming-to-ask-for-the-girl's-hand is a solemn and highly formalized piece of ritual, in which the boy and the girl have no part. Finally, it is only a few years in this village since the custom disappeared whereby after the betrothal the boy served his parents-in-law in their house for a year before marriage. And Mr. Villa's information from Quintana Roo indicates that this last custom is still general there. At this point we are in effect back in the early sixteenth century, for this last-mentioned mode of marriage is substantially the same as that described for the ancient Maya by Bishop Landa.

The comparison of these three communities—city, town and village—can therefore be expressed in terms of a process of transition. I think of this process as a shift from one type of society, which the most isolated village represents, toward another type, illustrated by the Yucatecan capital city but even better by our more mobile northern cities. But the process is also, as I have just indicated, in large measure an actual historical process, in that the sequential changes made manifest by the comparison are actual events that have taken place in the chronological development of certain members of the series. In the summary statement of some points of this comparison immediately to follow, the description may be understood in either way: as an account of a general trend in social or cultural type as Western civilization has entered Yucatan, or as a somewhat schematic recapitulation of the cultural history of any town in Eastern Yucatan that began as an isolated homogeneous village and became progressively modified by contact with the city and the wider economy and society.

Beginning, then, with more general and obvious differences, I will say that as one moves from the village through the town to the city one finds the communities increasingly mobile and heterogeneous. The increasing heterogeneity is not merely a function of the size of the community, for there are remote villages that are five times as large as the town we have been studying but are much more homogeneous. By this I mean that the mental world of one individual is much like that of any other; or, to put the same thing in other words, objects and acts have much the same meaning to everyone. Correspondingly, the division of labor becomes more complex; in the village every man is an agriculturalist and performs the necessary domestic tasks to supply himself with what he needs, while town and city are increasingly constituted of interdependent specialists Such specialists as exist in the village are chiefly "sacred specialists"— midwives, shamans, and reciters of ritual prayers—who perform their functions as matters of prerogative and public duty. But as one goes to town and city the proportion of secular specialists increases; their functions are discharged as matters of livelihood, and their fees, instead of being nominal or traditional, are dependent upon the fluctuations of free economic competition. Communal labor, which is a powerful instrument in maintaining the solidarity of the village community, breaks down with the introduction first of money-substitute, for personal labor, and then with the development of hired and prison labor. Lending of money, at first without interest, becomes subject to exorbitant interest rates; land comes to be regarded as subject to individual sale and then as security for debt; and later banking begins. In the village, estates are maintained intact until the death of the surviving spouse, even if the children and grandchildren are married; this is an aspect of the unity of the extended domestic family group. But moving to the town and then to the city, one finds distribution of a deceased man's property among the children and the widow more and more common; and testamentary disposition of property becomes familiar.

This same cityward progression sees the gradual breakdown of a familial organization in which the essential features are the subordination of women to men, and of young people to older people, and the responsibility of the individual to his kindred on both sides and of them to him. Marriage ceases to be an arrangement of two groups of kin to become connubially united and to provide for the adult security of two young people just leaving adolescence and becomes gradually an enterprise of youth and maiden in which the elders are less concerned and little influential. The sometimes elaborate and always religious rituals in support of marriage decrease in complexity and solemnity and at last disappear: the solemn asking for the hand of the bride; the ceremonious delivery of the bride-price with the admonishment of the marriage-intermediary; the ceremony after the wedding wherein the bride formally acknowledges her subservience to her parents-in-law, the groom acknowledges his respectful relation to his parents-in-law, and the two sets of parents-in-law pledge their new relation to each other and their obligation to the sponsors of the wedding.

Similarly, the godparental and *compadre* relationships, which in the village parallel and support the parental and parent-in-law relationships, become less important as institutions of control. With the development of class- and wealth-differences, godparents come to be selected for practical or prestige advantage, and, as the *compadres* are no longer on the same social level, the reciprocity of the relationship is broken down. The requesting the-godparent-to-act ceases to be a religious ritual and becomes perfunctory; and the ceremony of hand washing whereby the parent acknowledges his obligation to his *compadre* disappears. At the same time, because of the disparity in mental worlds between the generations, young people cease to show respect for their godparents, and the latter are less and less expected to intervene in the control of the godchild's conduct.

One of the most striking changes is the diminishing importance of religious belief and ritual. This applies as well to those elements which are of European Catholic origin as to those which are pagan. In the villages practical acts and needs are closely supported by sacred sanctions. Ritual is an immediate expression of an anxiety or a need, and, as all men are similarly interested and engaged, this need is often general throughout the community. But in the town and in the city, there are the very Catholic and the less Catholic, as well as Protestants and skeptics; and there are men in the community—few in the town and many in the city—who are not agriculturalists and for whom therefore the anxieties of sowing and drought are not acute. This topic is of course a very long and involved one; I can only mention a few of the conspicuous differences. The novena, for example—the Spanish or Latin prayer recited before the effigy of the saint or the symbol of the cross—is in the village a spontaneous individual or familial utterance of prayer: a man and his wife organize a novena when their child is sick or the crop is threatened or in gratitude for the recovery of the one or the safety of the other. But in the town the annual name-day novena becomes the dominant type, and its performance no longer is an expression of religious mood. It is a social occasion, with a religious flavor, performed, as much as anything, to maintain prestige. And in the city the novena tends to disappear entirely. Furthermore, in the town and in the city men take less and less part in religious activity, whereas in the village they lead.

In the village the solidarity of the local community is expressed in the paramount importance of the village *santo*; other saints are of small consequence. But in the town the patron suffers from competition with individual patrons and with miraculous *santos* of other communities; and this individuation of the gods is still further developed in the city, where the patron saint of the community almost completely disappears. In town as in village the pagan gods of the cornfield are the objects of worship, for the townsman is, generally speaking, a farmer, as is the villager. In the city these deities are largely gone, except in the peripheral communities where agriculture is still practiced. But village and town exhibit notable differences. In the village the agricultural rites are acts of piety; in the town they are acts of safeguard. They become less the direct responses to crisis, and more matters of traditional performance. In the village the forms are still full of meaning; the layman understands and follows what the shaman-priest says and does. In the towns this is less true. The shaman-priest is not a member of the town community; he is brought in from a village, and the symbolism of what he does is less understood. It is simply an act of prudence to have him perform his ceremonies: otherwise the crop might fail. In a word, this functionary becomes less of a priest and more of a magician.

The same fact can be approached from a consideration of the pagan gods themselves. In the village these are close at hand, plainly defined, and worshiped in ritual of apparent symbolism. In the town they are more remote; and their individual differences are blurred. The lesser deities—those of the bees, deer and cattle—disappear entirely, while the rain gods lose their definite attributes and become confused with the guardians of the milpa and the forest. In the villages the mischievous goblin embodied in the ancient clay effigy—the alux—is fairly well kept distinct from the true gods; but in the town the alux becomes a principal recipient of offerings made in the fields. The effect of this is to reduce what was a true prayer to a being defined in terms of the awesome and the benign, to the mere humoring of a mischievous sprite. The villager and the townsman carry corn gruel to the fields in acts that have the same external appearance, but the townsman's act comes to have about the same meaning as the putting out of a pan of milk for the brownie by a Scotch rustic. In the city, finally, all these beings are hardly more than eerie characters in folktales told to amuse or frighten.

The same diminution of the religious element is to be observed in the changes that take place in the ideas as to the causation of diseases. In the village a man's sickness is most often brought about by his failure to perform the expected rituals; illness, in other words, is commonly the proof of a lapse from piety; physical well-being is an aspect of moral wellbeing. But in the town sickness too becomes secularized. Fidelity to ritual is not emphasized as insurance against sickness. Both villager and townsman believe in evil winds as a principal factor in disease, but the villager, constantly instructed and admonished by the shaman-priest, is apt to regard these winds as the punitive aspect of deity, while the townsman thinks of them as operating of their own malevolence or as encountering the stricken one by mere accident.

We have been struck, in studying this matter of disease and its causation, by the apparent increase of black magic as a cause of sickness and death as one moves away from the village toward the city. This is a matter requiring more investigation to confirm, for our information is drawn from a single village, which may not be typical. But unless further facts change the conclusion, it will appear that sorcery is commoner in the town than in the village, and commoner in the city than in the town. Certainly Dr. Hansen's materials from Mérida indicate a development of black magic much greater than that shown by our materials from the village. Tentatively we suggest that this situation is to be explained by two kinds of reasons. One, a historical explanation, points to the diffusion of West Indian magic, largely medieval European in origin and perhaps partly African, into the city, to which come many Cubans. The other explanation might be spoken of as sociological; this would regard the increase of sorcery in the city as an adaptation to the greater insecurity and instability of life in the city among a people still partly illiterate and primitive in habit of thought. In the city the familial and neighborhood controls are broken; one does not know one's neighbor; and the authority of ritual and religious belief is largely removed.

Each one of the topics to which I have referred in this summary invites further study, and I have not mentioned all that have presented themselves to us. There are interesting changes in the body of folktales and myths. The progressive secularization of the annual fiesta is a matter adapted to detailed investigation, for the rituals are many and well-defined, and the local variants are so numerous that it is possible to describe with some fullness the transition of a sacred ritual to a social entertainment—the change from prayer to party.

The transition which has been sketched in the foregoing paragraphs I conceive, I repeat, as a shift from one type of society, illustrated by the isolated primitive or peasant village, toward another type most nearly realized in our northern cities. In other words this particular historical change that has taken place and is taking place in one particular place, Yucatan, need not be regarded as a unique series of events. It can be compared with the effect of white civilization upon peripheral peoples in other parts of the world, and it can be compared with the gradual civilization of Europe as known to us from history.

The trend of this paper can therefore be summarized by asserting two advantages which inhere in the mode of defining a study of culture change which has been developed in the consideration of our materials. In the first place the simultaneous study of communities enjoying the same fundamental basic culture but exposed in different degrees to outside influences allows the study of culture change directly—the data are under immediate observation—and without the necessity of waiting until the lapse of time has brought about marked changes in a single community. And, in the second place, the changes observed can be compared with others like it so as to lead the student into scientific generalizations.

This comparison requires, of course, a terminology which will eliminate what is peculiar to one time and place and will emphasize what is alike in spite of these temporal and local differences. A review of the specific changes which I have mentioned for Yucatan will indicate the direction to be taken by this generalizing terminology. The one type of society, approached in the village, is a relatively immobile society, culturally homogeneous, in which the ways of life form a single web of interrelated meanings. This culture is closely adjusted to its local milieu. Relationships are personal, and the important institutional controls are familial. The sanctions which control conduct are prevailingly sacred, piety is emphasized, and custom has the force of moral rule. Ritual is highly developed and expresses vividly the wishes and fears of the people. On the other hand, as one leaves the village and moves through the town to the city, one goes toward a contrasting type of society. This society is much more mobile and culturally heterogeneous. The ways of life are less closely interrelated; group-habits exist more in terms each of itself and do not to the same degree evoke a body of closely associated and definatory acts and meanings. These ways of life rest upon, but are not of, their natural environment. Relationships are increasingly impersonal, and formal institutions qualify the acts of the individual. The familial organization is much reduced in importance as an instrument of control. Life is secularized; economic advantage and valuation have penetrated the social body; and the individual acts from constraint or convenience rather than from deep moral conviction. Religious belief and action are much reduced; the individual can no longer express himself in the comfortable grooves of sacred ritual.

I have found it convenient to speak of the former type of society as Culture and the latter types as Civilization. If this terminology be adopted, the study we are engaged upon is one of deculturalization, rather than of acculturalization. But as there are objections, at least those of usage, to denying the term "culture" to the life-ways of the city man, it may be more acceptable to describe this study as that of the change from folk culture to city culture.

Notes

1. [Editor's Note: Diego de Landa, *Yucatan before and after the Conquest*, 2d ed., trans. William Gates (Baltimore: Maya Society, 1937)].
2. It is still considered proper for a meeting to take place between the parents of the boy and those of the girl, but usually everything, even the date of the wedding, has been determined by the young couple before this.

8

The Folk Culture and Civilization

This essay represents the last chapter of The Folk Culture of Yucatan, *the book-length presentation of the findings from his series of Yucatan community studies. While it provides a succinct summary of the results, it also reflects difficulties Redfield had reconciling some of the empirical evidence his studies had turned up, particularly regarding Guatemalan communities that revealed themselves to be unexpectedly secular in character. Another interesting aspect of this chapter is Redfield's effort to ground his work in the theoretical work of Emile Durkheim, Ferdinand Tönnies, and Henry Sumner Maine. Redfield did not explore these linkages in depth, but the very fact that he was drawing upon such sociological theorists in an ostensibly anthropological work was distinct in the late 1930s and early 1940s, and his work served for many students of this era as a bridge to these theorists. Finally, this chapter represents the first full presentation of Redfield's influential "folk-urban continuum" construct, and the complete text served as standard reading for doctoral students in anthropology and sociology from the 1940s into the 1950s.*

Some novelty attaches to the method employed in this study: the approximately simultaneous investigation of a series of contemporary communities differing chiefly with respect to the degree to which each has been affected by communication with a single important center of modifying influence.[1] In this chapter there will be presented the author's conclusions as to the results of this method as applied in Yucatan.

The most general conclusion is that the same relative order—an order corresponding to their relative positions on the map: city, town, peasant village, and tribal village—serves to range the four communities studied so as to represent the progressively increasing or decreasing extent to which several general social or cultural characters are present. In a preliminary paper[2] it was asserted that the peasant village as compared with the tribal village, the town as compared with the peasant village, or the city as compared with the town is less isolated; is more heterogeneous; is characterized by a more complex division of labor; has a more completely developed money economy; has professional specialists who are more secular and less sacred; has kinship and godparental institutions that are

First published in *The Folk Culture of Yucatan* (Chicago: University of Chicago Press, 1941), 338-369.

less well organized and less effective in social control; is correspondingly more dependent on impersonally acting institutions of control; is less religious, with respect both to beliefs and practices of Catholic origin as well as to those of Indian origin: exhibits less tendency to regard sickness as resulting from a breach of moral or merely customary rule; allows a greater freedom of action and choice to the individual; and—a conclusion then more tentatively advanced—shows a greater emphasis upon black magic as an ascribed cause of sickness. In the present volume these conclusions are particularized by the reference to facts as to certain customs and institutions as they appear in the four communities. They are also further generalized in that most of the cultural characters as to which differences are found are grouped under three headings. The changes in culture that in Yucatan appear to "go along with" lessening isolation and homogeneity are seen to be chiefly three: disorganization of the culture, secularization, and individualization.

The contribution made by the present application of this method to research on the history of Yucatan is small. It is true that the investigation has revealed the persistence in a more peripheral community of certain elements of custom which documentary evidence or the oral testimony of old people shows to have been once characteristic of a less peripheral community. Examples are: the persistence of the vecino-indio distinction with emphasis on the status significance of Indian surnames in Dzitas after its disappearance in Mérida; ... the important and conspicuous features of Catholic ritual still present in Tusik of which many are attested to have existed in former years in less remote communities; the persistence of compulsory collective labor for the public benefit (fagina) in the villages with evidence of its earlier existence in Dzitas and even in Mérida; the use of separate oratories for domestic santos, which is a practice in Tusik but only a memory in Chan Kom; the decline and substantial disappearance in the city of the custom, usual in the villages, of choosing the child's baptismal name from among those of saints appropriate to the day of its birth. To the degree to which the investigators obtained information as to earlier custom in the communities they studied, there appears a certain rough overlapping of the courses of history of each, so that, if their accounts are superimposed on one another at the points where the past condition of one community coincides with the present condition of the next most isolated community, there results a single historical account, although a very rough one, of culture change in Yucatan. Even where confirmation is lacking as to the earlier presence in a less peripheral community of elements of culture now present in a more peripheral community, the different forms of custom and institution may be arranged in an order consistent with the spatial order of the communities so as to suggest a possible actual historical sequence. This was done [earlier in *The Folk Culture of Yucatan*] ... with reference to differences as to the conventional definition given to status and ethnic groups. This could be done more systematically with reference to many other aspects of Yucatecan life. It could be done with reference to differences in familial organization and ritual and with regard to many elements of religious and festal practice. It would be assumed that, because the more remote communities have had less contact with the one important center of influence, what is to be found in the more remote communities represents on the whole an earlier condition of the same general custom or institution than what is found in less remote communities. As with the definitions of ethnic and status groups, so these differences could be connected so as to suggest how each might have given rise to the next. There would result, as in the case of the general conclusion reached [earlier] ... a sort of generalized hypothetical account of the history of the culture of what might be called an "ideal type" of Yucatecan community, or of Yucatecan society taken as a whole. In a similar way it might be validly asserted that a comparative description of communities encountered as one goes from Paris southward through Marseilles, Algiers, the Sahara, and then the Sudan would provide the vague outlines of the culture history of western Europe. Such a method of reaching an approximate and generalized culture history probably comes somewhat nearer the facts as they might be determined by true historical research in such a region as Yucatan where the culture history is already known to have been very simple: a single Indian culture came in contact with Spanish colonial society four hundred years ago and remained largely undisturbed by other influences or local movements until the introduction of more modern ways through a single port and a single city. Nevertheless, that the more archaic feature is always preserved in the most peripheral community is not always true, and instances have been given in this volume where it was found not to be true. In Yucatan as elsewhere each community has its own special course of culture history. The method is certainly a crude way to derive even the most tentative historical conclusions.

The most that may be claimed is that the work of the professional historian in working out the history of culture in Yucatan through study of artifact and document may be to some degree supplemented by the student of the contemporary cultures—provided that student does as much local history as he can. There is doubt that the documents and the artifacts will ever yield decisive information on such problems as changes in the kinship system, on forms of courtship and marriage, or on the steps by which some of the saints were incorporated into the pagan pantheon while the pantheon in other respects also was changing its character. The opinion may be ventured that, if we are interested in the history of such changes as these in Yucatan, we are well advised to pursue historical inquiry through study of present-day communities. The outlines of historic trends of change in such institutions as were mentioned above might be expected to appear more clearly if carefully prepared histories of local cultures were written (by asking old people what they remember, and by comparing results with what informants report as more recent and with what is observed to be characteristic today), and if the results in one community were compared with the corresponding results in communities progressively less affected by recent influences. But in none of the four communities studied in the present connection was any systematic effort made to recover the older conditions of the local society by asking informants. Hanṣen's study of Mérida, as yet in the course of composition, comes closest to being an exception. On the whole the investigation of the course of historic change in any one community by consultation of either document or informant has been casual and unsystematic. On the whole the results here achieved follow a comparison of present conditions in one community with present conditions in the others. Attested historical changes in any one community supplement in a secondary fashion the results of the comparison of contemporary situations.[3]

In the preliminary paper there was shown a disposition,[4] here further developed, to seek through this method of comparison of differently affected communities some general knowledge as to the nature of society and of its changes. It has been discovered that the less isolated and more heterogeneous societies of the series of four in Yucatan are the ones which are more characterized by disorganization of culture, by secularization, and by individualization. These conclusions are generalizations on many particular facts. The assertions are "on the whole" true. To reach these conclusions it is not necessary to report the history of any one of the communities: they may be compared as if all existed at the same moment of time. At the same time, when questions come to be raised as to whether changes in any of the characters are related to or conditioned by changes in any of the others, and as to how they are interrelated, such knowledge as the writer has about particular events in the history of the communities is very welcome and he wishes he had more. The simple comparison of contemporary communities is not a method to be recommended to those wishing to do historical research in Yucatan, in view of the availability of documents and in view of the opportunity to determine the recent history of any community studied by consulting old informants as to earlier conditions, It is, however, a satisfactory way somewhat to clarify certain problems as to the nature of isolated-homogeneous society as compared with mobile-heterogeneous society.

In the preliminary paper it was suggested that the characters of the more isolated communities might be grouped to constitute a "type" in opposition to the "type" formed by assembling the opposite characters of the less isolated communities. The characters there asserted to identify the first "type" are: isolation; cultural homogeneity; organization of the conventional understandings into a "single web of interrelated meanings"; adjustment to the local environment; predominately personal character of the relationships; relative importance of familial institutions; relative importance of sacred sanctions as compared with secular; development of ritual expression of belief and attitude; tendency for much of the behavior of the individual to involve his familial or local group. These conceptions (which obviously derive much, as has been earlier remarked, from Maine, Durkheim, and Tönnies) were offered in that paper to point a direction in which studies of changes in primitive or peasant societies under influence from modern civilization or cities might be systematically and comparatively pursued. The line of thought suggested by the discovery or creation of these "types" leads to some hypotheses: (1) The primitive and peasant societies (which will be found to be, as compared with other societies,[5] isolated and homogeneous local communities) have in general characters of the first type. (2) When such societies undergo contact and communication with urbanized society (or at least with modern Western urbanized society), they tend to change in the direction of the opposite of these characters. (3) There is some natural or interdependent relation among some or all of these characters in that change with regard to certain of them tends to bring about or carry with it change with respect to others of them. The present study, an examination of four particular communities in Yucatan, does not, of course, establish the truth of any one of these possible hypotheses. It may be claimed that it moves a little distance toward their more precise formulation and toward the development of ways of bringing particular facts to bear upon them.

The problems suggested in that earlier paper are too comprehensive in scope and too vague in definition to be suitable guides for research. Nine or ten characters, each simply denoted by a phrase or two, are thrown together and called a "type." It is not clear how we are to determine how any particular society partakes more or less of any of these characters. It is not made clear how we are to determine which of these characters is naturally associated with any other. It is necessary to ask many more special questions, and relate them to particular facts, to define more precise lines of inquiry. The facts given in this report lend themselves to this effort.

The problem is seen as one of the relation among variables. No one of these is the sole cause of the others, but it is assumed, subject to proof, that, as certain of these vary, so do others. For the purposes of this investigation the isolation and homogeneity of the community are taken together as an independent variable. Organization or disorganization of culture, secularization, and individualization are regarded as dependent variables. The choice of isolation and homogeneity as independent variables implies the hypothesis that loss of isolation and increasing heterogeneity are causes of disorganization, secularization, and individualization. Even if this should be established, it would not follow that these are the only causes of these effects or that these are the only covariant or causal relationships to be discovered in the same data. There may be, for example, covariant or causal interrelations between disorganization and secularization or between disorganization and individualization.[6]

If these questions are to become guides to empirical research, the terms must be sufficiently general to make it possible to compare what is done in one field, as Yucatan, with what is done in another. But they must be sufficiently precise to enable the investigators, while operating within the definitions given him by the broad concept, to ask more special questions of particular fact and get answers which can be recognized as evidential for the more general question implied by the term. One must know how to find out whether the particular fact reported within a particular setting of time and place represents the presence or absence of some quality generalized in the concept.

As is, or ought usually to be, the case, the present investigation has involved some interaction between the guiding general term, on the one hand, and the particular facts, on the other, with resulting redefinition of the general terms and propositions. The use of the term "primitive," for the purposes of this study, as referring to the "enduring isolation" and the "homogeneity" of a society, arose from the attempt to specify just what sort of facts could be compared in the various communities in order to determine their relative primitiveness. The relative lack of emphasis placed on size of the community, development of the technology, degree of literacy, relative importance of sacred as compared with secular sanctions, or complexity of the division of labor does not mean that these characters might not be found to be variables interdependent with one or more of the others already mentioned or with each other. It means merely that the four communities were found to be readily comparable with reference to their degree of isolation and homogeneity and that it is assumed that simple, easily verifiable facts, such as those given in the second chapter, are available to justify placing them in the order given with reference to these qualities. Also implied is the assumption that other communities, similarly situated in other parts of the world, might be similarly ranged according to the same guiding conceptions and so make possible a comparative study of the problems sketched in this report.

The conception of organization of culture with its reciprocal, disorganization, has undergone change and development in the course of the study.[7] The original question remains: To what extent may each of these four communities be described in terms of an organized body of conventional understandings? In the preliminary paper one character of the supposed type of society was asserted to be the fact that "the ways of life form a single web of interrelated meanings." As one leaves the village and goes toward the town, one encounters, it was stated, a situation in which "the ways of life are less closely interrelated; group-habits exist more in terms each of itself, and do not to the same degree evoke a body of closely associated and definitive acts and meanings."[8] As the matter is now considered, this contrasting characterization of cultural organization and disorganization appears valid but inadequate in that it covers what appears now to be a number of different though related characters no one of which has been adequately defined. Four of these may be recognized: (1) the unity of the culture of the society, that is, the extent to which it may be described as a single culture and to which it must be seen as a series of related subcultures, some subordinate to others; (2) the extent and nature of alternative lines of thought and action, conventionally made available to the individual; (3) the extent to which there exist relationships of interdependency between the various elements of culture; and (4) the extent of relationships of conflict and inconsistency between various elements of the culture.

The first of these has to do with the extent to which the society may be described in terms of a single—only one—organized body of conventional understandings. If the conventionalized activities of all the kinds of people making up the society—men, women, specialists, and nonspecialists—express meanings which have a relation one to another and which can be described as a whole, and if that whole represents the understandings of all these people, then to that extent there is but a single culture. This situation is never realized in fact. There is in the case of each society "an aggregate of subcultures,"[9] characteristic of local groups, classes, occupational groups, or other subdivisions of the entire society. The existence of subcultures in Dzitas, especially as characterizing indios in contrast to vecinos, in the society in which the present older generation was raised, has been mentioned [earlier in *The Folk Culture of Yucatan*] ... and the introduction of Protestantism into Chan Kom, as described [earlier] may be recognized to have resulted in a new subculture—that of the Protestant converts. But no systematic comparison of the four communities with respect to the relative number and importance of subcultures as compared with a possible general or "over-all" culture has been attempted. The writer supposes that in the more isolated homogeneous communities it is more nearly possible than in those less isolated and homogeneous to describe the society in terms of a single organized body of conventional understandings. The conclusion is indeed in part already reached by defining the former class of societies as homogeneous, for, if we say that the society is composed of the same kind of people doing the same kind of thing, we have probably also said that the behavior of these people has the same conventional character for all of them.

The second character comprised in the observation that as one goes from village to city in Yucatan it is less possible to describe the ways of life as a single web of interrelated meanings lies in the increasing number of what Linton has recognized under the name of "Alternatives." In Linton's book "Alternatives" is allowed to stand for what on closer analysis appear to be two different phenomena of culture: (1) elements "which are shared by certain individuals but which are not common to all members of the society or even to all the members of any one of the socially recognized categories[10] and (2) elements known to every normal adult or to all the members of a socially recognized group but among which the individual may "exercise choice."[11] The former (which, following a suggestion from Dr. Sol Tax, who pointed out to the writer this distinction, one might call "Variants") are elements known only to certain individuals of the society; each member of the society, so far as the Variants are concerned, has one way, conventionally shared with certain other individuals who do not together constitute any socially recognized group, to meet a certain situation; other members have other ways. Alternatives in the more restricted sense (as, for example, in the choice open to us to go by train or by bus) are two or more ways open to everyone in the society or socially recognized group to meet a certain kind of situation; they are, in fact, a kind of Universal. The increase of Variants and Alternatives as one goes from village to city has not been systematically investigated in the present work, but the fact of the increase is suggested many places in the manuscript; it is especially noted in the [earlier] chapter on "Medicine and Magic," where material is presented to show that in the town and city there is a much wider range and a larger number of elements of diagnosis and of treatment from among which the native has to choose, and it is shown that therefore the lines of conduct followed by neighboring individuals are in the city more variable, inconsistent, and unstable. It appears to the writer that the relative importance of alternative lines of conventionally recognized action may be inquired into in the manner suggested by the comparison of treatment of disease in Chan Kom as compared with Mérida: the collection of equivalent cases to which the same crisis, as observed first in the one community and then the other, gave rise. If, as in the case of the materials from Chan Kom, each individual tends to follow the same line of thought and action as does his neighbors, and tends to follow the same line in each recurrent instance of the same class of situation, while, as in the materials with regard to sickness from Mérida, each individual experiments and vacillates among a variety of lines of conduct so that the courses of action in the second group of cases are not parallel but inconsistent and various, then in the latter community there are, in respect to this class of situation, more Variants and more Alternatives. Denoting the primitive (and peasant) cultures as "folk cultures," Linton recognizes that the difference between the folk cultures and modern civilizations is "primarily a matter of the proportion which the core of Universals and Specialties bears to the fluid zone of Alternatives."[12] We may understand Linton to mean by "core of Universals" those elements of culture which are general for all the members of the society and which do not consist of conventional competing ways of acting in the same situation; we may understand him to mean "core of Universals which are not (in the restricted sense) Alternatives." Then the "core of Universals" is about the same as "the extent to which the entire society can be described in terms of a single organized body of conventional understandings." It is the breakdown or reduction of this core which is noted by the present writer in comparing the villages of Yucatan with the city and town, and that is declared by Linton to characterize modern civilization as compared with the folk societies:

> Folk cultures are borne by small, closely-integrated social units or by aggregates of such units which have already worked out satisfactory mutual adjustments. In such cultures, new items are not appearing with any great frequency and the society has plenty of time to test them and to assimilate them to its pre-existing pattern. In such cultures the core constitutes almost the whole.
>
> In modern civilization on the other hand, the small, closely integrated social units are being broken down, giving place to masses of individuals who are much more loosely interrelated than the members of the former local groups and classes.... In modern civilizations, therefore, the core of culture is being progressively reduced. Our own civilization, as it presents itself to the individual, is mainly an assortment of Alternatives between which he may or frequently must choose. We are rapidly approaching the point where there will no longer be enough items on which all members of the society agree to provide the culture with form and pattern.[13]

Following this line of thought we are made to see that the investigation in Yucatan has been, *in parvo*, a study of certain aspects of the historic process of civilization itself.

By way of digression it may be said that the two characters so far mentioned bear different relationships to the general problem of culture change and culture disorganization. The number of subcultures may increase in a society that develops a complex division of labor or may be increased by the inclusion of people with a different tradition or cult, but the presence of a large number of subcultures is not an indication of a rapid rate of social change. Any culture, "sub" or otherwise requires some isolation for its development. The materials with regard to the fusion of Catholic and pagan elements in Tusik, and the facts as to the adjustment of Protestantism to other elements of culture in Chan Kom, help to show how understandings become common, and develop interrelations among themselves, when a people are left alone to communicate freely with one another and not too much with outsiders. It does not seem appropriate to speak of an increase in the number of subcultures as an aspect of the disorganization of a culture. Indeed it is the conversion of both the universal elements of culture and those which are special to subcultures into Alternatives which is a feature of modern civilization and of Dzitas and Mérida as contrasted with Chan Kom and Tusik.

A correlative proposition is that we may expect to find a relatively large number of Alternatives associated with a relatively low degree of interdependence of the elements of the culture and of consistency among them. A review of the materials from Yucatan does not yield a demonstration of this relationship in their case. Such a relationship is plausible. Where there are many alternative lines of conduct and thought open to the individual, the situation is favorable, one may argue, for the presence of inconsistencies between what he does on one occasion and what he does on another, and it is probably less likely that such lines of thought and action as he does follow will be found to be extensively and in many places interdependent.

The discussion may now be allowed to return to consideration of the characteristics of cultural organization. The last two characters of the four enumerated on a previous page of this chapter may be set forth in the form of questions. The first question is: "To what extent does any element of culture have interdependent connotations with others?" The answer to this question is to be found in the act of reducing the culture to written description. If the elements of a culture require, for its full exposition, exposition of other elements, this aspect of culture organization exists. In describing the agricultural activities of the people of the villages one cannot deal fully with the subject without also dealing with sickness and its cure, and vice versa; but in reporting the bee cult there is no need to take account of the beliefs and practices with reference to death. There is an interconnection in the first case, and none in the second. But in Mérida little or no account of agriculture need be taken in dealing with sickness and so, where there is an interconnection in the villages, there is none in the city.

Finally, the investigator of cultural disorganization[14] may ask, "To what extent are there conventionally recognized lines of thought and action within the same culture which are inconsistent with one another in that they call for a choice whereby one must be abandoned in favor of another?" He may find conventionally recognized actions or attitudes which at least apparently contradict one another, as in the case of the belief that men who marry their deceased wife's sister go to hell, and the practice of contracting such marriages. The mere fact of apparent contradiction is itself probably an indication of imperfect operation of the tendency, here again asserted or assumed to exist, of cultures to develop consistency of parts. If the belief is a genuine belief and not a mere saying, and if the practice is general, then there must be, in the individuals who both believe and yet so marry, a sense of conflict. It is in the evidences for conflict and distress in such individuals that the existence of such deeper inconsistencies must be sought.

The study of these materials has thus led to an understanding that the matter of the organization of those elements of conventional understanding that make up the culture of a society may be studied in terms of more special questions each of which directs the investigator to the examination of corresponding particular sorts of facts; (1) the number and identity of cultures, some of which may be subordinated to others, going to make up the total conventional life of the society; (2) the extent and nature of alternative lines of thought or action conventionally made available to the individual; (3) the extent to which the elements of culture are connotatively interdependent; (4) the presence and nature of conventionally recognized elements which are inconsistent apparently as asserted or even in that one calls for a course of behavior which makes impossible the other.[15]

In order that societies may be more precisely compared as to the degree to which they are sacred or secular, a clearer understanding of the meaning of these terms is required than has been expressed in the preceding pages. The conclusion has been reached that the city and town exhibit greater secularization than do the villages. The principal facts offered in support of this conclusion are (in the order in which they have been presented): the separation of maize from the context of religion and its treatment simply as a means of getting food or money; the increase in the number of specialists who carry on their activities for a practical livelihood relative to those that carry on traditional activities which are regarded as prerogatives and even moral duties to the community; the change in the character of the institution of guardia whereby from being an obligation, religiously supported, to protect a shrine and a god it becomes a mere job in the town hall; the (almost complete) disappearance of family worship; the decline in the sacramental character of baptism and marriage; the conversion of the pagan cult from what is truly religious worship to mere magic or even superstition; the decline in the veneration accorded the santos; the change in the novena in which from being a traditional form expressive of appeal to deity it becomes a party for the fun of the participants; the alteration in the festival of the patron saint in which it loses its predominant character as worship and becomes play and an opportunity to profit; the separation of ideas as to the cause and cure of sickness from conceptions as to moral or religious obligation.

What definition of "sacred" will embrace all of the first members of the pairs of facts implied in the foregoing summary and direct the investigator to particular data relevant to a comparative study of secularization? Durkheim's formulation of the antithesis is that of an absolute differentiation of two realms of human thought: the sacred is to be recognized in distinction from the profane (secular) by the very fact that one may not be brought in contact with the other; we are to look, apparently, for those rites of transition, purification, and interdiction which will mark for us the boundary between the two realms.[16] But the materials from Yucatan have not yielded to the present writer any confirmation of the possibility of distinguishing the sacred from the secular by attention to such ritually guarded portals. Rather it seems that objects and sanctions may be more or less sacred. The secularization of maize, or of the festival of the patron, or of the loh ceremony,[17] is a gradual change, not a leap from one realm of thought to another. And in each of the four communities studied it seems to make sense to say that certain things are more sacred than other things. Indeed, the people themselves will approximately say it: "Maize is more to be respected than beans."

The statement just quoted recalls the customs, to which at least the older people in the villages adhere, not to step on maize kernels or crack them idly between the teeth or in other ways treat them with disrespect. The reluctance to do so is supported by the connection maize has with the gods and with other conceptions regarding the virtuous life. It is not good to treat any food wastefully or rudely, and especially not maize. The reluctance is not merely a matter of practical convenience; it is just believed, and there is a feeling of distress which cannot be fully accounted for in terms of practical advantage or disadvantage that attaches to a violation of the injunction. It may be suggested, therefore, that an object is sacred to the extent that there is reluctance, emotionally supported, to call the thing rationally or practically into question. Secular objects are treated in a practical or even critical manner without reluctance. What makes it appropriate to say that maize is sacred as it grows in the fields in Chan Kom and secular when it gets to market is that in the fields reasons of practical advantage are not enough to make a man decide whether or not to step on the kernels or even to plant or not to plant: he just feels uncomfortable, his words and actions lead us to believe, if the corn is stepped on or if, though able-bodied and free to do so, he does not make milpa. But the actions with regard to maize in the market are readily adapted to considerations of expediency: show the man how to get a better price, and he will follow the suggestion.[18]

Of course, it is in the area where the gods are that lie most of the objects and actions which give rise to strong reluctance if rational or practical criticism of them is entertained. So in the materials here presented it is decline of the gods or the separation of one element of custom or another from religious thought and sanction that make up the largest part of the evidence for secularization. The great cross at X-Cacal we conclude to be more sacred than many of the crosses encountered in Yucatan because of the evidences in customary action of the awe in which it is held: the screen which stands before it, the armed guards, the requirements to take off shoes and make offerings, the belief that it talks and that it gives signals of its displeasure, etc. But moral conceptions are sacred too, as the word is here defined. So also are those elements of the nonrational which are impure rather than pure, and which Durkheim recognizes as one of the poles of the sacred,[19] to be included within the definition. The decline in the sacred in Yucatan includes also—although the matter has not been discussed in these pages—the diminution or disappearance of belief in the danger of menstrual flow and of corpses.

The recognition of some such definition for the sacred as has just been suggested should help to bring about a more effective comparison of societies, and of the succeeding phases of change in an element of culture, with respect to secularization. It is a good thing not to have our attention too attentively drawn to matters of formal religion in connection with the sacred. In our own society, for example, some of the most sacred elements, in this sense, are probably some outside of the usually recognized religion. The definition gives some promise of guiding investigation; it should be possible to devise more special interrogations to ask of more special facts.[20]

The third general conclusion that has been reached with respect to the differences among the four communities in Yucatan is that the least isolated and the most heterogeneous of these are the most individualized (or individualistic). The principal facts which support this conclusion are the following (again expressing the progressive differences among the four communities as if a single historic change were involved): the relative decrease in importance of specialized functions which are performed on behalf of the community and the relative increase of specialties discharged for the individual's own benefit; the development of individual rights in land and in family estates; the diminution or disappearance of collective labor and of the exchange of services in connection with civic enterprises and religious worship; the decreasing concern of the family or of the local community in the making and the maintaining of marriages; the becoming less common of the extended domestic family; the lessening of emphasis and of conventional definition of the respect relationships among kin; the decline in family worship and the disappearance of religious symbols expressive of the great family; decrease in the tendency to extend kinship terms with primary significance for members of the elementary family to more remote relatives or to persons unrelated genealogically; the increasing vagueness of the conventional outlines of appropriate behavior toward relatives; the change in the nature of the marriage and baptismal rites so as less to express the linkage of the families and more to concern the immediately involved individuals only; the decline in relative importance of the santo patron of the local community; the suggested relation of the increase in sorcery to the separation of individuals, especially of women, from the security of familial groups.

We may understand a society to be individualistic to the extent that the socially approved behavior of any of its members does not involve family, clan, neighborhood, village, or other primary group. The villages in Yucatan, as compared with the town and the city, are relatively more "collectivistic" or "nonindividualized" in that such important and recurrent situations as labor, ownership, selection of spouse, entering upon the married state, and religious worship are more controlled by and have greater consequences for the family and the local community. In the villages it is relatively easy to say "the family did this" or "the community did that"; in Mérida it is not so easy.

It may be pointed out that a comparison of two societies as to their relative individualistic character, on the one hand, and to their collectivistic character, on the other, does not necessarily involve a consideration of the degree to which either is undergoing change. It is the impression of the writer that the society of the rural Ladinos of the midwest highlands of Guatemala is a little-changing society which is much more individualistic than is the society of Tusik: families have a much smaller share in the arrangement and maintenance of marriages, and individuals are free to make occupational choices and enter into business enterprises at their own sole responsibility, to cite only two respects in which the statement just made could be shown to be true. In the Guatemalan case the social norms allow for much independent action by the individual; in the case of the Yucatecan villages less such allowance is contained within the conventions. The rural Ladino society of Guatemala and the society of Tusik are alike in that in both the existing social rules are followed by most people; the difference between them is in the character of the rules. In the one case the rules give the individual much independent liberty of action; in the other case they give less. In considering the matter in such a more changing society as that of Dzitas, we encounter situations in which norms of the latter sort are giving way to norms of the former sort. The older people lament the fact that young people do not obey familial controls. There is, in Dzitas, what Thomas and Znaniecki call "social disorganization: decrease of the influence of existing social rules of behavior upon individual members of the group."[21] But if the ways of the younger people should become the customs of the succeeding generations without further change there would result a society without social disorganization but more individualistic than that which had existed before. In the materials from Yucatan it is not possible to recognize such an outcome; both social disorganization and the development of more individualistic norms are apparently occurring together in the town and in the city. The modes of conduct shift toward the more individualistic pole of the collectivistic-individualistic scale, but there is a decrease in the degree to which the courses of conduct of the members of the society tend to conform to whatever mode there is.

The foregoing discussion of the three major conclusions of this volume should make it possible by review of the materials on which this study is based or by collection of new materials to verify the general conclusion that in Yucatan the long-isolated, homogenous society is the sacred, collectivistic society characterized by well-organized culture, as compared with the less isolated, more heterogeneous society. If this is established, questions of greater significance arise. One question, created by the attempt to universalize the conclusion, may be stated: "Are all long-isolated, homogenous societies sacred, collectivistic, and characterized by well-organized cultures?" The question invites examination of the primitive societies and their comparison with reference to the three qualities here stressed, a comparison to be made with each other and then with at least that less isolated, heterogeneous society that we know best—our own. A reading knowledge of some of the primitive societies suggests that in general the answer to the question is likely to be in the affirmative and that there is indeed a natural association between long isolation and homogeneity, on the one hand, and sacredness, collectivism, and the organization of culture, on the other. In various ways this has been declared in the antithetical concepts offered by Maine, Durkheim, and Tönnies, already referred to (Preface). But it may well turn out that the correspondence is limited by special circumstances, that the association among some of the various characters is more necessarily close than among others, and that besides the long-isolated society with its attendant characters, on the one hand, and the less-isolated, heterogeneous society with its characters, on the other, we may recognize subtypes, or types in which various kinds of compromises or combinations of character are found. A recent paper by Dr. Sol Tax[22] points out that, while certain Guatemalan nonliterate societies of which he has some knowledge are characterized by local cultures (presumably well organized), are homogeneous, and are isolated at least in the sense that the contacts with persons outside the local community are not intimate, nevertheless family organization is low, and on the whole the conventions allow for much individualistic behavior, and the secular character of the social life is great (he also points out the impersonal nature of many institutions and controls in these communities, a matter not much discussed in the present pages with reference to Yucatan). These Guatemalan societies are, as has been remarked above in connection with the rural Ladinos, in relative equilibrium, that is, social disorganization is relatively small. Tax concludes that a primitive (long-isolated, homogeneous) society can be "mobile, with relationships impersonal, with formal institutions dictating the acts of the individuals, and with familial organization weak, with life secularized, and with individuals acting more from economic or other personal advantage than from any deep conviction or thought of the social good."[23] His conclusion requires much more analysis of particular facts in Guatemala to enable us to regard the results of the comparison as established, but the avowedly tentative conclusion may be rephrased: There are long-isolated, nonliterate, homogeneous, culturally well-organized local communities in relative equilibrium which are characterized by predominance of secular and impersonal behavior and sanctions and by individualism with relative unimportance of kinship institutions.

It is hardly possible long to pursue the task of classifying societies in such terms as these without developing an interest in problems of becoming. Reverting to the conclusion reached with reference to the four communities in Yucatan, one asks, once that the general conclusions as to the differences among them are at all accepted, "What has brought about these differences?" One possible answer would be that the four communities differ in the respects mentioned according to their degree of isolation from the single important center of influence, which center has been transmitting to the various communities, first the ways of the Spaniard, and later the ways of the modern city, in proportion to the degree of isolation of the communities from that center. It might be argued that the differences between Tusik and Chan Kom, and between Chan Kom and Dzitas, are merely the different degrees to which Spanish and modern elements of culture have diffused, as the anthropologist says, to these communities. It might be said that there is no natural interrelation among the various changes that have apparently occurred in the four communities, that each is independent of the other and, to give a single example to illustrate the whole possible line of argument, that Dzitas has both a less well-organized culture and a more secular society as compared with an earlier condition in that community simply because its people have borrowed from the city a set of customs which happen to have less organization, and at about the same time, following example from the same source, have learned to take religion less seriously. It might be contended that all that has been accomplished in this study is to summarize the events of diffusion into the hinterland of Yucatan and that the results that have here been expressed in general form depend upon the accident that the societies that exerted influence over the peripheral communities were characterized by less well-organized culture, by secularism, and by individualism. Such a line of argument, if consistently followed, would involve the contention that the extension of these three kinds of social behavior or qualities of society into the peripheries of the modern Euro-American area has no more significance for the understanding of the general nature of society and its changes than has the spread of trousers or the gasoline tin.

If this should be the only conclusion to which the study leads, it might, nevertheless, have a value in providing a general guide for the comparative study of the extension of modern Euro-American ways into other societies. It is certainly to be recognized that the present study does not establish that any isolated, homogeneous society, or that of the hinterland of Yucatan in particular, would have become less well organized culturally, more secular, and more individualistic if it had become less isolated and more heterogeneous through contact with some other kind of society—a society, let us say, that was also sacred and collectivistic and well organized culturally. Recent history does not readily provide us with opportunities to study such a situation. It is probable that different readers will find different values in the materials herein presented with reference to possible contribution to the understanding of general problems of social change. It seems to the writer that the materials indicate that there is some interrelation of the characters which constitute the progressive differences noted. It seems to him impossible to report the situation in Yucatan simply in terms of different degrees of diffusion of elements of culture. Account has also to be taken of the consistency of the total social situation with the new element of culture that is presented by example. If it appears that in Mérida as compared with Dzitas there is less bargaining and more disposition to announce a fixed price for goods offered for sale, it is significant to point out that merchants in the city imitate foreign standards. It is also significant to point out that, where the stores are large, the employees are more impersonal, and the saving of time is important, the fixed price instead of the protracted haggle is more adaptive, more "natural." Perhaps the merchants of Mérida, once having developed their business in other respects to its present point, would have begun to announce fixed prices even if they had not heard of the custom. We cannot say as to this. But we can say that the borrowing, if it was a borrowing, was made easier by the fact of the other changes. There is no necessity for a clear choice between an explanation in terms of borrowing, on the one hand, and in terms of necessary interrelation of changes, on the other. Contact and communication initiate changes which go on partly under the guidance example provided by the source of the communications and partly of the adaptive necessities of the social situation as it comes to be.

It would be difficult to support an assertion that the lesser organization of culture in the town and the city is due simply to the fact that the people of the city have learned how to have less organization in their conventional life. The comparison of the four communities indicates that the greater disorganization comes about as a cumulative result of many particular changes, some of which are not on the level of communication at all. What is borrowed are particular tools, modes of conduct, and ideas; these in turn do things to the lives of the borrowers so that the total result is a kind and degree of disorganization. The appearance of opportunities to make a livelihood in ways other than agriculture causes some men in the community to give up agriculture. Having given up agriculture, they do not participate in agricultural rituals. In this way they cease to share in the attendant understandings as to, for example, the relations between agricultural ritual and disease. But meanwhile the pressure of city opinion has made it difficult for the shaman-priest to practice his calling in the town community. So he moves away, and the people of the town are without his immediate and frequent example and instruction. At the same time new ways of treating illness, without reference to agricultural piety and ritual conformity, are introduced from the city. So far as these are followed the individual is in this way also led aside from the interrelated patterns of thought and action which characterized the older way of life. The connections between sickness and ritual practices are broken down. In many such interacting and cumulative ways as this the phenomenon that has here been called the disorganization of culture has come about in Yucatan. It is also to be emphasized that the complementary process of reorganization of culture is certainly not brought about by learning to have organized customs and institutions in direct imitation; rather it is brought about by living in isolated intimacy for a long time. This is attested most convincingly by the fact that it is in the isolated communities that elements of Catholic origin are most closely integrated with elements of the pagan religion. Organization and disorganization of culture are not directly learned. They are aspects of society which "go with," respectively, isolation and outside communication and heterogeneity.

Similar questions can be raised about secularization and individualization. Do the people of Dzitas (for example) come to take a more secular view of life and to recognize the rights of the individual to act on his own independent account because they are presented with the example of citizens of Mérida, whom they perhaps admire, and who are skeptical and behave in a more individualistic manner? Can there be effective education and propaganda to inculcate a generally secular view? Perhaps there can be. Or perhaps, until the experience of an individual is such as to impair his conception of the sacredness of an act or an object, his observation of skepticism in others will have little effect on him. Whether or not secularization and individualization may be directly and generally learned or inculcated is not established by the materials from Yucatan. The materials do suggest that these results may come about more indirectly. The specialized activities in Dzitas are on the whole more secular than those of Tusik partly because new arts unconnected with religion have been introduced to Dzitas and partly because old arts have lost those connections for a variety of reasons. It was probably the advent of a more general literacy that made the secretary, as a sacred specialist, unnecessary. If we attempt to explain the fact that guardia is a sacred duty in Quintana Roo and a secular chore in Chan Kom, we cannot say much that is convincing as to the effect of an example of a secular government upon the people of Chan Kom as an influence that may have caused them to take a less religious view of guardia. It is more probable that, when the ancestors of the Chan Kom people ceased to guard a shrine containing a talking cross, or some equivalent symbol of great religious power, they continued to carry on guardia, but now without the religious connection. Or it may be that guardia, once more secular among the Quintana Roo people, became more sacred when, after the War of the Castes, they became organized tribally in defense of their isolated land from the whites.

The impossibility of describing all the differences among the four communities solely in terms of different degrees of diffusion from the city appears from an attempt to offer such an explanation for the facts with reference to black magic. It may be argued that black magic is regarded with less horror in the city than in Quintana Roo because the people of the city, even the lower class, are more exposed to examples of rational and skeptical thinking and especially to disbelief in magic. But the fact that in the city black magic is more frequently believed to have occurred than it is in Quintana Roo cannot be accounted for in such terms. The explanation offered in the preceding chapter in terms of the breakdown of the family and other primary group controls, with attendant personal insecurity, will seem to many readers more acceptable. Nor can it be plausibly argued that there are more family quarrels in Dzitas than in Quintana Roo because the people of Dzitas have directly imitated the example of Mérida in this respect.

It appears to the writer that interrelation between the disorganization of culture and secularization is rather strongly suggested by the Yucatan materials. One of the principal implications of chapter ix ["The Decline of the Gods"] is that people cease to believe because they cease to understand, and they cease to understand because they cease to do the things that express the understandings. The community is so large that not all the men can participate in a single rain ceremony. Or new arts have been introduced which give some men employment other than in agriculture; as a result some of the men, having no milpa, have no occasion to participate in the ceremonies. Or the shaman-priest moves away from the local community. For any or all of these reasons, and for others, fewer of the people find themselves participating in the rituals and hearing or reciting the prayers. As they do not do these things, they cease to understand them. There remains merely the feeling that, if the rites are not performed, misfortune will follow. The disorganization of culture has also involved secularization, for the content of belief, myth, and ritual which expressed and supported the emotionally colored attitude—the sacredness of the agricultural activities—has been lost. The materials are no more than suggestive at this point, but they seem to the writer sufficient to point out the likely possibility that, whatever might have been the effect of direct example upon the religious cults of the villages, the mere increasing heterogeneity and complication of the division of labor would have brought about some secularization. It is notable that the secularization proceeds, as one compares the four communities, with regard to both the Christian and the pagan cults and in not very different degrees.

Pursuit of these questions fails for the lack of sufficient historical data on the course of change in each of the communities. The comparison of the four communities as they were found to be at the time of investigation suggests general hypotheses for the study of cultural disorganization, secularization, and individualization, now considered as processes, not simply as characters of unchanging societies. While such investigations are awaited, further guidance in the formulation of these hypotheses may be derived from a widening of the comparison. Once more the reader's attention is called to the much more briefly reported societies in the highlands of Guatemala. The question may be asked how these Guatemalan societies came to be (if they are) secular and individualistic, while being culturally well organized and homogeneous. Again the question cannot be answered without greater knowledge of history than we now have.

Some speculations as to alternative possibilities may be offered as a guide to historical research. In the first place, it is a probable assumption that at some time in their early history the Indian societies of Guatemala were more sacred and collectivistic than they now appear to be.. This assumption is an application of the generalization already offered, subject to examination, that most primitive societies tend to have these characteristics. One possibility is that the Guatemalan societies became more secular and individualistic due to contact with the Spanish society following the Conquest. If this were true, the situation there would be similar to that in Yucatan, with the differences that, though becoming secular and individualistic, the Guatemalan societies retained their local, nonliterate, homogeneous, and culturally well-organized characteristics and reached an equilibrium retaining these characters. However, another and different assumption might be made: that the Guatemalan societies, even before the Conquest, were relatively secular and individualistic. To this assumption we are directed by the fact that the secular and individualistic character of these societies appears to be dependent on aspects of those societies which we have reason to suppose existed before the Conquest: the complex and important system of trade with some use of money and the form of political organization whereby an elite secures the participation of all members of the group in ceremonial and practical activities of the state by the exercise of impersonal controls. By this second assumption the Spanish invasion, by increasing the division of labor, extending the use of money, the system of markets, and further enlarging the impersonal state, merely carried further a secularization and individualization that had already begun.

Both the secular quality of contemporary Guatemalan life and its individualistic character are bound up both with the important commerce and with the highly developed political institutions. Almost everybody buys and sells, and everyone goes to market. Haggling for goods in terms of one outstanding measure of value—money—is carried on by man, woman, and child. So doing, anyone, even a young unmarried girl, will act independently to secure a practical advantage. Success in such dealings is readily measured in monetary terms. It is understood by the people how the possession of money increases freedom and personal mobility, and its acquisition is freely employed to secure these results. Where most goods are measurable in terms of money, and where much time and attention are devoted to practical, competitive bargaining by means of a mundane and universal measure of value and of achievement, it is easy to add the conclusion that intense personal religious life and a nonrational sanctification of social objects are not likely to occur.

Another striking feature of the societies of at least the midwestern highland part of Guatemala is the large part played by impersonal political and juridical institutions in social control. Public opinion and family organization do not have the greatly dominant roles in controlling the individual that they have in many simple societies. Much use is made of the courthouse machinery; many quarrels lead quickly to complaints before the local authorities; in the case of hamlets these courts are not even in the local settlement but in a village or town some distance away; in these formal actions and litigations brother may be pitted against brother, and father against son-in-law or even son.[24] As the ultimate sources of power that support these courts are in the city of Guatemala and in the national government, the individual who so easily resorts to them throws himself upon a very impersonal authority indeed. A related fact is the almost automatic character of public office in many of these Guatemalan communities. Participation in a hierarchy of office is a duty required of boys and men; the individual submits himself to the system, it might be said, passing through a graded series of public duties until he emerges, an old man, free of the necessity. It is not hard to see a connection between these exterior and impersonal systems of controls and the individualistic and secular behavior which appears to characterize this part of Guatemala.

These considerations suggest some possible causes, independent of the breakdown of cultural organization, for secularization and individualization: trade and a money economy and the development of a formal, hierarchical government with authority exercised by remote control. A consideration of some other societies, notably some in West Africa, might tend to reinforce these hypotheses or it might tend to contravene them. But, with reference to the Yucatecan and Guatemalan materials alone, the suggestions appear to have force, especially with regard to the influence of money and markets. The most isolated communities of Quintana Roo are like those of Guatemala in that they are primitive societies in equilibrium. They are unlike them in that they are more sacred and less individualistic. It has been seen that especially in Quintana Roo the market plays a small place in the life of the people and that money valuation of goods is much less general than in Guatemala. It has also been shown that in Quintana Roo as compared with Guatemala practically all social control is exerted by institutions arising from within the local community. The suggestion that a money economy is an agent of secularization is an old one in connection with the history of our own society. The line of thought suggested in this and the preceding paragraph indicates that it is important to determine the history, in both Guatemala and Yucatan, of the regional division of labor, of the system of trade and the use of money, and of the institutions of government, particularly of the civil-ceremonial government of Indian communities of the highlands of Guatemala. It is important to determine to what extent these institutions existed in pre-Columbian times and what was the effect of the Conquest and of later events upon them.

The indicated hypothesis is that the secular and individualistic character of highland Guatemala life is a result, in part, of the great regional division of labor and of trade. These features were in turn dependent, we may suppose, on the topographic and geographic diversity. Yucatan does not have this diversity. Yet apparently before the Conquest, Yucatan participated in the trade[25] and was perhaps characterized by greater regional division of productive labor than it now is. Cacao and cotton were grown; the coast people exported salt. Perhaps Quintana Roo was before the Conquest more commercial than it is now because a form of society based on regional division of labor, trade, and even money, and characterized by impersonal, hierarchical government, developed in the highlands where the habitat made such development possible, and was then extended to the Yucatan peninsula. And perhaps when the Maya state broke up before the Conquest, and when after that event contact with Guatemala largely ceased, such villages of Maya as remained relatively remote from the later modern civilization of the white man reverted from a secular, individualistic condition to a more sacred, less individualistic condition.[26] In such case the Maya of Quintana Roo have taken elements from two civilizations—one Christian, the other pagan—and have gone back to the more usual sort of primitive society. The Indians of the Guatemalan highlands, on the other hand, according to this view, retain the characters of the mixed society—a secular, individualistic, primitive society—which they began to develop before the Conquest out of the social and technical conventions which their habitat favored.

The contribution of speculation-as-to-facts to the line of thought has now become large, and the argument has probably gone beyond the point where it is of value to science. The principal tentative generalizations to which we are led by the Yucatan materials, combined with some knowledge of the Guatemalan societies and of other societies less particularly denoted here, may be summarized. A consideration of Yucatan, set against a background of general impressions as to the primitive societies on the whole, and with limitation suggested by Guatemala, indicates that in the absence of a money economy, isolated, homogeneous societies tend to have well-organized cultures and to be sacred and collectivistic. A comparison of what Tax reports for Guatemala with the materials from Yucatan leads to the conclusion that there is no single necessary cause for secularization and individualization. The Yucatan materials, in spite of the possible objection that the differences are simply learned or diffused directly, induce the writer to propose that increase of contacts, bringing about heterogeneity and disorganization of culture, constitutes one sufficient cause of secularization and individualization. And the case of Guatemala, fortified by certain interpretations of the history of our society, suggests that the development of important commerce and a money economy may be another such sufficient cause.

Notes

1. T. E. Jones compared the results of questionnaires given residents in certain Japanese rural communities differing as to the degree to which they had been affected by modern urban influences (Jones, Doctor's thesis, Columbia University, 1926).
2. Redfield, "Culture Changes in Yucatan," *American Anthropologist* 36 (January-March, 1934): 57-69.
3. Recent work has indicated the possibilities of a combination of ethnological and documentary historical method in reaching conclusions as to the historic trend of change with respect to kinship terminology and institutions. Eggan (*American Anthropologist*, 39: 34-52) reached the conclusion that a once widespread Crow type of kinship structure has in the cases of several tribes in the North American Southwest been progressively modified in the same direction as in degrees of change closely correlated with the degree of general change brought about in the Indian societies through contact with white civilization. Eggan compared societies differing as to the relative degree of change undergone, but he made his conclusion possible by reference also to documentary records of the state of kinship terms and practices of certain of the tribes at periods beyond recall of informants. Spicer (*Pascua: A Yaqui Village in Arizona*, 1940, 86-88) indicates the possibilities of reporting recent changes in kinship terminologies by comparing current practice of younger people with more conservative usage of older people. An important application of mixed documentary-historical and ethnological methods to these same problems of changes in kinship institutions has been made by Han Yi Feng in his monograph on "The Chinese Kinship System" (*Harvard Journal of Asiatic Studies*, Vol. II, No.2 [1937]).
4. Redfield, "Culture Changes in Yucatan," 68.

5. A discussion of the city as a type of society characterized by large, dense, permanent settlements of heterogeneous people, in which appear other characteristics consistent, on the whole, with that "type" as opposed to that of the folk, including impersonal relations and disorganization of culture, and the weakening of the bonds of kinship, occurs in Louis Wirth's paper, "Urbanism as a Way of Life," *American Journal of Sociology*, 44: 1-24.
6. Hook, *Encyclopaedia of the Social Sciences*, 3: 114.
7. In this connection I have been helped—but probably not enough—by Dr. Leo Srole.
8. Redfield, "Culture Changes in Yucatan," 69.
9. Ralph Linton, *The Study of Man* (New York: D. Appleton-Century Co., 1936), 275.
10. Ibid., p. 273.
11. Ibid., p. 275.
12. Ibid., p. 283.
13. Ibid., pp. 283-84.
14. The word "disjunction" may be more suitable than "disorganization."
15. For some readers the suggestions contained in these pages may be made more acceptable if "integration" or "configuration" should be substituted for "organization." If such a substitution be made, it should be noted that "integration" has had recent important use in connection especially with the social relationships making up societies, and also that what is discussed in the present pages is not what Benedict [*Patterns of Culture*, 1934], for example, is chiefly concerned with in dealing with configuration. She also recognizes cultures as more than the sums of their parts, but while she is particularly interested in distinguishing and perhaps classifying the cultures, so seen as wholes, in terms of aspects of their particular custom or content—what kinds of behavior they emphasize—the present writer is concerned with the phenomena of organization (or configuration) themselves. Thus the Zuñi culture and that of the Northwest Coast are by Benedict sharply distinguished in that the former emphasizes quite other virtues and ideals than does the latter. But it might appear that, with respect to the four characteristics of organization enumerated on a foregoing page of this chapter, the Zuñi and the Kwakiutl cultures are closely alike.
16. Durkheim [*The Elementary Forms of the Religious Life*] (trans. G. W. Swain), 1915, 38 ff.
17. [Editor's Note: the loh ceremony was a ritual of purification undertaken to cleanse one from contamination by winds believed to be evil]. Redfield, *Chan Kom* (1934), 175-77.
18. This is substantially the understanding of secularization given by Walter Bagehot [*Physics and Politics*] (1890, 156 ff.), who has argued that the discussion of principles is a means to the breakdown of sacred custom.
19. Ibid., 409 ff.
20. For example, the relative sacredness of two collections of tales and myths might be determined somewhat more precisely than would result from the expression of the investigator's general impression if each story were considered with reference to such questions as: Does the story refer back to remembered action or forward to anticipated action? If it does, what is the role of that action in custom and belief? Are there recognized limitations on the time or place of telling the story or as to who may tell it? What is the response if the story is mocked or treated lightly?
21. Thomas and Znaniecki, [*The Polish Peasant*] 1920, 4: 2-3.
22. Tax, *Scientific Monthly*, 48: 463-67.

23. Ibid., p.467
24. Tax, *American Anthropologist,* 39: 423-44; also Tax, *ibid.,* 40: 27-42.
25. Blom [*Commerce, Trade, and Monetary Units of the Maya*], 1932, 533-56.
26. In a personal communication Ralph L. Roys suggests that in the century before the Conquest the communities may have reverted to a more independent, self-sufficient condition. He writes: "Just now I am occupied with the idea that this condition was the result of an attempt at social revolution of a sort in 1441, when the age of the real cities ended, that the big cities were ruled by a warrior-trader caste, but after the fall of Mayapan, the agriculturalist got the upper hand. Although I admit this was not the case everywhere, I think it was so in the Cupul area at least. I don't know whether I will ever be able to convincingly show this, but I am trying to construct a foundation for it." If this should be proved to be the fact, the version in eastern Yucatan toward a more sacred society with few impersonal sanctions might have begun before the Conquest.

9

The Folk Society and Culture

In 1938, Redfield's University of Chicago sociology colleague Louis Wirth published a classic description of urban society, "Urbanism as a Way of Life." This article quickly came to have widespread recognition as the definitive description of the urban experience. Redfield considered his expertise to lie in study of societies at the opposite pole from the urban, the traditional or "folk" societies as he called them. In 1940, the University of Chicago Social Sciences Division, in an action that reflected a strong sense of the importance of the influence of Chicago social science, especially sociology, staged a celebration of the tenth anniversary of its impressive Social Science Research Building located at 1126 East 59th Street in Chicago. At this commemorative event, Louis Wirth read his already classic paper "Urbanism as a Way of Life." In juxtaposition, Redfield read an essay that described the polar opposite of urban society, "The Folk Society and Culture," which was published shortly thereafter in the American Journal of Sociology. *This essay represents an important stage in Redfield's formulation of his influential "folk-urban" construct.*

The familiar oriental fable of the blind men and the elephant ends just at the point where it becomes interesting to students of scientific method. If the man who approached the animal through a consideration of the legs later compared his results with those achieved by the special investigators of ears, trunk, tail, and body, it is likely that the combined and reconsidered results gave an excellent understanding of elephant nature and of the role played by each of the principal organs. There may be an advantage in studying something first as if it were a whole in itself and then coming to see it as a part or aspect of a larger whole.

Without stressing the unfortunate infirmity of these oriental investigators, I propose an analogy between the course of their investigations and those that have been carried on by the anthropologists and by the sociologists. So far as these two groups of students have not been distracted by the operation of museums or bureaus of marital advice or by other secondary enterprises but have been concerned with learning about the nature of society they have, by reason of accidents of subject matter, dealt with contrasting aspects of a whole. The whole is society. Anthro-

---

First published in *American Journal of Sociology* 45 (March 1940): 731-742.

pologists in studying primitive life have been concerned with aspects of society which are there emphatically present, while sociologists, in dealing chiefly with modern urban peoples, have especially made known to us other and contrasting characteristics of human association. The two disciplines, as far as they are social sciences at all, are in method alike: they attempt, by dealing with all of social life as organized wholes, to describe its nature in general terms. Their differences are largely functions of their different subject matters. They have developed corresponding differences of concept, problem, and field procedure. But, put together, their methods and results give a larger understanding of the nature of society. The very contrast between society seen in terms of the primitive groups, on the one hand, and society seen in terms of the industrialized city, on the other hand, evokes new problems and gives better understanding of old ones. The suggestion here made is that anthropology and sociology are not so much parallel as they are complementary. To bring problems and concepts of the two disciplines into the same field of discussion is to take a step in the direction of a unified science of society.

This is an appropriate platform from which to report something of the contribution to social science that is resulting from the joint study of primitive cultures and urban civilizations. For over forty years on this campus anthropological and sociological research have been carried on in the same or in closely related departments. The convergence of anthropological and sociological interest on this campus found an early recognition in the publication in 1918-20 of W. I. Thomas and F. Znaniecki's *Polish Peasant*.[1] For a dozen years vigorous programs of field research have been maintained here with the joint knowledge and supervision of anthropologists and sociologists. The retiring chairman of the department of sociology, Ellsworth Faris, spent years with primitive peoples and took the lead in bringing about a renewal of anthropology in the teaching and research programs of the university. The present chairman of that department wrote a first book[2] which was received even more enthusiastically by anthropologists than by sociologists. One member of the department of anthropology received his training in part in the one field and in part in the other, and another member holds appointment in both departments. For five years members of the two departments have maintained a joint seminar for the study of problems of racial and cultural contacts.

The essential identity of anthropology and sociology is becoming ever more apparent. In England and on certain campuses of the United States the contribution to this single enterprise from the study of the primitive societies is rediscovered under such names as "social anthropology" or "comparative sociology." Sociology continues its development from a speculative to an empirical discipline and sociologists seek to do field work even with primitive peoples. When Wissler hailed the Lynds' *Middletown*[3] as an application of anthropological method to modern society, he did not mean that at last one sociologist had discovered or achieved strong and secret tools of research that had before been in the control of anthropologists alone. It was rather that in that case a sociologist was reporting human behavior in terms of the entire community in which it occurred. The unit of investigation was society seen as a whole and studied through intimate and intensive acquaintance with its members. Anthropology and sociology have converged.

My purpose here is to point out some illumination shed upon society through a comparison of the experiences of the students of primitive societies with those of students of urbanized life. It seems to me that this illumination appears when one deals with groups that do not clearly belong either to the category of the primitive or to that of the urbanized. As this has been my own experience, I venture to make it the point of departure. Professor Warner brought here from Harvard a way of combining anthropology and sociology by studying first the Australian aborigine and then the New England industrialist. While he has been playing both ends against the middle, some of us have been playing the middle against both ends by concerning ourselves especially with peoples intermediate between tribe and city or with primitive groups changing under urban influence.

These intermediate and marginal peoples are critical in this connection. They call our attention to a picture by failing to fit it. Even Lewis H. Morgan, many years ago, felt a difficulty in the fact that the Iroquois Indians, modified by the white man's civilization, did not retain their ancient culture and presented a practical problem as to what to do with them. The last chapter of *The League of the Iroquois*[4] is perhaps the first of American "acculturation studies." Many years later Rivers pointed out some of the effects of civilization upon certain Oceanic peoples.[5] He attributed the depopulation of certain areas in part to the loss of the will to live. He found that in parts of the islands where head-hunting and pagan religion were preserved "the old zest and interest in life" persisted and the people were "still vigorous and abundant." But where European influence was strong "the people were deprived of nearly all that gave interest to their lives." If culture, as Benedict has said,[6] provides the individual with goals and with reasons for existence, then Rivers was discovering that those Melanesians were experiencing not simply a change in their culture but a loss of culture. The changing tribe does not fit the picture of a typical primitive society; to a less extent does it have culture.

Twelve years ago I made a study of a Mexican village,[7] having in view the primitive societies described by my anthropological teachers and also in mind the urban societies with which the sociologists were chiefly concerned. There resulted an account which suggested respects in which that village combined features characteristic of modern city life with characteristics of the primitive tribe. The life of that village, furthermore, turned out to include a double world one group of natives lived in terms of the local folk tradition, while others saw themselves and their fellows in relation to conception held by the city dweller. In that village the two groups, folk people and urbanized class, bore different names and so clamored for separate investigation. A comparison of the two distinctive ways of thinking and acting—there present within the same community—called attention to a process which might turn out to be recurrent and widespread: the process whereby the primitive man becomes a civilized or urbanized man.

Since then a number of investigators originating here have made studies of intermediate societies with this interest in mind. Miner[8] studied a French-Canadian village where the folk community is articulated with the urban and international world in large part through the Catholic Church. Embree has recently reported on a village of Japanese peasants,[9] where a local folk society is managed and directed by a national state in such a way as both to preserve the local culture and also to serve the national purpose. It appears that a society may be, under certain circumstances, literate and yet essentially primitive and stable.

It now appears that the peasant society (which might in a narrower sense be spoken of as folk society, as a terminological alternative to the use of "folk" to denote both tribal and peasant societies together) allows us to recognize a societal type, relatively stable intermediate between primitive society and urban society. The peasant, like the tribesman, "lives in terms of common understandings which are rooted in tradition and which have come to form an organization."[10] The sanctions that control conduct are likely to be prevailingly sacred. The familial organization is strong. There is little disorganization and little crime. On the other hand, the peasant "participates in money economy, produces a surplus for sale in city markets, pays taxes, sometimes goes to school, votes and otherwise participates in a wider economic and political structure which includes not only the peasant but the townsman."[11] The peasant makes some use of literacy, while the aborigine does not. The peasant makes some use of "machine technology, while the primitive man does not. Moreover, peasant and city man constitute one single society that is organized in terms of status. ... It is the nature of the peasant that he accords prestige to the city man and to the sophisticated members of his own group. The peasant may, through education, enter the world of the city, while the city man has kinsmen among the peasants."[12]

The significance of these interstitial societies appears when they are considered from the point of view of antitheses suggested to us by certain earlier students who also tried to see primitive and civilized society within a common framework. Maine compared earlier forms of Greek, Roman, and East Indian society with later forms.[13] In his terms, the peasant society represents a balance between familial and territorial society; it is a compromise adjustment between a society of status and a society of contract. In Durkheim's[14] terms the peasant society forms a special type of relatively stable compromise between the social segment and the social organ. It is the adjustment of local culture to the civilization of cities. The solidarity of the tribe is preserved in conjunction with the market and within the nation. And, as Ferdinand Tönnies[15] would have put it, the peasant group is a form of society in which neither Gesellschaft nor Gemeinschaft is strongly present at the expense of the other; both are to be observed in a condition of equilibrium.

Thus once again we are reminded of that interaction between concept and new particular fact which is the mainspring of advance in social science. Maine and Durkheim, studying certain more ancient or more primitive societies with an eye to modern life, hit upon ways of describing the differences which were apparently widely applicable. Later students, aware of these formulations, make more intensive studies of societies that stand midway between the antithetical extremes proposed. They are thus led to generalize upon their materials so as to enlarge the classification of societal types and so as to raise questions as to the forms of compromise that may occur and as to the processes of change from one form to another. This in turn leads to a reconsideration of the subject matter of anthropology as compared with that of sociology. The hints given us by Maine, Durkheim, and others may now be assembled and made more explicit. There results a characterization of primitive society as an ideal type of society, never completely realized in fact but approximated in the experience of the anthropologist.

This society is, as Sumner put it, composed of "small groups scattered over a territory."[16] The population of any one group is homogeneous in that in race and custom any individual is much like any other. The group is isolated from others. The technology is simple. The community approaches economic self-sufficiency. The division of labor is simple; activities appropriate to the sexes are sharply distinguished, but activities carried on by any one member of a sex-and-age group are much the same as those carried on by others of that group. There is little or no use of writing, or if writing is used it is a mere adjunct to oral tradition and, like the latter, serves to conserve the local heritage. The habits of members of the society tend to correspond with customs. The society is relatively integrated in that the component groups are closely interdependent and the ways of life are correspondingly interrelated and consistent with one another. Change in the society is slow. The prevailing forms of control are informal and traditional, and control to the members of the society appears in large degree spontaneous. The intimate and primary institutions, such as the family and the local group, play relatively large parts in that organization of the groups and institutions which make up the society. Many objects, conceptions, and forms of control partake of those qualities of unquestionable power and prestige which we denote as "sacred."

This is the implicit conception of society which follows from a study of the primitive or folk societies because, seen in comparison with the results of study of modern urbanized societies, it is a distinguishing generalized description of all of them. In so far as the anthropologist studies more complex societies or more changing societies his results may be expected to depart from this ideal type. In West Africa he will find societies with a well developed and pervasive familial organization combined with commerce, legal tribunals, and something approaching a national policy. Such groups as these lead the investigation—still guided by the general concepts—into the formulation of more special questions capable of less imprecise answers. In Guatemala, Tax,[17] another student associated with this university, is comparing societies, with the result that he is brought toward a conclusion that a local folk culture may remain relatively stable although associated with commercialism and an individualistic habit of mind but that there may be a necessary or natural connection between commerce and money, on the one hand, and individualism and decline in the importance of familial organization, on the other hand. If these investigations continue as they are going, we may determine some of the extensions of application of propositions suggested by Simmel and Sombart and some of the limitations upon them. In the meantime, still influenced by these considerations and in association with other workers, I have been comparing four communities in Yucatan in an effort to learn something of the necessary or likely interrelations among elements as a primitive society becomes more urbanized. These investigations, still unpublished, also give some small degree of understanding of the manner in which, under conditions of isolation, a society, after receiving influences from the outside, may build up a new culture and thereby revert toward the type of the ideal primitive society, only again to face the disorganizing influences of modern civilization.

I return now to the statement I made earlier in this paper to the effect that anthropology and sociology have developed different problems, concepts, and methods because of differences in subject matter. The point here is that these differences, as between the two things the two disciplines talk about, are to be understood in part as recognitions of the differences between the primitive society, on the one hand, and urban society, on the other. Put together, they widen our understanding of society in general.

Perhaps the central fact here is the development of the concept of culture at the hands of anthropologists rather than of sociologists. The students of primitive societies were making general use of the term for a generation before it became of great importance in sociology. To the anthropologist "a culture" implies an integral. The phrase has reference to organized, traditional ways of life in which all members of a self-sufficient, continuing, and complete society participate and which are adequate for all recurrent needs of the individual from birth to death and of the community through successive generations. Justification for this concept is to be found in the manner of living of isolated primitive peoples rather than in the big city. I remember how queerly the word "culture" fell upon my ears when, coming back from an Indian society where the organized ways of life provided those goals for existence of which Benedict speaks, I heard certain students here speak of two Chicago districts, Woodlawn and Englewood, as different "culture areas." A further point exists in the fact that anthropologists commonly use the terms "community," "society," and "culture" interchangeably; while the distinctions among these concepts may be of significance in dealing with the modern and urbanized and industrialized society, in using them in reference to the primitive societies there is often no need felt to make them, for the reason that there the group of people who live physically together are the same people who share those common understandings we call culture, and they are very nearly the same people who produce and consume their own goods. Spatial, personal, and economic relations tend to coincide.

The same difference between culture as an organization or system as seen in the folk societies, on the one hand, and culture or society seen as an agglomeration of individuals and institutions, on the other, as seen in the city, may be recognized in comparing either the written products of anthropology with those of sociology or in considering differences in their methods of achieving those products. It is the anthropologist, not the sociologist, who characteristically presents the social relations and the values and institutions of society in the form of a diagram. The student of the city may diagram ecological order or economic organization but hardly the relations of family life to ritual. (In so far as Warner's forthcoming works belie this remark, we shall be further enlightened.) It is the student of the folk who uses words like "pattern," "configuration," and "structure." It is the anthropologist who sets out to produce a "rounded picture of the society." The same degree of "roundness" is not possible in studying Chicago or even Middletown. The conception of a unified and comprehensive analysis-synthesis of a society so that every part is seen in relation to the whole has thus naturally developed in anthropology.

A related circumstance is that while the students of urbanized society have been engrossed with matters of special procedure, ethnologists, until very recently, have not attempted to formulate systematically the ways they have of getting facts and of analyzing them. Excellent descriptions of primitive life have appeared in which the writer says much about the customs of the group he studied but little about how he determined that these were indeed the customs. In such works we may find no more clue of how the trick was done than the mere mention of the names of the anthropologist's principal informants. In dealing with an isolated and relatively stable folk society, the problem of sampling may be almost ignored or at least treated in a common-sense and casual manner. What one adult male knows is enough like what the others know to make it possible to learn much about the whole society from no more than a single case Also it is true that, by beginning with a single individual and considering all the connections he has with others, most of the total primitive society can be laid bare. A student of Chicago or even of some special area such as the near North Side could not hope to approach success by dealing solely with, let us say, a single rooming-house occupant. In studying urban society the necessity early appears of defining the aggregate studied and of fixing upon ways systematically to sample it and to standardize information obtained from the samples. The student of primitive societies comes to this kind of problem much later when he is concerned with the less formalized aspects of culture, such as, to mention one example, the way in which the demands of adult life are met by adolescents or when he is studying acculturative change. On the whole, anthropological research into community life lays its emphasis upon direct and personal participation in the life of the community, because to know a few people well and directly yields results, while the sociological students of the city make much greater use of census, schedule, questionnaire, and formal document, not only because such are available, but because a wider range of behavior must be considered and must be properly sampled.

This paper must be brought to an end without more than mentioning many other respects in which the problems and concepts of the two disciplines have been differently shaped by the difference between folk culture and urban civilization. The student of a primitive society is likely to begin with the kinship institutions and to describe them as a system. Perhaps the greatest advance in the determination of valid compendent general propositions as to the nature of society yet reached by anthropologists has been attained in the field of kinship institutions and terminologies. In urban societies kinship institutions have a far less systematic character and do not occupy a corresponding place of central importance; the student of the city is concerned with the political, economic, and ecological aspects of the community rather than the familial. When the sociologist studies the family, he characteristically begins with the family in so far as it is affected by social problems such as divorce and juvenile delinquency, just as he studies not religion but the church or the failure of the church. Where the anthropologist is concerned with religion, with myth, and with ritual, the student of the city is concerned with the church, with reading habits, and with the law. These differences reflect the fact that in the folk societies it is the sacred and undeliberate aspects of society that are important, whereas in the urbanized societies more important are the secular and deliberate forms of control. The very language of social science has different shades of meaning, depending on whether the usage has grown up with reference to the one kind of society or to the other. The different connotations of "culture" have already been mentioned. The word "status" suggests to the student of primitive peoples the social system as it is implicit in the role and evaluation accorded anyone individual. In the city, however, a man's status is less a reflection of a system into which he is born and more a matter of his individual and unique experiences. Similarly, to a student of primitive society a "class" is a persisting status group, including both sexes and all ages, and articulating in amiable equilibrium with one or more corresponding status groups. The word does not suggest a conflict group; the "class" of "the class struggle" is a phenomenon of urbanism.

What I have attempted chiefly to say is that the convergence of anthropology and sociology, as a unified way of studying societies as wholes, which has been occurring in method —speculative sociology becoming empirical while fact-collecting anthropology comes to develop a conceptual apparatus—is also occurring in the establishment of a common subject matter. If all the "vanishing peoples" of the world should indeed vanish, we would still have to study the acculturated people, the folk people changing under the impact of urban growth. In these changing people, and in the intermediate peasant societies, we have abundant materials for the study not only of societal types, but also of social process. A study of the differences between the folk societies and the urban societies directly, and not merely as indirectly represented in the differences between anthropology and sociology, and a study of the intermediate societies give promise of developing better knowledge of this process. I think we shall come to see in many instances of social change the operation of two opposing tendencies. By one of these the ultimate values of a society develop an organization and consistency which gives a group moral solidarity. By the other the technical and economic system expands, while the moral organization is correspondingly impaired. In so far as the latter process gains at the expense of the former, we recognize the general and apparently irreversible historic process of civilization. In the various forms of social equilibrium we may see varying adjustments of these two tendencies. The church offered in the Middle Ages one solution of the problem of combining the two aspects of society in a single system; and in the totalitarian societies of recent times we may be able to recognize another attempted solution, this time, however, under the deliberate demand of secular government.

Notes

1. Boston: Richard C. Badger, 1918-20.
2. William F. Ogburn, *Social Change* (New York: Viking Press, 1928).
3. Robert S. and Helen Lynd (New York: Harcourt, Brace & Co., 1929).
4. Lewis H. Morgan, *League of the Ho-dé-no-sau-nee or Iroquois* (New York: Dodd, 1904).
5. W. H. R. Rivers, "The Psychological Factor," in *Essays on the Depopulation of Melanesia* ed. W. H. R. Rivers (Cambridge: University Press, 1922).
6. Ruth Benedict, *Patterns of Culture* (New York: Houghton Mifflin Co., 1934), 46.

7. Robert Redfield, *Tepoztlán: A Mexican Village* (Chicago: University of Chicago Press, 1930).
8. Horace M. Miner, *St. Denis: A French-Canadian Parish* (Chicago: University of Chicago Press, 1939).
9. John Embree, *Suye Mura: A Japanese Village* (Chicago: University of Chicago Press, 1939).
10. Robert Redfield, "Introduction" to Miner, *St. Denis,* xiii.
11. Ibid., xv.
12. Ibid.
13. Henry Maine, *Ancient Law* (London: J. Murray, 1861) and *Village-Communities in the East and West* (7th ed.; London: J. Murray, 1895).
14. Emile Durkheim, *De la division du travail social* (Paris: F. Alcan, 1932).
15. *Gemeinschaft und Gesellschaft* (Leipzig, 1887).
16. W. G. Sumner, *Folkways* (Boston: Ginn & Co., 1907), 12.
17. Sol Tax, "Culture and Civilization in Guatemalan Societies." *Scientific Monthly,* XLVIII, No. 5 (May, 1939): 463-67.

10

The Folk Society

Although Redfield offered an initial description and definition of "folk society" in his 1940 article "The Folk Society and Culture," he continued to refine his conception of folk society following publication of this essay. In 1942, he presented an expanded conception in the lecture "The Folk Society" delivered to students in the College at the University of Chicago. This essay was translated into Spanish and published in the Revista Mexicana de Sociología *in 1942 and only later, at the urging of the editors of the* American Journal of Sociology, *was it published in the English version included here. This article came to have almost iconic significance from the late 1940s through 1960s and was frequently republished in sociology and anthropology readers, usually paired with Louis Wirth's "Urbanism as a Way of Life." It remains as Redfield's most formal statement of the characteristics and significance of folk society.[1]*

I

Understanding of society in general and of our own modern urbanized society in particular can be gained through consideration of the societies least like our own: the primitive, or folk, societies.[2] All societies are alike in some respects, and each differs from others in other respects; the further assumption made here is that folk societies have certain features in common which enable us to think of them as a type—a type which contrasts with the society of the modern city.[3]

This type is ideal, a mental construction. No known society precisely corresponds with it, but the societies that have been the chief interest of the anthropologist most closely approximate it. The construction of the type depends, indeed, upon special knowledge of tribal and peasant groups. The ideal folk society could be defined through assembling, in the imagination, the characters which are logically opposite those which are to be found in the modern city, only if we had first some knowledge of non-urban peoples to permit us to determine what, indeed, are the characteristic features of modern city living. The complete procedure requires us to gain acquaintance with many folk societies in many parts of the world and to set down in words general enough to describe most

---

First published in *American Journal of Sociology* 52 (January 1947): 293-308.

of them those characteristics which they have in common with each other and which the modern city does not have.

In short, we move from folk society to folk society, asking ourselves what it is about them that makes them like each other and different from the modern city. So we assemble the elements of the ideal type. The more elements we add, the less will any one real society correspond to it. As the type is constructed, real societies may be arranged in an order of degree of resemblance to it. The conception develops that any one real society is more or less "folk." But the more elements we add, the less possible it becomes to arrange real societies in a single order of degree of resemblance to the type, because one of two societies will be found to resemble the ideal type strongly in one character and weakly in another, while in the next society strong resemblance will lie in the latter character and not in the former. This situation, however, is an advantage, for it enables us to ask and perhaps answer questions, first, as to whether certain characters tend to be found together in most societies, and then, if certain of them do, why.

Anyone attempting to describe the ideal folk society must take account of and in large degree include certain characterizations which have been made by many students, each of whom has been attentive to some but not to all aspects of the contrast between folk and modern urban society. Certain students have derived the characterization from examination of a number of folk societies and have generalized upon them in the light of contrast provided by modern urban society; the procedure defined above and followed by the writer. This is illustrated by Goldenweiser's characterization of five primitive societies. He says that they are small, isolated, nonliterate; that they exhibit local cultures; that they are relatively homogeneous with regard to the distribution of knowledge, attitudes, and functions among the population; that the individual does not figure as a conspicuous unit; and that knowledge is not explicitly systematized.[4]

In other cases the students have compared the state of certain societies at an early time with the same, or historical descendant of the same, society at a later time. In this way Maine arrived at his influential contrasts between society based on kinship and society based on territory, and between a society of status and one of contract.[5] In the case of this procedure, as in the case of the next, broad and illuminating conceptions are offered us to apply to folk societies as we contrast them with modern urban society. We are to find out if one of the contrasting terms is properly applicable to folk society and the other term to modern urban sociey.

In the work of still other students there is apparent no detailed comparison of folk with urbanized societies or of early society with later; rather, by inspection of our own society or of society in general, contrasting aspects of all society are recognized and named. This procedure is perhaps never followed in the unqualified manner just described, for in the instances about to be mentioned there is evidence that folk or ancient society has been compared with modern urbanized society. Nevertheless, the emphasis placed by men of this group is upon characteristics which, contrasting logically, in real fact coexist in every society and help to make it up. Here belongs Tönnies' contrast between Gemeinschaft and Gesellschaft, or that aspect of society which appears in the relations that develop without the deliberate intention of anyone out of the mere fact that men live together, as contrasted with that aspect of society which appears in the relations entered into deliberately by independent individuals through agreement to achieve certain recognized ends.[6] Comparable is Durkheim's distinction between that social solidarity which results from the sharing of common attitudes and sentiments and that which results from the complementary functional usefulnesses of the members of the group. In the "social segment"—the form of society existing in terms of "mechanical solidarity"—the law is "repressive"; in the "social organ"—the form of society existing in terms of "organic solidarity"—the law is "restitutive."[7]

It may be asked how closely the constructed type arrived at by any one investigator who follows the procedure sketched above will resemble that reached by another doing the same. It may be supposed that to the extent to which the real societies examined by the one investigator constitute a sample of the range and variety of societies similar to the sample constituted by the societies examined by the other, and to the extent that the general conceptions tentatively held by the one are similar to those held by the other, the results will be (except as modified by other factors) the same. For the purposes of understanding, which are served by the method of the constructed type, however, it is not necessary to consider the question. The type is an imagined entity, created only because through it we may hope to understand reality. Its function is to suggest aspects of real societies that deserve study, and especially to suggest hypotheses as to what, under certain defined conditions, may be generally true about society. Any ideal type will do, although it is safe to assert that that ideal construction has most heuristic value which depends on close and considered knowledge of real folk societies and which is guided by an effective scientific imagination—whatever that may be.

II

"The conception of a 'primitive society' which we ought to form," wrote Sumner, "is that of small groups scattered over a territory."[8] The folk society is a small society. There are no more people in it than can come to know each other well, and they remain in long association with each other. Among the Western Shoshone the individual parental family was the group which went about, apart from other families, collecting food; a group of families would assemble and so remain for a few weeks, from time to time, to hunt together; during the winter months such a group of families would form a single camp.[9] Such a temporary village included perhaps a hundred people. The hunting or food-collecting bands considered by Steward, representing many parts of the world, contained, in most cases, only a few score people.[10] A Southwestern pueblo contained no more than a few thousand persons.

The folk society is an isolated society. Probably there is no real society whose members are in complete ignorance of the existence of people other than themselves; the Andamanese, although their islands were avoided by navigators for centuries, knew of outsiders and occasionally came in contact with Malay or Chinese visitors.[11] Nevertheless, the folk societies we know are made up of people who have little communication with outsiders, and we may conceive of the ideal folk society as composed of persons having communication with no outsider.

This isolation is one half of a whole of which the other half is intimate communication among the members of the society. A group of recent castaways is a small and isolated society, but it is not a folk society; and, if the castaways have come from different ships and different societies, there will have been no previous intimate communication among them, and the society will not be composed of people who are much alike.

May the isolation of the folk society be identified with the physical immobility of its members? In building this ideal type, we may conceive of the members of the society as remaining always within the small territory they occupy. There are some primitive peoples who have dwelt from time immemorial in the same small valley, and who rarely leave it.[12] Certain of the pueblos of the American Southwest have been occupied by the same people or their descendants for many generations. On the other hand, some of the food-collecting peoples, such as the Shoshone Indians and certain aborigines of Australia, move about within a territory of very considerable extent; and there are Asiatic folk groups that make regular seasonal migrations hundreds of miles in extent.

It is possible to conceive of the members of such a society as moving about physically without communicating with members of other groups than their own. Each of the Indian villages of the midwest highlands of Guatemala is a folk society distinguishable by its customs and even by the physical type of its members from neighboring villages, yet the people are great travelers, and, in the case of one of the most distinct communities, Chichicastenango, most of the men travel far and spend much of their time away from home.[13] This does not result, however, in much intimate communication between those traveling villagers and other peoples. The gypsies have moved about among the various peoples of the earth for generations, and yet they retain many of the characteristics of a folk society.

Through books the civilized people communicate with the minds of other people and other times, and an aspect of the isolation of the folk society is the absence of books. The folk communicate only by word of mouth; therefore the communication upon which understanding is built is only that which takes place among neighbors, within the little society itself. The folk have no access to the thought and experience of the past whether of other peoples or of their own ancestors, such as books provide. Therefore, oral tradition has no check or competitor. Knowledge of what has gone before reaches no further back than memory and speech between old and young can make it go; behind "the time of our grandfathers" all is legendary and vague. With no form of belief established by written record, there can be no historical sense, such as civilized people have, no theology, and no basis for science in recorded experiment. The only form of accumulation of experience, except the tools and other enduring articles of manufacture, is the increase of wisdom which comes as the individual lives longer; therefore the old, knowing more than the young can know until they too have lived that long, have prestige and authority.

The people who make up a folk society are much alike. Having lived in long intimacy with one another, and with no others, they have come to form a single biological type. The somatic homogeneity of local, inbred populations has been noted and studied. Since the people communicate with one another and with no others, one man's learned ways of doing and thinking are the same as another's. Another way of putting this is to say that in the ideal folk society, what one man knows and believes is the same as what all men know and believe. Habits are the same as customs, In real fact, of course, the differences among individuals in a primitive group and the different chances of experience prevent this ideal state of things from coming about. Nevertheless, it is near enough to the truth for the student of a real folk society to report it fairly well by learning what goes on in the minds of a few of its members, and a primitive group has been presented, although sketchily, as learned about from a single member. The similarity among the members is found also as one generation is compared with its successor. Old people find young people doing, as they grow up, what the old people did at the same age, and what they have come to think right and proper. This is another way of saying that in such a society there is little change.

The members of the folk society have a strong sense of belonging together. The group which an outsider might recognize as composed of similar persons different from members of other groups is also the group of people who see their own resemblances and feel correspondingly united. Communicating intimately with each other, each has a strong claim on the sympathies of the others. Moreover, against such knowledge as they have of societies other than their own, they emphasize their own mutual likeness and value themselves as compared with others. They say of themselves "we" as against all others, who are "they."[14]

Thus we may characterize the folk society as small, isolated, nonliterate, and homogeneous, with a strong sense of group solidarity. Are we not soon to acknowledge the simplicity of the technology of the ideal folk society? Something should certainly be said about the tools and toolmaking of this generalized primitive group, but it is not easy to assign a meaning to "simple," in connection with technology which will do justice to the facts as known from the real folk societies. The preciseness with which each tool, in a large number of such tools, meets its needs in the case of the Eskimo, for example, makes one hesitate to use the word "simple." Some negative statements appear to be safe: secondary and tertiary tools—tools to make tools—are relatively few as compared with primary tools; there is no making of artifacts by multiple, rapid, machine manufacture; there is little or no use of natural power.

There is not much division of labor in the folk society: what one person does is what another does. In the ideal folk society all the tools and ways of production are shared by everybody. The "everybody" must mean "every adult man" or "every adult woman," for the obvious exception to the homogeneity of the folk society lies in the differences between what men do and know and what women do and know. There differences are clear and unexceptional (as compared with our modern urban society where they are less so). "Within the local group there is no such thing as a division of labor save as between the sexes," writes Radcliffe-Brown about the Andaman Islanders. "Every man is expected to be able to hunt pig, to harpoon turtle and to catch fish, and also to cut a canoe, to make bows and arrows and all the other objects that are made by men."[15] So all men share the same interests and have, in general, the same experience of life.

"We may conceive, also, of the ideal folk society as a group economically independent of all others: the people produce what they consume and consume what they produce. Few, if any, real societies are completely in this situation; some Eskimo groups perhaps most closely approach it. Although each little Andamanese band could get along without getting anything from any other, exchange of goods occurred between bands by a sort of periodic gift giving.

The foregoing characterizations amount, roughly, to saying that the folk society is a little world off by itself, a world in which the recurrent problems of life are met by all its members in much the same way. This statement, while correct enough, fails to emphasize an important, perhaps the important, aspect of the folk society. The ways in which the members of the society meet the recurrent problems of life are conventionalized ways; they are the results of long intercommunication within the group in the face of these problems; and these conventionalized ways have become interrelated within one another so that they constitute a coherent and self-consistent system. Such a system is what we mean in saying that the folk society is characterized by "a culture." A culture is an organization or integration of conventional understandings. It is, as well, the acts and the objects, in so far as they represent the type characteristic of that society, which express and maintain these understandings. In the folk society, this integrated whole, this system, provides for all the recurrent needs of the individual from birth to death and of the society through the seasons and the years. The society is to be described, and distinguished from others, largely by presenting this system.

This is not the same as saying, as was said early in this paper, that in the folk society what one man does is the same as what another man does. What one man does in a mob is the same as what another man does, but a mob is not a folk society. It is, so far as culture is concerned, its very antithesis.[16] The members of a mob (which is a kind of "mass") each do the same thing, it is true, but it is a very immediate and particular thing, and it is done without much reference to tradition. It does not depend upon and express a great many conventional understandings related to one another. A mob has no culture. The folk society exhibits culture to the greatest conceivable degree. A mob is an aggregation of people doing the same simple thing simultaneously. A folk society is an organization of people doing many different things successively as well as simultaneously. The members of a mob act with reference to the same object of attention. The members of a folk society are guided in acting by previously established comprehensive and interdependent conventional understandings; at any one time they do many different things, which are complexly related to one another to express collective sentiments and conceptions When the turn comes for the boy to do what a man does, he does what a man does; thus, though in the end the experiences of all individuals of the same sex are alike, the activities of the society, seen at a moment of time, are diverse, while interdependent and consistent.

The Papago Indians, a few hundred of them, constituted a folk society in southern Arizona. Among these Indians a war party was not so simple a thing as a number of men going out together to kill the enemy. It was a complex activity involving everybody in the society both before, during, and after the expedition and dramatizing the religious and moral ideas fundamental to Papago life.[17] Preparation for the expedition involved many practical or ritual acts on the part of the immediate participants, their wives and children, previously successful warriors, and many others. While the party was away, the various relatives of the warriors had many things to do or not to do—prayer, fasting, preparation of ritual paraphernalia, etc. These were specialized activities, each appropriate to just that kind of relative or other category of person. So the war was waged by everybody. These activities, different and special as they were, interlocked, so to speak, with each other to make a large whole, the society-during-a-war-expedition. And all these specialized activities obeyed fundamental principles, understood by all and expressed and reaffirmed in the very forms of the acts—the gestures of the rituals, the words of songs, the implied or expressed explanations and admonitions of the elders to the younger people. All understood that the end in view was the acquisition by the group of the supernatural power of the slain enemy. This power, potentially of great positive value, was dangerous, and the practices and rituals had as their purposes first the success of the war party and then the draining-off of the supernatural power acquired by the slaying into a safe and "usable" form.

We may say, then, that in the folk society conventional behavior is strongly patterned: it tends to conform to a type or a norm. These patterns are interrelated in thought and in action with one another, so that one tends to evoke others and to be consistent with the others. Every customary act among the Papago when the successful warriors return is consistent with and is a special form of the general conceptions held as to supernatural power. We may still further say that the patterns of what people think should be done are closely consistent with what they believe is done, and that there is one way, or a very few conventional ways, in which everybody has some understanding and some share of meeting each need that arises.[18] The culture of a folk society is, therefore, one of those wholes which is greater than the sum of its parts. Gaining a livelihood takes support from religion, and the relations of men to men are justified in the conceptions held of the supernatural world or in some other aspect of the culture. Life, for the member of the folk society, is not one activity and then another and different one; it is one large activity out of which one part may not be separated without affecting the rest.

A related characteristic of the folk society was implied when it was declared that the specialized activities incident to the Papago war party obeyed fundamental principles understood by all. These "principles" had to do with the ends of living, as conceived by the Papago. A near-ultimate good for the Papago was the acquisition of supernatural power. This end was not questioned; it was a sort of axiom in terms of which many lesser activities were understood. This suggests that we may say of the folk society that its ends are taken as given. The activities incident to the war party may be regarded as merely complementarily useful acts, aspects of the division of labor. They may also, and more significantly, be seen as expressions of unquestioned common ends. The folk society exists not so much in the exchange of useful functions as in common understandings as to the ends given. The ends are not stated as matters of doctrine, but are implied by the many acts which make up the living that goes on in the society. Therefore, the morale of a folk society—its power to act consistently over periods of time and to meet crises effectively—is not dependent upon discipline exerted by force or upon devotion to some single principle of action but to the concurrence and consistency of many or all of the actions and conceptions which make up the whole round of life. In the trite phrase, the folk society is a "design for living."

What is done in the ideal folk society is done not because somebody or some people decided, at once, that it should be done, but because it seems "necessarily" to flow from the very nature of things. There is, moreover, no disposition to reflect upon traditional acts and consider them objectively and critically. In short, behavior in the folk society is traditional, spontaneous, and uncritical. In any real folk society, of course, many things are done as a result of decision as to that particular action, but as to that class of actions tradition is the sufficient authority.

The Indians decide now to go on a hunt; but it is not a matter of debate whether or not one should, from time to time, hunt.

The folkways are the ways that grow up out of long and intimate association of men with each other; in the society of our conception all the ways are folkways. Men act with reference to each other by understandings which are tacit and traditional. There are no formal contracts or other agreements. The rights and obligations of the individual come about not by special arrangement; they are, chiefly, aspects of the position of the individual as a person of one sex or the other, one age-group or another, and as one occupying just that position in a system of relationships which are traditional in the society. The individual's status is thus in large part fixed at birth; it changes as he lives, but it changes in ways which were "foreordained" by the nature of his particular society. The institutions of the folk society are of the sort which has been called "crescive"; they are not of the sort that is created deliberately for special purposes, as was the juvenile court. So, too, law is made up of the traditional conceptions of rights and obligations and the customary procedures whereby these rights and obligations are assured; legislation has no part in it.

If legislation has no part in the law of the ideal folk society, neither has codification, still less jurisprudence. Radin has collected material suggesting the limited extent to which real primitive people do question custom and do systematize their knowledge.[19] In the known folk societies they do these things only to a limited extent. In the ideal folk society there is no objectivity and no systematization of knowledge as guided by what seems to be its "internal" order. The member of this mentally constructed society does not stand off from his customary conduct and subject it to scrutiny apart from its meaning for him as that meaning is defined in culture. Nor is there any habitual exercise of classification, experiment, and abstraction for its own sake, least of all for the sake of intellectual ends. There is common practical knowledge, but there is no science.

Behavior in the folk society is highly conventional, custom fixes the rights and duties of individuals, and knowledge is not critically examined or objectively and systematically formulated; but it must not be supposed that primitive man is a sort of automaton in which custom is the mainspring. It would be as mistaken to think of primitive man as strongly aware that he is constrained by custom. Within the limits set by custom there is invitation to excel in performance. There is lively competition, a sense of opportunity, and a feeling that what the culture moves one to do is well worth doing. "There is no drabness in such a life. It has about it all the allurements of personal experience, very much one's own, of competitive skill, of things well done."[20] The interrelations and high degree of consistency among the elements of custom which are presented to the individual declare to him the importance of making his endeavors in the directions indicated by tradition. The culture sets goals which stimulate action by giving great meaning to it.[21]

It has been said that the folk society is small and that its members have lived in long and intimate association with one another. It has also been said that in such societies there is little critical or abstract thinking. These characteristics are related to yet another characteristic of the folk society: behavior is personal, not impersonal. A "person" may be defined as that social object which I feel to respond to situations as I do, with all the sentiments and interests which I feel to be my own; a person is myself in another form, his qualities and values are inherent within him, and his significance for me is not merely one of utility. A "thing," on the other hand, is a social object which has no claim upon my sympathies, which responds to me, as I conceive it, mechanically; its value for me exists in so far as it serves my end. In the folk society all human beings admitted to the society are treated as persons; one does not deal impersonally ("thing-fashion") with any other participant in the little world of that society. Moreover, in the folk society much besides human beings is treated personally. The pattern of behavior which is first suggested by the inner experience of the individual—his wishes, fears, sensitivenesses, and interests of all sorts—is projected into all objects with which he comes into contact. Thus nature, too, is treated personally: the elements, the features of the landscape, the animals, and especially anything in the environment which by its appearance or behavior suggests that it has the attributes of mankind—to all these are attributed qualities of the human person.[22]

In short, the personal and intimate life of the child in the family is extended, in the folk society, into the social world of the adult and even into inanimate objects. It is not merely that relations in such a society are personal; it is also that they are familial. The first contacts made as the infant becomes a person are with other persons; moreover, each of these first persons, he comes to learn, has a particular kind of relation to him which is associated with that one's genealogical position. The individual finds himself fixed within a constellation of familial relationships. The kinship connections provide a pattern in terms of which, in the ideal folk society, all personal relations are conventionalized and categorized. All relations are personal. But relations are not, in content of specific behavior, the same for everyone. As a mother is different from a father, and a grandson from a nephew, so are these classes of personal relationship, originating in genealogical connection, extended outward into all relationships whatever. In this sense, the folk society is a familial society. Lowie[23] has demonstrated the qualification that is to be introduced into the statement of Maine[24] that the primitive society is organized in terms of kinship rather than territory. It is true that the fact that men are neighbors contributes to their sense of belonging together. But the point to be emphasized in understanding the folk society is that, whether mere contiguity or relationship as brother or as son is the circumstance uniting man into the society, the result is a group of people among whom prevail the personal and categorized relationships that characterize families as we know them, and in which the patterns of kinship tend to be extended outward from the group of genealogically connected individuals into the whole society. The kin are the type persons for all experience.

This general conception may be resolved into component or related conceptions. In the folk society family relationships are clearly distinguished from one another. Very special sorts of behavior may be expected by a mother's brother of his sister's son, and this behavior will be different from that expected by a father's brother of his brother's son. Among certain Australian tribes, animals killed by a hunter must be divided so that nine or ten certain parts must be given to nine or ten corresponding relatives of the successful hunter—the right ribs to the father's brother, a piece of the flank to the mother's brother, and so on.[25] The tendency to extend kinship outward takes many special forms. In many primitive societies kinship terms and kinship behavior (in reduced degree) are extended to persons not known to be genealogically related at all, but who are nevertheless regarded as kin. Among the central Australians, terms of relationship are extended "so as to embrace all persons who come into social contact with one another. ... In this way the whole society forms a body of relatives."[26] In the folk society, groupings which do not arise out of genealogical connection are few, and those that do exist tend to take on the attributes of kinship. Ritual kinship is common in primitive and peasant societies in the forms of blood brotherhood, godparental relationships, and other ceremonial sponsorships.[27] These multiply kinship connections; in these cases the particular individuals to be united depend upon choice. Furthermore, there is frequently a recognizedly fictitious or metaphorical use of kinship terms to designate more casual relationships, as between host and guest or between worshipper and deity.[28]

The real primitive and peasant societies differ very greatly as to the forms assumed by kinship. Nevertheless, it is possible to recognize two main types. In one of these the connection between husband and wife is emphasized, while neither one of the lineages, matrilineal or patrilineal, is singled out as contrasted with the other. In such a folk society the individual parental family is the social unit, and connections with relatives outside this family are of secondary importance. Such family organization is common where the population is small, the means of livelihood are by precarious collection of wild food, and larger units cannot permanently remain together because the natural resources will not allow it. But where a somewhat larger population remains together, either in a village or in a migratory band, there often, although by no means always, is found an emphasis upon one line of consanguine connection rather than the other, with subordination of the conjugal connection.[29] There results a segmentation of the society into equivalent kinship units. These may take the form of extended domestic groups or joint families (as in China) or may include many households of persons related in part through recognized genealogical connection and in part through the sharing of the same name or other symbolic designation; in the latter case we speak of the groups as clans. Even in societies where the individual parental family is an independent economic unit, as in the case of the eastern Eskimo, husband and wife never become a new social and economic unit with the completeness that is characteristic of our own society. When a marriage in primitive society comes to an end, the kinsmen of the dead spouse assert upon his property a claim they have never given up.[30] On the whole, we may think of the family among folk peoples as made up of persons consanguinely connected. Marriage is, in comparison with what we in our society directly experience, an incident in the life of the individual who is born, brought up, and dies with his blood kinsmen. In such a society romantic love can hardly be elevated to a major principle.

In so far as the consanguine lines are well defined (and in some cases both lines may be of importance to the individual),[31] the folk society may be thought of as composed of families rather than of individuals. It is the familial groups that act and are acted upon. There is strong solidarity within the kinship group, and the individual is responsible to all his kin as they are responsible to him. "The clan is a natural mutual aid society.... A member belongs to the clan, he is not his own; if he is wrong, they will right him; if he does wrong, the responsibility is shared by them."[32] Thus, in folk societies wherein the tendency to maintain consanguine connection has resulted in joint families or clans, it is usual to find that injuries done by an individual are regarded as injuries against his kinship group, and the group takes the steps to right the wrong. The step may be revenge regulated by custom or a property settlement. A considerable part of primitive law exists in the regulation of claims by one body of kin against another. The fact that the folk society is an organization of families rather than an aggregation of individuals is further expressed in many of those forms of marriage in which a certain kind of relative is the approved spouse. The customs by which in many primitive societies a man is expected to marry his deceased brother's widow or a woman to marry her deceased sister's husband express the view of marriage as an undertaking between kinship groups. One of the spouses having failed by death, the undertaking is to be carried on by some other representative of the family group. Indeed, in the arrangements for marriage—the selection of spouses by their relatives, in bride price, dowry, and in many forms of familial negotiations leading to a marriage—the nature of marriage as a connubial form of social relations between kindreds finds expression.

It has been said in the foregoing paragraphs that behavior in the folk society is traditional, spontaneous, and uncritical, that what one man does is much the same as what another man does, and that the patterns of conduct are clear and remain constant throughout the generations. It has also been suggested that the congruence of all parts of conventional behavior and social institutions with each other contributes to the sense of rightness which the member of the folk society feels to inhere in his traditional ways of action. In the well known language of Sumner, the ways of life are folkways; furthermore, the folkways tend to be also mores—ways of doing or thinking to which attach notions of moral worth. The value of every traditional act or object or institution is, thus, something which the members of the society are not disposed to call into question; and, should the value be called into question, the doing so is resented. This characteristic of the folk society may be briefly referred to by saying that it is a sacred society. In the folk society one may not, without calling into effect negative social sanctions, challenge as valueless what has come to be traditional in that society.

Presumably, the sacredness of social objects has its source, in part, at least, in the mere fact of habituation; probably the individual organism becomes early adjusted to certain habits, motor and mental, and to certain associations between one activity and another or between certain sense experience and certain activities, and it is almost physiologically uncomfortable to change or even to entertain the idea of change. There arises "a feeling of impropriety of certain forms, of a particular social or religious value, or a superstitious fear of change."[33] Probably the sacredness of social objects in the folk society is related also to the fact that in such well organized cultures acts and objects suggest the traditions, beliefs, and conceptions which all share. There is reason to suppose that when what is traditionally done becomes less meaningful because people no longer know what the acts stand for, life becomes more secular.[34] In the repetitious character of conventional action (aside from technical action) we have ritual; in its expressive character we have ceremony; the folk society ritual tends also to be ceremonious, and ritual-ceremony tends to be sacred, not secular.

The sacredness of social objects is apparent in the ways in which, in the folk society, such an object is hedged around with restraints and protections that keep it away from the commonplace and the matter-of-fact.[35] In the sacred there is alternatively, or in combination, holiness a dangerousness. When the Papago Indian returned from a successful war expedition, bringing the scalp of a slain Apache, the head-hairs of the enemy were treated as loaded with a tremendous "charge" of supernatural power; only old men, already successful warriors and purified through religious ritual, could touch the object and make it safe for incorporation into the home of the slayer. Made into the doll-like form of an Apache Indian, it was, at last, after much ceremonial preparation, held for instant by the members of the slayer's family, addressed in respect and awe by kinship terms, and placed in the house, there to give off protective power.[36] The Indians of San Pedro de la Laguna, Guatemala, recognize an officer, serving for life, whose function it is to keep custody of ten or a dozen Latin breviaries printed in the eighteenth century and read prayers from one or another of these books on certain occasion. No one but this custodian may handle the books, save his assistants on ceremonial occasions, with his permission. Should anyone else touch a book he would go mad or be stricken with blindness. Incense and candles are burnt before the chest containing the books, yet the books are not gods—they are objects of sacredness.[37]

In the folk society this disposition to regard objects as sacred extends, characteristically, even into the subsistence activities and into the foodstuffs of the people. Often the foodstuffs are personified as well as sacred. "'My granduncle used to say to me,' explained a Navajo Indian, 'if you are walking along a trail and see a kernel of corn, pick it up. It is like a child lost and starving.' According to the legends corn is just the same as a human being, only it is holier. ... When a man goes into a cornfield he feels that he is in a holy place, that he is walking among Holy People. ... Agriculture is a holy occupation. Even before you plant you sing songs. You continue this during the whole time your crops are growing. You cannot help but feel that you are in a holy place when you go through your fields and they are going well.'"[38] In the folk society, ideally conceived, nothing is solely a means to an immediate practical end. All activities, even the means of production, are ends in themselves, activities expressive of the ultimate values of the society.

III

This characterization of the ideal folk society could be greatly extended. Various of the elements that make up the conception could be differently combined with one another, and this point or that could be developed or further emphasized and its relations shown to other aspects of the conception. For example, it might be pointed out that where there is little or no systematic and reflective thinking the customary solution to problems of practical action only imperfectly take the form of really effective and understood control of the means appropriate to accomplish the desired end and that, instead, they tend to express the states of mind of the individuals who want the end brought about and fear that it may not be. We say this briefly in declaring that the folk society is characterized by much magic, for we may understand "magic" to refer to action with regard to an end—to instrumental action—but only to such instrumental action as does not effectively bring about that end, or is not really understood in so far as it does, and which is expressive of the way the doer thinks and feels rather than adapted to accomplishing the end. "Magic is based on specific experience of emotional states ... in which the truth is revealed not by reason but by the play of emotions upon the human organism." Magic is founded "on the belief that hope cannot fail nor desire deceive."[39] In the folk society effective technical action is much mixed with magical activity. What is done tends to take the form of a little drama; it is a picture of what is desired.

The nature of the folk society could, indeed, be restated in the form of a description of the folk mind. This description would be largely a repetition of what has been written in foregoing pages, except that now the emphasis would be upon the characteristic mental activity of members of the folk society rather than upon customs and institutions. The man of the folk society tends to make mental associations which are personal and emotional, rather than abstractly categoric or defined in terms of cause and effect. "Primitive man views every action not only as adapted to its main object, every thought related to its main end, as we should perceive them, but ... he associates them with other ideas, often of a religious or at least a symbolic nature. Thus he gives to them a higher significance than they seem to us to deserve."[40]

A very similar statement of this kind of thinking has been expressed in connection with the thinking of medieval man; the description would apply as well to man in the folk society:

> From the causal point of view, symbolism appears as a sort of short-cut of thought. Instead of looking for the relation between two things by following the hidden detours of their causal connections, thought makes a leap and discovers their relation, not in a connection of cause or effects, but in a connection of signification or finality. Such a connection will at once appear convincing, provided only that the two things have an essential quality in common which can be referred to a general value. ... Symbolic assimilation founded on common properties presupposes the idea that these properties are essential to things. This vision of white and red roses blooming among thorns at once calls up a symbolic association in the medieval mind: for example, that of virgin and martyrs, shining with glory, in the midst of their persecutors. The assimilation is produced because the attributes are the same; the beauty, the tenderness, the purity, the colours of the roses are also those of the virgins, their red color that of the blood of the martyrs. But this similarity will only have a mystic meaning if the middle-term connecting the two terms of the symbolic concept expresses an essentiality common to both; in other words, if redness and whiteness are something more than names for physical differences based on quantity if they are conceived of as essences, as realities. The mind of the savage, of the child, and of the poet never sees them otherwise.[41]

The tendency to treat nature personally has recognition in the literature as the "animistic" or "anthropomorphic" quality of primitive thinking and the contrast between the means-ends pattern of thought more characteristic of modern urban men and the personal thought of primitive man has been specially investigated.[42]

In the foregoing account no mention has been made of the absence of economic behavior characteristic of the market in the folk society. Within the ideal folk society members are bound by religious and kinship ties, and there is no place for the motive of commercial gain. There is no money and nothing is measured by any such common denominator of value. The distribution of goods and services tends to be an aspect of the conventional and personal relationships of status that make up the structure of the society: goods are exchanged as expressions of good will and, in large part, as incidents of ceremonial and ritual activities. "On the whole, then, the compulsion to work, to save, and to expend is given not so much by a rational appreciation of the (material) benefits to be received as by the desire for social recognition, through such behavior."[43]

The conception sketched here takes on meaning if the folk society is seen in contrast to the modern city. The vast, complicated, and rapidly changing world in which the urbanite and even the urbanized country-dweller live today is enormously different from the small, inward-facing folk society, with its well integrated and little-changing moral and religious conceptions. At one time all men lived in these little folk societies. For many thousands of years men must have lived so; urbanized life began only very recently, as the long history of men on earth is considered, and the extreme development of a secularized and swift-changing world society is only a few generations old.

The tribal groups that still remain around the edges of expanding civilization are the small remainders of this primary state of living. Considering them one by one, and in comparison with the literate or semiliterate societies, the industrialized and the semi-industrialized societies, we may discover how each has developed forms of social life in accordance with its own special circumstances. Among the polar Eskimos, where each small family had to shift for itself in the rigors of the arctic environment, although the ties of kinship were of great importance, no clans or other large unilateral kinship groups came into existence. The sedentary Haida of the Queen Charlotte Islands were divided into two exogamous kinship groups, each composed of clans, with intense pride of descent and healthy rivalry between them. Among the warring and nomadic Comanche, initiative and resourcefulness of the individual were looked on more favorably than among the sedentary and closely interdependent Zuñi. In West Africa, great native states arose, with chiefs and courts and markets, yet the kinship organization remained strong; and in China we have an example of slow growth of a great society, with a literate elite, inclosing within it a multitude of village communities of the folk type. Where cities have arisen, the country people dependent on those cities have developed economic and political relationships, as well as relationships of status, with the city people, and so have become that special kind of rural folk we call peasantry,[44] And even in the newer parts of the world, as in the United States, many a village or small town has, perhaps, as many points of resemblance with the folk society as with urban life.

Thus the societies of the world do not range themselves in the same order with regard to the degree to which they realize all of the characteristics of the ideal folk society. On the other hand, there is so marked a tendency for some of these characteristics to occur together with others that the interrelations among them must be in no small part that of interdependent variables. Indeed, some of the interrelations are so obvious that we feel no sense of problem. The smallness of the folk society and the long association together of the same individuals certainly are related to the prevailingly personal character of relationships. The fewness of secondary and tertiary tools and the absence of machine manufacture are circumstances obviously unfavorable to a very complex division of labor. Many problems present themselves, however, as to the conditions in which certain of these characteristics do not occur in association, and as to the circumstances under which certain of them may be expected to change in the direction of their opposites, with or without influencing others to change also.

A study of the local differences in the festival of the patron village saint in certain communities of Yucatan indicates that some interrelationship exists in that case.[45] In all four communities, differing as to their degrees of isolation from urban centers of modifying influence, the festival expresses a relationship between the village and its patron saint (or cross) which is annually renewed. In it a ritual and worship are combined with a considerable amount of play. The chief activities of the festival are a novena, a folk dance, and a rustic bullfight. In all four communities there is an organization of men and women who for that year undertake the leadership of the festival, handing over the responsibility to a corresponding group of successors at its culmination. So far the institution is the same in all the communities studied. The differences appear when the details of the ritual and play and of the festal organization are compared and when the essential meanings of these acts and organizations are inquired into. Then it appears that from being an intensely sacred act, made by the village as a collectivity composed of familially defined component groups, with close relationship to the system of religious and moral understandings of the people, the festival becomes, in the more urbanized communities, chiefly an opportunity for recreation for some and of financial profit for others, with little reference to moral and religious conceptions.

In the most isolated and otherwise most folklike of the communities studied, the organization of the festival is closely integrated with the whole social structure of the community. The hierarchy of leaders of the community, whose duties are both civil and religious, carry on the festival: It is the chiefs, the men who decide disputes and lead in warfare, who also take principal places in the religious processions and in the conduct of the ceremonies. The community, including several neighboring settlements, is divided into five groups, membership in which descends in the male line. The responsibility for leading the prayers and preparing the festal foods rests in turn on four men chosen from each of the five groups. The festival is held at the head village, at the shrine housing the cross patron of the entire community. The festival consists chiefly of solemnly religious acts: masses, rosaries, procession of images, kneeling of worshipers. The ritual offerings are presented by a special officer, in all solemnity, to the patron cross; certain symbols of divinity are brought from the temple and exposed to the kneeling people as the offerings are made. The transfer of the responsibility to lead the festival is attended by ceremony in an atmosphere of sanctity: certain ritual paraphernalia are first placed on the altar and then, after recitation of prayers and performance of a religious dance, are handed over, in view of all, from the custodians of the sacred charge for that year to their successors.

In the villages that are less isolated, the festival is similar in form, but it is less well integrated with the social organization of the community, is less sacred, and allows for more individual enterprise and responsibility. These changes continue in the other communities studied, as one gets nearer to the city of Mérida. In certain seacoast villages the festival of the patron saint is a money-getting enterprise of a few secular-minded townspeople. The novena is in the hands of a few women who receive no help from the municipal authorities; the bullfight is a commercial entertainment, professional bullfighters being hired for the occasion and admission charged; the folk dance is little attended. The festival is enjoyed by young people who come to dance modern dances and to witness the bullfight, and it is an opportunity to the merchants to make a profit. What was an institution of folk culture has become a business enterprise in which individuals, as such, take part for secular ends.

The principal conclusion is that the less isolated and more heterogeneous communities of the peninsula of Yucatan are the more secular and individualistic and the more characterized by disorganization of culture. It further appeared probable that there was, in the changes taking place in Yucatan, a relation of interdependence among these changing characteristics, especially between the disorganization of culture and secularization. "People cease to believe because they cease to understand, and they cease to understand because they cease to do the things that express the understandings."[46] New jobs and other changes in the division of labor bring it about that people cannot participate in the old rituals; and, ceasing to participate, they cease to share the values for which the rituals stood. This is, admittedly, however, only a part of the explanation. The conception of the folk society has stimulated one small group of field workers to consider the interdependence or independence of these characteristics of society. In Yucatan isolation, homogeneity, a personal and "symbolic" view of nature, importance of familial relationships, a high degree of organization of culture, and sacredness of sanctions and institutions were all found in regular association with each other. It was then reported that in certain Indian communities on or near Lake Atitlan in Guatemala this association of characteristics is not repeated.[47] As it appeared that these Guatemalan communities were not in rapid change, but were persisting in their essential nature, the conclusion was reached that "a stable society can be small, unsophisticated, homogeneous in beliefs and practices," have a local, well-organized culture, and still be one "with relationships impersonal, with formal institutions dictating the acts of individuals, and with family organization weak, with life secularized, and with individuals acting more from economic or other personal advantage than from any deep conviction or thought of the social good." It was further pointed out that in these Guatemalan societies a "primitive world view," that is, a disposition to treat nature personally, to regard attributes as entities, and to make "symbolic" rather than causal connections, consists with a tendency for relations between man and man to be impersonal, commercial, and secular, as they tend to be in the urban society.[48]

These observations lead, in turn, to reconsideration of the circumstance, tending to bring about one kind of society or one aspect of society rather than another. The breakdown of familial institutions in recent times in Western society is often ascribed to the development of the city and of modern industry. If, as has been reported, familial institutions are also weak in these Guatemalan villages, there must be alternative causes for the breakdown of the family to the rise of industry and the growth of the city, for these Guatemalan Indians live on or near their farms, practice a domestic handicraft manufacture, and have little or nothing to do with cities. It has been suggested that in the case of the Guatemalan societies the development, partly before the Conquest and partly afterward, of pecuniary economy with a peddler's commerce, based on great regional division of labor, together with a system of regulations imposed by an elite with the use of force, may be the circumstances that have brought about reduction in the importance of familial institutions and individual independence, especially in matters of livelihood.[49]

The secular character of life in these highland villages of the Lake Atitlan region is not so well established as in the individuated character of life, but, if life is indeed secular there, it is a secularity that has developed without the influence of high personal mobility, of the machine, and of science. In a well-known essay Max Weber showed how capitalistic commercialism could and did get along with piety in the case of the Puritans.[50] So it may appear that under certain conditions a literate and, indeed, at least partly urbanized society may be both highly commercial and sacred—as witness, also, the Jews—while under certain other conditions an otherwise folklike people may become individualistic, commercial, and perhaps secular. It is, of course, the determination of the limiting conditions that is important.

Notes

1. Margaret Park Redfield, headnote to "The Folk Society," by Robert Redfield, in Margaret Park Redfield, ed., *Human Nature and the Study of Society: The Papers of Robert Redfield*, vol. 1, 231.
2. Neither "primitive" nor any other term is denotative, and none has sufficient generally accepted precise meaning to allow us to know in just what characters of a society to discover the degree to which it is or is not "primitive," "simple," or whatever. The words "non-literate" or "preliterate" do call attention to a particular character, literacy, but understanding is still required as to when a society is "literate" and as to what form or degree of literacy has significance. There are head-hunting tribes, in other respects as primitive as were the Pawnee Indians in the seventeenth century, that have knowledge of writing. In certain Mexican villages most children and many adults have formal knowledge of the arts of reading and writing, but in most other respects these village societies are much more like tribal societies than they are like our Western cities.

    The word "folk," which will be used in this paper, is no more precise than any other. It is used here because, better than others, it suggests the inclusion in our comparisons of peasant and rustic people who are not wholly independent of cities and because in its compounds, "folklore" and "folk song," it points, in a rough way, to the presence of folklore and folk songs, as recognized by the collector of such materials, as a sign of a society to be examined in making up the characterization of the ideal type with which we are here concerned. But the question of the word to be used is of small importance.
3. The reader may compare the conception developed in this paper with the ideal "sacred society" characterized by Howard Becker in "Ionia and Athens" (Ph.D. diss., University of Chicago, 1930), pp. 1-16; with similar conceptions developed in chapter i of *Social Thought from Lore to Science* by Harry Elmer Barnes and Howard Becker (Boston, New York: D. C. Heath & Co., 1938); and with the application of the conception in *The Sociology of the Renaissance* by Alfred von Martin (London: Kegan Paul, Trench, Trubner & Co., Ltd., 1945).
4. A. A. Goldenweiser, *Early Civilization* (New York: Alfred A. Knopf, 1922), pp. 117-18.
5. Henry Maine, *Ancient Law* (London: J. Murray, 1861).
6. Ferdinand Tönnies, *Gemeinschaft und Gesellschaft* (first published, 1887), trans. and ed. Charles P. Loomis as *Fundamental Concepts of Sociology* (New York, Cincinnati, etc.: American Book Co., 1940).
7. *Émile Durkheim on the Division of Labor in Society*, a translation by George Simpson of *De la division du travail social* (New York: Macmillan Co., 1933);

Howard Becker, "Constructive Typology in the Social Sciences," *American Sociological Review,* V, No. 1 (1940), 40-55, and reprinted in Harry Elmer Barnes, Howard Becker, and Frances Bennett Becker (eds.), *Contemporary Social Theory* (New York: Appleton-Century-Crofts, Inc., 1940), Part 1.
8. W. G. Sumner, *Folkways* (Boston: Ginn & Co., 1907), p. 12.
9. Julian Steward, *Basin-Plateau Aboriginal Sociopolitical Groups* (Smithsonian Institution, Bureau of American Ethnology, Bull. 120 [Washington: Government Printing, Office, 1938]), pp. 230-34.
10. Julian Steward, "Economic and Social Basis of Primitive Bands," *Essays in Anthropology Presented to A. L. Kroeber* (Berkeley: University of California Press, 1936), pp. 341-42.
11. A. R. Radcliffe-Brown, *The Andaman Islanders* (Cambridge University Press, 1933), pp. 6-9.
12. A. L. Kroeber, *Handbook of Indians of California* (Smithsonian Institution, Bureau of American Ethnology, Bull. 78 [Washington: Government Printing Office, 1925]), p. 13.
13. Robert Redfield, "Primitive Merchants of Guatemala," *Quarterly Journal of Inter-American Relations,* I, No. 4, 42-56.
14. Sumner, *Folkways,* pp. 13-15.
15. Radcliffe-Brown, *Andaman Islanders,* p. 43.
16. Herbert Blumer, "Mass Behavior and the Motion Picture," *Publications of the American Sociological Society,* XXIX, No.3 (1935), 115-27.
17. Ruth Underhill, *The Autobiography of a Papago Woman* ("American Anthropological Association, Memoirs," No. 46 [1936]).
18. Ralph Linton, *The Study of Man* (New York: Appleton-Century-Crofts, Inc., 1936), chap. xvi, esp. p. 283.
19. Paul Radin, *Primitive Man as Philosopher* (New York: Appleton-Century-Crofts, Inc., 1927).
20. A. A. Goldenweiser, "Individual, Pattern and Involution," *Essays in Anthropology Presented to A. L. Kroeber* (Berkeley: University of California Press, 1936), p. 102.
21. Ruth Benedict, *Patterns of Culture* (Boston and New York: Houghton Mifflin Co., 1934).
22. Ruth Benedict, "Animism," *Encyclopedia of the Social Sciences.*
23. Robert H. Lowie, *The Origin of the State* (New York: Harcourt, Brace and Co., 1927), pp. 51-73.
24. Maine, *Ancient Law.*
25. A. W. Howitt, *The Native Tribes of Southeastern Australia* (New York: Macmillan Co., 1904), p. 759.
26. A. R. Radcliffe-Brown, "Three Tribes of Western Australia," *Journal of the Royal Anthropological Institute,* XLIII, 150-51.
27. Benjamin Paul, "Ritual Kinship: With Special Reference to Godparenthood in Middle America" (Ph.D. diss., University of Chicago, 1942).
28. E. C. Parsons, *Notes on Zuñi,* Part II ("American Anthropological Association, Memoirs," Vol. IV, No.4 [1917]).
29. Ralph Linton, *The Study of Society* (New York: Century Co.), p. 159.
30. Ruth Benedict, "Marital Property Rights in Bilateral Societies," *American Anthropologist,* XXXVIII, No. 3 (July-September 1936), 368-73.
31. Peter Murdock, "Double Descent," *American Anthropologist,* N.S., XLII, No.4, Part I (October-December 1940), 555-61.
32. Edwin W. Smith and Andrew Murray Dale, *The Ila-Speaking Peoples of Northern Rhodesia* (London: Macmillan & Co., Ltd., 1920), I, 296.

Social Anthropology

33. Franz Boas, *Primitive Art* (Oslo, 1927), p. 150. 6
34. Robert Redfield, *The Folk Culture of Yucatan* (Chicago: University of Chicago Press, 1941), p. 364.
35. Emile Durkheim, *The Elementary Forms of the Religious Life* (London: Allen & Unwin, 1926).
36. Underhill, *Autobiography of a Papago Woman,* p. 18.
37. Benjamin Paul, unpublished MS.
38. W. W. Hill, *The Agricultural and Hunting Methods of the Navaho Indians* ("Yale University Publications in Anthropology," No. 18 [New Haven: Yale University Press, 1938]), p. 53.
39. Bronislaw Malinowski, "Magic, Science and Religion," in *Science, Religion and Reality,* ed. Joseph Needham (New York: Macmillan Co., 1925), p. 80.
40. Franz Boas, *The Mind of Primitive Man* (New York: Macmillan Co., 1938), p. 226.
41. J. Huizinga, *The Waning of the Middle Ages* (London: Arnold & Co., 1924), pp. 184-85. This "symbolic" kind of thinking is related to what Levy-Bruhl called "participation" (see L. Levy-Bruhl, *How Natives Think* [New York: Alfred A. Knopf, Inc., 1925], esp. chap. ii).
42. Hans Kelsen, "Causality and Retribution," *Philosophy of Science,* VIII, No. 4 (1941), 533-56; and Kelsen, *Society and Nature* (Chicago: University of Chicago Press, 1944).
43. Raymond Firth, *Primitive Economics of the New Zealand Maori* (New York: E. P. Dutton & Co., 1929), p. 484. See also, Firth, *Primitive Polynesian Economy* (London: George Routledge & Sons, 1939), esp. chap. x, "Characteristics of a Primitive Economy."
44. Robert Redfield, "Introduction," in Horace Miner, *St. Denis: A French-Canadian Parish* (Chicago: University of Chicago Press, 1940).
45. Redfield, *The Folk Culture of Yucatan.*
46. *Ibid.,* p. 364.
47. Sol Tax, "Culture and Civilization in Guatemalan Societies," *Scientific Monthly,* XLVIII (May, 1939), 467.
48. Sol Tax, "World View and Social Relations in Guatemala," *American Anthropologist,* N.S., XLIII, No.1 (1941), 27-42.
49. Redfield, *The Folk Culture of Yucatan,* pp. 365-67.
50. Max Weber, "Protestant Ethics and the Spirit of Capitalism," cited in Kemper Fullerton, "Calvinism and Capitalism," *Harvard Theological Review,* XXI, 163-95.

Part II

Peasants

11

The Intermediate Community

As he embarked upon his dissertation study of Tepoztlán, Redfield displayed a keen awareness that he was attempting to apply anthropological methods to the study of peoples previously not examined by anthropologists or sociologists. The people of Tepoztlán represented, he argued, people intermediate between the very isolated "primitive" villagers typically studied by anthropologists and the townspeople or city dwellers examined by sociologists. The villagers of Tepoztlán demonstrated many characteristics of remote undeveloped peoples, yet they had formal ties to the urban centers beyond their borders and were already in the process of moving beyond a way of life that could be defined as fully traditional. Redfield recognized the intermediate status of these peoples and suggested that distinct vocabulary and methods of study were needed to study and characterize such societies. In this essay, which served as the concluding chapter of Tepoztlán, A Mexican Village, *Redfield summarized his efforts to define a social anthropological rather than mere ethnological approach to study of transitional societies and intermediate or peasant peoples. The interest Redfield expressed here in defining a workable approach for the study of intermediate or peasant peoples served along with his interest in theorizing the dynamics of social change as a guiding motif for Redfield over the course of his career.*

The culture of Tepoztlán appears to represent a type intermediate between the primitive tribe and the modern city. It has, one would venture, its nearest analogues in the peasant communities of the more backward parts of Europe, of the Near East, and of the Orient. To the extent that Tepoztlán is economically and mentally self-sufficient, to the extent that its social heritage is local and is transmitted without the use of writing, to the extent that all knowledge is intimate and personal and is closely associated with the ancient habitat of the people, the community resembles a primitive tribe. But just to the degree that Tepoztlán conceives itself as a part of the outside world, and that the Tepoztecans define their personal problems in terms of modern city civilization, it is unlike a tribal society. The Tepoztecans are primarily Tepoztecans, but they are also, if somewhat more remotely, Mexicans. Their society might be called a "folk" community, in a more special sense than that in which the term is often used.

First published in *Tepoztlán, A Mexican Village: A Study of Folk Life*. (Chicago: University of Chicago Press, 1930), 217-223.

So little, outside of the material culture, are elements of pre-Columbian custom preserved that it presents small opportunity to a culture historian interested in the character of the aboriginal society. Only from the point of view of history or of romantic appreciation is Tepoztlán an "Aztec *pueblo*." The elaborate ritual and philosophic scheme that distinguished the pre-Columbian culture was carried by the priestly class; and these meanings were practically extirpated by the conquerors. The society was, one might say, decapitated. The ancient household techniques remain, but the ancient values are gone.

But if the interest is not in depiction, but in studying social change as it takes place—in social anthropology as contrasted with ethnology, in the terminology of Radcliffe-Brown[1]—then Tepoztlán presents an excellent opportunity. This opportunity is for the study of the change whereby a folk community is slowly becoming more like the city. This change is a case of diffusion, occurring in an easily observed situation, so slowly as not to accomplish the disorganization of the community, and under practical circumstances that liberate the student from responsibility to record the fragmentary vestiges of a disappearing culture.

The frontier of this change is between *los correctos* and *los tontos*.[2] This frontier is a geographical, not merely a figurative, frontier. The diffusion of city traits can be observed and expressed in spatial terms. The point from which changes originate is the central *plaza*. This is at first confusing to one accustomed to examples of the diffusion process taken from tribal societies. There the changes that originate in the center of an area are those modifications locally developed in accordance with the characteristic type of the area, while the changes that take place because of contact with another culture take place on the periphery. But here, with a paradox that is only apparent, the periphery of change is at the center. This is because the contact with the city takes place here. Here visitors come. Here are trade, machinery, and print, so far as these come at all to Tepoztlán. And here, by a sort of selection, are drawn the tradespeople whose roles have been determined by urban competition and who are familiar with city ways. These people—the tradespeople and other *correctos*—on the one hand, communicate by direct face-to-face relations with *los tontos* on the periphery, and, on the other hand, through their memories of the city, and by means of letters, newspapers, and visits to the capital, communicate with the city. It is as though there were, in this central zone where live *los correctos*,[3] two overlapping culture "areas": a culture of the folk, with communication by direct contact, and a culture of the city, which impinges on the other culture in another dimension, by means of communication which transcends space.

The ways of the city diffuse outward from the central *plaza*. They are not carried outward by migration, because the interests and activities of *los correctos* cause them to live near the *plaza* and so keep out *los tontos*, and also because people continue to occupy the house sites of their ancestors. By spotting the traits on a map of the community the distribution of city traits as compared with folk traits could be indicated. ... On the one hand are those specialists—tradespeople and artisans—who practice European techniques and who mostly acquired their specialties through economic competition. These are in general found near the *plaza*. On the other hand are the midwives, herb doctors, and fireworks-makers, who practice more ancient, traditional techniques and who in more cases came into their roles by birth. These tend to be found toward the periphery.

The upper three *barrios*, San Pedro, Los Reyes, and San Sebastian (and, to a somewhat less extent, Santa Cruz), are the most remote from the *plaza* and are *barrios* of *tontos*. These three contain the greatest proportionate number of magical specialists and not a single rational specialist of the sorts listed. The people in these *barrios* have a different "mentality" from those that dwell around the *plaza*. Racially they are no different, but the experiences they undergo are different. They are "timeless" for one thing; few up there have watches, and they are too far away to hear the clock on the *plaza*. Illiteracy is greater up there. The mail-carrier in the months of these observations never delivered a letter to one of these three *barrios*.

These statements, and those that follow, need of course the support of a more substantial body of materials and more careful exploration into the facts. They are made merely to define a problem for further work. In this sense it may be stated that the distributions of various aspects of city ways rather strikingly coincide. Those elements of material culture which were more recently taken over from the city and are still exterior to the Spanish-Indian folk culture, such as forks, felt hats, and metal beds, are to be found in the inner zone of *los correctos*. Here also is most marked the tendency toward secularization of holiday celebration. It is *los correctos* who promote the carnival, with its strongly secularized, commercialized aspect; while it is *los tontos* who control the religious *fiestas*, with their greater detail of ritual and remoteness from commercial activity. The three most important *fiestas* commemorating santos occur respectively in San Pedro, San Sebastian, and Ixcatepec, on the peripheries of the community. It is *los tontos* who preserve the most traditional ritual on practical occasions of crisis, such as birth or death. One might venture to guess that the nearer a birth occurs to the central plaza the less the proportion of merely ritualistic, expressive behavior and the greater the proportion of purely practical behavior which attends the occasion. If the difference between *los correctos* and *los tontos* increases during periods of disorder, it decreases during periods of peace. And during these latter times the progressive advance of city ways, the influence of *los correctos* over *los tontos*, can be observed. This process, it has already been sufficiently suggested, is a process of diffusion. It remains only to point out that this diffusion process may be thought of somewhat more broadly than is usually possible in the instances of diffusion ordinarily considered by ethnologists, where the bare facts have to be reconstructed or learned at second hand.

In the first place, it may be supposed that the diffusion is not merely the communication, between contemporary groups, of the traits usually listed, of technique and ritual. There pass also what can rather awkwardly be called "subjective" traits: mental form as well as mental content. It is not merely that the group comes to employ a new artifact or to adopt a new attitude toward marriage or toward a religious practice. It may be said that the whole mentality correspondingly changes, if by "mentality" is understood a complex of habits employed in meeting unfamiliar problems. Mentality in this sense too is an aspect of culture. If the individual undergoes experiences of a very different sort from those undergone before, he develops a correspondingly new organ, a new mind. The patterns of thinking of a city man, where a multitude of unfamiliar experiences are dealt with by relegating them to convenient classes, are different from those of a remote rural dweller whose social objects are all unique and known by their individual characters. So, if it can be shown that *los correctos* tend to reject traditional magical ways of curing disease, for instance, and accept instead the ways of modern life, it might be that such a change be not entirely due to the prestige of city cures but due also to a general tendency to solve problems by means wherein the mechanisms involved are understood.

In the second place, the diffusion is not merely the borrowing of ethnological traits, because the diffusion is accompanied by a change in the attitude that the people have toward themselves. The just-preceding chapter suggests that a study of diffusion here is not merely enumerating elements of culture which the group has or has not, but also involves a consideration of striking changes in the type of personality to be expected in the group. The sensitiveness, pride, and zeal for reform that characterize the individual described in that chapter are perhaps traits that typify the culture of his group (*los correctos*), but they were not borrowed from the city. They are changes that have resulted in him out of the conflict between the two cultures in which, mentally, he is living at the same time. The way a people feel about themselves and about other people is a datum that may be included in a direct study, such as this might be, of the culture process.

Notes

1. A. R. Radcliffe-Brown, art., "The Methods of Ethnology and Social Anthropology."
2. Editor's Note: Redfield defines earlier in his text his usage of the terms *los correctos* and *los tontos*. *Los correctos* "are the small group of townspeople who are richer, better educated, and more accustomed to city ways than the others. These men are the shopkeepers and many of the artisans. They are *los correctos*—the 'correct' people—as contrasted with *los tontos*—the 'ignorant' people. The former wear shoes and dark trousers; the latter, sandals and white trousers." (*Tepoztlán*, 68.)
3. Of course there is no definite zone, but merely a tendency for *los correctos* to dwell, and for city traits to occur, near the *plaza* rather than near the outskirts.

12

Introduction to *St. Denis: A French Canadian Parish*

> *Over the course of his career, Redfield progressively refined his vocabulary for discussing intermediate peoples who lay between tribal villagers and civilized urbanites. Although starting in 1930 with Tepoztlán he had used the term "folk" to refer to such intermediate peoples, he had at times not clearly distinguished in his writings the definition of peasants from folk or tribal peoples. But in his 1939 introduction to his student Horace Miner's* St. Denis: A French Canadian Parish, *Redfield articulated a definition of peasantry that sharply distinguished peasants from tribal peoples. Peasants, he argued, represented a middle position between tribal and civilized peoples and, as such, they offered a useful vantage point for study of all levels of society ranging from the most simple to complex. Redfield continued into the 1950s to elaborate his conception of peasantry and to formulate a methodology to characterize these people that borrowed from both anthropology and sociology. This essay represented a major step in his effort to define peasant studies as an independent field of inquiry within social anthropology.*

For the comparative study of societies the peasant peoples occupy a strategic position. They form a sort of middle term in the equation of culture and civilization. On the one hand, they resemble the primitive peoples with whom the ethnologist is characteristically acquainted; and on the other, they belong to that modern urbanized world which lies in the foreground of attention of most American sociologists. To study the peasant peoples is to help to draw into a single field of investigation all the societies of the earth from the simplest to the most complex. This unity of subject matter must be realized if we are to develop the science of society and culture, whatever that science may be called. For their importance the peasant societies have been relatively neglected; careful field studies of such groups are to be welcomed.

First published as introduction to *St. Denis: A French Canadian Parish*, by Horace Miner (Chicago: University of Chicago Press, 1939), xiii-xix.

The reader of Dr. Miner's excellent book will note the respects in which this French-Canadian peasant society resembles the primitive peoples. The *habitants* live in terms of common understandings which are rooted in tradition and which have come to form an organization. The fundamental views of life are shared by almost everyone; and these views find consistent expression in the beliefs, the institutions, the rituals, and the manners of the people. In a word, they have a culture. Furthermore, the sanctions which support conduct are strongly sacred: the faith which all share provides endorsement of certain behavior and condemnation for other behavior. The priest tells them this is right and that is wrong; but the point here is that the people feel the right and the wrong and act from such a feeling, not from mere expediency. And, also, this society, like many others more primitive and outside of the European world, is strongly familial. The fabric of society is woven of threads of consanguineous and connubial connection; the family system is strong, pervasive, and certain in its effects. The activities which the individual will perform—in work, in getting married, in finding a career, in politics—are largely determined by his position in a family. The familial organization, as analyzed by Dr. Miner, though made up of no exotic elements but of terms and customs perfectly familiar to most readers, has the definition of outline, the importance of role in the total society, and the intimacy of connection with other parts of the total social structure which we are accustomed to find in the study of aboriginal simple societies. There is little disorganization and little crime. "The only death by violence in the parish happened so long ago that even the ballad about it is forgotten." Viewed in one light, the isolated peasant group is comparable with American Indian or native African societies. Even the political behavior of the people of St. Denis may be so regarded; the division into two political parties the members of each of which exhibit strongly expressive and competitive behavior toward each other suggests the dual divisions of some simpler folk.

But to look at these *habitants* as another Melanesian or American Indian society would be, of course, to ignore the fact that they form a part of the modern urbanized world. The peasant participates in a money economy, produces a surplus for sale in city markets, pays taxes, sometimes goes to school, votes, and otherwise participates in a wider economic and political structure which includes not only the peasant but the townsman. The peasant makes some use of literacy, while the aborigine does not. Moreover, peasant and city man constitute one single society that is organized in terms of status. Each is aware of the other; each allows a place for the other in his world of recognized social relations; each accepts the other as a member of a larger society in which both are members. It is the nature of the peasant that he accords prestige to the city man and to the sophisticated members of his own group. The peasant may, through education, enter the world of the city while the city man has kinsmen among the peasants. In the case of St. Denis the immediate connection between the *habitant* and the city of Quebec is made by certain residents of the local community: the *curé* and his relatives, and the senator and his kinsmen. ... These persons, having risen from the people, are nevertheless "socially so far removed from the society of the parish that they can not carry on normal social life with the other parishioners. ... These persons do not owe their position to anything within the immediate society. Their position is due to contacts which they have had with the world outside the parish, from which sphere they have received recognition far higher than anything the parish can give." The *habitants*, in turn, accord them the prestige which these educated persons have won in the city.

In Durkheim's terms the peasant society forms a special type of relatively stable compromise between the social segment and the social organ. It is the adjustment of local culture to the civilization of the cities. The solidarity of the tribe is preserved in conjunction with the market and within the nation.

The condition of the peasant is often regarded as something to be escaped, an ignominy to be shunned. A consideration of the French Canadians herein described, who are almost the only North American peasants, may give pause to such a judgment. Certainly their form of life invites comparison with other rural agriculturalists with low standards of living. If the sharecropper be brought to mind, the difference between the mode of life of the latter and that of the *habitant* is evident, and who will say that the comparison is to the disadvantage of the latter? If the habitant has order and security and faith and confidence, it is chiefly because he has a culture. It cannot be validly said that his advantages arise from a relatively greater wealth of natural resources in the region he occupies; it is doubtful if such an advantage could be demonstrated. It is not simply that the one owns land and the other does not. The *habitant's* life is orderly and relatively secure largely because it is lived in terms of an organized body of common understandings that authorize his conduct and explain and justify his impulses. Culture is not to be identified with the artifacts of a tribe or the tools of a farmer. The *habitant* has culture not because he has something to live with but because he has something to live for.

The double character of peasant societies brings it about that they offer to students of social change a combination of advantages of which, in this case, Dr. Miner has not failed to avail himself. Like other primitive or folk societies they have a definiteness of outline and a relative simplicity which facilitates the work of the reporter and student. One can say what their institutions are, one can fix upon the essential characters of their culture, and one can often recognize the elements that are today promoting change. On the other hand, being a part of a literate nationality, these societies have each a recorded past. One can consult documents about them and learn something about how they have come to be what they are. The histories of nonliterate peoples are far less accessible. But when one has trustworthy information on the past, the present is clarified and one may venture to consider probable future trends.

In the case of the French-Canadian rural communities Dr. Miner's account makes plain some of the special circumstances that have there tended to preserve the local and traditional organization and some other factors that are tending to disrupt it. Like the members of other societies on the peripheries of expanding civilization, the *habitant* has been exposed to the existing and disorganizing example of the outsider and more citified person. There has been the usual tendency to modify old local ways and take over customs and points of view of the outsider. But here the Catholic Church has acted as a regulator upon this tendency. She has stood between the changing world and the *habitant*, preventing the admission of elements which she condemns and interpreting admitted elements in accordance with the faith and with the local culture. The reader of this book cannot fail to be impressed with the completeness with which this local folk culture is articulated with the doctrines and the practices of the church. The church provides sacred justifications and explanations for the necessary toil of the native, offers rituals to carry the individual from birth to death, and supports and sanctifies the large-family system. In its local institutions and in the local priest it provides the framework for community government and the moral leader of the community. And when the local ways are threatened by such a danger as the example of the summer colony, the church is there, in the sermons of the priest, to minimize the danger of contagion. The church has gradually eliminated from the magic of the people those forms which are not consistent with Catholic Christianity, while allowing the society to accept certain approved novelties, such as scientific agriculture. One might think that under this tutelage the traditional culture of the French Canadian, preserving its essentials, might continue substantially intact for many centuries.

Dr. Miner's analysis indicates some of the important reasons why, nevertheless, the traditional organization is threatened. The system, as a body of beliefs and practices, is static; but as an adjustment between sources of wealth and means of exploitation, it is expansive. It required the settlement of excess children upon marginal lands. The large-family system produced more children than could be established in the local community. The culture could persist without important change so long as there were marginal lands. In Dr. Miner's language, "French-Canadian culture was one which had a high degree of internal social integration based on a short-term adjustment to the environment." As accessible lands gave out, a readjustment had to be made. In old France the large-family system gave way to one of small families. So far, in Quebec, this adjustment has not taken place. Other adjustments have. Some of the children have been placed in the professions; some have immigrated to the factories of the outside world. But to educate children requires money, and the need for money has brought changes of technology and dependence upon a wider economy. And the children that go out to factories return to bring city ways into the rural community. The old organization was one of land and church; the new ways of dealing with excess children, turning them into factory hands abroad or into local day-laborers, puts them outside of the land-church system. And this tends to disrupt the system. It is the same thing that happens when an oceanic native is given a job and a daily wage on a plantation: it disrupts the tribal life. Only, in this case no invader with a plantation was necessary. The system based on expansion into new lands, contained its own future problems. The *habitant* had a folk culture, but he came as a pioneer into a new world. It is this combination of a self-consistent and well-organized culture with a new habitat and open resources that makes the situation of the French Canadian particularly interesting. A study such as we have here preserves our confidence that social change may be subjected to orderly study and reduced to a more systematic understanding.

13

Later Histories of the Folk Society

As Redfield continued to refine his notions of folk and peasant societies, he also refined his conception of urban societies. By the early 1950s, Redfield came to view the notion of urban society as too limited to capture fully the characteristics of complex society that represented the sophisticated pole of his developmental continuum. He thus came to view the developmental progression as moving from traditional folk society to complex pluralistic civilization rather than urban society. This focus on civilization reflected an important historical shift in Redfield's thinking, a shift which signaled his movement beyond a strictly synchronic sociological conception of the dynamics of social change. In this essay, delivered first by Redfield as a lecture at Cornell University in 1952 and then published in 1953 as a chapter in The Primitive World and Its Transformations, *Redfield examined the dialectical relationship between civilization and folk societies, focusing especially on the forces and events that transform folk societies into peasant societies. Civilizations reach out and act upon folk societies within their orbits, he argued, and if this interaction is sufficient, folk societies are transformed into peasant societies. These peasant societies then become dependent in part upon the urban centers of the civilizations in critical economic, political, and moral dimensions. The construction of the relationship between peasant society and civilization that Redfield expressed in this essay represented a significant advancement in his evolving conception of the socio-historical role of peasantry.*

In the long view of human affairs, the food-producing revolution and the urban revolution of Childe form into one mighty event: the transformation of the folk society into civilization.[1] The first revolution appears as a prelude and precondition of the second. Taken together, they are one major turning point. Only "the mutation of sub-man into man, which was accomplished in circumstances of which we have no record, was a more profound change."[2] Connecting this second great event, civilization, with the dynamic aspect of existence known to the Chinese as Yang as opposed to Yin, Toynbee remarks that for 98 percent of all human history mankind reposed on the "ledges" of primitive human nature "before entering on the Yang-like activity of civilization."

From the position we occupy on a higher ledge, looking down on what Toynbee conceives as the dead or apparently paralytic societies

---

First published in *The Primitive World and Its Transformations* (Ithaca, N.Y.: Cornell University Press, 1953), 26-53.

remaining or resting on lower ledges, his foremost question is: How did *we* get *here?* The question is as to the genesis of civilization. Toynbee seeks the general circumstances which attend the birth of a civilization, and the characteristic developments in that class of societies which are civilized. From this point of view it is asked to what extent civilizations show recurrences in their developmental phases. To this group of questions different answers have been given by Spengler, Toynbee, and Sorokin. The question takes on a multitude of special forms as attention is fixed on particular aspects of the phenomenon of civilization, or is guided by particular interests and hypotheses. The origins of civilization may be seen, as Wittfogel sees them,[3] in the specific necessity to control waters for irrigation and other human use. Or they may be found in a more inclusive and generalized successful response to some sort of challenging difficulty, as Toynbee finds them. The many more special questions as to the origins of civilization may be illustrated by reference to the old problem as to the origins of the state, which some have found in the conquest of one people by another. It is also illustrated in the view that formal law, another aspect of civilization, tends to develop either where there is surplus wealth, unevenly distributed, or where there are major communal enterprises, such as the hunt, war, or public works, requiring regulation.

These great questions are for those who have the scholarly competence which they demand. The enquiry initiated in this chapter starts from the humbler viewpoint of the folk societies themselves. The question here is not, How does civilization come about? but, What becomes of the folk society? Instead of addressing the main outlines of the human adventure from the point of view of civilized men who look back on their beginnings, let us view that adventure from the position of all mankind, originally folklike in its manner of life, and fairly recently transmuted into societies with new and different manners of life. Here begins a sketchy review of the transformations of the folk societies. Some of these societies have remained on the lower ledges of Professor Toynbee's precipice. How did others come to clamber to higher ledges? What were the influences of civilized peoples upon some of them that caused some precivilized societies to move to different ledges from those they occupied in precivilized times? Toynbee's insights into some of these transmutations are guides in recognizing many of the new forms of human living. Others require new efforts to discern them.

At the time we attempt some account of the transformations of the folk societies, there is not very much left of them. The civilizations of the last five thousand years have destroyed them or have altered them with very small exception. One civilization that developed in Western Europe during very recent times indeed has reached into almost all of even the remote comers where they most successfully persisted in the primary condition. "In this worldwide Western offensive against the rear-guard of the primitive societies, extermination or eviction or subjugation has been the rule and conversion the exception."[4] Most of the folk societies of precivilized times are no more. Such as survive are a mere handful of the population, relative to the immense numbers of the civilized. Anthropology, a product of the Western civilization which, chiefly, has destroyed the folk societies, is the chief agency to bring the survivors to general notice. The anthropologist sees these survivors as marginal to civilization, either because they lie on the outer edges of the continental masses where the civilizations arose (the Australian blackfellow; the Eskimo), or because civilization, swirling around them, leaves them in some relatively inaccessible valley or mountain side (the Vedda of Ceylon; the Ainu; the Cora Indians).[5] In some of the anthropological reports, the surviving folk society is presented as if it were less influenced by civilization that is actually the case at the time of the study; many an ethnological report is something of a reconstruction, a description of the people at the time of their grandfathers or an account of life at the time of the investigation with the influence of the trader, the mission, or the school somewhat underemphasized. When the purpose of the investigation is to provide the comparative science of society or culture with another independent case to compare, this is proper. In the present connection, however, it is just the kinds of changes that have been brought about in the folk societies that are the center of interest.

With the exception of the few isolated survivors, the rise of the civilizations transformed the precivilized peoples into other kinds of peoples. We may think of civilization as a remaking of man in which the basic type, the folk man, is altered into other types. Some of these types can be recognized as common and perhaps relatively stable. But with later history, the types become so many, so intergraded, and so rapidly changing as to defy analysis.

This remaking of man was the work of the city. As suggested in the first chapter, the archaeology of the Middle East may make it necessary to recognize a period of town life before that of city life. There are sites which suggest that populations intermediate in size between that characterizing the neolithic farming settlement and the ancient city existed in Iraq before Eridu and other cities were distinctly cities. In such towns, says Braidwood, he would suspect that there were administrators, specialists, and an outer clustering of peasants. This is again the question as to the rapidity of acceleration of the curve of that technological development which culminated in city life.

But whether or not we distinguish town from city in this period, the first important differentiation of societal types took place in these cities and proto-cities. Rather than say each time "town and city," I shall say simply "city." In the city appeared the administrative elite, the literate priest with his opportunities for reflection and cultivation of esoteric knowledge, the specialized artisan, detached from the local community. These are new kinds of men, not only because they have found new kinds of economic support, but because, in the greater impersonality of their relations with others and in their relative independence of the village community with its local culture and "inward-facingness," these city men have a new world view and essential style of life.

The developing city required economic support from a wider and wider area of production, and so affected, at first only in terms of labor, tribute, and sale, peoples as yet not civilized, or only partly civilized. The process of differentiation of societal types took place also outside of the city, by extension of its influence on folk societies. I suppose that a Sumerian city, or an Egyptian kingdom, drew its supplies from peoples in all kinds and degrees of transformation of their style of life, from more remote peoples still primitive and tribal to the city-dominated farmers at their very gates. And the early city extends its influence by procreation of other cities: Byblos, in Syria, becomes a semi-Egyptian city; after Assyrian merchants have settled in Cappadocia, a variant of Mesopotamian civilization develops there.[6] So secondary centers of urban influence came into being. This process of transformation of folk peoples into urban peoples or partly urbanized peoples has never ceased. It continues today on the Western-managed tropical plantation, in the African kraal, the American Indian reservation, the Macedonian village, and the Ozark mountain valley.

Our historians of the ancient civilizations, when they come to describe cities so old and highly developed as stood in Egypt or in Mesopotamia in the third millennium before Christ, use the word "peasant" for those peoples close at hand whose labors made the city possible. The word points to a human type. Rather than use it, as some have,[7] for any community of small-scale producers for market, let us reserve it for this new type. It required the city to bring it into existence. There were no peasants before the first cities. And those surviving primitive peoples who do not live in terms of the city are not peasants. The Siriono Indians are not peasants; nor are the Navajo. But it is possible positively to characterize those peoples who are.

The peasant, like the primitive tribesman, is indigenous. He lives where he has always lived, and the city has grown up out of a kind of life which, in fundamental custom and belief, is his too. Perhaps its influence came to him from near at hand, and he has walked to the city to sell his produce or to contribute his labor; or perhaps the nearest city is so far away that its influence has reached him only after long delay. But in either case he is long used to the existence of the city, and its ways are, in altered form, part of his ways. The peasant is a rural native whose long established order of life takes important account of the city.

The account that the peasant takes of the city or town is economic, political, and moral. The peasant has some product which the city consumes, and there are products of the city—metal tools, guns, patent medicines, or electric flashlights—which the peasant takes from the manufacturers in the city. Since the coming of money into the world, the peasant village has come in great degree to define its economic affairs in terms of this measure. In Oriental peasant villages the extraordinary expenditures required by the marriage of a child or the advent of a festival are met by cooperative credit associations, "a mechanism for collective saving and lending,"[8] and these institutions function in terms of money. They exist in villages in China,[9] in Japan,[10] and in India.[11]

The relations between peasant and town or city are expressed in part in financial institutions. Gain is calculated; some crop or other product is sold, in the village or elsewhere, to a buyer of a more urbanized community who pays in money. Taxation is also present; when tribute is regularized into taxation, a tribal people is on the way to becoming peasantry. In certain East Indian villages the accountant is an important specialist.[12] In the Chinese villages described by Fei,[13] the peasant requires the assistance of townsman or city man to finance his agriculture. A town collector of rice sends an "agent boat" to the villages; the agent gets the townsman collector to lend rice to the peasant when the peasant has no more; the agent guarantees the return of the rice to the townsman by the peasant when his new rice comes to market. Or village people borrow money from wealthy people in the towns with whom they have connections; the rate of interest is very high. In East Indian villages the moneylenders that interested Henry Maine when he wrote of Indian village life eighty years ago[14] still flourish; recently their operations have come to be regulated by modern law; they still function "and in a highly sophisticated way; they generally cover vast areas, working in teams and visiting their fixed villages along the bus and rail lines at least twice a year; they establish credit ratings by systematic interviewing and by taking help from local agent-spies."[15] Pawnbrokers in the towns probably account for a significant part of the village credit in India.[16] We may summarize the economic character of the peasant village by saying that it combines the primitive brotherhood of the precivilized folk community with the economic nexus characteristic of civilized society. So far as the peasant community faces inward, the relationships that compose it are still personal and familial, but now they are modified by a spirit of pecuniary advantage.

This pecuniary spirit contributes to the formation of an added dimension of the peasant's social life: in the peaceful and stable relationships with outsiders. The peasant village maintains its local solidarity, its folklike inward-facingness, but now qualifies the sharp exclusiveness of the primitive settlement with institutionalized forms for admitting strangers. In the idealized typical folk society all members of one's own community are kinsmen; all others are enemies. In some real primitive societies, under original conditions of isolation, this condition is approximated; we remember Professor A. R. Radcliffe-Brown's account of how, to gain admittance to a settlement of unfamiliar aborigines, this anthropologist's guide had first to establish, by that dialectic of the kinship term so important there, his connection by kinship with the group into which admission was sought.[17] But in the peasant village there is institutionalized provision for the stranger. When he is a specialist in the business, the East Indian moneylender is in the village by right and necessity, but he is not of it. The village fathers discuss their problems without him. The simple agriculturalist will be admitted fully into the moral life of the community. But for him to be admitted there may be some ritual of acceptance, of adoption. In some villages settler may be admitted as a "soil brother." Such persons are admitted at par. They become like the native born.

But the admission of one who will not become a full participant in the local life, but will merely live there and serve it in a specialized and instrumental capacity, is a more serious matter. I was present in a village of Mayan Mexican peasants when the question was debated as to whether a certain traveling vendor of city goods and buyer of locally produced swine should be allowed, on his petition, to settle in the village and open a store. The villagers had themselves already established small stores in which to sell city products they themselves imported. The admission to the community, however, of one who would not be a farmer like themselves and who would presumably have no part in the religious and moral life with which the agriculture was bound up, was a momentous step, and they took it only after due consideration. The institutionalized resident stranger is a feature of peasant life. At any earlier stage of that process whereby the tribal community becomes a peasant community, the question may be as to the admission of traveling vendors from the outside, who are not even allowed to pass a night in the settlement. So, among the more primitive Maya of Quintana Roo, Villa, my associate ethnologist, had to appear as a traveling peddler of cloth, medicine, and gunpowder as a first step in getting permission to reside for a season among them. With established peasantry, however, the traveling merchant, the caravan trade, the permanent store kept by Arab, or Syrian, or Chinese, or urbanite from Tyre or Sidon, come to be familiar.

The economic interdependence of peasant village and city finds political expression in institutions for control of the local community by power exerted from the city. The established relations of the peasant village with the urban world are political as well as economic. Where the local community is still more or less tribal, the urban control may be exercised through punitive expeditions, actual or threatened, but when peasantry are fully present, the secular and impersonal control of the city is continuous and precise. The representative of the central power may be someone derived from the village itself, as when the literate Chinese villager who has passed an examination deals on behalf of the village with the bureaucrats in the yamen. Or the village leaders, the panchayat, or the elders of the mir, will deal with the outside power in ways to which they have become adjusted. These varying forms of political adjustment to the central power come into being whether the central power is a city-state, a kingdom, or an empire. The peasantry of feudalism have their own patterns of political relationship to power that is above them, although in this case the influence of the city appears in the manor and ruling elite, even in the immediate absence of the city itself.

This relatively stable relationship between peasant and city is in part shaped by the cultural advances of the city and the incorporation into the peasant life of institutions developed in the course of this advance. Entertainment is one form of city-born activity. In the precivilized society the dramatic and lyric arts are inseparable from the religion or from the mythic content of the local culture, and secular professional entertainment is unknown. This is a creature of the city. Peasants look in part to town or city for their entertainment; the conditions of peace and relative freedom of movement make it possible for traveling entertainers to come to the peasant villages, entertainers whose models are in part urban. The migratory professional entertainers of medieval Europe are well known. Writing of East Indian villages, Altekar tells us how the agricultural labors of the villagers are interrupted by traveling singers and dancers.[18] In China dramatic performances entertain the villagers; the companies may consist of amateurs organized locally, or they may be made up of more professional players who travel from community to community.[19] The Mexican peasant at festivals receives musicians employed from a town, or is amused by a traveling circus. The festival is better, the prestige of the village is the higher, if the musicians hired come from a more urbanized town.

The peasant is also adjusted, in ways that characterize his style of life, to that outstanding feature of civilization, writing. The precivilized hunter or villager is preliterate; the peasant is illiterate. The existence of the art of writing has become an element in his mode of life, although he himself perhaps cannot read or write. He must take account of those who can, and things written are meaningful objects in his life. The sociology of literacy has not yet been written. But it should be possible to recognize the characteristic forms of adjustment to literacy. It may be too much to say that in the ancient civilizations writing remained "a mystery, a specialized profession too abstruse to combine with manual avocations";[20] some of the earliest uses of writing were in connection with purposes apparently exoteric and secular. But it is probably correct to say that in the early civilizations of the Old World, as among the Maya of the New, there developed a higher learning dependent on literacy; and the literate specialists, in many cases priestly in function, were not also artisans. The literate man tended to become, until modern times, a kind of professional. In many a peasant village literacy is confined to the few, and these few use their knowledge either to communicate what is held in sacred books—traditional writings of moral and religious force—or to communicate with the city world in secular matters. In the villages of Quintana Roo, among Indians not yet become peasants, the art of literacy at the time when Alfonso Villa Rojas studied these people was entrusted in each sub-tribe to only two individuals, who passed on the esoteric art to successor-acolytes. The art was used to read certain sacred writings treasured by the tribe, or to read communications from God conveniently reduced to writing.[21] In the fully developed Mayan peasant village we found the use of literacy as the sacred specialists' medium of communication with tradition to be represented by certain specialists who knew how to read traditional prayers. But there literacy had come also to have secular significance. Certain men learned to read in order to understand written communications from the town or city, and to keep the records and accounts necessitated by the economic and political relationships with the city.[22] Finally, in the villages stimulated to that effort by urban leaders, these Yucatecan peasants began to undertake the extension of literacy to everyone. But it was noticeable then how greatly the motivation of the villager lay in matters of status. The townsman's ways were looked up to, and the townsman was literate; therefore the peasant wished to learn to read. Yet the view persisted that insofar as literacy was a practical necessity, it was enough that somebody in the village should be literate. Today when men plan to make all the world's peoples literate, the attempts to do so encounter, among other difficulties, the limited motivations of the peasant. Nor is it clear that universal literacy would of itself change the peasant style of life. Where the uses of literacy are limited, the localism and traditionalism of the village is not much affected.

Much of what I have said about the peasant life can be related to the fact that in his case, as contrasted with that of the precivilized hunter or agriculturalist, city people or townspeople are included in his system of relationships of status. The tribesman or dweller in a precivilized band or hamlet looks across at other such people to whom he does not accord a special status within his own plan of life. To precivilized man the outsider is, perhaps, useful, different, hostile, dangerous, amusing, contemptible. But the peasant knows himself as a part of a moral world in which the city man is also included. The city man expresses certain values, as of material success, or religious authority, or special access to the meaning of life, which he, the peasant, also cares about. Peasant and urbanite are, in certain things, one society, and the peasant knows it. It does not follow that the peasant looks upward to the city man in everything. Indeed, among such peasants as I have known or have read about, there is characteristically present the attitude that in certain important moral qualities, as for example industry, physical endurance, honesty, and sexual morality, the peasant is superior.

Undeterred by Sorokin's conclusion[23] that there is little evidence of a typical rural mind, E. K. L. Francis has turned to the specifically peasant form of life, and, through a study of Hesiod's *Works and Days,* has attempted a characterization of the Boeotian peasant of that time which might stand for all peasantry.[24] Francis seeks the personality type of the peasant, or the peasant's "integrated pattern of dominant attitudes"—his style of life. In Hesiod's pages, Francis finds a pattern of dominant attitudes emphasizing a practical and utilitarian attitude toward nature, yet with such a positive valuation of work as sees it as not only materially productive but also a fulfillment of divine command; a de-emphasis of emotion; a concern with security rather than adventure; a high valuation of procreation and children; a desire for wealth; and the joining of social justice with work as basic ethical notions. The type of thought and feeling which emerges seems to me readily applicable, for the most part, to the Polish peasant as made known to us in both science[25] and literature,[26] to the Chinese peasant insofar as I know about him, to the Kurdish peasant as Braidwood knows him, and to the Mayan Indian and Guatemalan Hispanic peasants with whom I have direct acquaintance. If there is such a peasant style of life, the comparison of it with that of pastoral warrior nomads, already attempted,[27] might be developed.

The peasant appears as a human type that is recognizable, widespread, and long enduring, brought about by the development of civilization. Presumably it is such a mode of existence as permits continuation of many of the adaptive characteristics of the folk society with the new necessities brought about by the city. The peasant society exists by virtue of the traditional moral solidarity to be found in any isolated folk society; kinship relationships are still of first importance; the ends of living are implicit and strongly felt. On the other hand the peasant makes certain elements of civilization a part of his life: a trading spirit, money, formal and impersonal controls, whether economic or political. In many peasant communities the division of labor has produced many kinds of specialists. The peasant community has developed in very important respects indeed away from the ideal type of folk society. The peasant style of life is a balanced adjustment between moral order and technical order. It is, probably, a form of living which is adaptive in periods and places where the influence of the city has spread, but not very rapidly, into precivilized communities. The necessary condition of peasant life is that the system of values of the peasant be consistent, in the main, with those of the city people who constitute, so to speak, its other dimension of existence. Peasants "constitute part-societies with part-cultures."[28] Writing of the Russian gentry at the turn of the nineteenth century, Henri Troyat says that in spite of serfdom and the French education of these gentry, "their faith, their tastes, their essential fears and hopes were the same (although they little suspected it) as those of the common people whose ignorance they sneered at."[29]

With these thoughts to guide us, we may speculate as to the origins of the peasantry out of precivilized folk. We may imagine that not all precivilized peoples were characterized by systems of values amenable to a peasant life. The values of the uncivilized Comanche would have to undergo very great change to suit a peasant condition. Some precivilized people were probably more inclined than others to fill the role of peasantry. Even among neighboring communities of Melanesian gardeners we are told that there are great differences as to the values emphasized. Presumably among the precivilized Asiatics and Europeans there were similar differences. Some of these were perhaps already more practically disposed toward nature, already sober and unemotional in emphasis. Yet we know that the ethical system of a people—at least of a civilized people—can undergo marked change in not a great many generations; the case of England in the last three hundred years is commonly cited. At any rate, the introduction of agriculture presumably bent the ethical system of many people who became farmers into ways of thought and feeling that were congenial to peasantry. The development of the market and the coming of the city completed the transformation.

In the historic processes whereby the folk societies were transformed, we may distinguish a primary phase in which the transformations were local and within a single cultural tradition, from that much more complex secondary phase in which peoples of widely differing traditions and cultures were brought into contact, modified and uprooted. In a published map of the distribution of civilization about 3000 B.C.,[30] the civilized areas of the world appear as "three tiny patches of the earth's surface."[31]

At this time only the primary phase in the transformation of the folk societies had occurred. Some of the agriculturalists near the new cities had become peasants. Within the new cities new kinds of men were coming into being: the administrative and power-holding elite, the literati, certain kinds of artisans detached from rural local communities. Farther away from the cities more remote peoples had acquired products and inventions of the cities without losing their essential independence of the city, without becoming peasants. The peasants then in existence were peasants on the main line, so to speak; their descendants are familiar to us in Asia, the Middle East, Eastern Europe. But in the later phase, at the periphery of civilizational expanse, other kinds of peasants came into existence, especially in Latin America. In this latter case the folk peoples that became peasants had cultures very different from those who, beginning as their conquerors, came to be the ruling elite of the folk now transformed into peasantry. But here the transformation required the adjustment of the indigenous Indian folk to a way of life consistent with that of their

Spanish or Portuguese conquerors. The Latin American Indian begins as a member of a morally independent folk society whose people look across at invader and conqueror; he becomes a peasant, looking up—and down—toward a ruling class. All stages of the process of transformation of tribal folk into peasantry culturally homogeneous with their urban elite are to be observed in Latin America.

Of the types of men brought about within the city itself, I say little, for lack of knowledge of ancient history. In Harper's translation of the Code of Hammurabi, I see mentioned a great many different kinds of the specialists that existed in Babylon—freemen and slaves, landlords and tenants, agents and merchants, wine sellers, priestesses, physicians, veterinaries, boatmen, herdmen, brickmakers, tailors, and carriers. And in the city appeared social classes, not merely people differing in prestige and power while identical in culture (as the social classes of the Kwakiutl Indians), nor classes represented by the difference between invading conqueror and invaded native people, but social classes in conscious protest against their contrasting positions in what Max Weber calls "life chances." And the specialization of function within the ruling elite of the city provided special types of men within that more inclusive group. The typical functions developed by those specialists in reading and writing who appear in civilization, the styles of life that come to be developed out of these functions, and the characteristic positions occupied by the literate in the new civilization and in its contacts with other peoples, less or differently civilized, may some day be described in a future sociology of civilizational types.

In emphasizing two contrasting aspects of the functions and roles of the literate in the early and later civilizations Childe and Toynbee point to a difference that might deserve the distinguishing terms that these writers give to the two kinds of literate people. Childe[32] is impressed with the separation between craftsmanship and literacy in the early civilizations, and with the "scholastic attitude" developed by those clerks who used writing to set down traditional lore and knowledge and who came to develop the exact sciences and philosophy. Some of these became custodians and interpreters of sacred books. In this aspect of their functions, internal to the developing civilization, we might speak of the new type of men as the literati. The literate elite of old China illustrate the type. These persons are enclosed within the culture that has become civilization. They carry it forward into a more systematic and reflective phase. Called into being by a revolution in the technology, they are themselves to become the agents of distant transformations of the moral life.

Toynbee,[33] on the other hand, writes of the functions of those literate persons who mediate between the society out of which they arose and some other and alien civilization which is impinging upon it. These people have learned something alien to the culture of their native community; they "have learnt the tricks of the intrusive civilization's trade so far as may be necessary to enable their own community, through their agency, just to hold its own in a social environment in which life is ceasing to be lived in accordance with the local tradition and is coming more and more to be lived in the style imposed by the intrusive civilization upon the aliens who fall under its dominion."[34] Such are the Oriental diplomatists who learn to deal with Westerners, "the civil servant who has picked up the practice of conducting the public administration according to Western forms," and so forth. We may add the educated African or the American Indian with a literate knowledge of the white man and his ways. These people Toynbee calls by the word which developed for them in Russia, the intelligentsia. In contrast to the literati, the member of the intelligentsia "is born to be unhappy." He belongs to two worlds, not one; he is a "marginal man."[35] In the Mayan village of peasants which I knew best, some years ago, the literati were represented by the *maestros cantores* reading and interpreting the sacred prayers; the intelligentsia were appearing in those men who learned the ways and the writing of the city world the better to deal with it. The former used literacy to carry on the local sacred tradition; the latter used it to admit the ways of the world outside. But at this early stage of differentiation of literate types, the two tendencies may appear in the same individual.[36]

This mention of the intelligentsia, like the reference to the formation of peasants through conquest of folk peoples by alien civilizations, has carried the story of the transformation of the folk societies into the second phase, in which the expanding civilization reaches out to folk societies with cultures different in traditional content from those which gave rise to that civilization. By the diffusion of elements of civilization to peripheral peoples there resulted, of course, changes in the modes of life of such peoples; the story is familiar in the effects of Mediterranean civilization upon peoples north of these centers. Here we may try to think of the effects of the expansion, not as diffusion of civilization, but as the production of distinguishable social types.

We start again from the politically and morally independent folk society. The expansion of civilization in some cases pushed up to such societies, or flowed around them, leaving them politically and morally independent. The Lolos on the Chinese frontier, or certain American

Indians not yet put on reservations, illustrate this situation. These became enclaved folk. In some cases, as illustrated by the Hopi Indians, the political independence may be partly lost while the moral independence is largely maintained. Or the folk society may be taken into the society of the invading civilization, as a partner, yet retaining for a long time its cultural distinctness. This is apparently an uncommon outcome. Toynbee[37] mentions three such cases: the Scottish Highlanders, the Maoris of New Zealand, the Araucanians of Chile. Such peoples are more than mere enclaves; they are minority peoples; they make an adjustment which retains their own traditional moral order in considerable degree while yet they take part in the engulfing society. A commoner and not entirely different outcome is represented by the imperialized folk, if so we may call the many folklike peoples who came to be dominated by either the political rule or the economic exploitation of an invading civilization. In most of these cases the old moral order of the folk is thrown into confusion, and gives way; it may not do so for some time, however. The Indonesians working on the Dutch plantations, described by Boeke,[38] illustrate such a people. There are many such in Africa today as well.

In the long run, however, the folkways of most of these peoples are transformed into a manner of life which approximates that of the invader. If such peoples are not early destroyed, by force, or by such disorganization as breaks down the will to live,[39] they are assimilated. On the other hand, invasion and conquest commonly stimulate reaction in which local culture is reorganized. ...

The foregoing has been written as if the separate isolated folk societies merely remain where they are and are transformed *in situ,* as the archaeologist says. But this is not the case. The expansion of civilization results in vast and complex migrations of peoples. The effects of these movements upon the transformation of the civilizations themselves constitute a great theme in Toynbee's study of history. Here, in continuing this rough typological account of the transformation of the folk societies, I mention aspects of these effects on the periphery of the civilizations, from the point of view of the folk societies themselves. And the changes in the moral order that Toynbee discusses are highly instructive to me when I try to consider the later relations between technical and moral order.

The expanding civilization may in cases remove whole populations of folk peoples and set them down in some distant land. Occasionally the transplantation may be accomplished in such a way as to establish in the new home enough representatives of the folk society so that the indigenous culture may resume its life in the new land. The Bush Negroes of Dutch Guiana[40] approximate such a condition. The Arizona Yaqui suggest it;[41] they are a transplanted folk. The causes of the migration of the ancestors of the Gypsies from their home in India is unknown. But the outcome has been an oddity: a world-nomad folk. "They certainly have an ethos all their own."[42] They have adopted vagrancy as a style of life. When the folk are removed in such a way as to mingle in the new land of people of notably different languages and cultures, and are thrown down in conditions of isolation, they make a new folk life, but now chiefly out of elements of living provided by their conquerors. The plantation Negroes of America are remade folk. The process of making folk is not something that went on once only before the advent of the civilizations. To a degree it continues wherever the conditions of isolation exist. One of the things learned in the course of a study of culture in the Yucatan peninsula[43] was that these Indian peoples who, having been peasantlike serfs on plantations, retired into the bush after their unsuccessful war against the white conqueror became in a century of chosen isolation more folklike than they had been. The folk culture that continued to develop in the bush was made up of more European than of Indian elements. Yet in the integration of custom and institution, in the presence of strong implicit conceptions of the purpose of life, the manner of life grew more folklike, not less. So too we recognize in the development of folklore, and a certain style of life, that isolated occupational groups from civilized communities represent, in some aspects, the process of formation of folk. Lumbermen, cowboys, river boatmen are quasi folk. And the resemblances of the isolated sectarian communities to the folk societies is a familiar fact.

We seem to see, in the varying transformations of the primary folkness of mankind, the effects of opposing tendencies in the construction and stability of the moral order. It may be repeated that the folk society is that society in which the technical order is subordinated within the moral order. The moral order is there, self-consistent and strong. As the technical order develops with the food-producing and urban revolutions, as the civilizations produce within themselves a differentiation of human types, and as they also reach out to affect distant peoples, there is a double tendency within the moral order. On the one hand, the old moral orders are shaken, perhaps destroyed. On the other, there is a rebuilding of moral orders on new levels. The rebuilding may be within the peripheral local community, as in the case of freshly isolated Indians of the forests of Quintana Roo, or among isolated American Negroes. Or the rebuilding may occur so as to include more and different peoples, who have been brought into some kind of relationship already by the expansions of the technical order. The moral order grows by death and rebirth. Or, to change the figure, within the life of the moral order of mankind there is a perpetual anabolism and catabolism.

The coming of the civilizations disturbed, probably forever, the primordial relation between these tendencies. Then the technical order underwent such an acceleration as to throw the ancient moral orders into profound confusion. The civilizations brought many kinds of different peoples together. We read of archaeological evidence for an Indian cult celebrated in a Sumerian city.[44] There were Egyptian foreign colonies in Syrian cities.[45] Heterogeneity is the first characteristic of the city, ancient or modern. And with heterogeneity come doubts as to the moral order. Civilization is deracination. Within the city the roots are torn through the heterogeneity of populations, the exploitation of minorities, the specialization of knowledge and function. On the edges of expanding civilizations the civilization meets with people of whom it makes half-converts to the city way of life, or whom it employs as mercenaries, seizes as slaves, or sends as merchants to distant lands. Now, telling our lesser story from the bottom up, we have met with those kinds of peoples whom Toynbee calls—in an unusual extension of meaning—"the proletariats."[46] These are in part within the civilization itself, the "internal proletariat." This proletariat is made up, he tells us, "of the disinherited and uprooted members of the society's own body social; partially disinherited members of alien civilizations and primitive societies that were conquered and exploited without being torn up by the roots; and doubly disinherited conscripts from these subject populations who were not only uprooted but were also enslaved and deported in order to be worked to death on distant plantations."[47] These words refer to the internal proletariat of the Hellenic civilization; other proletariats Toynbee finds to be similar. The "external proletariats" are composed of peoples marginal to a civilization, who have ceased to follow the cultural leadership of the civilization and have turned against it, using, in the violent form of the response, the new instruments of the technical order of the civilization. "The surrounding primitive peoples are no longer charmed but are repelled."[48] They cease a disposition to enter a moral order of a civilization whose moral order is not simple and compelling, and react against that civilization. Here the anthropologist thinks of one of the many groups of whom Toynbee thinks in conceiving the external proletariat, partly civilized American Indian peoples on the American frontier, acting either as warriors against the whites, or as creators of new nativistic religions.

The point about Toynbee's proletarians in our present connection is that they have ceased to live within the ambit of their ancient moral orders. "The true hallmark of the proletarian is ... a consciousness—and the resentment that this consciousness inspires—of being disinherited from his ancestral place in society."[49] The reaction Toynbee finds may be an explosion of savagery, or it may take the form of a religious movement. The proletarian is a product of the city, of civilization. What is new about him is that he is aware of the blow dealt to his moral order, and reacts to this awareness. With civilization the problems of the moral order move to a new level of struggle and achievement. It is the level marked by self-consciousness, of sense of deprivation, and of conscious creativeness.

Internal growth, and the effects of the meeting of peoples, are two aspects of the whole of cultural development that are ever of interest to anthropologists. These two played their parts in the transformations of the folk societies. Of the many folk peoples that existed in many parts of the earth five to ten thousand years ago, a few, already provided with granaries or with food animals, built themselves cities and so made a style of life new to humanity. This style of life was characterized by a development and complexity of the technical order theretofore unknown. And it was characterized by both disorganization and regrowth of the moral order. While the literati were using reading and writing to transmute the old sacred tradition of the folk into science and philosophy, the old tradition was being broken down under the influence of commerce, specialization of useful function, and the movements and mixings of peoples. The style of life of the city included doubt and dissent, and ultimately the displacement and dissatisfactions of those new and city-made kinds of peoples, the proletariats. Meanwhile, as the civilizations moved outward to meet peoples still tribal and folklike, they slowly transformed the country people nearest at hand into peasantry. Farther away, the city men dealt with tribesmen and rulers of barbarian states, and here still other styles of life came into being: folk enclaved within civilization, policed or protected, and yet retaining the moral predominance of folk life; peoples subordinated to the rule of the city men or in long continuing warfare with them: peoples transplanted by their captors to new lands, there in ignorance and isolation again to become folk, perhaps to be taken into the technical and moral orders of their conquerors, or perhaps, in the discovery of the preciousness of the ancient tradition which they were losing, creating, out of the very anguish of their loss, a new cult, a new sense of the separateness and importance of their style of life.

The phrase "style of life" has come into this discussion to meet the need for a term that will suggest what is most fundamental and enduring about the ways of a group persisting in history. "Ethos," "basic culture patterns," "values," "configuration of culture," and "modal personality" are other terms which have arisen among anthropologists in response to this need. If "culture" itself does not seem to meet the need, it is because that word may suggest too narrowly the items of institutions and belief which go to make up the anthropologist's account of, say, the Hopi Indians as contrasted with the Navajo Indians.

"Style of life," as used here, includes the ways of getting a living insofar as these contribute to the shaping of ideas of the good life. The term emphasizes the judgments, implicit or expressed, as to what right conduct is. And not excluded are the lesser tastes and preferences that give to a people its characteristic flavor, so to speak. When Lionel Trilling writes of *manners*, as "a culture's hum and buzz of implication ... half-uttered or unuttered or unutterable expressions of value,"[50] he is thinking of the style of life.

The phrase has a usefulness here; it need not be continued. Better than "culture," "style of life" admits the possibility that people with very different specific contents of culture may have very similar views of the good life. As the anthropologist would ordinarily put it, the cultures of the Lapp and of the Bedouin are very different. These two peoples are differently fed and housed; they have different religions, customs, and institutions. Nevertheless it may prove to be true that in certain general ways of looking upon the world, in the emphasis on certain virtues and ideals, in certain manners of independence and hospitality natural to a free-roaming people, Lapp and Bedouin have the same style of life. But "style of life," like "culture," does imply some harmony of parts and some continuity through time, the generations looking backward to their own lives in the past and again to their own lives in the future. Toynbee's internal proletariats are for a time without style of life. The disinherited who followed Spartacus as he raged up and down the Italian peninsula were then without style of life. But a shepherd on the hills of Galilee has a style of life; so has a Hopi Indian; so too had an aristocrat of the *ancien régime*.

And extending the term to forms of human existence still more general, one might say that folk life, in contrast to civilized life, is one style of life, in spite of the very great specific cultural differences among precivilized or primitive societies. Peasantry then, whether Mexican or Chinese or Polish, is that style of life which prevailed outside of the cities and yet within their influence during the long period between the urban revolution and the industrial revolution. The specific styles of life that civilization creates are beyond my powers to discern and distinguish. On the outskirts of American cities at least two kinds of people with two distinct styles of life are to be found living together physically but separate morally: rural farmers and suburbanites. In the cities themselves ways of living develop in which the continuity from generation to generation is impaired or almost lost. If continuity is lost, if people see no clear lines for the development of their careers, certainly not for their children's careers, do we still speak of a style of life? What sort of style of life is "other-directedness"?[51] In modern civilization the making of new forms of man takes new turns, which may demand new terms for their description.

Notes

1. [Editor's Note: Redfield is referring here to the two major prehistoric revolutions postulated by V. Gordon Childe; these ideas were best developed in his books *Man Makes Himself*, 2d ed. (London: Watts & Co.) and *What Happened in History* (Harmondsworth, Middlesex: Penguin Books, 1942).
2. Arnold J. Toynbee, *A Study of History,* abridgement of Volumes I-VI by D. C. Somervell (New York and London: Oxford University Press, 1947), p. 49.
3. Karl A. Wittfogel, "Die Theorie der orientalischen Gesellschaft," *Zeitschrift für Sozialforschung,* VII (1938), 90-122.
4. Toynbee, *A Study of History*, p. 414.
5. A. L. Kroeber, *Anthropology* (rev. ed.; New York: Harcourt Brace and Co., 1948), pp. 418-425.
6. V. Gordon Childe, *What Happened* in *History*, p. 133.
7. Raymond Firth, *Malay Fishermen: Their Peasant Economy* (London: Kegan Paul, Trench, Trubner & Co., 1946), pp. 22-27.
8. Hsiao-Tung Fei, *Peasant Life in China* (New York: E. P. Dutton & Co., 1939), p. 267.
9. Ibid.
10. John F. Embree, *Suye Mura, A Japanese Village* (Chicago: University of Chicago Press, 1939), pp. 138-153.
11. McKim Marriott, personal communication, "In the far south, and especially on the Malabar side."
12. A. S. Altekar, *A History of Village Communities in Western India* (Bombay: Oxford University Press, 1929), p. 11.
13. Fei, *Peasant Life in China,* pp. 274-280.
14. Henry S. Maine, *Village-Communities in the East and West* (3rd ed.; London: John Murray, 1907).
15. McKim Marriott, personal communication.
16. Ibid. However, as to the present situation in villages of India, Marriott adds that the largest part of the villagers' credit is provided by landlord, shopkeepers, or well-to-do peasants of the peasant's own or neighboring community.
17. A. R. Radcliffe-Brown, "Three Tribes of Western Australia," *Journal of the Royal Anthropological Institute,* XLIII (1913), 150-151.

18. Altekar, *A History of Village Communities in Western India*, p. 114.
19. Arthur H. Smith, *Village Life in China* (New York: Fleming H. Revell Co., 1899), pp. 54-69.
20. Childe, *What Happened in History*, p. 111.
21. Alfonso Villa Rojas, *The Maya of East Central Quintana Roo* (Washington: Carnegie Institution of Washington, 1945), pp. 48, 161 ff.
22. Robert Redfield and Alfonso Villa Rojas, *Chan Kom, A Maya Village* (Washington: Carnegie Institution of Washington, 1934).
23. P. Sorokin and C. Zimmerman, *Principles of Rural-Urban Sociology* (New York: H. Holt & Co., 1929), p. 332.
24. E. K. L. Francis, "The Personality Type of the Peasant according to Hesiod's *Works and Days*," *Rural Sociology*, X (September, 1945), 275-295.
25. W. I. Thomas and Florian Znaniecki, *The Polish Peasant in Europe and America* (1st ed.; Boston: Richard C. Badger, 1918-1920; 2nd ed.; New York: Alfred A. Knopf, 1927).
26. W. Reymont, *The Peasants* (New York: Alfred A. Knopf, 1925).
27. Christopher Dawson, *The Age of the Gods* (London: Sheed & Ward, 1933).
28. Kroeber, *Anthropology*, p. 284.
29. Henri Troyat, *Pushkin, A Biography*, tr. by Randolph T. Weaver (New York: Pantheon, 1950), p. 13.
30. *Time, Space and Man*, prepared by the Department of Anthropology of the University of Chicago under the direction of R. J. Braidwood, W. M. Krogman, and Sol Tax (Chicago: University of Chicago Press, 1946). (A new edition is in preparation under the direction of R. J. Braidwood, Sol Tax, and S. L. Washburn.)
31. Childe, *What Happened in History*, p. 123.
32. *Ibid.*, p. 126 ff.
33. Toynbee, *A Study of History*, p. 394 ff.
34. *Ibid.*, p. 394.
35. Robert E. Park, *Race and Culture* (Glencoe, Ill.: Free Press, 1950), pp. 345-392.
36. See the career of Don Eustaquio Ceme of Chan Kom, as recorded in Redfield and Villa, *Chan Kom*, and in Robert Redfield, *A Village that Chose Progress* (Chicago: University of Chicago Press, 1950). Don Eus, in his deliberate cultivation of the townsman's knowledge and in his reading of secular technical literature, led the intelligentsia of Chan Kom. Yet, in his continuing interest in and sympathy with the traditional sacred lore of his village, his attempts to reflect upon and systematize this lore, he belonged also to the literati. The circumstances under which the reconciliation can be made in a single personality might be investigated. The appearance of the literati in early Mesopotamian civilization is expressed in "school tablets" going back to the beginning of the third millennium B.C. See Samuel Noah Kramer, "The Sumerian School: A Pre-Greek System of Education," *Studies Presented to David Moon Robinson on his Seventieth Birthday*, ed. by G. E. Mylonas (St Louis: Washington University, 1951), Vol. 1.
37. Toynbee, *A Study of History*, p. 414.
38. J.. H. Boeke, *The Evolution of the Netherlands East Indies Economy* (New York: Netherlands and Netherlands Indies Council, Institute of Pacific Relations, 1946).
39. W. H. R. Rivers, ed., *Essays on the Depopulation of Melanesia* (Cambridge, Eng.: The University Press, 1922).
40. Melville J.. Herskovits and Frances S. Herskovits, *Rebel Destiny among the Bush Negroes of Dutch Guiana* (New York and London: Whittlesey House, 1934).

41. Edward Spicer, *Pascua, A Yaqui Village in Arizona* (Chicago: University of Chicago Press, 1940).
42. Kroeber, *Anthropology*, p. 279.
43. Robert Redfield, *The Folk Culture of Yucatan* (Chicago: University of Chicago Press, 1941).
44. Childe, *What Happened in History*, p. 90.
45. Childe, *Man Makes Himself* (2nd ed.; London: Watts and Co., 1941), p. 171.
46. Toynbee, *A Study of History*, p. 375 ff.
47. Ibid., p. 378.
48. Ibid., p. 405.
49. Ibid., p. 377.
50. Lionel Trilling, "Manners, Morals and the Novel," *The Liberal Imagination* (New York: Viking Press, 1950), pp. 206-207.
51. David Riesman, with the collaboration of Reuel Denney and Nathan Glazer, *The Lonely Crowd: A Study of the Changing American Character* (New Haven: Yale University Press, 1950).

14

Peasantry: Part Societies

> *Redfield advanced his most mature expression of the definition and socio-historical significance of peasant societies in a series of lectures he presented in 1956 at Swarthmore College, which were then published as* Peasant Society and Culture. *In the essay "Peasantry: Part Societies," Redfield articulated a definition of peasantry that was to exercise great influence among anthropologists and sociologists from the 1950s through the 1970s. Redfield argued that while anthropology had come of age by conducting studies of remote, isolated tribal peoples, which they described as functionally self-sufficient cultures, this perspective would not suffice for study of peasant societies. Peasant societies were not self-sufficient wholes but rather "part societies" and could only be studied by taking into account the larger civilizations in which they were embedded. Redfield urged anthropologists to go beyond the bounds of their traditional studies and examine the entire network of connections which linked peasant societies to urban centers, and his influence served as one of the prime motivators for anthropologists to expand their range of interests to include study of societies at all levels of size and complexity, an expansion of interest that eventually culminated in the rise of the sub-field of urban anthropology.*

In the course of their studies of small and self-sufficient primitive societies, anthropologists came to think of each such community as a system of elements in relationship to one another. Each was an analyzable whole. Each could be looked at by itself, without necessary reference to things outside of it, and could be understood as parts working together within a whole. Radcliffe-Brown showed how myth, ritual, and daily life worked together in the Andaman Islands. Malinowski made a name, "functionalism," out of his success in showing the many interrelations of custom, institution, and human need in Trobriand life. In *Patterns of Culture* Ruth Benedict showed us four primitive views of the good life as distinct and equivalent patterns—systems of another kind in which customs and institutions conform to implicit choices of basic values from the range of human possibilities.

Anthropologists have seen the primitive isolated community as several kinds of complete and self-contained systems.[1] It can be seen as a system of customs and institutions. It is sometimes seen, as in

---

First published in *Peasant Society and Culture: An Anthropological Approach to Civilization* (Chicago: University of Chicago Press, 1956), 23-39.

Benedict's book, as the fundamental ideas of good and bad which guide a people's life. And often, as in the important work of the British anthropologists in studying especially the native peoples of Africa, it is seen as a system of characteristic relationships between the kinds of people characteristic of that community. Although the phrase has several distinguishable meanings in anthropology,[2] let us here use "social structure" for the total system of persisting and important relationships that distinguish a community from others. Here we shall be concerned with social structure.

In studying a primitive society as social structure, the anthropologist looks at the kinds of roles, with attendant statuses, that tradition recognizes in that community. There are fathers and sons; perhaps it is important that mothers' brothers bear some special relationship to sisters' sons; there may be priests and laymen, chiefs and other people, buyers and sellers, and so on. These roles and statuses persist while the particular individuals who fill them enter them and leave them. The community is conceived as the arrangement of the more persistent and important of these roles and the conventional relationships between them. If the community is relatively compact and isolated, the investigator finds these roles and relationships within the band, settlement, or tribe that he studies. He does not have to go outside it.

Now I raise the question: Considering a peasant community as a system of social relations, as social structure, how shall we describe its relations with the world outside of that community? What are the modifications of concept and procedure that come about if we study a peasant village, thinking of it as a system of persisting important relationships among people? For peasantry ... are such by reason in part of their long-established interdependence with gentry and townspeople.

It may be that a peasant village, related as it is to people and institutions outside of it, is so incomplete a system that it cannot well be described as social structure. Perhaps we anthropologists shall come to describe not the peasant village but the larger and more nearly complete system: the feudal society, the complex region, the national state. Primitive states, complexly developed tribes, have been anthropologically described; Herskovits' *Dahomey* is one such account.[3] W. Lloyd Warner and his associates have made studies of American urban communities as representative of much in the national life. Margaret Mead and others, working very differently, have studied the national characters of modern peoples. Recently Julian Steward has proposed that any complex society might be regarded as composed of three kinds of parts. He distinguishes first such local groups as households, neighborhoods, and communities; these he calls "vertical divisions." Second, he sees the groups which are not local but which appear in many local communities and arise from some common qualities among the dispersed members, as occupation, class, caste, race, or special interest. These he calls "horizontal" divisions or segments. And third, he recognizes the formal institutions such as banking, trade, school systems, and official doctrine, which run through the whole large society affecting it at many points. This way of looking at a large complex society sees it as a kind of lattice in which the local units run in one direction and the groups that are not local run in the other direction, while the formal institutions of centralized authority and widespread influence, like the vines growing upon the lattice, perhaps, tie the whole together.[4]

Steward has used this set of conceptions in describing one modern state—Puerto Rico on its island.[5] The conceptions are not directed necessarily to societies with peasants in them. I suppose they could be used in describing Denmark or New Zealand. Their use puts anthropologists to work on complex societies in ways to which they are accustomed, for it breaks down these big wholes into two kinds of smaller groups each of which is thought to have something of a culture which the anthropologist can study. He can make studies of small local communities, of samples of the social classes, maybe, or of the religious groups. And the formal institutions—the law, the church, school or taxation systems—can still be studied from the center by the other kinds of social scientists who are used to that kind of thing; the anthropologist will, I suppose, attend especially to the local modifications of these national institutions.

The development of procedures appropriate to anthropology for studying large modern societies will go forward, and the very different ways of doing so provided by Julian Steward, Lloyd Warner, and Margaret Mead are evidences that the science puts forth its shoots on different sides of the growing tree. Here I look only at the growth outward from the local community study. I try to distinguish some of the kinds of social relations that one comes to describe if one begins with some local peasant community and tries to do justice to the fact that many of its relations are with outsiders.

In identifying three kinds of systems of social relations that we find it necessary to study if we leave the primitive isolate and attempt to describe a peasant society as social structure, I have been helped by a short publication of J. A. Barnes,[6] an anthropologist trained by British students of the social structures of primitive communities. Barnes, however, went to Norway and made a study of an island parish of that country. He found that he could not keep his attention solely on what happened within the parish: he had to follow the social relations of these rural Norwegians outside of their local community. Yet he saw that what he learned about the parish of Bremnes could "lead directly to knowledge of only a very small sector in the social life of the nation." Thus Barnes studied his little rural community not as a self-contained isolate (which it obviously is not), nor as a sample fully representative of the whole (as anthropologists study the Sudanese Nuer or the Tiv of Nigeria), nor yet as one element in a comprehensively planned study of a modern state (as did Steward). Rather, Barnes pushed outward from the local community, recognizing in the parish he studied kinds of systems of social relation in part new to the anthropologist of the primitive isolate, systems that connect the small community with other such communities, with the Norwegian nation, and with industrial systems wider than the nation.

The Norwegian parish is today probably not a peasant community. It is outside of but not very far away from the cluster of little communities to which I have here applied the word "peasant." Of every ten men in Bremnes three are fishermen, one is in the merchant marine, two are industrial workers, two are in other occupations or are retired, and only two are in agriculture. One might say that Bremnes is partly seafaring, partly agricultural, and partly a rural community in a modern nation. The people are educated and take a large part in their national life. Yet just because Bremnes is farther away from the primitive isolate community than are the rural communities of less modernized countries, what Barnes found there in the way of social relations will help us to learn what to look for in peasant societies of Asia or Latin America. We need a basis for comparison on the more modernized side of peasantry as well as on the more primitive side.

Barnes finds that these rural Norwegians are members of many kinds of social groups. The groups are so many and so variously related to one another that it might be difficult to arrange them very strictly according to Professor Steward's lattice.[7] Barnes collects them into what he calls "social fields" of three different kinds. Each social field is a conceived system of activities and social relations somewhat separable from the other two. Each has, I think, a lesson for us in our effort to push beyond the self-contained community to the understanding of the social structure of peasant societies.

First, "there is the territorially-based social field, with a large number of enduring administrative units, arranged hierarchically, one within the other."[8] This ascending series of local groups includes hamlets or neighborhoods, wards, and the parish itself, which is then a part of several larger ascending series of units with administrative, judicial, or ecclesiastical functions each including other parishes of Norway.

It is at the level of the parish that we can see a transition from local life to national life. Looked at from the point of view of one studying the nation, the parish of Bremnes is a unit of civil and ecclesiastical administration. There is, for instance, a grouping of parishes of that region which in turn belongs within an archdeaconry which is part of a diocese. These groupings are formal and serve very special functions and relationships. Within the parish, relationships are more personal and involve more of human life. Nevertheless, in modern Norway the separation between local life and national life has become obscured by education and the full articulation of local and national institutions. In societies in which the rural people are still clearly peasantry, the territorially based social field or system which Barnes describes for Bremnes unites local life and the life of the feudal system or the state; and in peasant societies the two parts are clearly distinguishable. At the bottom the series of units consists of people in personal and traditional relationship to one another; there kinship and neighborhood are the prevailing connections. At the top of the series are people in more impersonal and formal institutional relationship to one another. As a system of hierarchically arranged social relations, a peasant society is two connecting halves. We may be able to see a sort of link or hinge between the local life of a peasant community and the state or feudal system of which it is a part. In an Indian community of western Guatemala, where the local life and the national life are wide apart, the link or hinge is very obvious; it consists of the administrative officers sent down from the city to relate the Indian community, which is organized within itself, to the national life.[9] The parish priest and some shopkeepers may be other parts of the hinge. In the Andalusian town, a community of town-dwellers with peasant characteristics, the hinge is also present in a conspicuously different group of professional and wealthy people who live their mental lives in part away from the town where they dwell, in the city, and "who represent the government to the pueblo, and who represent the pueblo to the government."[10] In the old-fashioned Chinese peasant community one would find the hinge in the mandarin negotiating between the *yamen* of the imperial power and the village elders. In the Balkan village the line between the local life and the national life, between the two parts of the ascending territorial-political series, is held by the priest and the mayor.[11] Later something will be said here about the functions in the cultural life of the people who hold the hinge.

Even in Bremnes, though the people are for the most part no longer peasants, it is the territorially organized local life that gives the society stability. "The same fields are cultivated year after year, and new land comes into cultivation only slowly ... for the most part people go on living in the same houses and cultivating the same land from year to year."[12] A century and a half ago, we may suppose, this was the social system of dominant importance; only the fishing, not yet industrialized, modified the peasant life of that time.

But fishing has now been industrialized in Norway to the degree that for the man of Bremnes parish it is an activity fairly independent of his life on the land. Fishing is highly competitive; "herring fishing is war," people say. Here loyalties to kinsmen operate to only a limited extent. "Any man can try to get himself included in a crew and each owner seeks to engage the crew that will catch most fish. During the herring season, men from Bremnes sail in vessels belonging to other parishes, and vessels registered in Bremnes sometimes have on board fishermen from as much as six hundred miles away. In effect, there is something like a free labour market."[13] The social field through which the Bremnes man moves in his role as fisherman is composed of unstable relations with many kinds of men in many different places—shipowners, skippers, net bosses, cooks, and others—with whom he has happened to become linked; and each man's social field for fishing intersects the vast, world-wide organized fishing industry.

This is the second lesson from Barnes's account. It is the market, in one form or another, that pulls out from the compact social relations of self-contained primitive communities some parts of men's doings and puts people into fields of economic activity that are increasingly independent of the rest of what goes on in the local life. The local traditional and moral world and the wider and more impersonal world of the market are in principle distinct, opposed to each other, as Weber[14] and others[15] have emphasized. In peasant society the two are maintained in some balance; the market is held at arm's length, so to speak. We may see the intermediacy of the peasant community in this respect also if we suggest a series of societies in which the separation of the world of the market is progressively greater. The Andamanese band approximates a self-contained isolate. But from time to time people of one band will take up some of their bows and baskets and go to visit another band. There they will make presents of what they have brought and receive from their hosts presents of some of their artifacts.[16] The economic life is not even distinguishable as such: it is a casual exchange between friendly persons on a basis of good will. In rural India, in a society with a great division of labor, much of the exchange of services is involved in hereditary status in the form of caste. There are also markets where trading is relatively free. In the Guatemalan American Indian community of Chichicastenango, a peasant society except for the cultural separation between the Indian and the urban elite, most of the men devote large parts of their lives to commercial travel; they walk about a wide circle of markets buying and selling.[17] But this commercial life is separate from the social and political life of the town and hamlet. Observers have been struck with the insulation of the Guatemalan trader from the influences of the many other local cultures through which he moves.[18] As a trader, this Indian semi-peasant leads a separate life; he enters a distinct "field of activity." The Bulgarian peasant buys from and sells to the city, but we are told that his weekly trips to town and city introduce few changes to the village.[19] In the city the peasant is an onlooker; he talks chiefly with other peasants. So in this case too peasant world and city world are kept apart, though in apparent contact. Inside a peasant village commercial life and agricultural life may fall into separate patterns of thought and action. In the intensely agricultural Yucatecan village, the Maya, more of a peasant than is the western Guatemalan Indian, carries on his agriculture as a mode of life, indeed, as religious activity, as does the Hopi or the Zuñi. But he sells half his maize to market. Growing in the field or offered to the gods, maize is traditional, sacred, moral. But once made ready for sale, the people call it by a different name; and the commercial dealings with maize have a certain separateness from the local dealings with it.[20] And trade with hogs or cattle is a secular activity in which one joins with any buyer or seller one happens to meet.

Every peasant society offers for our study some field of economic activity which is to some degree separated out from that closely integrated union of all activities which characterizes the primitive isolate community. The economic field comes to have, as Barnes says, a different "analytical status." One has to make a special study of that field. In studying rural Swedish life of a century ago, B. Hanssen describes[21] the relations of those villagers, chiefly cotters, with those gentry of the manor with whom they took service, as a distinct field of activity. In that case the field was not wholly economic: the cotters entered into the domestic life of the manor; some of the peasants had for parts of their lives persisting relationships, of utility and also more or less cultural, with some of the gentry. A connection between the two halves of the double society, peasantry-gentry, was made by a field with separate analytical status, but a field in which, no doubt, the examples of custom and manners provided by gentry life were made to influence the peasantry. The fishing field of modern Norway is fully industrialized; the rural fisherman is largely separated off from the life on the land, and the fishing field is fluid, competitive, increasingly independent of the ties formed in the local life.

"Market" means both a state of mind and a place to trade. We can use both conceptions in studying peasant and rural life. Barnes refers to the industrialized fishing of the Norwegian as a "social field." The field is not spatially defined; it is a set of activities, attitudes, and relationships that belong together wherever and whenever the Norwegian enters industrialized fishing. Such a field we may study as a more or less coherent body of things done and thought. Also, of course, we may study those markets which do have geographical definition. McBryde has described one kind of market in western Guatemala: the people who come together in one town at one time to buy and sell.[22] One can also describe the people who move about the country from one market, in the former sense, to another town market. Taken together, these ambulatory merchants in all their relationships of trade are another kind of market with definition upon the land. Students of rural sociology and economics describe the regions in which goods of one kind or another are sold, and the regions from which are drawn the buyers who come to centers of sale and distribution. Arensberg and Kimball, anthropologists, have well described such markets, centering on crossroads, fairs, and shops, in rural Ireland.[23]

The third "social field" which Barnes recognizes in the Norwegian parish he calls a "network." All the relations of all kinds of the rural people with one another and with people elsewhere are thought of as a network in which people are the knots or points, and relationships, of whatever kind, are the threads or lines. Barnes, however, here thinks in particular of that part of the total network that is left if the relationships of the territorial and the industrial systems are removed. To distinguish this residual part of the network, and to give it a name suggestive of its presence in every society that is more than the imagined primitive isolate, let us call it "the country-wide network." The simple fact that creates this network is that every person, through kinship, friendship, acquaintance, or some common interest, "is in touch with a number of people, some of whom are directly in touch with each other and some of whom are not."[24] In Bremnes this kind of network of relationships not only knits together people of the parish but connects them with people of other parishes. There it has no boundaries; there is no way of defining a group with membership; "each person sees himself at the center of a collection of friends."[25] But sometimes defined groups are formed, fishing crews or committees, out of clusters of people in such boundless networks.

In every society, however primitive, some attention is paid to the connections of one kinsman to another or of one friend to another. People are nowhere organized only into lineages or other formed and bounded social groups. So there are always boundless networks in so far as genealogical kinship is extended outward or as mere acquaintance or other occasional personal association creates a relationship. In the primitive societies it is kinship that largely contributes to the qualities of such networks as there are. In some of them there is a kind of latency in the kinship which allows it to expand at the edges of the local community to include individuals newly encountered. One remembers the way in which in central Australia strangers to one another establish friendly relations through identification of some third individual to whom each applies a kinship term.[26]

If the tribe is large and dispersed, its people not settled in distinct villages, as is true of the Tiv of Nigeria, the whole tribe is one great country-wide network. But if we study the early Plains Indians, or the Indians of the Amazon, or the tribesmen of Luzon, we do not find ourselves much concerned with country-wide networks. The band, the camp, the village, or the tribe is a relatively discrete social system. Between it and other such systems there are no very impressive and persisting networks of relationship. One unit may join another or separate off, and one individual may be captured or otherwise become a part of a local society to which he was once a stranger.

But the communities are compact, and relationships for the most part institutionalized in kinship or other kinds of groups. As to the compactness, Barnes puts the point well when he says that in primitive societies the mesh of the network is small, in civilized, urban, or mass societies the mesh is large. "By mesh," he writes, "I mean simply the distance round a hole in the network ... in primitive society many of the possible paths leading away from any A lead back to A after a few links; in modern society a smaller proportion lead back again to A."[27] In Zuñi the links go right back to the man with whom you started. In rural Norway the links carry one outside of the parish to distant communities. In peasant societies as in primitive, many links are those of kinship, but the mesh is wider and looser. In French Canada the peasant travels, but travel is to visit relatives. If there is no relative in the neighboring parish, the peasant does not go there, but he may make a pilgrimage to the shrine of St. Anne de Beaupre and make his stay with relatives in Quebec.[28]

This fact of the developed and widespread country-wide network in societies that are not primitive gives the anthropologist another kind of system of social relations to study. He cannot keep his attention solely on the peasant village or scattered rural community of neighboring farmers. He finds himself looking down on village tied to village, farm to distant relative, and town to countryside, in a web of social relations. The connections that people have with one another, apart from the system of relationships that begins in the family and the neighborhood and grows upward to the formal government of the state, are in peasant and in rural communities so significant as to demand description in their own right. Where the relations continue to have localization, and constitute a system of ties relating people to one another although they dwell apart, then they seem to emerge from the societal map to meet our scientific imaginations. Points and lines meet the concept-forming eye of the mind. We begin to wonder what will be the ideas by which we shall characterize that class of social systems, that aspect of social structure, that might be called country-wide networks.

Plainly the purpose or interest which relates people in the network is an important matter of similarity or difference. Oscar Lewis has compared Mexican and East Indian rural societies to stress a difference of this kind.[29] If we look down on the Mexican countryside we see village connected with village chiefly through trade, visiting at festivals, and, less, important, through performance of governmental duties and through pilgrimages to shrines. The local communities tend to be endogamous, each has a more or less homogeneous culture, and the sense of local community loyalty is strong. The people who go out from one local community to another, or to a town, on the whole do so as separate individuals or family parties carrying on perhaps similar but parallel and independent activities. The activities are incidental to a familial and cultural life lived within the village. We do not find whole groups with culture and social structure that have persisting relationships along the country-wide network with other such groups in other local communities.

This is what we do find in India. Should we look down on the countryside of India, we should see each local community connected with many other local communities through caste. The internal unity of the village is qualified or balanced by the unity that is felt by the villager with a fellow caste member of another village. In times of stress the fellow caste member of the other village will come to one's aid. In the cases of the higher castes this unity may be felt over wide areas, and it may be institutionalized by genealogists and caste historians.

Furthermore, the country-wide network of rural northern India is composed of widespread connections of marriage. The villages are exogamous. In the Punjab, for example, "each village is said to have a traditional set of villages to whom its girls regularly go in marriage and another set from which it regularly receives wives." Here there is a country-wide marital network. With reference to the Punjabi villages studied by Marian Smith "the marital community to be considered would start four miles away and have to include at least those villages up to eight miles distant."[30] In Kishan Garhi, a village southeast of Delhi, again there is no marriage within the village. "Daughters of the village move out and wives of the village move in at marriage, moving to and from more than three hundred other villages."[31] When Marriott studied this village, he found that fifty-seven marriages then connected Kishan Garhi with sixteen towns and cities. The connection a villager has with other villages than his own remains very strong. In another village in northern India if a lower-caste man gets into trouble with the upper-caste landowner he "may still take refuge with his mother's, his wife's or his sister's relatives." "Often a child spends two or three years with his mother on a long visit to his mother's father's household in another village."[32]

In short, the principal elements of the country-wide networks of India consist of familial and caste associations that persist through generations. These associations connect one set of villages with another or some of the families in one village with families corresponding in culture and social status in other villages. It is as if the characteristic social structure of the primitive self-contained community had been dissected out and its components spread about a wide area. Rural India is a primitive or a tribal society rearranged to fit a civilization.

The closeness or openness of the mesh, the range or scope of the network, the kinds of human interests served by the relationships that make up the mesh, the stability of the relationships, whether occasional or permanent—these are all elements to be considered in understanding country-wide networks.

In these remarks I have perhaps extended and generalized the three kinds of sets of social relations which Barnes notes in rural Norway beyond his meaning and intention. I see in them exemplars for many who will study societies that very plainly are more complex, more interrelated with others, than are the primitive tribal communities. I think we will find it helpful to look for the three kinds of systems or "fields" which Barnes found in Bremnes: the hierarchy of territorially based groups; the more or less independent economic fields of activity; and the country-wide networks of relationship. These three kinds will not be found in peasant societies only. Their beginnings occur also in primitive and non-European societies, and they occur in modern states. One can think of them as three ways in which the primitive isolate is exceeded or in which it breaks down, is pulled apart and extended over the social landscape. Country-wide networks are notable within those African tribes that grow in size till they occupy a wide area with scattered houses and settlements. These are networks involving no peasantry. Such networks must have developed as between villages in the highlands of Mexico before the Spaniard came, and, in so far as the Aztec capital was an urban center with its elite, the networks were becoming truly rural. Wherever civilization has fully arisen we may speak of the networks as rural, for now there is an *urbs*. Yet local differences within the great civilizations in this respect are to be recognized: the networks of intimate peasant-elite relationships continued in England until very late to maintain something of the manorial form of medieval times, for the English gentry were countrymen themselves in contrast to their equivalents in France or Italy who lived the civilization of the city and kept farther apart from their peasantry.

The economic field is already present in the "silent market" of which German writers on primitive economy made much, and it grows in preliterate societies to the great markets of Abomey—we are told that ten thousand people might take part in such a market.[33] But it is industry outside of the indigenous local life, especially capitalistic and highly technological industry, that takes the Camar worker from his Indian village to work in the cotton or jute mills, the African tribesman to labor in the diamond mines, and the New Guinea tribesman to toil on the distant plantation. The distinct economic "fields" of the peasant are on the whole less distinct and less disruptive of the local life than are those that affect the tribesman. The more primitive man is the man likely to enter modern industry when it is established in his country; the landowning peasant, with a way of life already in stable adjustment to many aspects of civilization, is more resistant to industrialization.[34]

The political autonomy of the local community is much qualified in many non-European societies by chieftainship, councils, and other authorities affecting more than one band or settlement. In many an African society political and administrative authority is hierarchical, and there are non-territorially organized attachments to power, as instanced by the "sectors" and the loyalties to queens and storehouses among the Lozi: men of different settlements are united by the fact of a common tie to a center of power, itself subordinate to the king.[35] In the African kingdoms, such as Dahomey, units of the political system intermediate between kinship groups and the state are in part territorially defined, and so the "hierarchy of territorially based groups" that Barnes identifies for Norway is present. There is, however, one feature of this hierarchy that characterizes peasant societies. Indeed, it follows from the very basis of my choice in grouping as peasant societies those in which there are long-established relations with an elite whose culture is that of the peasant carried to another level of development. I have remarked on the two halves that compose the total society; there are two kinds of people, peasants and a more urban (or at least manorial) elite. The two kinds of people look at each other, at that joint or hinge in the total society, and have for each other attitudes that complement (but not always compliment) each other. The relationships between the two kinds of people define the relative status of one to the other. The lower kind of people recognize, in certain respects, the political authority of the other and also their "guidance in the moral sphere."[36]

The anthropologist who comes to peasant society through the study of the social structure of a peasant village will find that important parts of that structure are represented in the village by a few individuals or, perhaps, by people who are not in the village but somewhere else. In peasant communities remote from town, city, or manorial country estate, the elite may not be immediately present. In the Brazilian peasant village described by Pierson and his associates, there were none. The villagers managed their own local affairs. But they had relations with the elite when the villager went to the city or the officials came to them.[37] In the Yucatecan village that I studied the people were more or less peasantry; the relations they had with a more urban elite (*dzulob*, they called them) were many and frequent, but the schoolteacher was then the only resident from that upper and outer world. In many a European peasant village live a few people with urban manners and some learning who manage those affairs of the peasants which relate to the national state. To these administrative and cultural intermediaries between local life and wider life the word "intelligentsia" has long been applied. Sanders uses it to denote the small group in the Bulgarian village composed of the mayor, the doctor, and the schoolteachers. These people associated with one another, showed their separation from the peasantry, talked politics and perhaps literature, organized and led all the patriotic celebrations, and provided something for the peasants to recognize as better than themselves. Sanders writes: "The *intelligentsia* ... had more importance than their village duties seemed to indicate. They were the channels through which the national state, the national church, and the national school system expressed themselves. ... Their high status rested not only upon the influence they wielded as representatives of powerful institutions, but also upon the fact that they were educated."[38] Much the same is said by Miner of the curé and the senator in the peasant parish of French Canada. These two, and their relatives, "are so far removed from the society of the parish that they cannot carry on personal social contacts with the other parishioners. ... Their position is due to contacts which they have with the world outside the parish, from which sphere they have received recognition far higher than anything the parish can give."[39] In early Norway most of the priests lived in the country and each parish had its bureaucrat; these persons were part of an urban elite.[40]

The Andalusian town of Alcalá recently described by Pitt-Rivers provides a striking instance of the two kinds of people, each representing one distinguishable half of a double society, and both dwelling in the same compact community.[41] As the agricultural people live in the town and identify themselves with it, and not a rural village or dispersed settlement, they are not typically peasants, although in many respects their manner of life and thought is like that of Bulgarian or Italian peasants. In the town lives also an educated class, called *señoritos* by those of the town who work the land or otherwise live the socially inferior kind of life. The *señoritos* are distinguished by superior manners, acceptance of responsibility to protect inferior dependents, a higher sense of honor, and the fact that they do not participate in the local customs. They provide the small ruling group; they serve as the intermediaries, administrative, and also cultural, between near-peasant and city. The *señoritos* identify themselves with the common people as against a rival pueblo or against a predatory bureaucracy from outside, but identify themselves with *señoritos* of other pueblos in the business of administration and commerce. Within the pueblo the investigator discerns two contrasting ways of life corresponding to the two social classes: "one can see, in place of the sanctions of law, the sanctions of the pueblo's mockery; in place of the food-control, the clandestine mills and the black market ... in place of the Civil Guard, the bandit and the smuggler. In place of the schools, the *maestros rurales*; in place of the doctor, vet and chemist, the *curanderos*; in place of the ... trained nurse, the ... country midwives. And for the purpose of invoking the powers of religion in such matters, in place of the priest, the *sabia*."[42] Here we have the folk in the town, the urban elite in common habitation and in one social structure with a more folklike people.

The social structure of peasant and peasant-like societies includes then, the relations of cultural influence and example between the elite half and the peasant half of the whole larger social system. It will not do to describe these relations only as relations of ruler and ruled or of exploiter and exploited, although these elements an likely to be present. The student will want also to describe the prestige or contempt, the feelings of superiority or inferiority and the examples of excellence to be emulated or of baseness to be avoided that may be present in the relations between peasant and elite. The peasant is a rustic and he knows it. The educated man, whose life is in part in the local community and in part—at least mentally—in more urban circles, looks down on the peasant. "Oh what a rogue and peasant slave am I!" exclaimed Hamlet in one of his frequent moods of self-depreciation. All over the world the terms applied to rural people by urban people imply contempt, condescension, or—and this is the opposite face of the attitude—a certain admiration for the virtues of the simple, the primitive, and the hardy. On his side the peasant admits his relative inferiority as to culture and manners but naturally claims the virtues accorded him and sees the city man as idle, or false, or extravagant. He see himself as low with regard to the common culture but nevertheless with a way of life morally superior to that of the townsman.

The isolated primitive community presents the student of social structure with a simpler and smaller system. There social relations are compact, congruent, and largely personal. With the growth and the spread of civilization social relations extend themselves out from the local community, lose much of their congruence (as in the development of industrial fields of activity), and develop many kinds of impersonal and formal varieties of connection. In peasant societies we see a relatively stable and very roughly typical adjustment between local and national or feudal life, a developed larger social system in which there are two cultures within one culture, one social system composed of upper and lower halves. The cultural relations between the two halves are to be emphasized. Sjoberg puts it well: "the elite exhibits to the peasant the highly valued achievements and provides the peasant's social system with a sophisticated justification for its existence and survival."[43] The priest and the senator in the French Canadian parish, the intelligentsia of the Bulgarian village and the *señoritos* of Andalusia, in East Indian peasant communities the pundits and the gurus, show by their examples and tell by their teaching of another and higher version of that same life which the ordinary peasant lives. We may think of peasant culture as a small circle overlapping with much larger and less clearly defined areas of culture, or we may think of the peasant life as a lower circle unwinding into the upward-spreading spiral of civilization. If the student of peasant society is to describe the systems of social relations of that society, he will study those social relations that communicate the higher dimension of the civilization to the lower or peasant dimension. ...

Notes

1. Robert Redfield, *The Little Community: Viewpoints for the Study of a Human Whole* (Chicago: University of Chicago Press, 1955).
2. Raymond Firth, "Social Organization and. Social Change," *Journal of the Royal Anthropological Institute of Great Britain and Ireland*, LXXXIV, Part 1 (January-June, 1954), 1-17.
3. Melville Herskovits, *Dahomey: An Ancient West African Kingdom* (New York: J.J. Augustin, 1938).
4. Julian H. Steward, *Area Research, Theory and Practice;* (Social Science Research Bull. 63 [New York: Social Science Research Council, 1950]).
5. Julian H. Steward *et al.* (forthcoming).
6. J. A. Barnes, "Class and Committees in a Norwegian Island Parish, *Human Relations*, VII, No. 1 (1954), 39-58.
7. In Steward's words, the local units are "vertical" and the groups formed by common occupation, caste, etc., are "horizontal sociocultural subgroups." Apparently some groups are both vertical and horizontal: in Bremnes the local fishermen's associations are territorially defined. In many an East Indian village the caste groups are also neighborhoods.
8. Barnes, "Class and Committees in a Norwegian Island Parish," p. 42.
9. Ruth Bunzel, *Chichicastenango: A Guatemalan Village* ("Publication of the American Ethnological Society," Vol. XXII [New York: J. J. Augustin, 1952]).
10. J. A. Pitt-Rivers, *The People of the Sierra* (London: Weidenfeld & Nicolson, 1954), pp. 32-33.
11. Irwin T. Sanders, *Balkan Village* (Lexington, Ky.: University of Kentucky Press, 1949).
12. Barnes, "Class and Committees in a Norwegian Island Parish," p. 41.
13. Ibid., pp. 41-42.
14. Max Weber, *General Economic History* (Glencoe, Ill.: Free Press, 1950).
15. R. H. Tawney, *Religion and the Rise of Capitalism* (New York: Harcourt, Brace & Co., 1937).
16. A. R. Radcliffe-Brown, *The Andaman Islanders* (Glencoe, Ill.: Free Press, 1948), p. 42.
17. Bunzel, *Chichicastenango: A Guatemalan Village.*, pp. 67 ff.
18. Robert Redfield, "Primitive Merchants of Guatemala," *Quarterly Journal of Inter-American Relations*, I, No. 4 (October, 1939), 42-56.
19. Sanders, *Balkan Village*, pp. 105-6.
20. Robert Redfield, *The Folk Culture of Yucatan* (Chicago: University of Chicago Press, 1941), p. 163.
21. Börje Hanssen, *Österlen* (Stockholm: L.T.'s Förlag, 1952).
22. Webster McBryde, *Sololá* (New Orleans, La.: Department of Middle American Research, Tulane University, 1933).
23. Conrad Arensberg and Solon T. Kimball, *Family and Community in Ireland* (Cambridge: Harvard University Press, 1940), chap. xiii.
24. Barnes, "Class and Committees in a Norwegian Island Parish," p. 43.
25. Ibid., p. 44.
26. A. R. Radcliffe-Brown, *The Social Organization of Australian Tribes* ("Oceania Monographs," No. 1 [Melbourne: Macmillan Co., 1931]), p. 95.
27. Barnes, "Class and Committees in a Norwegian Island Parish," p. 44.
28. Horace Miner, *St. Denis: A French-Canadian Parish* (Chicago: University of Chicago Press, 1939), pp. 69-70.

29. A. M. Shah, "A Dispersed Hamlet in the Panchmahals," *Economic Weekly* (Bombay) (January 26, 1955), 115.
30. Marian W. Smith, "Social Structure in the Punjab," *Economic Weekly* (Bombay), II, No. 47 (November 21, 1953), 97.
31. McKim Marriott, "Little Communities in an Indigenous Civilization," *Village India* (Chicago: University of Chicago Press, 1955), p. 175.
32. Bernard Cohn, "Changing Status of a Depressed Caste," *Village India*, p. 57.
33. Herskovits, *Dahomey: An Ancient West African Kingdom*, p. 57.
34. Wilbert E. Moore, *Industrialization and Labor* (Ithaca: Cornell University Press, 1951).
35. Max Gluckman, "The Lozi of Barotseland in Northwestern Rhodesia," in *Seven Tribes of British Central Africa*, ed. Elizabeth Colson and Max Gluckman (London: Oxford University Press, 1951).
36. Gideon Sjoberg, "Folk and Feudal Societies," *American Journal of Sociology*, LVIII, No. 3 (November, 1952), 234.
37. Donald Pierson (with the assistance of Levi Cruz *et al.*), *Cruz das Almas* ("Smithsonian Institution, Institute of Social Anthropology Publications," No. 12 [Washington, D.C.: Government Printing Office, 1948]).
38. Sanders, *Balkan Village*, p. 11.
39. Miner, *St. Denis: A French-Canadian Parish*, pp. 250-51.
40. "Thus a hundred and fifty years ago there were in each rural parish one or two bureaucrats living at a much higher standard from the rest of the population, speaking a different language, and moving from post to post without developing marked local affiliation. Below them in status were a few traders, usually burghers of a town; they had more local ties and were not so mobile as the bureaucrats. The rest of the population were peasants . . ." (Barnes, "Class and Committees in a Norwegian Island Parish," p. 56).
41. Pitt-Rivers, *The People of the Sierra*.
42. Ibid.
43. Sjoberg, "Folk and Feudal Societies," p. 234.

Part III

Comparative Study of Civilizations

15

The Villager's View of Life

From his earliest work in Tepoztlán through his late-career work in India, Redfield focused primarily on the mental preoccupations of his subjects. His critics, especially Oscar Lewis and those he inspired, faulted Redfield's privileging of the mental worlds of his subjects over their social concerns. Nevertheless, Redfield found the mentalist orientation a rich vein, and he mined it deeply. A central feature of his magnum opus, The Folk Culture of Yucatan, *was the chapter that portrayed the mental world of the Yucatecan villager. In this chapter, "The Villager's View of Life," which functions well as a standalone piece, Redfield provided an insightful example of what he later came to call world view studies. Here he presented an integrated view of how the peasants of the Yucatecan villages looked out upon the world, describing specifically the way in which they defined themselves versus other peoples, conceived of the gods, and thought about natural resources, health, sickness, and death. Redfield subsequently came to regard world view studies as a key methodology to be used in the comparative studies of civilizations, and he devoted much effort to defining how these studies might be constructed.*

The historical analysis [presented earlier in *The Folk Culture of Yucatan*] concluded ... that it is in the peripheral communities that Spanish and native elements of religious ritual are most closely articulated into a single whole. This observation may be extended to the entire conventional life represented in the four communities. It is in the more isolated villages that the ways of living exhibit to the greatest degree an interrelation of parts and inner consistency. The mode of life of Tusik rather than of Chan Kom, and of Chan Kom rather than of Dzitas, can, therefore, be described as an organized body of conventional understandings. The reference here is not, essentially, to the fact that in the peripheral communities the habits of individual men conform most closely to the customs of the community. This is, of course, also true. In Tusik the outlook on life which one man has is very like that of any other, making allowances for temperamental differences. Even in Chan Kom this may still be said, in spite of the differing degrees to which influences from the

---

First published in *The Folk Culture of Yucatan* (Chicago: University of Chicago Press, 1941), 110-131.

city have modified the ideas and practices of individuals. In Dzitas the heterogeneity of mental worlds and of corresponding overt behavior is much greater, while in Merída the range of interest, knowledge, belief, and general sophistication is so wide that in describing the life of the city it is necessary to deal with one social class or interest group at a time, and even then general statements as to the thoughts and behavior of any one of these are more approximate than are corresponding statements for the entire subtribe in Quintana Roo. This progressive difference as to the heterogeneity among the mental worlds of individuals in the same community is, of course, to be anticipated from such general information as to the four communities as has already been presented. To demonstrate its truth is probably unnecessary. The ethnologist quickly perceives the differences. If, for example, he inquires as to the meaning of the word "balamob" among members of the Quintana Roo settlements, he will find that to everyone he approaches the word connotes those incorporeal guardians of men, villages, and cornfield, awesome beings, beneficent but also dangerous, who enter into many repeated situations involving the safety of man and of his crops and who are to be propitiated and appealed to in well-defined and well-understood ways. In Dzitas, on the contrary, appeal to a corresponding number of individuals will yield not one but several varying views. To one man the balamob are the awesome beings just described; to another, they are recognized, intellectually, as the guardians of the fields but are not appealed to, propitiated, or genuinely feared; while, to a third, their very existence is a matter of doubt or denial. One man has lived in the city; another has not. The run of experience varies so much in Dzitas and so little in Tusik.

Students of the primitive peoples have used the phrase "design for living" in connection with the cultures of these peoples. The quality suggested, to the writer, at least, by this phrase is to be found not in the extent to which the modes of living of members of the community are alike, but in the organized character of the elements that make up the view of life of anyone of them. If one considers the people of the city and even of the town, this quality of organization and consistency is much less notable. And this is true even if one considers a single class, a neighborhood, or a single individual. In comparison with the isolated villager, two observations may be made as to the life-view of the lower-class Meridano studied by Hansen. In the first place, instead of a single significant connotation for an act or an object, in many cases several are possible. In Linton's terms, there are more "alternatives" in the case of the mode of life of the city man.[1] If a conservatively thinking native of

Chan Kom falls ill and does not soon recover, he calls the shaman-priest. A Meridano of the working class in similar circumstances may call an herbalist, buy a patent medicine, see a spiritualist, or visit a doctor. These are all well known ways of dealing with the practical problem of illness. In the second place, the ideas of the city man, in comparison with those of the villager, are more discrete. Each connotation tends shortly to end. If one is sick, then one should do one thing or another to be cured. The experience has few further connotations. To the villager, however, sickness suggests that he has offended against the gods or the souls of the dead by some omission of ritual or pious duty; the diagnosis of the shaman-priest is likely to remind him of this conventional connection between sickness and religion; the religious connotations in turn depend upon the agricultural or beekeeping practices of the native. Thus, approaching the complex of ideas from the other end, when he cares for his bees or plants his corn, he will perform the customary rituals with a thought to the preservation of his health and that of his family.

In referring to this quality of organization and inner consistency, which one apprehends in entering into the mental world of the participant in the life of a well-established isolated community, it is difficult to avoid the use of terms referring properly to physical qualities. The system of ideas and practices is a "structure." It is a "web "or a "network." The villager's view on life has "depth," while that of the urbanite is relatively "shallow." Such terms do not denote qualities that may be precisely limited and compared; they merely suggest them. It will be useful to devise ways by which the conventional modes of living of two communities can be more objectively and exactly compared with reference to this quality of organization. The present pages merely record the insight obtained by students of four communities felt to differ significantly in this regard. The differences are clearly felt as the student proceeds to organize his impressions and his notes. In the case of the town, or still more the city, the customs, beliefs, and institutions remain an aggregation; they must be presented topically, almost one by one. In the case of the isolated community the knowledge obtained by the student proceeds to fall together so that one subject becomes closely linked with others and so that a consistency or even symmetry becomes apparent. In this case it is easy, or even necessary, to see the life-view of the native as a whole; and a presentation of materials in terms of separate topics, while convenient, seems, to one enjoying a close acquaintance with the community, to do violence to reality.

Such a violence is done by the monographs on Chan Kom and the cacicazgo of X-Cacal. They are convenient compromises among a number of claims upon the authors. These include the responsibilities to report the presence or absence of elements of custom, to present specialized knowledge, such as that of the shaman-priests, and to take account of individual differences among contemporary natives. Furthermore, these monographs include much matter outside the life-view of the native, such as data on population and historical information. These assorted data are exhibited in chapters and section heads involving categories in part suggested by consideration of the particular societies studied and in part by traditions of ethnographic reporting. Volumes result which present in an orderly way many facts about the communities involved, but which obscure the outlines of that design for living which controls and stimulates the native's conduct. The facts in the monograph cannot be fitted back upon the mind of any native, or upon that of an "average" native, with any success.[2]

In this chapter an attempt is made to indicate some of the outlines of the design for living which is to be recognized in the thought and action of the native of Chan Kom. Most of the facts to be involved have appeared in the Chan Kom monograph;[3] they are here stated with different connections and emphases. In order to make clear the qualities of organization and internal consistency with which this chapter deals, the materials used are those drawn from the older people, and particularly from those older people who appeared to have the most thoughtful and penetrating view of the world around them. The attempt is, therefore, to present part of the conception of the world and of life held by the more reflective members of the older generation in Chan Kom at the time just before the recent period of expansion, increasing mobility, and education—in let us say, 1928. The sample of life-view that appears in the following pages has been selected with a view toward showing its organization and consistency. Points at which the organization is not apparent are neglected. ... None knows better than the author how incomplete is this presentation and how much it would be corrected through more intimate knowledge of the people. The view of life of the Quintana Roo native would offer a better opportunity to draw a design for living except that the author has much less direct knowledge of the southern communities.[4]

As the view of life of the older native is a whole, there is no single appropriate point of beginning. Adopting the figure of a network for the organized conceptions and practices, one may say that one may lay a finger upon the fabric at any point and find an entrance. Any one thread leads to other threads, and some threads wind their way through most of the texture. Such a thread, in the network of ideas governing the native of Chan Kom, is the milpa. An account of village life must recur often to the milpa; the connections of the milpa with other elements in the design are manifold.

Four chief terms define the terrestrial world within which man moves: the bush, the cenote, the village, and the milpa. The first two are of nature, that is to say, of the gods, while the village and the milpa are what man has made out of nature with the permission and protection of the gods. The bush covers almost everything; it is the background within which lie all other special features of earth's surface. It is never reduced permanently to man's use; the milpas are but temporary claims made by men upon the good will of the deities who animate and inhabit the bush; after a few years each planted field returns to its wild state and becomes again an undifferentiated part of the forest. Therefore, each new invasion of the tall bush must be accomplished with prudent and respectful attention to the gods of the bush, the *kiulob-kaaxob*. For the same reason—that it is only when the gods grant to man the use of a piece of bush that is then wild, that is theirs—a man makes the ceremony of recompense ("dinner of the milpa") and makes the offering of first fruits only in respect to the first crop grown on land he has cleared.

The milpero marks off only so much bush for felling as will correspond with the future milpa. Thus an understanding is reached between the kuilob-kaaxob and the milpero: the milpero respects the bush, making use of only so much as he needs and wasting none; in return the gods of the bush will refrain from deflecting the swung ax against the milpero's foot. All relations with the gods have this character of a contract or, rather, of mutual expressions of good faith. The ceremonies that attend the fields and the beehives are essentially renewed pledges of pious respect and temporary discharges of a persisting obligation that is reciprocal between gods and men. Whenever a man takes from the fields or from the hives their yield, it is felt that he owes an appropriate return to the deities for what they have granted him. The first-fruit ceremonies and the rituals called "dinner of the milpa" and "dinner of the hives" formally return to the gods what they have granted. If the return is not at once made, the agriculturalist recognizes the existence of a debt that must be discharged. For each yield a certain return is due. Thus a large fowl and a small one should be offered for each springtime yield of honey. But the return need not be made at once; the debt may accumulate. But, when at last the appropriate ceremony is performed, the fowls sacrificed equal in number and kind the amount of the total obligation. So man keeps an account with the gods. Yet it is not simply a matter of arithmetical accounting. Good will must be present too. A man who scrimps against the deities is "haggling"; his health will suffer and his crops will fail. So one does not too long accumulate a debt to the deities. As another year passes without the performance of the proper ceremony, as the harmonious adjustment between man and the gods is by that much more disturbed, so increases the danger of sickness and crop failure, misfortunes by means of which the gods punish.

The obligation not to fell more bush than one needs is a part of the more general obligation never to take from the gods all the yield that is available. When the honey is taken from the hives, a little is left. When the ripe corn is taken from the field, some ears must be offered to the gods before man eats of them. When a deer is slain, certain parts must first be given to the spiritual protectors of the deer before the hunter eats his venison. For all the yield of bush and field is the gods', because the bush and the animals therein belong to the gods. These offerings return in part and in symbol what is essentially the property of the gods and which is by them ceded to men of pious conduct.

The bush is, then, the principal lodging-place of the supernatural beings. All aspects of nature have their spiritual aspect; each tree or knoll or cave may hold an invisible being and should therefore be approached with circumspection and without irreverence; and some natural features are more particularly associated with supernatural beings. The silk-cotton tree is the haunt of the x-tabai, the being in woman's form who may entice men to their death. The mounds of red earth made by the leaf-cutter ant are the abiding-place of the devil and are therefore likewise to be avoided. And throughout the bush and especially along the roads may pass the balamob, the invisible protectors of the cornfield and of the village. In certain places the bush is taller; there grow wine palms, and then the milpero finds mounds built by the ancients. Here especially lurk the *aluxob,* little mischievous beings, who are not the owners of wood or field, as are the gods, but who must on some occasions be propitiated. The bush teems with unseen inhabitants. Especially at night does the native hear a multitude of rustlings, murmurings, and whistlings that make known the presence of the many beings who people the bush. And each of these is disposed, well or ill, toward man, and of them man must take account.

Of all natural features, that attended by the most important considerations is the cenote —the natural well perforated by erosion through the limestone upon which grows the bush. The bush, even in the rainy season, is tough and thorny and after months without rainfall is a sere and dusty tangle of brittle branches and vines. But the cenote, a shaft down to the distant water, is ringed with fresh verdure. From its mouth emerges air, moist and cool; swallows twitter about its sides. The plants about the cenote are green and soft and luxuriant; they are, therefore, the plants used in the ceremonies to the rain-gods. Similarly the frogs, toads, and tortoises that are found near the cenotes are the animals of the rain-gods. The cenotes are the places of the rain-gods, the chaacs. These, residing behind a doorway in the eastern sky, come to earth and are also thought of as dwellers in these natural wells. The land is known largely by the cenotes; they are the points by which are located other features of the bush. In the prayers uttered by the shaman-priest in the agricultural ceremonies all the cenotes in the region in which the native moves and makes his milpas are mentioned by name; thus the priest calls, one by one, upon the chaacs associated with the cenotes. For the chaacs have within their power the granting or the withholding of the rain upon which the maize and, therefore, the life of the people depends. Of all the gods of nature, the chaacs come first in importance.

The chaacob, the balamob, and the kuilob-kaaxob are guardians, respectively, of the rain, the village and the milpa, and the bush. Lesser features of nature have also their protectors. The deer are watched over by spiritual beings called "zip," who have the form of deer; and the cattle have their guardian who is in the form a great steer. Certain birds who frequent the milpa but appear not to eat the grain are the *alakob* of the balamob, as the frogs are the alakob of the rain gods. The principal wild animals are the domestic animals of their protectors; they are yielded to man only under appropriate conditions, as crops are yielded and the honey which the bees make. The bees, too, are under the tutelage of special deities. All these wild animals are, therefore, referred to in prayers as alakob, "domestic animals"; and, when man makes an offering to the gods, he offers his own alakob, hens or turkeys.

All these supernatural beings are not of the substance of which this world is made. They are, the native says, "of wind." The wind that blows suggests these beings and may, in fact, be them. The wind that blows from the cenotes, or from dry caves, comes from the sea to which all winds return. The winds, as they blow to refresh the land or to fan the flames at burning time, are beneficent; but there abound innumerable winds, often not felt at all—winds only in the sense of incorporeal spirits—that are evil, actually or potentially. These winds may go about of themselves, but also they attend all supernatural beings and all critical, dangerous, or morally wrong situations and human beings involved in such situations. Together the gods of bush, milpa, rain, and village are "the Lords," the yuntzilob. Wherever the yuntzilob go, the winds go too. So the gods are a source of danger to men; their sacred quality involves a peril. Also the Lords may send the evil winds to punish the impious or those careless of their obligations to the deities. So the ceremonies, besides propitiating the deities, ward off the evil winds or, in certain cases, clear from the bodies of the afflicted the evil winds that have attacked them.

The cenotes are particularly the sources of the winds. As the water makes its cycle, carried by the rain-gods from the cenotes up into the sky to fall as fertilizing rain upon the milpa, so the winds have their sources in the sea and pass up through the cenotes. Therefore, in certain ceremonies offerings are thrown into the cenotes to propitiate the winds. The cenotes are also the openings to the underworld; the suicide, worst of sinners, hurls himself into the cenote to pass directly into hell.

Except for rainfall, the cenotes are the only source of water. They determine the position of human settlements. Each cluster of milpas that has any permanency of settlement, each established village, centers about a cenote. The cenotes in the uninhabited bush retain more of their sacred quality; some indeed, may not be approached by women and are visited by men only when water of that high degree of sacredness is to be fetched for use in the most important ceremony. But the cenote of the village becomes a part of the mundane and human life. To it the women and girls come for water; there they exchange gossip and talk, and there the cattle are driven to water.

The village, like the world itself, is a square with its corners in the four cardinal directions. The cenote is its center. So five crosses should be set up in each village: one at each corner and one at the cenote. Each village has its five (some say four) protecting balamob. Four hover above the four entrances to pounce upon noxious beast or evil wind that might attempt to enter. The fifth stations himself above the center point. The milpa also is square, and similarly oriented, and provided with its five balamob. Five rain-gods occupy, respectively, the cardinal points of the sky and the center of the heavens. In all these sets of five the smallest of the five occupies the position either at the east or at the center. Though he is the smallest, he is the most powerful. The word for him (*thup*) suggests to the native the smallest and the most powerful of a series; by the same adjective is known the kind of corn that produces small ears early in the season; for this corn, because of its special virtue in ripening before other corn, a special ceremony must be made.

Of the four cardinal directions, the east is dominant. From the east blow the principal winds, out of the east arise sun, moon, and planets; and from the east, in springtime, the first clouds and rains, carried by the chaacs, emerge. In the dense forests to the east dwell the bee-gods and a number of lesser supernatural beings; and inconceivably far, somewhere to the east, lies Jerusalem, where Jesus Christ lived. When a man prays, therefore, he faces east; and every altar, from the little table of poles set up by a milpero in his field, when he makes an offering at the time of sowing, to the altar elaborately laid out by the shaman-priest for the rain ceremony, is oriented to the points of the compass and so arranged that the worshiper kneels before it to face the east. At the rain ceremony the rain-gods of the cardinal directions are impersonated by men placed at the four corners of the altar, and four boys, impersonating frogs, alakob of the rain-gods, sit at the four supports of the altar.

The milpa, also, is thought of as square, and its four corners are protected by four balamob; a fifth, the thup, is sometimes conceived as occupying the central point. When the agriculturalist makes an offering in the milpa, he sets one bowl of cornmeal-in-water in each corner of the milpa and may add a fifth in the center. In the center of the field he builds his granary, and here he leaves his corn for months, it may be, coming there after the harvest only from time to time to supply the needs of his household. There the maize is safe, for who would take it from under the eyes of the unseen gods who have set a watch upon it? The milpa is, indeed, not only a workplace, but also a place of worship. It is a place that must not be sullied. One works, eats, talks, and prays in a milpa. But one should not act boisterously in a milpa. Though one may take one's wife to a milpa, one should not have sexual intercourse under the sky out in a milpa but only within a house or shelter.

That the milpa, like the cenote and the bush, is set aside from the ordinary life of the village is indicated when the native says that the milpa is *zuhuy*. Everything that is protected from or is not exposed to the contamination of the ordinary, the earthly, the profane, is zuhuy. What is held from contaminating experiences is zuhuy: a girl who does not go about with other people, especially with men; a fowl penned by itself to make it ready for offering to the gods; a tablecloth that has never been used; water in a cenote to which women have not had access. What is appropriate to or associated with the gods is zuhuy: balche, the bark beer offered to the gods at the rain ceremony; the piece of ground upon which the ceremony has just been held; a milpa. The maize is zuhuy, especially as long as it is growing in the milpa. One does not rudely grasp a growing maize plant; one does not wantonly throw kernels of maize on the ground or crack them between the teeth. The Virgin herself is one of the guardians of the maize; by such a term she is addressed in the prayers used in agricultural ceremonies. So long as the maize is in the milpa it is not referred to by the word used for maize as it is prepared for eating or as it is sold in the market (*ixim*) but by the same word (*gracia*) used to denote the spiritual essence of offerings made to the gods.

Not only have the gods their special functions and their special positions in the quadrilaterals of village, milpa, earth, and sky but they have also their positions in a hierarchy of power and authority. When the offerings are laid out on the altar of the agricultural ceremonies, this relative order of power and importance is expressed in the placing of the offerings: the largest breads are committed to the highest beings and are closest to the candle that marks the central point of the eastern side of the table altar, while the smaller breads, for the lesser gods, are placed farther away from the candle. There are, the native recognizes, two hierarchies, but the two interlock, and there is one supreme head to them both. This is the *Hahal Dios*, the Great God, who sits in a place, called Glory, very remote, beyond the sky. Nothing happens but that he has it so; yet he is too remote to deal directly with men. The great saints sit high, but below him, and below them are the lesser saints and the souls of the virtuous and baptized dead. Some of the saints are protectors of the animals of the forest and are to be propitiated along with the wind-like supernatural deer who watch their corporeal kinds. The saints have their embodiment in their effigies, but these are also saints, with personalities and powers in their own right, especially those of miraculous origin. Each family may have a saint of this sort, but every village must have one. This saint is the protector of the entire community and the intermediary between the people and the Hahal Dios, as the balamob of the village protect it from terrestrial invasion by evil winds and marauding animals. One of the great saints, St. Michael, is chief of the chaacs. Through him the Hahal Dios controls the rain. Captain of the chaacs when they ride across the sky is the *Kunku-Chaac*, the great rain-god. Under orders from St. Michael, he leads the other rain-gods, who are subordinated to him down to the least chaac, the thup, who, being the least, has special powers to produce rain in torrents.

As it is with the gods, so it is the proper condition of men that they respect their proper order of duty and responsibility. One must be chief and father, expecting and receiving respect and obedience, while he gives protection and dispenses justice. So it is with the family, where the father is the head; so with the village where the comisario (chosen by the people more frequently than was the old batab who held his office for life) leads his people, composes their disputes, and determines punishments; and so it is with the state, where the governor has this role. Under each such leader come others who are next in authority. Everyone in a post of authority has supporters—his *noox*. When one stick is set up to support another, it is a noox. So the comisario has his *suplente*, and so the *cargador*, who is in principal charge of the annual festival of the patron saint, has his *nakulob* to help him. The municipal officers are a hierarchy, and so are the men composing the organization that maintains the festival of the patron; in each case there is one head and a distribution of authority and responsibility downward. In the case of the organization maintaining the festival this hierarchy is expressed in the ritual wherein certain festal foods are solemnly and publicly transferred from the outgoing cargador to his successor and are then distributed among the supporters of the new cargador, first to the three next responsible, and then among the lesser followers and votaries.

In the natural order of authority men are above women, and the old above the young. So, when a married couple leave the church, the bride walks ahead of her husband to show that he is to command; and so they walk afterward on the trail. A woman's activities center around the hearth; her usual path is from the house to the cenote. The path of men leads to the milpa and to the town; men and not women are concerned with public affairs. At all gatherings for the discussion of affairs outside the large family only men are present, or, if women are present, they do not take part. When the ceremony of *hetzmek* is performed to assure that an infant will develop as it should, the objects placed in its hand to symbolize its future capacities include a needle if it be a girl, an ax if a boy.

Among one's kinsmen one occupies, at every age, a well understood position in an order of respect, authority, and responsibility. To one's father one owes the greatest obedience and also respect; while he cares for you, his commands are to be obeyed. To one's father's or mother's brothers, but especially to the former, respect and obedience, but less, are due. One's older brother is distinguished from one younger than one's self by a different term that implies the obedience due him. If the father dies, the oldest brother will take his place at the head of the family. To an older brother (*zucuun*) one may go for help and advice as one would to a father or an uncle. But these kinsmen by blood are not the only members of this constellation of duty and obligation. By baptism and by hetzmek ceremony the parents provide *padrinos* for the child, older persons who stand ready to aid, to advise, and, if necessary, to chide their godchild. To these persons one shows the greatest respect, and this respect is expressed, throughout life, in gestures of greeting and in the making of gifts. Upon marriage one's parents-in-law become still another pair of these older persons to whom respect is due. So the younger person is enclosed, so to speak, within pairs of older persons. And the older persons, linked with one another through the sponsorship involved in baptism or hetzmek, and in the marrying of their respective offspring, are linked with one another in bonds of mutual respect and trust. After one marries and has children, one arranges, for each, the padrinos of the baptism and of the hetzmek and later sees to it that one's son finds a wife. And each of these undertakings to complete the social position of that child for whom one is responsible creates a new tie between one's self and one's wife and the person or the couple chosen to sponsor one's child or with the parents of the child's spouse. Or, at the least, it solemnizes and sanctifies a relation of intimacy and trust that has already come into existence through kinship or friendship.

Each of these relationships is created in ritual and sanctioned by tradition; some are renewed or later recognized in other rituals. When parents come to ask a couple to sponsor their child at baptism, they express their solemn petition through formal speech expressed through an intermediary, and the unbreakable relation established is signalized by the offering and acceptance of certain traditional foods and by eating and drinking together. The petitioner kisses the hand of the man he seeks as compadre, for, though the respect is to be mutual, the gratitude moves from the child's parents to the godparents. This gratitude later receives formal recognition in a special ceremony when the parents kneel before their compadres and wash their hands and in which the tie between the child and his godparents is expressed by placing the child in the godparents' arms. The responsibility assumed by the godparents of the baptism is paralleled by that assumed by the person who "makes hetzmek" with the child, first placing it astride the hip, where it will therefore be carried until it learns to walk; and a short domestic ceremony expresses this relationship and the assurance which performance of the ritual gives of the future sound development of the child. The relationships established by marriage are likewise signalized in procedures that are formal, solemn, traditional, and appropriate. Marriage is not only an arrangement for the adult condition of two young people; it is also the forging of a new relationship between two groups of kindred. As men take the leadership, so the parents of the boy come to the parents of the girl to ask for the girl's hand. As formal matters should be expressed through third persons, it is well to engage one specializing in the negotiation of marriages to express the petition and prosecute the negotiations. As every petitioner brings a gift, those coming with the petition bring rum, chocolate, cigarettes, and bread. And as the matter under consideration is important and concerns relatives on both sides, as well as the boy and girl, four visits are made and negotiations are extended. In the determination of the amount and nature of the gift to be made to the girl by the boy's parents and in the settlement of the details of the marriage arrangements, grandparents and perhaps godparents have an appropriate place, as well, it may be, as have uncles on both sides or elder brothers. If the old-style marriage is followed, a ceremony will be held in which the boy's parents are hosts. In this, by an order of kneeling and of offering rum, by the formal speeches made by the sponsor of the marriage, and finally by the offering of cooked turkeys by the boy's father to the girl's father and by the boy's father to the sponsor of the marriage, all the new relationships of obligation and respect are expressed and appropriately sealed.

So each new tie in the web of social relationships is fastened with rituals meaningful of the character and importance of the relationships. As ties are broken by death, new ones are formed. The new ties bring in new individuals, but they merely repeat the old patterns so that the design in the texture is always the same.

Death does not quite break the old ties. After the soul has been released from the body it does not go directly to its destination (whether *metnal* in the underworld, Purgatory, or Glory above). The behavior of the living, after a death, is such as to conduce the soul, by appropriate stages, to its ultimate destination in the other-world, where it will no longer trouble the living. If dying is difficult, chants will be sung to loosen the soul from the body. An opening must be left in the roof for the soul to pass through. The soul will return once to visit its home before it sets off on the road to the other-world. To make sure that it will not lose the way, in the event that the death takes place away from home at some settlement in the bush, corn may be scattered along the path to the village that the soul may not go astray in the woods. The soul may be addressed in speech and charged to come to the place of burial. Of the nine days of prayer which follow a death, that held on the third day tells the soul that it has left the body and must take the road away from earth; on this day the soul returns to its home to collect its sins, which it must carry to judgment. Therefore, the house must not then be swept; nothing must be done to make it difficult for the soul to collect the sins. The prayers on the seventh day commend the soul to God and start it on its journey. The living should not cry; this might wet the road of the dead and delay its passage.

Thereafter the souls of the baptized will no longer remain near their old homes. At certain times after the death, and at last on the anniversary of the death, prayers must be held for the repose of the souls of the recently dead. But only on All Souls' Day do the dead return; on this day food is to be set out for them, their names are to be called, and prayers are to be said for them. This the souls ask, and, if it is denied, they will visit the living with sickness and misfortune. Cases are known, and stories are told, of people who have neglected these obligations and who have been punished accordingly. To make sure that no soul is overlooked, a special offering is set out on All Souls' Day for "the nameless souls." The relation between the presence of the souls of the dead and danger to the living is apparent in the fact that, when, two or three years after interment, the bones of the dead are removed from the cemetery to make room for other interments, the people feel free to express their sorrow and mourning. To have done so earlier when the soul was about would have been to induce the soul to remain.

The proper course of man is set by piety and a prudent application of practical knowledge. The first need of man is to plant maize that one may eat. So, beginning as a small boy, one learns how this may best be done. In choosing the place in which to make milpa, one learns to seek the wine palm and the *uaxin* tree and to avoid the aloe. In felling the bush, one learns to leave certain trees and how to cut the others. In burning the felled trees, one comes to judge the signs of coming rain and to make use of the weather prognostications of the h-men. So each activity by which a livelihood is gained or by which life and health are kept involves much knowledge as to how to act if certain results are to follow. A fruit tree had best be planted just after a full moon; one should drive two cross-shaped sticks through a papaya tree to cause it to bear; the proper part of the plastron of a tortoise, tied around a child's neck, will protect it from whooping-cough. But many of these courses of action, felt to be in themselves direct and practical lie within a context of piety. There are many things one should do if one is wise; there are more important things one must do because it is virtuous. Yet virtue and prudence are so closely intertwined in thought and action that they can hardly be separated. The good man is the fortunate man. The man whose soul is at peace can expect his body to be in good health. The maize must be cared for, and the gods of the maize must be attended. To fail in the latter is to sin; one's fellows will condemn one, and, furthermore, misfortune will visit one. The milpa is a working-place; it is also a place in which approach is made to the powerful unseen beings. To make milpa is also to participate in those acts by which one establishes good relations with the gods. Not to make milpa is to put one's self outside that round of action, partly individual, partly communal, by which, in prayer and offering, the good will of the yuntzilob and of the saints is kept. A man who has enough maize to last him for a year or more will make at least a little milpa so as to maintain his part in these acts of virtue and of responsibility to the gods. A man personally incapacitated to make milpa will make milpa by employing the labor of others, even at economic loss. To give up making milpa entirely is to take a step serious for the soul as well as for its practical consequences.

Health of body and peace of soul depend upon the maintenance of conditions of balance. Extremes, and the meeting of extremes, are to be avoided. The relationships with the saints and with the yuntzilob rests, as already stated, upon preservation of a balance expressed in offering and ritual performance, on the one hand, and in protection and favor, on the other. To let the account go too long unpaid is to court misfortune. One's body, too, is best off if equable conditions are maintained. Excessive exercise or the excitement attendant upon association with the other sex, as at dances, carries with it the danger of sickness. "The evil winds come at such times." A menstruating woman, or even a person with a wound, carries the danger to others of the contagion inherent in such abnormal conditions. The shaman-priest who leads a ceremony in which are invoked the yuntzilob exposes himself to the winds the nearness of deity involves; he must be appropriately purified. When the men come back from lassoing the bulls at a festal bullfight, their lassos are loaded with these winds, and a ceremony is performed to cleanse them. To sick persons, especially to newborn infants, these dangers of attack from winds are greatest; and from such persons everyone who has been exposed to winds, even the man who has walked in the bush where a balam may have passed, will prudently keep away.

Good health involves also the maintenance of that median condition which the native expresses in terms of heat and cold. Some persons are naturally hot, others cold. Two persons representing the extremes of such natural conditions should not marry; the outcome will not be fortunate. Nor should a man whose blood is "hot" attempt to raise kinds of domestic animals known to be characteristically "cold." The foods one eats and the beverages one drinks are known to have their characters in terms of these opposites. Something that is a little too "hot," as beef, may be made safer for consumption by adding a little lime juice, which is "cold." But it is dangerous to bring the greatest extremes together: honey is very "hot," and it should not be followed by water, which is "cold." If a man has a fever, he is hot, and he may be treated with moderate amounts of herbs or foods which are cold. On the other hand, a person who is weak is "cold" and should be given "hot" things to eat and drink. The plants that are "cold" are, in some cases, the plants that grow near the cenote and that are used in the rain ceremony. For drought is the fever of the milpa. As man's fever may be treated with cold plants, so it is appropriate to use "cold" plants in seeking an end to drought.

The word "taman" expresses for the conservative native those appreciated qualities that may be roughly identified with our "piety." A man who is taman maintains faithfully the ceremonies of the field and of the hive. He is respectful of the maize, and in his milpa his behavior is decent and circumspect. Such a man takes his part when the offerings are made to the patron saint. He does not forget his dead and makes for them occasional novenas and sets out for them the dinner of the souls on All Souls' Day. When his harvest has been good, when his beans are ripe, or when the new ears of maize are ready to eat, he sees to it that cooked beans or new ears are hung in his yard for the yuntzilob to partake of. He participates in the new-corn ceremony over which the shaman-priest presides; and, if his harvest is good, he makes a novena in his house for the patron saint and the Hahal Dios. When he takes the honey from his hives, he is careful not to injure any bee, and, if he moves his hives, he secures permission of the bee-gods by making the proper ceremony. A man who is taman does not throw maize grains on the ground or throw water onto a dog. He does not quarrel or raise his voice against children.

The kind of valued behavior implied by the word "taman" represents an ideal that few attain but with which everyone feels his own conduct should in some degree correspond. Some of the norms of virtue are more compelling than others. Industry, for example, and obedience to authority, whether that of the comisario or of one's father, are expected of everyone, and a serious failure in these respects is not compatible with continued residence in the community. A man may be slow to set out the offerings for the yuntzilob, but he will certainly work in his milpa, and he will certainly not omit entirely his ritual obligations. Nor is the virtue implied by "taman" inclusive of all conduct that the society applauds. One may seek to lead his fellows in public office, provided always one works for the good of the entire community. One may seek recognition at festivals, as a leader of the dancing, or by providing fierce bulls for the festal bullfights. Certainly it is good to acquire corn and cattle, provided one is generous. If one is so inclined, a man may learn to play a cornet, and a woman may distinguish herself at embroidery. But none of these achievements will be attended with the approval of one's fellows if it involves significant departure from the normal ways of life. The success of the bullfighter or the wealth of the fortunate agriculturalist must be regarded as attained through piety and right conduct, and indeed too much success in any line of endeavor is likely to arouse the suspicion that the conduct of the successful one has not always been right.

The pattern of meanings and standards that has here been sketched is a background, a mold of conduct, within which individual interests and enterprise must work themselves out. The conceptions here presented as the view of life of the villager are not, of course, present in the form here offered with any degree of entirety at most times, or even, probably, at any time. Men and women go about as they do elsewhere, attending to immediate concerns. They solve the present difficulty. They do the day's work; they plan to sow or to harvest; they laugh at something that amuses them, or they worry over illness or misfortune. Yet the scheme of ideas is there, nevertheless. It is forever implicit in their conduct. It provides the goals of their action. It gives a reason, a moral worth, to the choices they make. It says: "Yes, this is right" and "This is why." With such a charter they may be unhappy because unfortunate, but they cannot feel themselves lost.

Notes

1. Ralph Linton, *The Study of Man* (New York: D. Appleton-Century Co., 1936), pp. 273-274.
2. [Editor's Note: Redfield is referring in particular here to his earlier work written in conjunction with Alfonso Villa Rojas, *Chan Kom: A Maya Village* (Washington, D.C.: Carnegie Institution of Washington, 1934).]
3. [Editor's Note: Ibid.].
4. [Editor's Note: Redfield suggests that the village of Quintana Roo would have been a more suitable village than Chan Kom for exploration of the world view of the villager specifically because Quintana Roo, as the most remote village in his controlled set of community studies, was the least influenced by city ways and was characterized by the most integrated culture and world view. Nevertheless, Chan Kom was decidedly remote and folklike, in Redfield's conception, and since he had spent far more time in this village, he felt much more equipped to present an in-depth holistic depiction of the villagers' world view.]

16

The Primitive World View

> *In the early 1950s, Redfield undertook to formalize and institutionalize the conception and execution of world view studies. His first step in this endeavor consisted of the publication of his article "The Primitive World View" in the* Proceedings of the American Philosophical Association. *In this article, he delineated the aims and intentions of world view studies. Here he did not discuss methods of study. Rather, he focused on defining what he meant by world view studies and argued for the value such studies held for cross-cultural comparison. He took pains to distinguish world view studies from other related comparative analyses, such as studies of values, ethos, and national character. Whereas all these analyses portrayed a culture as an outsider looked in upon it, world view studies portrayed how the world or universe appeared to those within the culture looking outward. Redfield expressed great faith that a limited number of universal elements could be found to allow orderly comparative analyses not only among cultures but also civilizations. This article expressed the core of his philosophical conception for such studies and served as an influential launching point for the work of many anthropologists in the 1950s who were to undertake world view studies of specific cultures. He expanded upon this article, moreover, in his 1953 book* The Primitive World and Its Transformations.

By "world view" is here meant that outlook upon the universe that is characteristic of a people. The phrase names one of a group of concepts that allow us to describe a way of life and to compare ways of life with one another. Of this group of concepts, the anthropologist's *culture* is the most familiar, comprehensive, and flexible. Using it, we may describe a people's way of life in terms of all the customs and institutions that distinguish it. Or, as did Ruth Benedict,[1] we may seek the most fundamental and persistent values of a people and describe them in terms of these values, their idea of the good life. The word "ethos" has been used for this more special conception. Still others, as Professor F. S. C. Northrop,[2] and also certain students of the relations between language and culture, seek to characterize the modes of thought that distinguish one people from another. And yet a different way of conceiving a people's way of life appears in studies of what is called "national character": in these a people is seen as if it were the personality of a single individual. The

First published in *Proceedings of the American Philosophical Society* XCIV (1952): 30-36.

national character of the French or the Chinese is the kind of person that is typically found among the French or the Chinese.

"World view" differs from culture, ethos, mode of thought, and national character. It is the picture the members of a society have of the properties and characters upon their stage of action. While "national character" refers to the way these people look to the outsider looking in on them "world view" refers to the way the world looks to that people looking out. Of all that is connoted by "culture," "world view" attends especially to the way a man, in a particular society, sees himself in relation to all else. It is the properties of existence as distinguished from and related to the self. It is, in short, a man's idea of the universe. It is that organization of ideas which answers to a man the questions: Where am I? Among what do I move? What are my relations to these things?

To use the concept is to assume certain human universals. It is at least to imply that in every society all men are conscious of self. Self is the axis of world view.[3] Every man distinguishes himself from all else. Beyond this first truth may be made other assertions as to the elements universal in all world views. As we go forward in making them they cease to be unquestionable assumptions and become hypotheses, propositions to be tested by looking for world views of which these things may not be truly said.

I will make some of these assertions. Every world view distinguishes not only the self from the not-self, but distinguishes parts of the self from each other: what G. H. Mead[4] meant by "the I and the Me" is a universal phenomenon; every man looks at a part of himself that is able to address another part. Outside of self, every man separates other human beings one from another, accords the property of self to them too, and looks upon other human beings as significantly different from all else that is not human. Though the degree and kind of partial identification of human beings with animals or other elements of what we in our society call "Nature" differ from world view to world view, we can assert, I think, that some distinction of the human from that which is not human is made in all of them. Every world view implies some conception of human nature.[5] Further, in every world view human beings, at least, are seen as grouped in classes or categories, and some of the properties of these categories are universal: the distinction between men and women, old and young, those who are near me and have a stronger claim on my sympathies as distinguished from those who are farther from me and have less claim. While, of course, the particular arrangement of categories, as to kindred, neighbors, nationals, or racial or religious groups, differs very greatly, the existence of some such categories and some of the qualities of attitude and sentiment which place every self in relation to whatever categories exist in his society are among the elements which every world view has in common with every other.

Turning from that part of the universal world view which attends primarily to the human to that part which is distinguished, if not completely at least partly, from the human, we find ourselves looking at that which in the language appropriate to the world views we know best is often identified by the two words "God" and "nature." The separation of God from nature and of these two together from man is, I venture to assert, made in some degree and in some sense in every world view; on the other hand, the kinds and degrees of separations made of these things from one another differ very widely among the societies known to history and ethnology; and I suppose that it is in understanding and defining the ways in which these distinctions are made that we shall come to some ordered comprehension of the range of variety of world views and of the types of world view. I think that in every society people look out at some things which are just things, being neither wholly human nor wholly of the qualities we call divine or spiritual: they are nature not much identified with the qualities that characterize human beings nor with those which characterize God. In working with the ordinary domestic tools, for example, I should suppose that every people recognizes a part of its world view in which things are seen as not the same as either people or divinities, "spirits." On the other hand, the kind of separation of man, God, and nature which characterizes much of the world view of Western man in historic times is, I think, by no means universal. And there is, I shall suggest later, something to be said on this point as to the world views of the primitive peoples.

If we look now still more restrictedly toward that part of the Not-Self which is Not-Man, and of the Not-Man toward that which is, as we say, nature—something with apparent physical qualities—I see some universals hardly to be contraverted, but I see more matters for investigation. The distinctions between earth and sky, between water and other things, between day and night; the recognition of the horizon—these, I suppose, are present in every world view. So, too, I suppose that every world view includes some spatial and temporal dimensions, some conceptions of place and of past and future. Man is necessarily oriented to a universe of extension and duration. Furthermore, the movements of the heavenly bodies set for everyone measures and metronomes of life that vary only within certain limits. But from such easy generalizations as these one moves into unanswered questions. To what extent do all the peoples of the world group the fixed stars in the same groupings? Holmberg[6] tells us that the Bolivian Siriono, inhabitants of a tropical forest, make no groupings of stars into constellations whatsoever. In such a more special question as this, we have probably arrived at something as to which it will prove possible to discover, by comparison of world views, generalizations true of almost all, or many, or some peoples, but not of all peoples everywhere. The recognition of the lunation may be, as I can believe, a universal element of world view, while the recognition of a series of lunations fitted within the approximate solar year is, I am sure, not universal, but only very common.

Before closing these introductory remarks on the universal elements of world view, I should admit the effect of certain universal experiences in setting the world stage of Everyman. Birth and death are events for everyone; every people looks out upon a universe in which these events are important elements, and certain aspects of attitude, as that death is unavoidable and on the whole undesirable, must be parts of the way every people look upon their universe. Sexual intercourse, menstruation, menopause, and senescence are experiences only somewhat less commanding of universal attention, and toward these human experiences too the attitudes of men, while differing widely, as M. Mead and many others have abundantly shown, include some elements which are universal, or at least overwhelmingly usual: the taboo, slight or severe, attending menstruation is one of these; the view that birth is an occasion of hazard is another.

This sketch of the universal world view could hardly be more brief. It indicates a common basis for all humanity in the common elements of the stage on which each society, each culture, performs life's drama. I have suggested that these common elements include among other things recognition of the self and others; groupings of people, some intimate and similar to oneself, others far and different; some usual ways of attending the inevitable experiences of the human career; a confrontation of the Not-Man seen in some ordered relationships of component entities, this Not-Man including both some observed features, such as earth, sky, day, and night, and also invisible beings, wills, and powers.

As with other phenomena which science seeks to understand, so in understanding world view we seek the universal to understand the particular, and we compare the particulars to understand the universal. The sketch of what is universal in world view that I have just given may lead us to some of the categories by which we shall understand particular world views, and come to classify them and then perhaps to understand the circumstances that give rise to world view of one type rather than another. From even this brief sketch I derive suggestions as to some of these categories. Following a suggestion made to me by Professor Daniel Boorstin, I attend to the fact of confrontation as a general idea useful in understanding world views. If, as I said, every world view begins with the distinction of the self from all else, every world view is a confrontation of that which is not the self and is outside of one's self. Then it might be possible to consider every world view with regard to two questions: What is confronted? What is the attitude man takes as to his relation to that which is confronted?

To the first question, what is confronted, I have already suggested the answer that the self confronts both man and that which is not man, and that the Not-Man, in our own Western world view (and in the work views of many other peoples), includes nature and God in varying kinds of separation of identification. It is probably true that a world view in which there is no element of God is a peculiarity of certain world views of secular minds of modern times. The Existentialism of Sartre is such an entirely godless world view. But it may at once be remarked that in the philosophies of individual literate and reflective minds world views are encountered which much increase the variety of known world views; I am in this paper attending to those world views which characterize whole peoples and have been, on the whole, developed without the specialized philosopher. For world view as developed through the systematic reflections of the specialized thinker, the word "cosmology" is conveniently at hand.

I think we shall find that the world views of primitive and ancient peoples differ a great deal as to the emphasized kind of thing which is confronted. In her account of the Arapesh of New Guinea,[7] Margaret Mead has described a people who confront, essentially, their own human nature. This people recognizes nature in land, water, and woods, as do all other peoples, and their universe includes certain gods or spirits associated with certain parts of this nature. But these beings are on the fringes of their interest and attention. In the case of these Melanesians "their whole attention has centered upon an internalized struggle between man and his human nature,"[8] the struggle between aggressive and dangerous sexuality on the one hand and parental and beneficent sexuality on the other. This world view centers on man; the rest of the universe is a hazy hinterland; there are almost no origin myths, and the outlines of the universe are not defined. A theory of human nature and the application of this theory in conducting life are the main parts of this world view. If we were to represent the Arapesh version of the Man-Nature-God relationships as a triangle, we would draw a triangle in which the human base was by far the longest line of the three. Should we compare the Arapesh world view with that of the Zuñi, we should see, in the case of these Indians, I think, a more nearly equilateral triangle; the Zuñi confront man, nature, and God about equally, regard the relations of the three as intimate, and see the maintenance of these relationships as the duty of man. The ancient Hebrews, especially after the development of their ideas as to an absolute God, had a world view in which the confrontation of deity was paramount; man's nature and nature's nature were subordinated entities; the triangle to represent this world view would be still differently drawn. And still different from the three world views I have just mentioned is that of the ancient Mesopotamians as described by Thorkild Jacobsen.[9] These people conceived of the universe as "an order of wills," as a great state. All things—salt, fire, sky, earth, man, and also such notions as justice, righteousness, and the form of the circle—had will, character, and power. All things were arranged in a vast hierarchy of power. In this world view man confronts man, nature, and God, as in the world view of the Zuñi. Zuñi world view and Mesopotamian world view are more alike than is either like the world view of the Arapesh. But the Mesopotamian conception of the universe is far more systematic and elaborately detailed than is that of the Zuñi. And the nature of the relationship of man to that which is confronted differs very markedly in the two cases.

This last assertion brings us to the second question that I have suggested may be asked of all world views: What is the attitude man takes toward that which is confronted? There are many ways, no doubt, in which this question could be understood. We may understand it to ask us as to the relative emphasis on the cognitive and the affective in man's attitude toward the Not-Man. The passion of the Hebrews, the more intellectual attitude of the Greek, illustrate this difference, as does the emotional way in which Margaret Mead's Arapesh relate themselves to their world in contrast to the more cognitive conception of it which I should say, from my study of the Maya of Yucatan, characterizes the way of that people in relating themselves to that which is outside themselves. Second, the question might cause us to attend to the degree to which and the way in which the universe is conceived as structured, as having a defined order. The Yucatan Maya, like their ancient forbears, conceive of a universe neatly and firmly structured in a system of layered quadrilaterals: field, sky, and village, are four-cornered and oriented to the compass. The

Polynesians, on the other hand, order their universe in terms chiefly of its past history: genesis and development are the axes of their system of cosmic ideas; they tell the genealogical story of creation from chaos down to the man who tells the story. And the Arapesh, to mention once more that helpfully contrasting people, order their universe very loosely; their universe is not much structured, either in terms of time or in terms of space.

Of the ways in which we may ask the question, what is the relation which man sees between himself and that which he confronts, I choose, as one that will probably yield illumination of world views, that meaning which makes the question ask what that relation calls on man to do. The question may then be restated: in the relation seen between man and what man confronts, what is the duty or purpose of man toward that which he confronts? World view can be seen as a characteristic attitude of purpose or obligation toward that which is confronted, whether that be human nature or God-Nature. I think it will be found to be true that there is no people in history or ethnology that has not such an attitude of purpose or obligation. Indifference toward the universe is probably incompatible with a persisting human way of life. I think, further, that it will be found that this attitude exists whether the Not-Man is conceived as two things, Nature and God, or whether the one of these two prevails over the other or is involved with the other.

The content of this attitude is, however, one of those things as to which world views differ importantly from one another. Just what it is that man feels he is called upon to do in relation to the universe is something that we cannot surely predict of a people before we have come to know that people. The range of possibilities is probably suggested by the verbs accept, maintain, become one with, yield to, obey, appropriate, transform. Man does or feels he may or should do some of these things with regard to the world around him. It may be possible to relate world views of primitive, historic, and contemporary peoples to one another by comparing the verbs called for in describing the predominating conception held in those world views as to man's relationship with his own nature and with the Not-Man.

A small beginning in the development of categories useful here may be made simply by comparing some particular world views that have been described by those who have studied them. If I read Mead on the Arapesh, I find that Arapesh man is called upon to keep the opposing kinds of sexuality in situations appropriate to each. If I read Bunzel on the Zuñi,[10] I learn that while here man, God, and nature are closely associated, the attitude is again one of obligation to maintain: the duty of man consists chiefly in the performance of rituals of the tribe that maintain a perpetual and harmonious relationship between man, nature, and the gods. The cosmos is seen as a perpetually self-repeating system embracing both the physical universe and the supernaturals; man himself is a part of this system and his part in the maintenance of the unending cycle that ensures well-being is discharged in private good conduct and in public ritual. In this world view one does not alter the universe, and one does not so much obey an authority as enact one's share of the whole sacred drama of life. If I read Jacobsen on the ancient Mesopotamians,[11] I find that it is just obedience which is stressed: the duty of man is to obey the authority of the gods as in everyday mundane affairs man obeys the ruler. Existence is not, as with the Zuñi, an endless round of repeating natural and divine events of which man is a part, an aspect of God-Nature. Among the Mesopotamians, where earthly power was great and society complex, life was, as Jacobsen puts it, "a pretty arbitrary affair."[12] Man's relation to the Not-Man was to follow its orders, and the gods were thought of as meeting from time to time to make new orders. If I read Professor Boorstin on the world view of Thomas Jefferson's circle,[13] I find that man's part in the drama of existence was to build, develop, and change. Nature manifested the divine plan; its evident existence made plain the provision for man on this American continent; man had the joyous task of acting upon nature to shape it, to make it produce still more, reveal the wealth and possibilities God had stored in it. These three attitudes toward the Not-Man, exhibited in the cases of the Arapesh and the Zuñi, the ancient Mesopotamians, and the early Americans, are distinguishable: to maintain it, to obey it, or to act upon it. I suppose that all of these three attitudes might be recognized in any careful examination of anyone of the three world views; yet the predominance of one over the others, and of a different one, in the three cases, seems to me clear from the accounts given. And so the little comparison suggests one way of reaching some orderly understanding of the great variety of world views.

I now give a last turn to my remarks in the direction of the world views of peoples who never became civilized. I ask: What is the nature of the primitive world view? In this context "primitive" may be understood to refer to the peoples who lived before the rise of the civilizations, and also to those peoples who never received the influences of any civilization and lived, until recent times, that kind of life which is studied by the ethnologist. So far as anything can be said as to the world views of the numberless societies that existed during the many tens of thousands of years before civilization appeared, it is said as an inference from what can be learned about the world views of the surviving primitive peoples. (There is one other possibility of supplementary evidence: the changes in the world views of ancient peoples, Egyptians, Mesopotamians, Chinese, so far as history tells us; to some extent it may be possible to read the record backward so as to draw conclusions as to the more nearly primary world view.) But in this brief paper I attempt only to say some things that, on the basis of some acquaintance with a few of the surviving primitive peoples, may turn out to be generally true of all or of most of them, and so also probably true of the peoples who lived before Thebes and Ur arose.

Here I have three assertions to offer as to the primitive or primary world view of mankind. In order to make two of them I need parts of the conceptions and categories which I have already offered as to the universal world view or as to some probably significant kinds of world view. In making the third assertion I introduce a conception not yet mentioned; but the complication that will result is not great. Here are the three assertions: One: in the primitive world view, that which is confronted and that which does the confronting are not sharply separated; they tend to be unitary. Two: in the primitive world view the predominating attitude toward the Not-Man is one of participant maintenance. Three: in the primitive world view the universe is morally significant. I will expand briefly each of these assertions and so end.

The unitary quality of that which is confronted has been recognized by many students of the life or the mentality of primitive peoples. E. B. Tylor[14] saw that in most primitive societies what civilized man distinguishes as "Nature" is by primitive man conceived as the dwelling place of spirits, as something possessed of will, intention, personal nature. This view, too simple for the facts, was modified by Marett,[15] who for Tylor's "animism" substituted "animatism"—a term created to point out that it is not so much that separate spirits are thought to live within a tree or hill as that a more generalized power and purpose are attributed to that which, to modern man, is more nearly will-less and purposeless. Later discussions of this same subject have put the point by saying that to primitive man the distinction between persons and things is not sharply made: all objects, not only man, are regarded somewhat as if they were persons. And in a recent work H. and H. A. Frankfort choose still a somewhat different formula: "for modern scientific man the phenomenal world is primarily an 'It'; for ancient—and also for primitive—man it is a 'Thou.'"[16]

The point may be made in the terms used in this present paper. For mankind there was, and is, a primary indistinction of personal, natural, and sacred qualities. The cosmos on which man originally looked out, and to which the surviving primitive peoples look out, is one partaking at once of the qualities of man, nature, and God. The triangle of man, nature, God is originally no triangle at all; the distinctness of its sides and the sharpness of the angles are a later development, a product of civilization. We know from the history of the Western world something of how that triangle came into clear being. The Hebrews made God transcendent beyond all else, the seat of all value, and so took God out of nature, The Greeks, conceiving a universe in which order was immanent without reference to God, began the thinking that put nature outside of man and independent of God. The reconciliation of the Hebrew and the Greek heritages has resulted in the modern world in many kinds of triangles but to the unitary view, in which the universe is no triangle, but a sort of circle from some undefined segment of which man looks out while yet he remains of it a part, modern men, save a few mystics, do not return. It follows from this that the verb "confront" does no justice to the primitive world view. "Primitive man is in nature already, and we cannot speak properly of man *and* nature."[17] Being in nature, man cannot fully confront it. Rather, he does his part within it. And with this we reach my second assertion: the predominant attitude of the primitive or primary world view is one of participant maintenance. I stress the adjective: the view is only predominant; primitive people, like other people, also work upon nature, shaping it to their ends; and there are occasions when a primitive person feels he should obey an order which is not fully predestined by the order of things but that issues from a source of authority that makes new orders. But to a very large extent, and in a degree that helps us to characterize the way of primitive peoples on the whole, the primitive person "works *with* the elements, not *against* them."[18] There is a sort of mutuality about what primitive people feel as to their relations with the universe, as I know such people or have read about them: man does his part, and the universe, the God-Nature, does its part.

The third assertion, that the universe is for primitive man morally significant, is hardly more than a corollary of the first two. In the primitive view man and nature and God are not sharply distinguished but constitute a single system of entities not entirely separable from one another. Also, these entities act, personally, with regard to each other. It almost follows that the relations among the entities—man, nature, and God however distinguished or merged—are not only personal but also, as personal relations always tend to be, moral. There is one moral order including everything. The Universe is not indifferent. It cares. The activities in which man has a part are not merely the applications of useful techniques, not merely blind obedience to orders given; they are scenes and acts in drama, the hopeful tragedy of existence. Whether it is the spirit-inhabited water hole and the still more important powerful sexuality of his own being, as in the case of the Arapesh, or the rain-gods and the maize plants of the Zuñi, or the divine authorities of the ancient Mesopotamian invisible state, these entities and dispositions are part of a man-including moral system. Even where, as among the very ancient Greeks, the gods do that which man should not do, the conduct of these gods is thought about in the moral terms that prevail on earth. To primitive man the universe is spun of duty and ethical judgment.

You will perhaps remark that the elements of the primitive world view that I have ventured to identify—the unitary nature of the cosmos; the prevailing attitude of participant maintenance; and the moral aspect of the Not-Man—did not die out with primitive man and characterize also civilized people, ancient and modern. And this is true, in that these aspects of world view were to be found in the ancient civilizations and are to be found in the world views of many people today. The moral significance of the universe, in particular, is slow to disappear; it may prove to be true that only in some modern world views, or parts of them, is it fully lost. But, I submit, the primitive world view is a broken thing. It persists in parts;[19] it strives to defend itself; among some modern men it is altogether gone. The ancient civilizations began its criticism and destruction. Man was separated out from his cosmos. He came increasingly to think of what was out there as something to be reduced to his practical purposes. In modern times this attitude of practical action has risen to dominance. Was it Descartes who first clearly stated it? And the universe becomes empty of person and personal caring. Man looks out from a humanity that is his alone, on a universe that is without moral implications. The struggle to find purpose and value is transferred to the theater of relations among men with each other only, or to that inner theater of the private soul. The primary world view was fashioned thousands of years ago in thousands of small communities. Civilization, among many other things, is the story of its destruction and its remaking.

Notes

1. Ruth Benedict, *Patterns of Culture* (Boston and New York: Houghton Mifflin Co., 1934).

2. F. S. C. Northrop, *The Meeting of East and West* (New York: Macmillan Co., 1934).
3. For a possible qualification of this assertion, see Dorothy Lee, "Notes on the Conception of the Self among the Wintu Indians," *Journal of Abnormal and Social Psychology,* XLV, No.3 (1950).
4. George H. Mead, *Mind, Self and Society* (Chicago: University of Chicago Press, 1934).
5. See, for example, Gladys Reichard, "Human Nature as Conceived by the Navaho Indians," *Review of Religion,* VII, No.4 (1943), 353-60.
6. Allen Holmberg, *Nomads of the Long Bow* (Smithsonian Institution, Institute of Social Anthropology, No. 10 [1936]).
7. Margaret Mead, "The Mountain Arapesh, II: Supernaturalism," *Anthropological Papers* (American Museum of Natural History), XXXVII, No.3 (1940), 319-451.
8. Ibid., p. 357.
9. Thorkild Jacobsen, "Mesopotamia," in *The Intellectual Adventure of Ancient Man,* by H. and H. A. Frankfort et al. (Chicago: University of Chicago Press, 1946).
10. Ruth Bunzel, *Introduction to Zuñi Ceremonialism* (Bureau of American Ethnology, 47th Annual Report [Washington, D.C., 1929-30]).
11. Jacobsen, "Mesopotamia."
12. Ibid., p. 207.
13. Daniel Boorstin, *The Lost World of Thomas Jefferson* (New York: Holt, Rinehart and Winston, Inc., 1948).
14. Edward B. Tylor, "Animism," *Primitive Culture* (7th ed.; New York: Brentano's, 1924), p. 10.
15. R. R. Marett, *The Threshold of Religion* (London: Methuen, 1909).
16. H. and H. A. Frankfort, *The Intellectual Adventure of Ancient Man,* p. 4.
17. Dorothy D. Lee, *Religious Perspectives of College Teaching* (New Haven: Edward Hazen Foundation, n.d.), p. 7.
18. Ibid., p. 13.
19. Sol Tax, "World View and Social Relations in Guatemala," *American Anthropologist,* XLIII, No.1 (1941), 27-42. Dr. Tax has described a world view in which, incident to a commercial life, relationships among men are individualized and secularized while nature is seen as personal and moral.

17

The Social Organization of Tradition

Few anthropologists of his generation were as conscious of method as Robert Redfield. Indeed, from his dissertation study of Tepoztlán to his final publications, he displayed a keen interest in methodology, particularly as related to the study of intermediate or peasant peoples. In the late 1940s to early 1950s, Redfield became interested in the study of complex civilizations. The study of civilizations had long been dominated by sociologists and humanists, whose investigations required written records and hence focused primarily on the activities and products of the elite. Redfield brought a unique perspective to the comparative study of civilizations, though, by calling attention to the need to expand the field to include examination of the masses of illiterate peasants that composed large portions of all complex civilizations. Most important, Redfield introduced a new framework for conceptualizing the role of peasants within civilizations. In this conceptualization, Redfield proposed that civilizations be seen as composed of two distinct but intertwined cultural traditions, the "great traditions" of the literary elite and the "little traditions" of the non-literate masses. Anthropologists had an important role to play in comparative civilization studies, Redfield argued, through their ability to study the little traditions. Redfield encouraged anthropologists to turn their attention toward studies of the little traditions of peasant peoples and to place these studies into the context of grand civilizational studies. Only through the composite efforts of sociologists and humanists in studying the literate great traditions and anthropologists in studying the non-literate little traditions, Redfield continued, could comparative civilization studies effectively proceed. Redfield elaborated his notion of the dialectical relationship between the great and little traditions over the course of the early to mid 1950s. This selection, a chapter taken from his short 1956 book, Peasant Society and Culture: An Anthropological Approach to Civilization, *offers Redfield's most succinct explanation of his ideas surrounding the great and little traditions and their application to the anthropological study of civilizations.*

Out of that anthropology which rested on studies of isolated primitive or tribal peoples arose the concept, "a culture." The Andamanese had a culture, as did the Trobrianders, the Aranda of Australia, and the Zuñi. Each culture came to be conceived as an independent and self-sufficient system. Recently words have been found to make clear this conception of an "autonomous cultural system." It is "one which is self-sustaining—that

First published in *Peasant Society and Culture: An Anthropological Approach to Civilization* (Chicago: University of Chicago Press, 1956), 40-59.

is, it does not need to be maintained by a complementary, reciprocal, subordinate, or other indispensable connection with a second system." Such units—such cultures as those of the Zuñi or the Andamanese—"are systems because they have their own mutually adjusted and interdependent parts, and they are autonomous because they do not require another system for their continued functioning."[1] The anthropologist may see in such a system evidence of elements of culture communicated to that band or tribe from others, but he understands that the system as it now is keeps going by itself; and in describing its parts and their workings he need not go outside the little group itself. The exceptions, where the band or tribe relies on some other band or tribe for a commodity or service, are small and do not seriously modify the fact that that culture is maintained by the communication of a heritage through the generations of just those people who make up the local community.

The culture of a peasant community, on the other hand, is not autonomous. It is an aspect or dimension of the civilization of which it is a part. As the peasant society is a half-society, so the peasant culture is a half-culture. When we study such a culture we find two things to be true that are not true when we study an isolated primitive band or tribe. First, we discover that to maintain itself peasant culture requires continual communication to the local community of thought originating outside of it. The intellectual and often the religious and moral life of the peasant village is perpetually incomplete; the student needs also to know something of what goes on in the minds of remote teachers, priests, or philosophers whose thinking affects and perhaps is affected by the peasantry. Seen as a "synchronic" system, the peasant culture cannot be fully understood from what goes on in the minds of the villagers alone. Second, the peasant village invites us to attend to the long course of interaction between that community and centers of civilization. The peasant culture has an evident history; we are called upon to study that history; and the history is not local: it is a history of the civilization of which the village culture is one local expression. Both points, in recognition of both generic aspects of the peasant culture, were clearly made by George Foster when he reviewed recently his experiences in Latin-American communities and wrote that there the local culture "is continually replenished by contact with products of intellectual and scientific social strata."[2] He said also that "one of the most obvious distinctions between truly primitive societies and folk [peasant] societies is that the latter, over hundreds of years, have had constant contact with the centers of intellectual thought and development. ..."[3]

This is a new experience for one whose ways of work were developed in studying such primitive isolates as Australian tribes, Andamanese, or Trobrianders. It calls for new thoughts and new procedures of investigation. For studies of villages, it requires attention to the relevance of research by historians and students of literature, religion, and philosophy. It makes anthropology much more difficult and very much more interesting.

How shall we begin to take mental hold of this compound culture that deserves a special word, "civilization"? Let us begin with a recognition, long present in discussions of civilizations, of the difference between a great tradition and a little tradition. (This pair of phrases is here chosen from among others, including "high culture" and "low culture," "folk and classic cultures," or "popular and learned traditions." I shall also use "hierarchic and lay culture.") In a civilization there is a great tradition of the reflective few, and there is a little tradition of the largely unreflective many. The great tradition is cultivated in schools or temples; the little tradition works itself out and keeps itself going in the lives of the unlettered in their village communities. The tradition of the philosopher, theologian and literary man is a tradition consciously cultivated and handed down; that of the little people is for the most part taken for granted and not submitted to much scrutiny or considered refinement and improvement.

If we enter a village within a civilization we see at once that the culture there has been flowing into it from teachers and exemplars who never saw that village, who did their work in intellectual circles perhaps far away in space and time. When George Foster looked at Latin-American villages with civilization in mind, he saw chiefly what had come into those villages from preindustrial Europe: irrigation wheels, elements of the Catholic religion from "theological and philosophical reflections of many of the best minds of history over a period of centuries," church organization, religious dramas, political institutions, godparenthood, the humoral pathology of Hippocrates and Galen, and dances and bullfights that had worked their way downward from Spanish gentry to little Indian-mestizo farmers in Mexico or Peru.[4] In every peasant village we see corresponding things.

The two traditions[5] are interdependent. Great tradition and little tradition have long affected each other and continue to do so. The teachings of Galen about the four humors may have been suggested by ideas current in little communities of simple people becoming but not yet civilized; after development by reflective minds they may have been received by peasantry and reinterpreted in local terms. Great epics have arisen out of elements of traditional tale telling by many people, and epics have returned again to the peasantry for modification and incorporation into local cultures. The ethics of the Old Testament arose out of tribal peoples and returned to peasant communities after they had been the subject of thought by philosophers and theologians. The Koran has the content it has because it arose among Arab not Chinese peoples, and the teachings of Confucius were not invented by him single-handed; on the other hand, both teachings have been and continually are understood by peasants in ways not intended by the teachers. Great and little tradition can be thought of as two currents of thought and action that are distinguishable, yet ever flowing into and out of each other. A picture of their relationships would be something like those "histomaps" we sometimes see, those diagrams of the rise and change through time of religions and civilizations.

The two traditions are not distinguishable in very isolated tribes or bands. In reading Radcliffe-Brown on the Andaman Islands we find nothing at all about any esoteric aspect of religion or thought. Apparently any older person will be as likely to know what there is to know as any other. This diffuse distribution throughout the population of knowledge and belief may be characteristic of very large primitive societies of much greater development of the arts of life than the Andamanese enjoyed. Thus, among the Tiv of Nigeria, a tribe including about a million agricultural people, "there is no technical vocabulary, because there are no professional classes, and little specialization beyond that which is the result of sex or age. Every aspect of tribal life is everybody's business."[6] This is a primitive society without a great tradition. Among the Maori, however, "two different aspects of all the superior class of myths were taught. One of these was that taught in the *tapu* school of learning, a version never disclosed to the bulk of the people but retained by the higher grade of *tohunga* (experts or priests) and by a few others. The other was that imported to the people at large, and this, as a rule, was of an inferior nature, more puerile and grotesque than the esoteric version."[7] And in West Africa, where aborigines had developed complex states, a distinction between what we might call a littler and a greater tradition appears in the control by certain priests of elements of worship, recognized by the people as recondite and esoteric. Initiates into these cults are secluded for seven months of instruction in secret. Also, there are differences as between layman and specialist in the understanding of the religion: the priests of the Skycult in Dahomey clearly see distinctions among deities and their characteristics about which laymen are very vague.[8] Among Sudanese peoples reported by Professor Griaule[9] there is extraordinary development of highly reflective and systematic specialized thought among certain individuals.

These instances suggest the separation of the two traditions in societies that do not represent the great world civilizations. The content of knowledge comes to be double, one content for the layman, another for the hierarchy. The activities and places of residence of the carriers of the great tradition may remain close to those of the layman, or the priests and primitive philosophers may come to reside and to work apart from the common people.

This series of non-European societies arranged according to the degree to which a distinguishable great tradition is or was present can be supplemented with some references to the ancient Mexican and Mayan societies. These fulfill the logical series, for there is little doubt that those Meso-American peoples had developed something that might well be called a civilization in so far as the growth of a great tradition is its sign. Adopting the words of a recent leading student of those civilizations, I identify the hierarchic culture of the Maya with the monumental stone architecture for temples and palaces, the highly sophisticated art, the hieroglyphic writing, complex arithmetic, astronomy and calendar, the deities not directly associated with the earth or the forces of nature, and the theocratic government. On the other hand, outside of the shrine-cities and in the little villages there was a lay culture of the subsistence activities, the crafts, the village, and related organization, and a religion based on the forces of nature. In the following words, I think Dr. Armillas somewhat exaggerates the separation of great and little traditions among the pre-Columbian Maya, but he does recognize just the conception that interests me: "a new concept of the classic Maya civilization ... that it was formed by two cultural strata or subcultures corresponding to two social groups: the dominant aristocracy of the ceremonial centers and the hamlet-dwelling farmers. The dominant group was apparently of religious origin, although martial or commercial segments of it might have been developed later. The village communities seem to have preserved their folk culture little affected by the culture of the upper class. The pseudo-urban character of the ceremonial centers, if it is true that they had not a large resident population and that some of the functions of real cities were lacking, and strong class barriers might have been the factors preventing the cultural influence of the ceremonial centers from filtering down to the rural masses, transforming their folk culture into peasant culture. If this view is correct, the world outlook and moral order of the Maya sophisticated aristocracy and the rural people must have been sharply different. In this light the collapse of the classic Maya civilization was in fact the disintegration of the pan-Maya upper stratum of society, leaving practically intact the underlying local folk cultures. That this actually happened has been made very apparent by Longyear's report on Copan, and the hypothesis is not in contradiction with the scanty data we have on this collapse from other places."[10]

There is a growing conviction that the development of aboriginal American civilization passed through phases and developed cultural and societal relationships similar to those that appeared in the independent beginnings of the civilizations of the Old World.[11] Elements in the development of civilization which are common to both the Old and the New World origins of civilization are those characteristics which are generic to indigenous civilizations: the separation of culture into hierarchic and lay traditions, the appearance of an elite with secular and sacred power and including specialized cultivators of the intellectual life, and the conversion of tribal peoples into peasantry. Some part of the course of events in the Meso-American instance can be recovered. But, of course, it is beyond our immediate observation, and the record of its events is overlaid with the strong impress of another civilization that invaded America from abroad.

In the case of the peasant societies of Latin America it is this impress of an invading civilization, one not indigenous but entering the local community from abroad, that is likely to strike the student of culture. It impressed George Foster: he saw elements of culture that had worked their way from Spanish gentry downward to communities perhaps founded by American Indians. But the Mexican and Peruvian cases are hybrid civilizations. We might call them "secondary civilizations" in contrast to the primary civilizations of India and China where the civilization is indigenous, having developed out of the precivilized peoples of that very culture, converting them into the peasant half of that same culture-civilization. (India and China, it is sure, have been strongly influenced since their founding by other civilizations; nevertheless, continuity with their own native civilization has persisted; Chinese and Indian peasants remain connected with their own civilizations.)

Some of the Latin-American local cultures are incomplete aspects of both the great tradition of Spain and the great tradition of that part of aboriginal America. Had I studied the villages of Yucatan as aspects of civilization, I should have conceived the culture of the village as referring to the Spanish-Catholic great tradition and also as referring to a now vanished great tradition that was once maintained in the shrine-cities of Yucatan by native priests-astronomers. The shaman-priests of the villages I studied carried on rituals and recited prayers that would have their full explanation only if we knew what were the ritual and the related body of thought at Chichen Itza or Coba. Certain prayers recited in the present-day Maya village include phrases that I am sure would have been more understandable to the Maya priest of the early sixteenth century than they were to the Indian whose praying I heard. The secondary civilizations, especially where one great tradition has supplanted, but incompletely, another and native great tradition, provide situations that the anthropologist may regard as instances of acculturation still going on. So far as the "decapitation" (as Kidder called it) that Spanish conquest brought about four centuries ago, they are also instances of "deculturation"—removal of a great tradition.

In the comments that follow I shall be thinking for the most part of the primary civilizations of the Old World. In coming to study peasant villages of primary civilizations, the anthropologist enters fields of study that have long been cultivated by historians and other humanistic scholars. He slips in by the back entrance: through the villages, by way of the little tradition, and after the fact of centuries of interaction of peasant and philosopher, both indigenous and so representatives of local culture, and both the makers of that civilization. He looks about him, he finds a mode of life that records this long interaction, and he sees people and institutions—priests, teachers, sacred books and tales, temples and schools—that still carry it on. To describe this village life at all fully will take him far from the village and, as he pursues the interactions of the traditions in the past, into sources of information relatively new to him. He becomes aware of the numerous and impressive studies by historians and students of art, literature, and religion. Do these studies have a relevance for him who makes a field study of a peasant village?

In their principal and important work, the humanist and historian stand somewhat remote from studies of present-day peasant life. A recent collection of excellent papers on what is called "Chinese thought"[12] is concerned with the reflective ideas of Chinese philosophers, poets, and moralists. It includes hardly a reference to what went on, in periods covered by the book, in the minds of Chinese peasants. It is probably impossible to know. It is, however, possible to know something of what goes on in the minds of Chinese peasants today—political conditions permitting. The scholars of the great traditions of India are concerned first with the development of the Vedic philosophy among a small number of reflective thinkers, ancient and modern. A recent English translation of the Upanishads[13] is provided with a commentary in which matters understood by Indian philosophers, not by peasants, are discussed, although those teachings distantly, and after much diffraction and diffusion, are reflected in the lives of peasants. In this particular book we are not told about this distant reflection in peasant life. We are told about the interpretation of certain Vedic texts by Sankaracharya, a thinker of the eighth century, and we are instructed on such matters as the differences between the strands of thought called non-dualism, qualified non-dualism, and dualism.

Nevertheless, in other writings or, at least, in passages of other writings an occasional historian-humanist seems to be coming forward to meet the anthropologist who is at work in the village. A recent student of Chinese religion, impressed with the mixture of teachings that have made up that religion and by the great differences between the beliefs and practices of peasants and those of educated Chinese, states that "instead of dividing the religious life of the Chinese people into three compartments called Confucianism, Buddhism and Taoism, it is far more accurate to divide it into two levels, the level of the masses and the level of the enlightened."[14] Reading this, one asks, how then did the enlightened come to transform popular belief into their own kind of religion, and how was it that with the presence of educated teachers in China for many centuries the masses transformed these teachings into their kind of religion? One might become interested in the ways in which the high tradition is communicated to the common people and how it becomes a part of the little tradition.

Every great tradition has its teachers, and the humanistic scholar of that tradition is in a position to tell us something about who these teachers are and about how their teachings reach the common people. For India these matters have been interestingly described by V. Raghavan.[15] He tells us something of the customs and institutions by which the Vedic lore and the religious and ethical instruction of the philosopher and religious thinker were and are communicated, by intention and organized effort, to the masses. He tells us of compositions, notably the epics and the Purana, which were made expressly to broadcast Vedic lore to the people at large. The prefaces of these compositions "were recited to vast congregations of people gathered at sacrificial sessions ... by a class of reciters called Sutapauranikas." Hindu culture was, he says, carried to Cambodia and other lands by endowments made by rulers for the recital, in temples they built, of Hindu epics. With regard to south India Raghavan traces an unbroken tradition of deliberate provision, by ruler and teacher, for recitation in the vernacular languages of the ancient Hindu epics, especially the *Ramayana*. Professor Raghavan, historically minded and familiar with the Sanskrit classics, follows their course through many centuries and languages and through modifications of institutionalized instruction. The stories were not only recited, they were also expressed in devotional hymns sung by traveling singer-saints. So this Sanskritist, pursuing the great tradition downward, comes into the villages of present-day India. He is thinking of peasant India when he writes that "hardly a day passes without some sweet-voiced, gifted expounder sitting in a temple, *mutt*, public hall or house-front and expounding to hundreds and thousands the story of the Dharma that Rama upheld and the Adharma by which Ravana fell."[16]

This same interest on the part of humanistic scholars in the relations between the hierarchic and the lay cultures is shown in a work about the relations between Islamic doctrine and the local cultures that became Islamized. In the introductory chapter Professor G. von Grunebaum considers different ways in which the conflict, coexistence, and interaction of the Islamic high culture and the local cultures can be described. Adopting the terms that are used in this book, he writes: "This is to say that one of the two patterns is recognized as the more advanced; it is assumed to make authority; it is almost exclusively represented in the writings as well as the public actions of the elite; social prestige is dependent on its adoption. In the *dâr al-Islâm* the Islamic pattern is in general in the position of the great tradition. In contrast, the little tradition is the catchment of the popular undercurrent; its effectiveness is still felt by the intelligentsia, but 'officially' it will be denied or deprecated. Where the hypotheses of the great tradition are considered beliefs, the hypotheses of the little tradition will be considered superstitions. In fact, the social position of a person may depend on which of the two traditions he determines to live by."[17]

Von Grunebaum distinguishes between two kinds of adjustment between these two patterns or traditions. They may become accommodated to each other, as when the Islamic teachers recognize the popular tradition as the religion of the ignorant or tolerate local practices which might have been considered heretical. Saladin sent a Christian cross to Baghdad; it was first despised but in the end was treated with reverence. In Turkey and Syria Muslims were or are permitted to resort to the invocation of Christian saints. The expounders of hierarchic Islam, says von Grunebaum, may integrate the local belief or practice with orthodoxy by interpretations of doctrine that provide a sanction for it. "The Prophet himself set the precedent for this procedure by giving an Islamic meaning to the heathen pilgrimage rites which he welded into the Muslim *hajj* to Mecca. ..." This integration or incorporation of the local culture is abundantly illustrated by "the justification within the framework of orthodoxy of the cult of the saints."[18] In spite of the apparently uncompromising monotheism of Islam, the saint "is interpreted as the possessor of gnostic knowledge" and so accepted, or Koranic evidence is found to prove the existence of familiars of the Lord, therefore of saints. Here the Islamist comes to meet the anthropologist. Professor von Grunebaum, discussing the interaction between local saint and Islamic orthodoxy, sees from the top, so to speak, the same interaction that Westermarck,[19] studying local saints in Morocco, saw from the bottom.

The Islamist can study a great tradition from its first origins, and the first interrelations of hierarchic and lay culture are relatively close to his own day and power of observation. Islam, a doctrine thrown up from local culture, itself became a secondary civilization as it moved into Persia and India. The Sanskritist and the Sinologist are concerned with much more ancient and complex interactions of great traditions, slowly developing from primitive thought and practice, themselves dividing and undergoing much modification and restatement, while influencing and being influenced by the thoughts and actions of millions of little people. All these scholars tell the story of the relationships between the two strands of culture in civilization from the point of view of the elite, of those who uphold the great tradition. Raghavan follows Vedic lore downward into the villages. Von Grunebaum reads the writings of Islamic thinkers and teachers and reports their struggles with the local and lay cultures. Both reach the village and the peasant in the course of their studies, and now they will find arrived there the anthropologist—a fellow ill prepared to report his villagers as terminal points in the long history of a great doctrine. Yet the anthropologist cannot ignore these connections with philosophy and with refined schools of thought. He sees their traces and their professional representatives in the villages. He may wish he had stayed with autonomous cultures, alone and undisturbed, in a community that is a world to itself and in which he, the anthropologist, is the sole student. But in considering peasantry, he has taken on something else.

He has taken on some part of the responsibility for the study of a composite cultural structure comprised of little and great traditions which have interacted in the past and which are still interacting today. He shares the responsibility with the historian and the humanist. Both can conceive of the civilization which they study as a persisting and characteristic but always changing interaction between little and great traditions. So conceived, the civilization is a content of thought with its expressions in action and symbol. The civilization is compound in that it has parts or levels, each present in some of the people who carry on that civilization more than in others. These people live similar but notably different lives, and they live them apart, some in villages, some in cities or shrine-centers, temples, or monasteries. These parts or levels are something other than local (regional) cultures; they are something different from the subcultures characterizing the occupational groups concerned with secular specialties. They are different because the learning of the great tradition is an outgrowth of the little tradition and is now an exemplar for the people who carry the little tradition. Great and little traditions are dimensions of one another; those people who carry on the lower layers and those who maintain the high alike recognize the same order of "highness" and "lowness."

Thought of as basic values, or as world view, the two layers or dimensions will be seen as similar and yet notably different. Even one who knows as little of India as I do may suppose that the world view of the little traditions of India is on the whole polytheistic, magical, and unphilosophical, while the different strands of the great Vedic tradition choose different intellectual and ethical emphases: the Vedas tend to be polytheistic and poetical, the Upanishads abstract, monistic, and not very theistic, while the important Vaishnavaism and Shaivism are theistic and ethical. Corresponding contrasts appear, to mention just one other great tradition, "when we compare Taoism as a philosophy ... with Taoism as a popular organized religion. Thus in philosophical Taoism the emphasis is on the subordination of man to nature, whereas in religious Taoism the goal is in the acquisition of human immortality through magical means, in other words, the gaining by man of control over natural forces; likewise in philosophical Taoism any idea of divine causation is rigidly excluded, whereas in religious Taoism the universe is peopled by a vast host of anthropomorphic deities."[20]

As we proceed to understand civilizations thus composed, we shall need to improve the communication between humanist-historian and anthropologist. The former may come better to understand the relations of the reflective thought he studies to the total life of that civilization; the latter may be helped to describe his small community in so far as its ways of life affect and are affected by the teachings of the great traditions. The forms in which the two kinds of research enterprises are conceived and carried on differ notably, of course; but their relevance to each other can be clarified and cultivated. We need the textual studies of the historian and student of art and literature. The student of the hierarchic culture has for his subject matter a corpus of texts. These texts are not only verbal. The world view of Hindu thought is written in the architecture of its temples as well as in its philosophies.[21] The studies of the anthropologist are contextual:[22] they relate some element of the great tradition—sacred book, story-element, teacher, ceremony, or supernatural being—to the life of the ordinary people, in the context of daily life as the anthropologist sees it happen.

The textual and the contextual studies will easily be found to come into connection with one another where the content of the text has important place in the context of village life. The *Ramayana* is the ancient source widely influential in village India today. Derived from oral tales, it was fashioned into a Sanskrit epic by some poet—it is said, one Valmiki—and so became part of India's great tradition. From the ninth century to the sixteenth century it was translated into many of the Indian vernaculars and in these forms was taught and sung by those professionals of the cultural structure about whom Professor Raghavan has told us. In the sixteenth century Tulsi-Das made a Hindi version which became the script for many a village celebration. This writer, an exponent of high culture, made a kind of basic text. We are told that this version is perhaps better known among the common people of India than is the Bible among rural English people. But then, as time went on, the Hindi of the Tulsi-Das version became hard for the peasants to understand. They added to it accretions from their local popular usage. And now, in village India, this basic text requires interpretation to be intelligible to the villagers. This is how it is done in connection with the festival of Ram Lila. There are two kinds of participants in the dramatic representation of the stories of Ram and Sita and the struggle with Ravana. The pundit, on behalf of the greater tradition, steps on the stage and reads from the Hindi text of the sixteenth century—with later popular interpolations. It is necessary that this text be read, because it is holy. But it is hard to understand. So, while the pundit is yet reciting, the impersonator (who is an unlettered villager) "starts to enact the deed which the recitation mentions. The pundit pauses, and the actor raising his voice, paraphrases in a speech in clear modern prose the verse which the audience has just heard."[23] So are the levels of the tradition linked in the actual arrangements for ceremonial moral instruction in the villages. So might we study Bible stories in the sermons of a rustic Western community or the actual communication and modification of Confucian teaching in Chinese villages.

When the anthropologist studies an isolated primitive community, the context is that community and its local and immediate culture. When he comes to study a peasant community and its culture, the context is widened to include the elements of the great tradition that are or have been in interaction with what is local and immediate. If he is interested in the transformations that take place through this interaction (diachronic studies), he will investigate the communication of little and great traditions with each other and the changes that may have resulted or come to result in one or both because of the communication. If he regards the peasant village as a persisting system, as synchronic studies (perhaps limiting his view of the lapse of time to the three generations that are sometimes said to constitute the period within which the recurrent changes that sustain the system take place), he will include in the analysis the persisting and expectable communications from the great tradition to the village as these are necessary to maintain the culture of the peasant. How is this to be done?

In some published accounts of peasant communities the reader does learn something of the ways in which local religious belief and ritual are like or unlike the belief and ritual of the hierarchic religious culture with which the villagers are in communication through their priests, teachers, or experiences in travel.[24] But procedures for the reporting and analysis of these communications and their effects, either in sustaining the local culture or in contributing to the history of its modifications and its effects on the great tradition, are yet to be developed. I suggest that it may be in the course of their work in India that anthropologists will come to develop them. It is in India that the great (Sanskritic) tradition is in constant, various, and conspicuous interaction with the life of the local communities. It is there that the teachings of reflective and civilized minds appear plainly in the festivals, rituals, and in the ideals of the peasantry. It is in India that a man's ascribed status, in the form of caste, is closely associated with the claim of that caste to participation in the rituals and ideals of life as inculcated in Sanskritic teaching. Professor Srinivas has given us an account[25] of the way that certain village people, the Coorgs, who had ways of life somewhat apart from the Sanskritic tradition, have been taking on, in part quite consciously, elements of Hindu culture. The Coorgs have come to think of themselves as Kshatriyas, people of the warrior *varna*, and have come under the influence of Hinduism to the point that four of their number have become *sanyasis*, dedicated holy men observing the teachings of the Indian high tradition. The Coorgs have taken a high place in the general Indian hierarchy of status; they have Hinduized their claims to status. So far does the great tradition reach and so much does it yet do in India to change the cultures of depressed or marginal peoples.

In very recent years Western anthropologists have come in considerable numbers to study the Indian peasant villages as they lie within Hindu, Moslem, or modern Western civilization. One such recent study begins to provide conceptions and ways of work for analyzing the mutual effect of hierarchic Hinduism and village culture on each other. This is a paper by McKim Marriott.[26] The viewpoint is "diachronic"; the subject is conceived not only in terms of social relations but also "culturally"—as customs and institutions in course of modification. In the village he studied, which he calls Kishan Garhi, in Uttar Pradesh, the religion consists of elements of local culture and elements of the high Sanskrit tradition in close adjustment and integration. He finds "evidences of accretion and of transmutation in form without apparent replacement and without rationalization of the accumulated and transformed elements." Fifteen of nineteen festivals celebrated in Kishan Garhi are sanctioned in universal Sanskrit texts. But some of the local festivals have no place in Sanskrit teaching; those that do are but a small part of the entire corpus of festivals sanctioned by Sanskrit literature; villagers confuse or choose between various classical meanings for their festivals; and even the most Sanskritic of the local festivals have obviously taken on elements of ritual that arose, not out of the great tradition, but out of the local peasant life.

This kind of syncretization is familiar to students of paganism and Christianity or to students of Islam in its relations to local cults in North Africa. Marriott proposes that the two-way interaction between little and great traditions be studied as two complementary processes to which he gives names. For one thing, the little traditions of the folk exercise their influence on the authors of the Hindu great tradition who take up some element of belief or practice and, by incorporating it in their reflective statement of Hindu orthodoxy, universalize that element for all who thereafter come under the influence of their teaching. Marriott cannot quite prove[27] that the following was indeed an instance of universalization, but he suggests that the goddess Laksmi of Hindu orthodoxy is derived from such deities as he saw represented in his village daubed on walls or fashioned in images of dung: the natures and meanings of the high goddess and the local godlings are similar, and some villagers identify the latter with Laksmi. Also, Marriott reports an annual festival in which wives go to visit their brothers in the villages of their origins and in which these women, leaving their brothers to return home, express their attachment to them by placing barley shoots on the brothers' heads and ears, the brothers reciprocating with gifts of small coins. One of the Puranas, a classic source of Sanskritic instruction, fixes the form for a Brahmanical ritual according to which, on the same day as that on which is held the village rite referred to, each village priest goes to his patron and ties upon his wrist a charm of many-colored thread, the patron then giving money to the Brahman. Did the local rite give rise to the ceremony fixed in the Purana, or is it an application of what the Purana teaches? Marriott inclines to the former explanation and thinks of this interaction between the two dimensions or layers of the religion as illustrating universalization.

The opposite process, which Marriott calls "parochialization," is that by which some Sanskritic element is learned about and then reformed by the villagers to become a part of their local cult. For example: a divine sage of the Sanskritic tradition, associated by the Brahman elders with the planet Venus, is represented by erection of a stone in the village. Brides are now taken here to worship with their husbands. But then the origins of the stone are forgotten; it comes to be regarded as the abode of the ancestral spirits of the Brahmans who put it there. Again, the Sanskritic tradition, as expressed in the great Indian myths, gives sanction to a festival celebrated in nine successive nights in honor of great goddesses of the pantheon of India's great tradition. In the village of Kishan Garhi the people include in the beings to be honored during the festival of Nine Nights a being they call Naurtha: each morning and evening during the nine days women and children worship this Naurtha by bathing, singing, and making figurines of mud. Naurtha has no place in the great tradition. Marriott is able to show that she has come into existence in the village through simple linguistic corruption—a misunderstanding of the phrase "Nava Ratra" which means "Nine Nights." So by mere linguistic confusion in the communication between the little tradition and the great tradition, a minor goddess has been created.

Marriott was able to learn something about the interaction of great and little traditions in bringing about the translation or substitution of meanings and connections of rite and belief because he has read some of the sources of Hindu orthodoxy and because in the village he studied he found some people much more than others in communication with those sources. The village includes the educated and the ignorant, and the villager himself is well aware of the difference. A more educated villager calls himself a *sanātāni*, a follower of the orthodox and traditional way; a Brahman domestic priest distinguishes "doers and knowers"; the ordinary villager says that a certain ritual is Narayan, a deity inseminating the mortar in which the family husks grain, but an educated man of the same village says that it is a symbol of the creation of the world.[28]

Where there are such differences as between villagers, the connections the village has with the philosopher or theologian can be traced in part by the anthropologist in his community study. The analysis then moves outward and upward to meet such investigations of the downward movement of orthodoxy or philosophy as is studied by von Grunebaum for Islam and by Raghavan for Hinduism.

One is encouraged to imagine the kinds of studies of the interaction of the two aspects of tradition that will develop in anthropology. Still thinking of India, where the material is abundant and interesting, I remark that the interaction may be conceived in a more cultural or in a more societal way. Marriott's study represents the former. Milton Singer, writing from India, is impressed with the importance of what he calls "the cultural media"—song, dance, drama, festival, ceremony, recitations and discourse, prayers with offerings—in expressing Indian culture. He is struck by the ways in which these forms constantly merge with one another and suggests that Indians, and perhaps all peoples, conceive of their culture as encapsulated in specific cultural forms which can be exhibited in "cultural performances" to outsiders and to themselves.[29] One may perhaps analyze how elements of high tradition are communicated to the villager in these cultural forms, and how the elements are modified as they are taken into the local culture.

Or it may become possible and important to study particular "cultural institutions," those activities and personnel that exist for the purpose of communicating the great tradition. In India it should be possible, as Marriott suggests, to study a temple at its points of contact with pilgrims or one of those many regional shrines which house the images of those deities that are intermediate between great and little traditions, being local forms of the one and universalized forms of the other. Where a fairly limited community contains institutions of formal instruction, the social organization of tradition can be studied, I should imagine, in those institutions.

The Muslim school differs from the Hindu temple as a religion based on fidelity to an ultimate perfect revelation recorded in one book differs from a religion of polymorphous symbolic expression of levels of the same truth. From what I read,[30] the Maghreb of Morocco even today provide an instance of an ancient and little changed structure of Islamic sacred tradition. We are told by Professor Le Tourneau that there is practically no difference there between a work written in the sixteenth century and one written in the twentieth, newspapers are unknown, and the intellectual life is confined to a small elite who are concerned ever with the same problems of interpreting Muslim orthodoxy. The peasant in the village is connected with Muslim orthodoxy by Koranic teachers and minor administrative employees; such people are taught in mosque-schools in the minor cities; a few then attend the mosque to learn Muslim law or elements of Arabic grammar; and a very few go to Muslim universities in Fez or Tunis. Here the stable connections between village and city life with regard to the cultivated sacred tradition can be defined.

In India one might study one of the sub castes whose functions are to cultivate the history and genealogy of their caste, or one might study a caste composed of entertainers and singers who sing traditional stories from the *Ramayana* or the *Mahabharata* to their patrons.[31] Such castes are corporate groups relating great and little traditions to each other. It seems that in India the structure of tradition is very complex indeed and provided with a great variety of specialists, often caste-organized, for communicating the greater traditions to the lesser. Milton Singer says that in Madras he finds three major groups of specialists associated with the Sanskritic tradition: the priests supervising domestic and temple rites; reciters, singers, and dancers who convey the popular Puranic culture; and Sanskrit pundits and scholars who cultivate different branches of Sanskritic learning.

Looked at in this way, the interaction of great and little traditions can be regarded as a part of the social structure of the peasant community in its enlarged context. We are concerned with those persisting and important arrangements of roles and statuses, in part appearing in such corporate groups as castes in sects, that are concerned with the cultivation and inculcation of the great tradition. The concept is an extension or specialization of the concept of social structure as used by anthropologists in the study of societies that are more nearly self-contained than are peasant villages. We turn now to consider, for the compound peasant society, a certain kind of the persisting social relations, a certain part of the social structure. The relations between Muslim teacher and pupil, between Brahman priest and layman, between Chinese scholar and Chinese peasant—all such as these that are of importance in bringing about the communication of great tradition to the peasant or that, perhaps without anyone's intention, cause the peasant tradition to affect the doctrine of the learned—constitute the social structure of the culture, the structure of tradition. From this point of view a civilization is an organization of specialists, of kinds of role-occupiers in characteristic relations to one another and to lay people and performing characteristic functions concerned with the transmission of tradition.

We might, as does Professor Raymond Firth, reserve the phrase "social organization"[32] in connection with concrete activity at particular times and places. Social organization is the way that people put together elements of action so as to get done something they want done. Social structure is a persisting general character, a "pattern" of typical relationships; social organization is described when we account for the choices and resolutions of difficulties and conflicts that actually went on in one particular situation. Accordingly we might withdraw the title of this chapter from its wider use and reserve it for the way in which elements of action are put together in any particular case of transmission of tradition. Thus we shall be studying the social organization of tradition when we investigate the way in which the school day is arranged in the conservative Islamic school, or when we study the way in which the festival of Ram Lila is brought about in an Indian community, the peasants and the literate pundit co-operating to the end that the sacred stories are acted out to the accompaniment of readings from the sacred text of the higher tradition. If there are problems of adjustment between what the more learned man would like to see done and what the lay people of the village think proper or entertaining, these cases of social organization of tradition will be the more interesting. I remember lost opportunities to study the social organization of tradition in my own field work, especially one occasion when the Catholic parish priest and the local shaman of the Maya tradition took part, successively, in a ceremony of purification in a Guatemalan village. There were then many pushings and pullings, many matters of doubt, conflict, and compromise, which I failed to record. In that case there were, of course, two more esoteric traditions, in some degree of conflict with each other, and both requiring some adjustment to the expectations of the villagers.

So we come to develop forms of thought appropriate to the wider systems, the enlarged contexts, of our anthropological work. In studying a primitive society, in its characteristic self-containment, its societal and cultural autonomy, we hardly notice the social structure of tradition. It may be present there quite simply in a few shamans or priests, fellow-members of the small community, very similar to others within it. In a primitive and preliterate society we cannot know much of the history of its culture. The structure of tradition in early Zuñi is seen as a division of function within the tribal community and is seen as something now going on, not as a history. But a civilization has both great regional scope and great historic depth. It is a great whole, in space and in time, by virtue of the complexity of the organization which maintains and cultivates its traditions and communicates them from the great tradition to the many and varied small local societies within it. The anthropologist who studies one of these small societies finds it far from autonomous and comes to report and analyze it in its relations, societal and cultural, to state and to civilization.

Notes

1. "Acculturation: An Exploratory Formulation" (The Social Science Research Council Summer Seminar on Acculturation, 1953 [Members: H. G. Barnett, Leonard Broom, Bernard J. Siegel, Evon Z. Vogt, James B. Watson]), *American Anthropologist,* LVI, No. 6 (December, 1954), 974.
2. George M. Foster, "What Is Folk Culture?" *American Anthropologist,* LV, No. 1, Part I (April-June, 1953), 169.
3. *Ibid.,* p. 164. In quoting this passage I venture to substitute "peasant" for "folk" to make the terminology fit that chosen for these chapters. I think Foster's "folk societies" are much the same as those I here call "peasant societies."
4. Ibid.
5. Of course there may be several great traditions, as Islam and Sanskritic Hinduism are present in India, and there may be numerous subdivisions of a great tradition: I speak of "two" for simplicity.
6. *Akiga's Story,* trans. and annotated by Rupert East (London: Oxford University Press, 1930), p. 11.
7. Elsdon Best, *Maori Religion and Mythology* (Dominion Museum Bulletin No. 10 [Wellington, N.Z.: W. A. G. Skinner, Government Printer, 1924]), pp. 31-32. See also B. Malinowski, "Baloma: The Spirits of the Dead in the Trobriand Islands," in *Magic, Science and Religion* (Glencoe, Ill.: Free Press, 1948), pp. 125-227, 231 ff.
8. Melville Herskovits, *Dahomey: An Ancient West African Kingdom* (New York: J. J. Augustin, 1938), Vol. II, chap. xxvi.
9. Marcel Griaule, *Dieu d'Eau* (Paris: Les Editions du Chêne, 1948).
10. Pedro Armillas, "The Mesoamerican Experiment," in "The Ways of Civilizations," ed. Robert J. Braidwood, MS.
11. Julian H. Steward, "Evolution and Process," in *Anthropology Today: An Encyclopedic Inventory,* ed. A. L. Kroeber (Chicago: University of Chicago Press, 1953), p. 323; "Cultural Causality and Law: A Trial Formulation of the Development of Early Civilizations," *American Anthropologist,* LI, No. 1 (January-March, 1949), 1-27.
12. *Studies in Chinese Thought,* ed. Arthur F. Wright. "Comparative Studies in Cultures and Civilizations," ed. Robert Redfield and Milton Singer (Chicago: University of Chicago Press, 1953).
13. Swami Nikhilananda, *The Upanishads: A New Translation* (New York: Harper & Bros., 1949).
14. Wing-tsit Chan, *Religious Trends in Modern China* (New York: Columbia University Press, 1953), pp. 141 ff. The distinction between the lay and hierarchic levels of Chinese religion and philosophy is made by Wolfram Eberhard, in a review article in the *Archiv für Religionswissenschaft,* XXXIII, No. 3 (1936), 304-44. For religions of the Middle East it is recognized by Raphael Patai, "Religion in Middle Eastern, Far Eastern, and Western Culture," *Southwestern Journal of Anthropology,* X, No. 3 (Autumn, 1954), 239-41.
15. V. Raghavan, "Adult Education in Ancient India," *Memoirs of the Madras Library Association* (1944), pp. 57-65; "Methods of Popular Religious Instruction, South India," MS; "Variety and Integration in the Pattern of Indian Culture," MS.
16. Raghavan, "Methods of Popular Religious instruction, South India," MS.

226   Social Anthropology

17. G. von Grunebaum, "The Problem: Unity in Diversity," in *Unity and Variety in Muslim Civilization,* ed. G. von Grunebaum (Chicago: University of Chicago Press, 1955), p. 28.
18. Ibid., pp. 28-29.
19. Edward Westermarck, *Ritual and Belief in Morocco* (London: Macmillan & Co., Ltd., 1926).
20. Derk Bodde, "Harmony and Conflict in Chinese Philosophy," in *Studies in Chinese Thought,* ed. Arthur F. Wright (Chicago: University of Chicago Press, 1953), p. 79, n. 46.
21. Stella Kramrisch, *The Art of India through the Ages* (London: Phaidon Press, Ltd., 1954).
22. For this way of contrasting the two kinds of studies, I am indebted to Milton Singer.
23. Norvin Hein, "The Ram Lila," *The Illustrated Weekly of India,* October 22, 1950, pp. 18-19 (provided by McKim Marriott).
24. Oscar Lewis, *Life in a Mexican Village: Tepoztlán Restudied* (Urbana: University of Illinois Press, 1951), pp. 273 ff.; John Gulick, *Social Structure and Culture Change in a Lebanese Village* ("Viking Fund Publications in Anthropology," No. 21 [New York: Wenner-Gren Foundation for Anthropological Research, Inc., 1955]), pp. 92 ff.
25. M. N. Srinivas, *Religion and Society among the Coorgs of South India* (Oxford: Clarendon Press, 1952). See also Bernard S. Cohn, "The Changing Status of a Depressed Caste," in *Village India,* ed. McKim Marriott ("Comparative Studies in Cultures and Civilizations," ed. Robert Redfield and Milton Singer [Chicago: University of Chicago Press, 1955]).
26. McKim Marriott, "Little Communities in an Indigenous Civilization," in *Village India,* pp. 171-222.
27. Mr. Marriott kindly tells me something of the strong evidence for the conclusion that Laksmi has entered the great tradition relatively late and from the folk cultures of India. He quotes Rhys Davids, Renou, and Filliozat to this effect. It appears that this deity was absent from early Vedic literature, that early statues to her were set in places reserved for popular deities, and that the Buddhist canon castigates Brahmans for performing nonsensical, non- Vedic rituals such as those to Siri Devi (Laksmi), etc.
28. Marriott tells me that in "Kishan Garhi" the more learned villager takes, in short, quite distinguishable positions toward great and little traditions. The latter, which he sees manifest in the doings of the uneducated villagers, is a matter of practice, of ignorance or fragmentary knowledge; it is confusion or vagueness and is expressed in concrete physical or biological images. The great tradition, which he thinks of himself as representing in larger degree, is theory or pure knowledge, full and satisfying; it is order and precision and finds for its expression abstractions or symbolic representations.
29. Personal communication.
30. Roger Le Tourneau, "The Muslim Town: Religion and Culture," MS.
31. Shamrao Hivale, *The Pardhans of the Upper Narbada Valley* (London: Oxford University Press, 1946).
32. Raymond Firth, *Elements of Social Organization* (London: Watts & Co. 1951), chap. ii, pp. 35 ff.

18

The Cultural Role of Cities

In the early 1950s, the University of Chicago emerged as one of the leading centers of modernization studies. One of the key leaders at Chicago was economic historian Bert Hoselitz, who published an influential journal, Economic Development and Cultural Change. *Hoselitz periodically held conferences to bring together government policy-makers and social scientists to discuss various aspects of development. In 1953, he organized a conference to explore the role of cities in economic development and cultural change. He proposed that the conference evaluate this influence from five different perspectives—cultural, demographic, economic, historical, and sociological—and he solicited leadoff papers from prominent scholars for each session. Hoselitz had collaborated closely with Redfield and Milton Singer in a variety of interdisciplinary ventures at the University of Chicago during the late 1940s to early 1950s, and he requested them to write the paper on the cultural influence of cities on development. Redfield and Singer wrote "The Cultural Role of Cities" in response to Hoselitz's request and published it subsequently in* Economic Development and Cultural Change. *In this article, Redfield and Singer advanced a unique taxonomy of cities as loci of change and influence and elaborated, in particular, upon the interplay of great and little traditions within cities. This article came to exercise an important influence among development theorists and, especially, among anthropologists interested in the new frontier of urban anthropology.*

This paper has as its purpose to set forth a framework of ideas that may prove useful in research on the part played by cities in the development, decline, or transformation of culture. "Culture" is used as in anthropology. The paper contains no report of research done. It offers a scheme of constructs; it does not describe observed conditions or processes; references to particular cities or civilizations are illustrative and tentative.

Time Perspectives

The cultural role of cities may be considered from at least three different time perspectives. In the long-run perspective of human history as a single career,[1] the first appearance of cities marks a revolutionary change: the beginnings of civilization. Within this perspective cities remain the symbols and carriers of civilization wherever they appear. In

---

Co-written with Milton Singer. First published in *Economic Development and Cultural Change* 3 (October 1954): 53-73.

fact the story of civilization may then be told as the story of cities from those of the ancient Near East through those of ancient Greece and Rome, medieval and modern Europe; and from Europe overseas to North and South America, Australia, the Far East, and back again to the modern Near East. In the short-run perspective we may study the cultural role of particular cities in relation to their local hinterlands of towns and villages.[2] The time span here is the several-year period of the field research or, at most, the life span of the particular cities that are studied. Between the long- and short-run perspectives, there is a middle-run perspective delimited by the life history of the different civilizations within which cities have developed.[3] This is the perspective adopted when we consider the cultural bearings of urbanization within Mexican civilization[4] or Chinese civilization or Indian civilization or Western civilization. It is a perspective usually of several thousand years and embraces within its orbit not just a particular city and its hinterland, but the whole pattern and sequence of urban development characteristic of a particular civilization and its cultural epochs.

While these perspectives are clearly interrelated, research and analysis may concentrate primarily on one of them. Empirical ethnographic, sociological, and geographical research on cities begins in the nature of the case with the short-run perspective, but the significance of such research increases as it becomes linked with ideas and hypotheses drawn from the other perspectives. One begins, say, with an empirical study of the origins, morphology, functions, and influence of an Asiatic city.[5] Then one may go on to look at this city as a link in the interaction of two distinct civilizations and see the problem of urbanization in Asia generally as a problem in Westernization,[6] or the problem of Spanish-Indian acculturation of Mexico after the Conquest as a problem of de-urbanization and re-urbanization.[7] Finally, the canvas may be further enlarged to show both Western and Eastern cities as variants of a single and continuing cultural and historical process.[8] In this paper we propose to concentrate on the middle-run perspective, i.e., we shall analyze the role cities play in the formation, maintenance, spread, decline, and transformation of civilizations. We think that links with the long- and short-run perspectives will also emerge in the course of the analysis.

In the many useful studies of cities by urban geographers, sociologists, and ecologists, we find frequent reference to "cultural functions" and "cultural centers."[9] Under these rubrics they generally include the religious, educational, artistic centers and activities, and distinguish them from administrative, military, economic centers and functions.

This usage of "cultural" is too narrow for the purpose of a comparative analysis of the role cities play in the transformations of the more or less integrated traditional life of a community. Economic and political centers and activities may obviously play as great a role in these processes as the narrowly "cultural" ones. Moreover, these different kinds of centers and activities are variously combined and separated and it is these varying patterns that are significant. In ancient civilizations the urban centers were usually political-religious or political-intellectual; in the modern world they are economic.[10] The mosque, the temple, the cathedral, the royal palace, the fortress, are the symbolic "centers" of the pre-industrial cities. The "central business district" has become symbolic of the modern urban center. In fact a cross-cultural history of cities might be written from the changing meanings of the words for city. "Civitas" in the Roman Empire meant an administrative or ecclesiastical district. Later, "city" was applied to the ecclesiastical center of a town-usually the cathedral. This usage still survives in names like "Ile de la Cite" for one of the first centers of Paris. With the development of the "free cities," "city" came to mean the independent commercial towns with their own laws.[11] Today, "the city" of London is a financial center, and when Americans speak of "going to town" or "going downtown" they mean they are going to the "central business district." They usually think of any large city as a business and manufacturing center, whereas a Frenchman is more likely to regard his cities—certainly Paris—as "cultural centers."[12]

This symbolism is not of course a completely accurate designation of what goes on in the city for which it stands. The ecclesiastical centers were also in many cases centers of trade and of craftsmen, and the modern "central business district" is very apt to contain libraries, schools, art museums, government offices, and churches, in addition to merchandising establishments and business offices. But allowing for this factual distortion, this symbolism does help us to separate two quite distinct cultural roles of cities, and provides a basis for classifying cities that is relevant to their cultural role. As a "central business district," the city is obviously a market place, a place to buy and sell, "to do business"—to truck, barter, and exchange with people who may be complete strangers and of different races, religions, and creeds. The city here functions to work out largely impersonal relations among diverse cultural groups. As a religious or intellectual center, on the other hand, the city is a beacon for the faithful, a center for the learning, authority, and perhaps doctrine that transforms the implicit "little traditions" of the local non-urban cultures into an explicit and systematic "great tradition."

The varying cultural roles of cities, so separated and grouped into two contrasting kinds of roles with reference to the local traditions of the non-urban peoples, point to a distinction to which we shall soon return and to which we shall then give names.

Types of Cities

In the studies of economic historians (Pirenne, Dopsch) and in the studies of the currently significant factors for economic development (Hoselitz),[13] the functions of cities are considered as they effect change; but the change chiefly in view is economic change. Our attention now turns to the roles of cities in effecting change in the content and integration of ideas, interests, and ideals.

The distinction Hoselitz takes from Pirenne between political-intellectual urban centers, on the one hand, and economic centers, on the other, points in the direction of the distinction necessary to us in taking up the new topic. But the distinction we need does not fully emerge until we refine the classification by (1) separating the political function from the intellectual and (2) giving new content to the term "intellectual." Delhi, Quito, and Peking are to be contrasted, as Hoselitz says, with Bombay, Guayaquil, and Shanghai because the former three cities are "political-intellectual centers" and the latter three are "economic centers." (The contrast of Rio to Sao Paulo is less clear.) Let us now add that there are cities with political functions and without significant intellectual functions: New Delhi (if it be fair to separate it from old Delhi), Washington, D.C., and Canberra (the new university there may require a qualification). Further, the intellectual functions of Delhi, Quito and Peking (and Kyoto, Lhasa, Cuzco, Mecca, and medieval Liége and Uaxactun) are to develop, carry forward, elaborate a long-established cultural tradition local to the community in which those cities stand. These are the cities of the literati: clerics, astronomers, theologians, Imams, and priests. New Delhi and Washington, D.C. do not have, significantly, literati; in spite of its schools and universities Washington is not a city of great intellectual leadership; these are cities without major intellectual functions. In respect to this lack, New Delhi and Washington, D.C., belong with cities with predominantly economic functions. On the other hand, not a few old cities with economic functions have also the functions associated with the literati (Florence, medieval Timbuktu, Thebes). We have taken into consideration, in this expanded grouping, both cities of the modern era and cities of the time before the development of a world economy. It may be useful now to separate the two historic periods, retaining the distinction between cities of the literati, cities of entrepreneurs, and cities of the bureaucracy. The following grouping results:

Before the Universal Oikoumenê (pre-industrial revolution, pre-Western expansion)

1. Administrative-cultural cities
   (cities of the literati and the indigenous bureaucracy)
   Peking
   Lhasa
   Uaxactun
   Kyoto
   Liége
   Allahabad (?)

2. Cities of native commerce
   (cities of the entrepreneur)
   Bruges
   Marseilles
   Lübeck
   Market towns of native West Africa
   Early Canton

   After the Universal Oikoumenê (post-industrial revolution, and post-Western expansion)

3. Metropolis-cities of the world-wide managerial and entrepreneurial class (Park's "cities of the main street of the world")
   London
   New York
   Osaka
   Yokohama
   Shanghai
   Singapore
   Bombay
   Lesser cities and towns, also carrying on the world's business, may be added here.

4. Cities of modern administration
   (cities of the new bureaucracies)
   Washington, D.C.
   New Delhi
   Canberra
   A thousand administrative towns, county seats, seats of British and French African colonial administration, etc.

What is the relationship of such a grouping to our topic: the role of cities in processes of cultural change?

The role of cities of Group 1 has already been stated. It is to carry forward, develop, elaborate a long-established local culture or civilization. These are cities that convert the folk culture into its civilized dimension.

But the cities of groups 2, 3, and 4 do not have, or do not have conspicuously and as their central effect, this role in the cultural process. They affect the cultural process in other ways. How? They are cities in which one or both of the following things are true: (1) the prevailing relationships of people and the prevailing common understandings have to do with the technical not the moral order,[14] with administrative regulation business and technical convenience; (2) these cities are populated by people of diverse cultural origins removed from the indigenous seats of their cultures.

They are cities in which new states of mind, following from these characteristics, are developed and become prominent. The new states of mind are indifferent to or inconsistent with, or supersede or overcome states of mind associated with local cultures and ancient civilizations The intellectuals of these three groups of cities, if any, are intelligentsia rather than literati.[15] The distinction that is then basic to consideration of the cultural role of cities is the distinction between the *carrying forward into systematic and reflective dimensions an old culture* and the *creating of original modes of thought that have authority beyond or in conflict with old cultures and civilizations*. We might speak of the orthogenetic cultural role of cities as contrasted with the heterogenetic cultural role.

In both these roles the city is a place in which cultural change takes place. The roles differ as to the character of the change. In so far as the city has an orthogenetic role, it is not to maintain culture as it was; the orthogenetic city is not static; it is the place where religious, philosophical and literary specialists reflect, synthesize, and create out of the traditional material new arrangements and developments that are felt by the people to be outgrowths of the old. What is changed is a further statement of what was there before. In so far as the city has a heterogenetic role, it is a place of differing traditions, a center of heresy, heterodoxy, and dissent, of interruption and destruction of ancient tradition of rootlessness and anomy. Cities are both these things, and the same events may appear to particular people or groups to be representative of heterogenesis. The predominating trend may be in one of the two directions, and so allow us to characterize the city, or that phase of the history of the city, as the one or the other. The lists just given suggest that the differences in the degree to which in the city orthogenesis or heterogenesis prevails are in cases strongly marked.

The presence of the market is not of itself a fact of heterogenetic change. Regulated by tradition, maintained by such customs and routines as develop over long periods of time, the market may flourish without heterogenetic change. In the medieval Muslim town we see an orthogenetic city; the market and the keeper of the market submitted economic activities to explicit cultural and religious definition of the norms. In Western Guatemala the people who come to market hardly communicate except with regard to buying and selling and the market has little heterogenetic role. On the other hand the market in many instances provides occasion when men of diverse traditions may come to communicate and to differ; and also in the market occurs that exchange on the basis of universal standards of utility which is neutral to particular moral orders and in some sense hostile to all of them. The cities of Group 2, therefore, are cities unfavorable to orthogenetic change but not necessarily productive of heterogenetic change.

The City and the Folk Society[16]

The folk society may be conceived as that imagined combination of societal elements which would characterize a long-established, homogeneous, isolated, and non-literate integral (self-contained) community; the folk culture is that society seen as a system of common understandings. Such a society can be approximately realized in a tribal band or village; it cannot be approximately realized in a city. What are characteristics of the city that may be conceived as a contrast to those of the folk society?

The city may be imagined as that community in which orthogenetic and heterogenetic transformations of the folk society have most fully occurred. The former has brought about the Great Tradition and its special intellectual class, administrative officers and rules closely derived from the moral and religious life of the local culture, and advanced economic institutions, also obedient to these local cultural controls. The heterogenetic transformations have accomplished the freeing of the intellectual, aesthetic, economic, and political life from the local moral norms, and have developed on the one hand an individuated expediential motivation and on the other a revolutionary, nativistic, humanistic, or ecumenical viewpoint, now directed toward reform, progress, and designed change.

As these two aspects of the effects of the city on culture may be in part incongruent with each other, and as in fact we know them to occur in different degrees and arrangements in particular cities, we may now review the classification of cities offered above so as to recognize at least two types of cities conceived from this point of view:

A. *The city of orthogenetic transformation; the city of the moral order;* the city of the culture carried forward. In the early civilizations the first cities were of this kind and usually combined this developmental cultural function with political power and administrative control. But it is to be emphasized that this combination occurred because the local moral and religious norms prevailed and found intellectual development in the literati and exercise of control of the community in the ruler and the laws. Some of these early cities combined these two "functions" with commerce and economic production; others had little of these. It is as cities of predominating orthogenetic civilization that we are to view Peking, Lhasa, Uaxactun, fourteenth-century Liége.

B. *The city of heterogenetic transformation, the city of the technical order*; the city where local cultures are disintegrated and new integrations of mind and society are developed of the kind described above ("The heterogenetic role of cities"). In cities of this kind, men are concerned with the market, with "rational" organization of production of goods, with expediential relations between buyer and seller, ruler and ruled, and native and foreigner. In this kind of city the predominant social types are businessmen, administrators alien to those they administer, and rebels, reformers, planners and plotters of many varieties. It is in cities of this kind that priority comes to be given to economic growth and the expansion of power among the goods of life. The modern metropolis exhibits very much of this aspect of the city; the town built in the tropics by the United Fruit Company and the city built around the Russian uranium mine must have much that represents it; the towns of the colonial administration in Africa must show many of its features. Indeed, in one way or another, all the cities of groups 2, 3, and 4 (*supra*) are cities of the technical order, and are cities favorable to heterogenetic transformation of the moral order.[17]

This type of city may be subdivided into the administrative city, city of the bureaucracy (Washington, D.C., Canberra), and the city of the entrepreneur (Hamburg, Shanghai). Of course many cities exhibit both characteristics.

"In every tribal settlement there is civilization; in every city is the folk society." We may look at any city and see within it the folk society in so far as ethnic communities that make it up preserve folklike characteristics, and we may see in a town in ancient Mesopotamia or in aboriginal West Africa a half-way station between folk society and orthogenetic civilization. We may also see in every city its double urban characteristics: we may identify the institutions and mental habits there prevailing with the one or the other of the two lines of transformation of folk life which the city brings about. The heterogenetic transformations have grown with the course of history, and the developments of peoples and especially those incident to the expansion of the West, have increased and accelerated this aspect of urbanization. The later cities are predominantly cities of the technical order. We see almost side by side persisting cities of the moral order and those of the technical order: Peking and Shanghai, Cuxco and Guayaquil, a native town in Nigeria and an administrative post and railway center hard by.

The ancient city, predominantly orthogenetic, was not (as remarked by W. Eberhard) in particular cases the simple outgrowth of a single precivilized culture, but was rather (as in the case of Loyang) a city in which conquered and conqueror lived together, the conqueror extending his tradition over the conquered, or accepting the latter's culture. What makes the orthogenetic aspect of a city is the integration and uniform interpretation of preceding culture, whether its origins be one or several. Salt Lake City and early Philadelphia, cities with much orthogenetic character, were established by purposive acts of founders. Salt Lake City created its own hinterland on the frontier (as pointed out by C. Harris). Other variations on the simple pattern of origin and development of a city from an established folk people can no doubt be adduced.

Transformation of Folk Societies: Primary Urbanization and Secondary Urbanization

The preceding account of different types of cities is perhaps satisfactory as a preliminary, but their cultural roles in the civilizations which they represent cannot be fully understood except in relation to the entire pattern of urbanization within that civilization, i.e., the number, size, composition, distribution, duration, sequence, morphology, function, rates of growth and decline, and the relation to the countryside and to each other of the cities within a civilization. Such information is rare for any civilization. In the present state of our knowledge it may be useful to guide further inquiry by assuming two hypothetical patterns of urbanization: primary and secondary.[18] In the primary phase a precivilized folk society is transformed by urbanization into a peasant society and correlated urban center. It is primary in the sense that the peoples making up the precivilized folk more or less share a common culture which remains the matrix too for the peasant and urban cultures which develop from it in the course of urbanization. Such a development, occurring slowly in communities not radically disturbed, tends to produce a "sacred culture" which is gradually transmuted by the "literati" of the cities into a "great tradition." Primary urbanization thus takes place almost entirely within the framework of a core culture that develops as the local cultures become urbanized and transformed into an indigenous civilization. This core culture dominates the civilization despite occasional intrusions of foreign peoples and cultures. When the encounter with other peoples and civilizations is too rapid and intense, an indigenous civilization may be destroyed by de-urbanization or be variously mixed with other civilizations.[19]

This leads to the secondary pattern of urbanization: the case in which a folk society, precivilized, peasant, or partly urbanized, is further urbanized by contact with peoples of widely different cultures from that of its own members. This comes about through expansion of a local culture, now partly urbanized, to regions inhabited by peoples of different cultures, or by the invasion of a culture-civilization by alien colonists or conquerors. This secondary pattern produces not only a new form of urban life in some part in conflict with local folk cultures but also new social types in both city and country. In the city appear "marginal" and "cosmopolitan" men and an "intelligentsia"; in the country various types of marginal folk: enclaved-, minority-, imperialized-, transplanted-, remade-, quasi-folk, etc., depending on the kind of relation to the urban center.

This discussion takes up a story of the contact of peoples at the appearance of cities. But here, parenthetically, it is necessary to note that even before the appearance of cities the relations between small and primitive communities may be seen as on the one hand characterized by common culture and on the other by mutual usefulness with awareness of cultural difference. The "primary phase of urbanization" is a continuation of the extension of common culture from a small primitive settlement to a town and its hinterland, as no doubt could be shown for parts of West Africa. The "secondary phase of urbanization" is begun, before cities, in the institutions of travel and trade among local communities with different cultures. In Western Guatemala today simple Indian villagers live also in a wider trade-community of pluralistic cultures;[20] we do not know to what extent either the pre-Columbian semi-urban centers or the cities of the Spanish-modern conquerors and rulers have shaped this social system; it may be that these people were already on the way to secondary urbanization before any native religious and political center rose to prominence.

While we do not know universal sequences within primary or secondary urbanization, it is likely that the degree to which any civilization is characterized by patterns of primary or secondary urbanization depends on the rate of technical development and the scope and intensity of contact with other cultures. If technical development is slow and the civilization is relatively isolated, we may expect to find a pattern of primary urbanization prevailing. If, on the other hand, technical development is rapid and contacts multiple and intense, secondary urbanization will prevail.

It may be that in the history of every civilization there is, of necessity, secondary urbanization. In modern Western civilization conditions are such as to make secondary urbanization the rule. But even in older civilizations it is not easy to find clear-cut examples of primary urbanization—because of multiple interactions, violent fluctuations in economic and military fortunes, conflicts and competition among cities and dynasties, and the raids of nomads. The Maya before the Spanish Conquest are perhaps a good example of primary urbanization.[21] The cases of the Roman, Greek, Hindu, Egyptian, and Mesopotamian civilizations, although characterized by distinctive indigenous civilizations, are nevertheless complex because little is known about the degree of cultural homogeneity of the peoples who formed the core cultures and because as these civilizations became imperial they sought to assimilate more and more diverse peoples. Alternatively the irritant "seed" of a city may have been sown in some of them by the conquering raid of an outside empire, the desire to copy another empire in having a capital, or simple theft from another people—with the *subsequent* development around this seed of the "pearl" of a relatively indigenous, primary urban growth, sending out its own imperial secondary strands in due time. Thus while Rome, Athens, Chang-An and Loyang in early China and Peking in later, Pataliputra and Benares, Memphis and Thebes, Nippur and Ur may have been for a time at least symbolic vehicles for loyalty to the respective empires and indigenous civilizations, it was not these relatively "orthogenetic" cities but the mixed cities on the periphery of an empire—the "colonial cities"—which carried the core culture to other peoples. And in such cities, usually quite mixed in character, the imperial Great Tradition was not only bound to be very dilute but would also have to meet the challenge of conflicting local traditions. At the imperial peripheries, primary urbanization turns into secondary urbanization.[22]

Similar trends can be perceived in modern times: Russian cities in southern Europe and Asia appear to be very mixed;[23] non-Arabic Muslim cities have developed in Africa and South Asia; and the colonial cities of the European powers admit native employees daily at the doors of their skyscraper banks. Possibly the nuclear cultures are homogeneous and create indigenous civilizations but as they expand into new areas far afield from the home cultures they have no choice but to build "heterogenetic" cities.

Modern "colonial" cities (e.g., Jakarta, Manila, Saigon, Bangkok, Singapore, Calcutta) raise the interesting question whether they can reverse from the "heterogenetic" to the "orthogenetic" role. For the last one hundred or more years they have developed as the outposts of imperial civilizations, but, as the countries in which they are located achieve political independence, will the cities change their cultural roles and contribute more to the formation of a civilization indigenous to these areas? Many obstacles lie in the path of such a course. These cities have large, culturally diverse populations, not necessarily European—for example, the Chinese in Southeast Asia, Muslims and Hindu refugees from faraway provinces in India; they often have segregated ethnic quarters, and their established administrative, military, and economic functions are not easily changed. Many new problems have been created by a sudden influx of postwar refugee populations, and the cities' changing positions in national and global political and economic systems. While many of these colonial cities have been centers of nationalism and of movements for revival of the local cultures, they are not likely to live down their "heterogenetic" past.[24]

The Cultural Consequences of Primary and Secondary Urbanization

The discussion of primary and secondary urbanization above has been a bare outline. It may be filled in by reference to some postulated consequences of each type of process. The most important cultural consequence of primary urbanization is the transformation of the Little Tradition into a Great Tradition. Embodied in "sacred books" or "classics," sanctified by a cult, expressed in monuments, sculpture, painting, and architecture, served by the other arts and sciences, the Great Tradition becomes the core culture of an indigenous civilization and a source, consciously examined, for defining its moral, legal, aesthetic, and other cultural norms. A Great Tradition describes a way of life and as such is a vehicle and standard for those who share it to identify with one another as members of a common civilization. In terms of social structure, a significant event is the appearance of literati, those who represent the Great Tradition. The new forms of thought that now appear and extend themselves include reflective and systematic thought; the definition of fixed idea-systems (theologies, legal codes); the development of esoteric or otherwise generally inaccessible intellectual products carried forward, now in part separate from the tradition of the folk; and the creation of intellectual and aesthetic forms that are both traditional and original (cities of the Italian Renaissance; development of "rococo" Maya sculpture in the later cities).

In government and administration the orthogenesis of urban civilization is represented by chiefs, rulers, and laws that express and are closely controlled by the norms of the local culture. The chief of the Crow Indians, in a precivilized society, and the early kings of Egypt were of this type. The Chinese emperor was in part orthogenetically controlled by the Confucian teaching and ethic; in some part he represented a heterogenetic development. The Roman proconsul and the Indian Service of the United States, especially in certain phases, were more heterogenetic political developments.

Economic institutions of local cultures and civilizations may be seen to be orthogenetic in so far as the allocation of resources to production and distribution for consumption are determined by the traditional system of status and by the traditional specific local moral norms. The chief's yam house in the Trobriands is an accumulation of capital determined by these cultural factors. In old China the distribution of earning and "squeeze" were distributed according to familial obligations: these are orthogenetic economic institutions and practices. The market, freed from controls of tradition, status, and moral rule, becomes the world-wide heterogenetic economic institution.

In short, the trend of primary urbanization is to co-ordinate political, economic, educational, intellectual, and aesthetic activity to the norms provided by the Great Traditions.

The general consequence of secondary urbanization is the weakening or supersession of the local and traditional cultures by states of mind that are incongruent with those local cultures. Among these are to be recognized:

1. The rise of a consensus appropriate to the technical order: i.e., based on self-interest and pecuniary calculation or on recognition of obedience to common impersonal controls, characteristically supported by sanctions of force. (This in contrast to a consensus based on common religious and non-expediential moral norms.) There is also an autonomous development of norms and standards for the arts, crafts, and sciences.

2. The appearance of new sentiments of common cause attached to groups drawn from culturally heterogeneous backgrounds. In the city,

proletariats are formed and class or ethnic consciousness is developed, and also new professional and territorial groups. The city is the place where ecumenical religious reform is preached (though it is not originated there). It is the place where nationalism flourishes. On the side of social structure the city is the place where new and larger groups are formed that are bound by few and powerful common interests and sentiments in place of the complexly interrelated roles and statuses that characterize the groups of local, long-established culture. Among social types that appear in this aspect of the cultural process in the city are the reformer, the agitator, the nativistic or nationalistic leader, the tyrant and his assassin, the missionary and the imported school teacher.

3. The instability of viewpoint as to the future, and emphasis on prospective rather than retrospective view of man in the universe. In cities of predominantly orthogenetic influence, people look to a future that will repeat the past (either by continuing it or by bringing it around again to its place in the cycle). In cities of predominantly heterogenetic cultural influence there is a disposition to see the future as different from the past. It is this aspect of the city that gives rise to reform movements, forward-looking myths, and planning, revolutionary or melioristic. The forward-looking may be optimistic and radically reformistic; it may be pessimistic, escapist, defeatist, or apocalyptic. In the city there are Utopias and counter-Utopias. In so far as these new states of mind are secular, worldly, they stimulate new political and social aspiration and give rise to policy.

Consequences for World View, Ethos, and Typical Personality

The difference in the general cultural consequences of primary and secondary urbanization patterns may be summarily characterized by saying that in primary urbanization, all phases of the technical order (material technology, economy, government, arts, crafts, and sciences) are referred, in theory at least, to the standards and purposes of a moral order delineated in the Great Tradition, whereas in secondary urbanization different phases of the technical order are freed from this reference and undergo accelerated autonomous developments. With respect to this development, the moral order, or rather orders, for there are now many competing ones, appear to lag.[25]

There is another way of describing these differences: in terms of the consequences of the two kinds of urbanization for changes in world view ethos, and typical personality.[26] To describe the consequences in these terms is to describe them in their bearings and meanings for the majority of individual selves constituting the society undergoing urbanization. We now ask, How do primary and secondary urbanization affect mental outlook, values and attitudes, and personality traits? These are in part psychological questions, for they direct our attention to the psychological aspects of broad cultural processes.

There are many accounts of the psychological consequences of urbanization. These have described the urban outlook, ethos, and personality as depersonalized, individualized, emotionally shallow and atomized, unstable, secularized, blasé, rationalistic, cosmopolitan, highly differentiated, self-critical, time-coordinated, subject to sudden shifts in mood and fashion, "other-directed," etc.[27] The consensus in these descriptions and their general acceptance by social scientists seem great enough to indicate that there probably is a general psychological consequence or urbanization, although it cannot be precisely described and proven. We should, however, like to suggest that the "urban way of life" that is described in the characterizations to which we refer is primarily a consequence of secondary urbanization and of that in a particular critical stage when personal and cultural disorganization is greatest. To see these consequences in perspective, it is necessary to relate them on the one hand to the consequences of primary urbanization and on the other to those situations of secondary urbanization that produce new forms of personal and cultural integration. Most of all it is necessary to trace the continuities as well as the discontinuities in outlook, values, and personality, as we trace the transformation of folk societies into their civilized dimension. The "peasant" is a type that represents an adjustment between the values of the precivilized tribe and those of the urbanite. The "literati" who fashion a Great Tradition do not repudiate the values and outlook of their rural hinterland but systematize and elaborate them under technical specialization. The cosmopolitan "intelligentsia" and "sophists" of the metropolitan centers have a prototype in the "heretic" of the indigenous civilization. And even the most sophisticated urban centers are not without spiritualists, astrologers, and other practitioners with links to a folklike past.[28]

The connections between the folk culture, the Great Tradition, and the sophisticated culture of the heterogenetic urban centers can be traced not only in the continuities of the historical sequence of a particular group of local cultures becoming urbanized and de-urbanized, but they also can be traced in the development of two distinct forms of cultural consciousness which appear in these transformations.

Cultural Integration between City and Country

From what has been said about primary and secondary urbanization it follows that city and country are more closely integrated, culturally, in the primary phases of urbanization than in the secondary phase. Where the city has grown out of a local culture, the country people see its ways as in some important part a form of their own, and they feel friendlier toward the city than do country people ruled by a proconsul from afar. The stereotype of "the wicked city" will be stronger in the hinterlands of the heterogenetic cities than in those of the orthogenetic cities. Many of these are sacred centers of faith, learning, justice, and law.

Nevertheless, even in primary urbanization a cultural gap tends to grow between city and country. The very formation of the Great Tradition introduces such a gap. The literati of the city develop the values and world view of the local culture to a degree of generalization, abstraction, and complexity incomprehensible to the ordinary villager, and in doing so leave out much of the concrete local detail of geography and village activity. The Maya Indian who lived in some rural settlement near Uaxactun could not have understood the calendrical intricacies worked out in that shrine-city by the priests; and the rituals performed at the city-shrine had one high level of meaning for the priest and another lower meaning, connecting with village life at some points only, for the ordinary Indian.

On the other hand, primary urbanization involves the development of characteristic institutions and societal features that hold together, in a certain important measure of common understanding, the Little Tradition and the Great Tradition. We may refer to the development of these institutions and societal features as the universalization of cultural consciousness—meaning by "universalization," the preservation and extension of common understanding as to the meaning and purpose of life, and sense of belonging together, to all the people, rural or urban, of the larger community. Some of the ways in which this universalization takes place are suggested in the following paragraphs. The examples are taken chiefly from India; they probably have considerable cross-cultural validity.

1. The embodiment of the Great Tradition in "sacred books" and secondarily in sacred monuments, art, icons, etc. Such "sacred scriptures" may be in a language not widely read or understood; nevertheless they may become a fixed point for the worship and ritual of ordinary people. The place of the "Torah" in the lives of orthodox Jews, the Vedas among

orthodox Hindus, the "Three Baskets" for Buddhists, the thirteen classics for Confucianists, the Koran for Muslims, the stelae and temples of the ancient Maya are all examples of such sacred scriptures, although they may vary in degree of sacredness and in canonical status.

2. The development of a special class of "literati" (priests, rabbis, Imams, Brahmins) who have the authority to read, interpret, and comment on the sacred scriptures. Thus the village Brahmin who reads the *Gita* for villagers at ceremonies mediates a part of the Great Tradition of Hinduism for them.

The mediation of a Great Tradition is not always this direct. At the village level it may be carried in a multitude of ways—by the stories parents and grandparents tell children, by professional reciters and storytellers, by dramatic performances and dances, songs and proverbs, etc.

In India the epics and *puranas* have been translated into the major regional languages and have been assimilated to the local cultures. This interaction of a Great Tradition and the Little Tradition of local and regional cultures needs further study, especially in terms of the professional and semiprofessional "mediators" of the process.

3. The role of leading personalities who because they themselves embody or know some aspects of a Great Tradition succeed through their personal position as leaders in mediating a Great Tradition to the masses of people. There is a vivid account of this process in Jawaharlal Nehru's *Discovery of India*, in which he describes first how he "discovered" the Great Tradition of India in the ruins of Mohenjo-Daro and other archeological monuments, her sacred rivers and holy cities, her literature, philosophy, and history. And then he describes how he discovered the Little Traditions of the people and the villages, and how through his speeches he conveyed to them a vision of *Bharat Mata*—Mother India—that transcended the little patches of village land, people, and customs.[29]

4. Nehru's account suggests that actual physical places, buildings and monuments—especially as they become places of sacred or patriotic pilgrimage—are important means to a more universalized cultural consciousness and the spread of a Great Tradition. In India this has been and still is an especially important universalizing force. The sanctity of rivers and the purifying powers of water go all the way back to the Rig-Veda. The Buddhists—who may have started the practice of holy pilgrimages—believed that there were four places that the believing man should visit with awe and reverence: Buddha's birthplace, the site where he attained illumination or perfect insight, the place where the mad elephant attacked him, and the place where Buddha died. In

the *Mahabharata*, there is a whole book on the subject of holy places (Aranyaka Book). Even a sinner who is purified by holy water will go to heaven. And the soul ready for *moksha* will surely achieve it if the pilgrim dies on a pilgrimage.[30] Today the millions of pilgrims who flock to such preeminent holy spots as Allahabad or Benares create problems of public safety and urban overcrowding, but they, like Nehru, are also discovering the *Bharat Mata* beyond their villages.

In India "sacred geography" has also played an important part in determining the location and layout of villages and cities and in this way has created a cultural continuity between countryside and urban centers. In ancient India, at least, every village and every city had a "sacred center" with temple, tank, and garden. And the trees and plants associated with the sacred shrine were also planted in private gardens, for the households too had their sacred center; the house is the "body" of a spirit (Virata Purusha) just as the human body is the "house" of the soul.[31]

At each of these levels—of household, village, and city—the "sacred center" provides the forum, the vehicle, and the content for the formation of distinct cultural identities—of families, village, and city. But as individuals pass outward, although their contacts with others become less intimate and less frequent, they nevertheless are carried along by the continuity of the "sacred centers," feeling a consciousness of a single cultural universe where people hold the same things sacred, and where the similarities of civic obligations in village and city to maintain tanks, build public squares, plant fruit trees, erect platforms and shrines are concrete testimony to common standards of virtue and responsibility.

Surely such things as these—a "sacred scripture," and a sacred class to interpret it, leading personalities, "sacred geography" and the associated rites and ceremonies—must in any civilization be important vehicles for the formation of that common cultural consciousness from which a Great Tradition is fashioned and to which it must appeal if it is to stay alive. It is in this sense that the universalization of cultural consciousness is a necessary ingredient in its formation and maintenance. Moreover, as the discussion of the role of "sacred geography" in the formation of Hinduism has intimated, this process does not begin only at the point where the villager and the urbanite merge their distinct cultural identities in a higher identity, but is already at work at the simpler levels of family, caste, and village, and must play an important part in the formation and maintenance of the Little Tradition at these levels.[32]

The integration of city and country in the secondary phase of urbanization cannot rest on a basic common cultural consciousness or a common culture, for there is none. Rural-urban integration in this phase of urbanization rests primarily on the mutuality of interests and on the "symbiotic" relations that have often been described.[33] The city is a "service station" and amusement center for the country, and the country is a "food basket" for the city. But while the diversity of cultural groups and the absence of a common culture make the basis of the integration primarily technical, even this kind of integration requires a kind of cultural consciousness to keep it going. We refer to the consciousness of cultural differences and the feeling that certain forms of intercultural association are of great enough benefit to override the repugnance of dealing with "foreigners." We may call this an "enlargement of cultural horizons" sufficient to become aware of other cultures and of the possibility that one's own society may in some ways require their presence. To paraphrase Adam Smith, it is not to the interest of the (Jewish) baker, the (Turkish) carpet-dealer, the (French) hand laundry, that the American Christian customer looks when he patronizes them, but to his own.

This is the practical psychological basis for admission of the stranger and tolerance of foreign minorities, even at the level of the folk society.[34] In a quotation from the *Institutions of Athens*, which Toynbee has, perhaps ironically, titled "Liberté-Égalité-Fraternité," we are told that the reason why Athens has "extended the benefits of Democracy to the relations between slaves and freemen and between aliens and citizens" is that "the country requires permanent residence of aliens in her midst on account both of the multiplicity of trades and of her maritime activities."[35]

When all or many classes of a population are culturally strange to each other and where some of the city populations are culturally alien to the country populations, the necessity for an enlarged cultural consciousness is obvious. In societies where social change is slow, and there has developed an adjustment of mutual usefulness and peaceful residence side by side of groups culturally different but not too different, the culturally complex society may be relatively stable.[36] But where urban development is great, such conditions are apt to be unstable. Each group may be perpetually affronted by the beliefs and practices of the other groups. Double standards of morality will prevail, since each cultural group will have one code for its "own kind" and another for the "outsiders." This simultaneous facing both inward and outward puts a strain on both codes. There may then be present the drives to proselytize, to withdraw and dig in, to persecute and to make scapegoats; there may even be fear of riot and massacre. In such circumstances the intellectuals become the chief exponents of a "cosmopolitan" enlarged cultural consciousness, inventing formulas of universal toleration and the benefits of mutual understanding, and extolling the freedom to experiment in different ways of life. But they do not always prevail against the more violent and unconvinced crusaders for some brand of cultural purity.

In primary urbanization when technical development was quite backward, a common cultural consciousness did get formed. The traveling student, teacher, saint, pilgrim, or even humble villager who goes to the next town may be startled by strange and wonderful sights, but throughout his journey he is protected by the compass of the common culture from cultural shock and disorientation. In ancient times students and teachers came from all over India and even from distant countries to study at Taxila, just as they came from all over Greece to Athens. In secondary urbanization, especially, under modern conditions, technical developments in transportation, travel, and communication enormously facilitate and accelerate cultural contacts. The effects of this on common cultural consciousness are not easy briefly to characterize. They make the more traditional cultural differences less important. They provide a wide basis of common understanding with regard to the instruments and practical means of living. It is at least clear that the integration of country and city that results is not the same kind of sense of common purpose in life that was provided to rural-urban peoples through the institutions mediating Little and Great Traditions referred to above. At this point the inquiry approaches the questions currently asked about the "mass culture" of modern great societies.

Cities as Centers of Cultural Innovation, Diffusion, and Progress

It is a commonly stated view that the city rather than the country is the source of cultural innovations, that such innovations diffuse outward from city to country, and that the "spread" is more or less inverse to distance from the urban center.[37] The objection to this view is not that it is wrong—for there is much evidence that would seem to support it—but that the limits and conditions of its validity need to be specified. It seems to assume for example that in the processes of cultural change, innovation, and diffusion, "city" and "country" are fixed points of reference which do not have histories, or interact, and are not essentially related to larger contexts of cultural change. Yet such assumptions—if ever true—would hold only under the most exceptional and short-run conditions. It is one thing to say that a large metropolitan city is a "center" of cultural innovation and diffusion for its immediate hinterland at a particular time; it is another to ask how that center itself was formed, over how long a period, and from what stimuli. In other words, as we enlarge the time span, include the rise and fall of complex distributions of cities, allow for the mutual interactions between them and their hinterlands, and also take account of interactions with other civilizations and their rural-urban patterns, we find that the processes of cultural innovation and "flow" are far too complex to be handled by simple mechanical laws concerning the direction, rate, and "flow" of cultural diffusion between "city" and "country." The cities themselves are creatures as well as creators of this process, and it takes a broad cross-cultural perspective to begin to see what its nature is. While this perspective may not yield simple generalizations about direction and rates of cultural diffusion, to widen the viewpoint as here suggested may throw some light on the processes of cultural change, including the formation and cultural "influence" of cities. In a primary phase of urbanization, when cities are developing from folk societies, it seems meaningless to assert, e.g., that the direction of cultural flow is from city to country. Under these conditions a folk culture is transformed into an urban culture which is a specialization of it, and if we wish to speak of "direction of flow" it would make more sense to see the process as one of a series of concentrations and nucleations within a common field. And as these concentrations occur, the common "Little Tradition" has not become inert; in fact it may retain a greater vitality and disposition to change than the systematized Great Tradition that gets "located" in special classes and in urban centers. From this point of view the spatial and mechanical concepts of "direction" and "rate" of flow, etc., are just metaphors of the processes involved in the formation of a Great Tradition. The cultural relations between city and country have to be traced in other terms, in terms of sociocultural history and of cultural-psychological processes. Physical space and time may be important obstacles and facilitators to these processes but they are not the fundamental determinants of cultural "motion" as they are of physical motion.

Under conditions of secondary urbanization, the spatial and mechanical concepts seem more appropriate because people and goods are more mobile and the technical development of the channels of transportation and communication is such as to permit highly precise measurement of their distributions and of "flows." But here too we may be measuring only some physical facts whose cultural significance remains indeterminate, or, at most, we may be documenting only a particularly recent cultural tendency to analyze intercultural relations in quantitative, abstract, and non-cultural terms. The assumption of a continuous and quantitatively divisible "diffusion" from a fixed urban center is unrealistic.

We may see Canton or Calcutta as a center for the diffusion of Western culture into the "East." We may also see these cities as relatively recent metropolitan growths, beginning as minor outliers of Oriental civilizations and then attracting both foreign and also uprooted native peoples, varying in fortune with world-wide events, and becoming at last not so much a center for the introduction of Western ways as a center for nativistic and independence movements to get rid of Western control and dominance. "Everything new happens at Canton," is said in China. We have in such a case not simple diffusion, or spread of urban influence from a city, but rather a cultural interaction which takes place against a background of ancient civilization with its own complex and changing pattern of urbanization now coming into contact with a newer and different civilization and giving rise to results that conform to neither.

The city may be regarded, but only very incompletely, as a center from which spreads outward the idea of progress. It is true that progress, like the ideologies of nationalism, socialism, communism, capitalism and democracy, tends to form in cities and it is in cities that the prophets and leaders of these doctrines are formed. Yet the states of mind of Oriental and African peoples are not copies of the minds of Western exponents of progress or of one or another political or economic doctrine. There is something like a revolution of mood and aspiration in the non-European peoples today.[38] The Easterner revolts against the West; he does not just take what can be borrowed from a city; he does sometimes the opposite: the Dutch language is set aside in Indonesia; there, anthropology, because associated with Dutch rule, does not spread from any city but is looked on with suspicion as associated with Dutch rule. Moreover, the influence of the West does not simply move outward from cities; it leapfrogs into country regions; a city reformer in Yucatan, Carrillo Puerto, arouses village Indians to join his civil war for progress and freedom against landowners and townspeople; Marxists discover that revolution can be based on the peasants without waiting for the development of an industrial proletariat.[39]

The conception of progress is itself an idea shaped by and expressive of one culture or civilization, that of the recent West.[40] What Toynbee and others have called the "Westernization" of the world may be the spread of only parts of the ideas associated in the West with the word "progress." Not without investigation can it be safely assumed that the spread of Western ideas from cities carries into the countryside a new and Western value system emphasizing hard work, enterprise, a favorable view of social change, and a central faith in material prosperity. In the cases of some of the peoples affected by modern urbanization, these values may be already present. In other cases the apparent spread of progress may turn out, on closer examination, to be a return to ancient values different from those of the West. Nationalistic movements are in part a nostalgic turning back to local traditional life. We shall understand better the varieties and complexities of the relations today between city and country as we compare the values and world views of the modernizing ideologies, and those of the Little and Great Traditions of the cultures and civilizations that are affected by the modern West. It may be that such studies[41] will discover greater "ambivalence" in the mood to modernize than we, here in the West, acknowledge; that the progressive spirit of Asia and Africa is not simply a decision to walk the road of progressive convictions that we have traversed, but rather in significant part an effort of the so-called "backward" peoples to recover from their disruptive encounters with the West by returning to the "sacred centers" of their ancient indigenous civilizations.

Notes

1. Robert Redfield, *The Primitive World and Its Transformations* (Ithaca, N.Y., 1953), ix-xiii. W. N. Brown and Others, "The Beginnings of Civilization," *Journal of the American Oriental Society,* Supplement No. 4, December, 1939, 3-61.
2. Robert Redfield, *The Folk Culture of Yucatan* (Chicago: University of Chicago Press, 1941). This study, short-run in description, also aims to test some general ideas. David G. Mandelbaum (ed.), "Integrated Social Science Research for India," *Planning Memo* (University of California, 1949).
3. Kroeber has recently discussed the problems of delimiting civilizations in his article, "The Delimitation of Civilizations," *Journal of the History of Ideas,* XIV (1953). Mark Jefferson, "Distribution of the World's City Folk: A Study in Comparative Civilization," *Geographica,* 1931.
4. Paul Kirchhoff, in "Four Hundred Years After: General Discussion of Acculturation, Social Change, and the Historical Provenience of Culture Elements," in *Heritage of Conquest* by Sol Tax and Others (Glencoe, Ill.: Free Press, 1952), p. 254: "It seems to me that the fundamental characteristic of Mesoamerica was that it was a stratified society, one like ours or that of China, based on the axis of city and countryside. There was a native ruling class, with a class ideology and organization, which disappeared entirely; there were great cultural centers which, just as in our life, are so essential that if you described the U.S. without New York, Chicago, etc., it would be absurd. The same thing happens when you describe these centers in ancient Mexico. ... It's not only the arts, crafts and sciences which constitute the great changes, but the basic form of the culture changing from a city structure to the most isolated form, which is, in my opinion, the most total and radical change anywhere in history. ... When the city is cut off what is left over is attached as a subordinate to the new city-centered culture. ..."
5. S. Ghosh, "The Urban Pattern of Calcutta," *Economic Geography,* 1950. J. Weulersse, "Antioche, un type de cite de l'Islam," *Congr. int. de Géographie* (Warsaw,

Social Anthropology

1934), III; D. R. Gadgil, *Poona, a Socio-economic Survey* (Poona, 1945, 1952).
6. "Urbanization is part of the Europeanization that is spreading throughout the world" (Mark Jefferson in reference [3] above). Kingsley Davis, *The Population of India and Pakistan* (Princeton, N.J., 1951), pp. 148-49; M. Zinkin, *Asia and the West* (London, 1951), chap. i, "Eastern Village and Western City."
7. Kirchhoff, "Four Hundred Years After."
8. See for this approach the books of V. Gordon Childe and his article in *Town Planning Review,* XXI (1950), on "The Urban Revolution."
9. Grace M. Kneedler, "Functional Types of Cities," reprinted in *Reader in Urban Sociology,* ed. Paul K. Hatt and Albert J. Reiss, Jr. (Glencoe, Ill.: Free Press, 1951); R. E. Dickinson, *The West European City* (London: Routledge & Paul, 1951), pp. 253-54; Chauncy Harris, "A Functional Classification of Cities in the United States," *Geog. Rev.,* 1943.
10. D. R. Gadgil, *The Industrial Revolution of India in Recent Times* (Oxford University Press, 1944), pp. 6-12. O. H. K. Spate and E. Ahmad, "Five Cities of the Gangetic Plain: A Cross-section of Indian Cultural History," *Geog. Rev.,* 1950. P. George, *La Ville* (Paris, 1952). B. Rowland, *The Art and Architecture of India* (Baltimore, Md.: Penguin, 1953). Map showing ancient and historic art and religious centers, p. xvii. Fei Hsiao-tung, *China's Gentry: Essays in Rural-Urban Relations* (Chicago: University of Chicago Press, 1953), pp. 91-117.
11. R. E. Dickinson, *The West European City.,* pp. 251-52; H. Pirenne, *Medieval Cities.*
12. See article on "Urbanization" by W. M. Stewart in 14th edition of *Encyclopaedia Britannica* for some cultural variables in the definition of "city."
13. B. Hoselitz, "The Role of Cities in the Economic Growth of Underdeveloped Countries," *The Journal of Political Economy,* LXI (1953), esp. 198-99.
14. Robert Redfield, *The Primitive World and Its Transformations,* chap. iii.
15. Ibid.
16. Robert Redfield, "The Natural History of the Folk Society," *Social Forces.* XXXI (1953), 224-28.
17. In the heterogenetic transformation the city and its hinterland become mutually involved: the conservative or reactionary prophet in the country inveighs against the innovations or backslidings of the city; and the reformer with the radically progressive message moves back from Medina against Mecca, or enters Jerusalem.
18. This distinction is an extension of the distinction between the primary and secondary phases of folk transformations in R. Redfield, *The Primitive World and Its Transformations,* p. 41.
19. Kirchhoff, "Four Hundred Years After."
20. R. Redfield, "Primitive Merchants of Guatemala," *Quarterly Journal of Inter-American Relations,* I, No. 4 (1939), 48-49.
21. Robert Redfield, *The Primitive World and Its Transformations,* pp. 58-73. See also Sylvanus G. Morley, *The Ancient Maya,* and Thomas Gann and J. Eric Thompson, *The History of the Maya* (New York, 1931).
22. The case of China is particularly striking, since the evidence for a dominant core culture is unmistakable but its relation to local cultures which may have been its basis is unknown. See Chi Li, *The Formation of the Chinese People* (Cambridge, Mass.: Harvard University Press, 1928), and Wolfram Eberhard, *Early Chinese Cultures and Their Development* ("Smithsonian Institution Annual Report," 1937 [Washington, D.C., 1938]). For a good study of imperial "spread" and "dilution," see A. H. M. Jones, *The Greek City from Alexander to Justinian* (Oxford University Press, 1940).

23. Chauncy Harris, "Ethnic Groups in Cities of the Soviet Union," *Geog. Rev.,* 1945.
24. D. W. Fryer, "The 'Million City' in Southeast Asia," *Geog. Rev.,* October, 1953; J. E. Spencer, "Changing Asiatic Cities," *Geog. Rev.,* XLI (1951). This last is a summary of an article by Jean Chesneaux. See also *Record of the XXVIIth Meeting of the International Institute of Differing Civilizations* (Brussels, 1952), esp. papers by R. W. Steel and K. Neys.
25. Robert Redfield, *The Primitive World and Its Transformations,* pp. 72-83.
26. For a further discussion of these concepts, see Redfield, ibid., chap. iv, and Redfield, *The Little Community* (Chicago: University of Chicago Press, 1955), chaps. v and vi, on personality and mental outlook.
27. See L. Wirth, "Urbanism as a Way of Life," and G. Simmel, "The Metropolis and Mental Life," both reprinted in Batt and Reiss, *Reader in Urban Sociology;* E. Fromm, *Escape from Freedom;* David Riesman and Others, *The Lonely Crowd;* and A. L. Kroeber, *Anthropology* (1948), sec. 121. For the effects of urban life on time-coordination, see H. A. Hawley, *Human Ecology,* chap. xv, and A. I. Hallowell, "Temporal Orientation in 'Western Civilization and in a Preliterate Society," *American Anthropologist,* XXXIX (1937), 647-76.
28. Robert Redfield, *The Folk Culture of Yucatan,* chap. xi; R. E. Park, "Magic, Mentality, and City Life," reprinted in Park, *Human Communities.* N. C. Chaudhuri, *The Autobiography of an Unknown Indian* (Macmillan Co., 1951), gives some interesting observations on the survival of "folk" beliefs and practices among, the people of Calcutta (pp. 361-62). P. Masson-Oursel, "La Sophistique. Etude de philosophic comparée," *Revue de metaphysique et de morale,* XXIII (1916), 343-62.
29. Jawaharlal Nehru, *The Discovery of India* (New York: John Day Co., 1946), pp. 37-40, 45-51.
30. D. Patil, *Cultural History from the Vāyu Puranā* (Poona, 1946), Appendix B.
31. C.P.V. Ayyar, *Town Planning in the Ancient Dekkan* (Madras, n.d.), with an Introduction by Patrick Geddes. See also Patrick Geddes, in *India,* ed. J. Tyrwhitt (London, 1947). N.V. Ramanayya, *An Essay on the Origin of the South Indian Temple* (Madras, 1930), and Stella Khramrisch, *The Hindu Temple* (Calcutta, 1946). B. Rao, "Rural Habitation in South India," *Quarterly Journal of the Mythic Society,* XIV. J. M. Linton Bogle, *Town Planning in India* (Oxford University Press, 1929). Mudgett and Others, *Banaras: Outline of a Master Plan* (Lucknow: Town and Village Planning Office).
32. See Robert Redfield, *The Little Community,* chap. viii, on the little community as "a community within communities." In addition to the above factors, it has been usual to single out special items of content of the world view and values of a Great Tradition as explanations of the "universalization" of Great Traditions. It has been frequently argued, e.g., that religions which are monotheistic and sanction an "open class" social system will appeal more to ordinary people and spread faster than those which are polytheistic and which sanction "caste" systems. (See, e.g., H. J. Kissling, "The Sociological and Educational Role of the Dervish Orders in the Ottoman Empire," in G. von Grunebaum [ed.], *Studies in Islamic Cultural History.*) F. S. C. Northrop and Arnold Toynbee both attach great importance to the ideological content of cultures as factors in their spread, although they come out with different results. It may be that such special features of content are important in the formation and spread of some particular religions at some particular time, but it is doubtful that they would have the same role in different civilizations under all circumstances. In his recent study of the Coorgs of South India, Srinivas argues with considerable plausibility that the spread of Hinduism

on an all-India basis has depended on its polytheism, which has made it easy to incorporate all sorts of alien deities, and on a caste system which assimilates every new cultural or ethnic group as a special caste. Another difficulty about using special features of content of some particular tradition as a general explanation of the formation and maintenance of any Great Tradition is that one inevitably selects features that have been crystallized only after a long period of historical development and struggle. These are more relevant as factors in explaining *further* development and spread than they are in explaining the cultural-psychological processes that have accompanied primary urbanization. The "universalization" of universal faiths takes us into a realm of secondary urbanization where diverse and conflicting cultures must be accommodated.

33. R. E. Park, "Symbiosis and Socialization: A Frame of Reference for the Study of Society," reprinted in *Human Communities.*
34. Robert Redfield, *The Primitive World and Its Transformations,* pp. 33-34, for the institutionalization of hospitality to strangers in peasant societies.
35. Arnold Toynbee, *Greek Civilization and Character* (Boston: Beacon Press, 1950), pp. 48-49. See also David G. Mandelbaum, "The Jewish Way of Life in Cochin," *Jewish Social Studies,* I (1939).
36. Robert Redfield, "Primitive Merchants of Guatemala."
37. P. Sorokin and C. Zimmerman, *Principles of Rural-Urban Sociology* (New York: Henry Holt and Co., 1929), chap. xvii, "The Role of the City and Country in Innovation, Disruption, and Preservation of the National Culture." G. Chabot, "Les zones d'influence d'une ville," *Congr. int. de Geog.* (Paris, 1931), III, 432-37. Mark Jefferson, "The Law of the Primate City," *Geog. Rev.,* 1939, pp. 226-32. O. H. K. Spate, "Factors in the Development of Capital Cities," *Geog. Rev.,* 1942, pp. 622-31. R. E. Park, "The Urban Community as a Spatial Pattern and a Moral Order," and "Newspaper Circulation and Metropolitan Regions," both reprinted in Park, *Human Communities.* E. T. Hiller, "Extension of Urban Characteristics into Rural Areas," *Rural Sociology,* VI (1941).
38. For further discussion of these concepts of "mood," "aspiration," and "policy" as they might figure in community studies, see R. Redfield, *The Little Community,* chap. vii, on the little community as "A History."
39. David Mitrany, *Marx against the Peasants* (London, 1952).
40. See A. L. Kroeber, *Anthropology,* secs. 127, 128, and Gerhart Piers and Milton Singer, *Shame and Guilt: A Psychoanalytic and Cultural Study,* for an examination of some of the evidence on this point for American Indian cultures. See also R. Redfield, *A Village That Chose Progress,* esp. chap. viii, "Chan Kom, Its Ethos and Success." Recent material on cross-cultural comparisons of value systems will be found in Daryll Forde (ed.), *African Worlds,* and in the publications of the Harvard Values Study Project directed by Clyde Kluckhohn.
41. Several such studies have been made. See, e.g., Paul Mus, *Viet-Nam, Sociologie l'histoire d'une guerre* (Paris, 1952); Shen-Yu Dai, *Mao Tse-tung and Confucianism* (Ph.D. diss., University of Pennsylvania, 1952); E. Sarkisaynz, *Russian Weltanshauung and Islamic and Buddhist Messianism* (Ph.D. diss. University of Chicago, 1953); V. Barnouw, "The Changing Character of a Hindu Festival," *American Anthropologist*, February, 1954.

19

Civilizations as Cultural Structures?

Redfield's interest in civilization studies culminated in the establishment by him and Milton Singer of the Comparative Civilizations program at the University of Chicago. Generously funded by the Ford Foundation, Redfield and Singer launched this program in 1951 to foster interdisciplinary comparative civilization studies. Through this program, they brought together a distinguished collection of graduate students and post-doctoral scholars who carried out over the course of the 1950s in-depth studies of the world's major civilizations. Redfield's health began to fail in the mid-1950s, however, and by 1958 he died of lymphoma. Despite illness during his last few years, he devoted himself to writing a final book on the aims and methods of civilization studies. Although he did not complete this book, he did finish three manuscript chapters, which his wife published following his death in the volumes of his collected papers that she edited. In the first of these chapters, "Civilizations as Things Thought About," Redfield examined the challenges associated with defining civilizations and argued that civilizations represented a construct that referred to a specific form of culture or society. In essence, he argued, civilizations were not fundamentally different from primitive societies, as many had proposed, but differed largely by degree of complexity. In the second chapter, "Civilizations as Societal Structures? The Development of Community Studies," he built upon ideas he had presented earlier in his 1956 book Peasant Society and Culture, *focusing particularly on the transformation of anthropological community studies from examinations of isolated villages conceived in functional terms to highly contextualized studies that took account both of the network of connections that existed between village and metropolis as well as historical factors shaping the village.*[1] *Finally, in the third chapter, "Civilizations as Cultural Structures, which is reprinted here, Redfield amplified ideas he had first presented in his article "The Primitive World View" (1952) and later book* The Primitive World and Its Transformations *(1953) regarding how explorations of great and little traditions and worldview analyses could be used as a basis for comparative civilization studies. Unfortunately, Redfield died before he could finish his book on civilization studies, but his ideas, especially his Great and Little Traditions construct, found wide application among students of comparative civilizations from the late 1950s through early 1970s.*

First published in *The Papers of Robert Redfield: Human Nature and the Study of Society*, Vol. 1, ed. Margaret Park Redfield (Chicago: University of Chicago, 1962), 392-401.

Such a "formed thing of the mind" as [described earlier by Redfield in his civilizations book manuscript]—a civilization conceived schematically as a persisting arrangement of kinds of communities or components of communities in characteristic interdependence with one another—is, of course, no "operational concept." The idea does not direct us to go and do just this at some point of observation or work with existing documents. It is, rather, a very embracing conception held in the mind as a framework for the understanding of that great thing, civilization, with reference to which one may undertake investigation of particulars. If, on the other hand, one studies how this tribal people is becoming peasantry, by accepting the self-judgments, manner of life and place in the social world in which a peasant is a peasant because there are townsmen or gentry there in terms of which he is seen by them and in terms of which he sees himself, then one may require concepts of operation. Srinivas' "Sanskritization"[2]—that process whereby in India a tribal people assumes ways of life appropriate to the Hindu tradition and expectation and so ceases to be tribal and becomes part of the caste structure of India—is a concept of operation. Milton Singer has referred to these two kinds of constructs, the one a formulation of a very wide scheme within which fit many particulars and the other a concept directly guiding and instructing particular investigations, respectively as "concepts of cogitation" and "concepts of observation."[3]

This chapter explores some further possible concepts of cogitation. Those now to be considered, like that almost reached in the second chapter, are "historic structures" —conceptions defining a civilizational entity through long periods of time. But now I turn from conceptions in which the entities making up the structure are kinds of people, communities or components thereof, to conceivable historic structures in which the entities making up the structure are ideas and the products of ideas.

A. The Structure of Tradition

The word "tradition" connotes the act of handing down and what is handed down from one generation to another. It means both Process and Product. A civilization may be thought of, then, as a structure of tradition that is, as a persisting form of arrangements for the handing down of cultural substance (idea and its products), within a great community, the community of that civilization, and as the characteristic processes of transmitting it. Just as we may think of a civilization as kinds of people in persisting forms of relationship, so we may think of it as kinds of things thought and done, with characteristic forms for communicating this substance from generation to generation, and from one part of the people to other parts.

In that local community which is and long has been within a civilization "the intellectual and often the moral life...is perpetually incomplete. ... To maintain itself peasant culture requires continual communication to the local community of thought originating outside of it."[4] Local culture "is continually replenished by contact with products of intellectual and scientific social strata."[5] The local community within a civilization is ideationally, culturally, intellectually, and often morally, "heteronomous"—dependent on norms coming to it from without.

This is the way that the conception of the structure of tradition may first appear to the anthropologist who begins his work within the dependent and heteronomous local community. But, to one who tries to look at a whole civilization, it begins to appear as that total structure of formed relationships for the communication of the tradition that is that civilization, throughout the length and breadth and the whole historic depth during which that civilization is recognizable as that civilization. How is so inclusive a conception to be further defined?

The fact (both societal and cultural), which appears at once to a mind that looks at civilizations and that entertains this question, is the large degree of distinction and separation between two aspects of knowledge, of what is thought and done, persistently and characteristically. It is, concretely, the difference between layman and priest, between peasant and philosopher or theologian, between local mythology and universal sacred doctrine, between the spontaneous developments of idea in the untutored and the considered teaching of the reflective.

We may note the development of this distinction and separation as we go from the less civilized to the more civilized peoples. Among the Andamanese there seem to be no specialists in tradition—older men know more than younger, that is all; among the Maori a special esoteric learning was carried on through time by a few special priests; in Dahomey priests of the Sky Cult had a more refined and penetrating knowledge of deities than did other people; in the shrine-centers of the ancient Maya a priesthood, separated now from ordinary people by their secluded places of work and thought and by the development of a mathematical and calendrical knowledge incomprehensible to the farmer, carried on their work; the world civilizations developed their Brahmins, Mandarins, or imams to expound, for the whole civilization, *dharma*, the Confucian ethic, or the *dar-al-Islam*.[6]

We may than attend to this distinction and separation and make it the axis of the formed thought for civilization as a structure of tradition. Most abstractly and schematically, a civilization is a form of relationship between these two components of tradition. I wrote: "In a civilization there is a great tradition of the reflective few, and there is a little tradition of the largely unreflective many."[7] This assertion evokes a diagram: a wide band to represent the whole-civilizational great tradition in reciprocal communication, through centuries, with a great many local and popular traditions, represented by small squares or circles. This, I think, is a concept of cogitation. It is so very schematic that it cannot begin to represent the real complexity of these relationships. As soon as we get to work, as we begin to study the relations of local tradition to widespread, reflective Brahminical tradition in India, we are at so particular and so small a part of the whole civilization that we develop and complicate the diagram, converting the concept of cogitation into concepts of observation. Writing of the structure of religious tradition in India, Marriott and Cohn say: "there are chains of specialists from the expert masters of authoritative texts down to semiliterate domestic priests; all may be classed as 'Brahmin,' but generally they will belong to several different Brahmin castes."[8] The real structure of tradition, in any civilization or part thereof, is an immensely intricate system of relationships between the levels or components of tradition, which we enormously oversimplify by referring to as "high" and "low" or as "great" and "little."

In approaching a civilization as a structure of tradition we have (as Milton Singer has pointed out[9]) several choices of subject matter to emphasize, of aspects of this structure to make our subject matter. We can think of the *content of thought*, the Vedic thought of the Upanishads versus the ideas of the villagers; the *kinds of specialists* (roles and offices) that maintain the communication among the parts; the *media* (and institutions) in which the communications are effected (MS); the *processes of modification* between components or levels (Marriott[10] on parochialization and universalization); the *works*, textual or oral, in which the components of tradition find expression. And no doubt others. But I think, whichever we choose, we are recognizing a large, overarching conception of a civilization as an arrangement for communication between components that are universal, reflective, and indoctrinating, and components which are local, unreflective, and accepting.

This conception will lead us, I think, to comparisons of civilizations in these terms. What was the general nature of the relationship between high tradition and little local traditions among the ancient Maya? So far as we know, the calendrical texts are works of highly specialized content without story or ethic, cultivated and developed by specialists for their own "life of the mind"—an arcane understanding of time and man. In China there were (or are) classical works with ethical content cultivated by the educated and drawing little on local popular tradition but strongly influencing the ordinary people by precept and example. Popular works in China appear to be notably separate from Confucian classics. In India there are both classical and popular works, with both story and ethical content, in frequent interaction so that substance of story and of moral has been interchanged and reworked by the intellectual and the common people. Such considerations might become a comparison of civilizations, each of which is seen as a persisting characteristic set of relationships among works expressing components of tradition.

B. The Structure of World View

This conception of civilizations as structures of tradition can be given a somewhat different cast or emphasis so that another and possibly useful variant conception arises for the future comparative student of civilizations. I now indicate this variant: a system or structure of "world views."

In writing of the structure of tradition of a civilization, I have been looking at the content of knowledge and thought of the people of that civilization through centuries of time during such a period of time as might allow the student to see different kinds of cultivators and transmitters of that knowledge and thought in persisting formal relationships to one another. It has been a view of a civilization through a long stretch of time. And it has been a view enjoyed—if at all—by us students mostly from outside of that civilization, or, if we are looking at Western civilization, looking at it with the eyes of people who know it with some detachment, as scholars know it, thinking about its content and its parts so as to render our descriptions sufficiently abstract and formal to bring about comparisons with other such structures of tradition. Structure of tradition is an outside view of a historic structure. In forming it, one of course attends to what the people of that civilization have in their minds of their tradition, but, in describing its "total structure," the outside observer puts together as best he can what he has learned about many of its parts from perhaps very many people and sources.

Suppose now that we attend to some community, small or large, a tribe, a peasant village, a nation, a civilized people, at some moment or period of time, and ask ourselves the question: How, right now, do these people experience the content of tradition as it is presented to them, in their moment of time, from their point of view within that community? If they happen to be historians, or include in their knowledge something about local traditions or tribal myths, there will be for them too a historical dimension in what they know. Whether there is or not, every individual's view of the universe around him has, for him, some organization, structure, or system. Chaos cannot be lived with. Attending to these inside views of everything as held by members of that community we study, could we ask the following questions: To anyone of those members, to all of them, to this group of them as compared with that other group of them, what is the view they have of all the thought and knowledge they have? In short, can we conceive of a structure or system of world view?

The question "*What* is that view?" asks too much. It raises all the questions about discovering and describing "value systems" or the even more basic assumptions made by that people about the nature of things or the nature of knowledge. I pass over these very difficult matters as to finding out and rightly representing the full substance of a world view to fix attention on the possibility that we may recognize different *kinds of organizations, structures, systems* among the ideas held by anybody as to everything, so as to distinguish, in these terms, between more primitive people and more civilized people and perhaps between one civilization and another. Ideas that come to me about this possibility are very ill-defined and explorative; I may, however, expose them for development. I do so now in a short series of comparisons.

The question, I repeat, is: With what kind of organization of thought and judgment does the member of that community look out upon his universe? Is it, I ask myself especially, a unified or a not unified view, and if there are parts or separations in it of which that member is aware, what are they? I proceed to speculate as to possible answers from some reports known to me of the views of everything of a few very different kinds of peoples.

In very simple and homogeneous societies, such as the Siriono or the Andamanese, the accounts do not suggest to me that the native is aware either of different layers or levels of knowledge or that what he himself thinks about everything presents conflicts or problems of doubt or difficulty. According to Holmberg,[11] Siriono Indians have very little interest or time to think about the nature of the universe, and it is safe, I think, to suppose that any one of them is aware of a world around him not much structured and felt to be the same for his fellow Siriono. There is not much structure of world view and what there is is one thing for everybody, more or less.

In other primitive societies with specialization of knowledge in older men or in priests or shamans, there is at least a distinction between everyday and common knowledge and deeper levels of knowledge enjoyed by some people of the community. So the ordinary Maori must have had an awareness of a dimension of understanding of the nature of things which he did not have but which the *tohunga* had—and vice versa. For the Maori the world view, of either layman or specialist, includes a hinterland, knowledge that there is a knowledge more than or less than his own but nevertheless knowledge about the same things. There is here a structured world view corresponding to the difference between layman and specialist.

In some societies not easily called civilized, and yet in these respects more highly developed, the structure of world view is more complex, but still held within the tribal or other local community. The example that has much interested me is provided by the reports of Professor Griaule and his associates with regard to the Dogon, a Sudanese people.[12] The Dogon have an elaborately complex conception of the nature of all things. Their accumulated tradition has become an impressive work of the mind. All things—plants, animals, tools, man's social life, his rituals, and the divine beings—are linked together in an intricate system of interrelated meanings. The linkage is both genetic and static; everything has some connection with events going back to creation; for example, the village is a human body; this body is also the primordial body of the first god; the house represents man's pedigree back to the gods; even pots are images of the universe. Moreover, for our interests here, this knowledge is conceived to be constituted of four aspects or levels of understanding: the first three degrees are called respectively "knowledge in front," "on one side," and "behind," but the fourth is "clear knowledge"—this is all knowledge in its ordered complexity. These degrees of knowledge are imparted by organized instruction according to the development of the young person to old age and provide for the intellectual powers and aspirations of the few—about 6 per cent of the adults, Griaule tells us—who attain to "clear knowledge." There is a special series of intellectual attainments for women. We are given examples of the different levels of understanding in such domains of knowledge as insects, heavenly bodies: rituals.[13] My comment on all this should be obvious: there is here a structure (or system, if you prefer) of world view in which any individual knows what he knows and also knows that there is some part of that structure or system which he does not or does not yet know. The structure or system is held within the tribal society and community; and the system of ideas corresponds closely to the day-to-day life of the Dogon—apparently of all Dogon, the more as well as the less enlightened; it corresponds also to the social structure (in the British sense). Its own structural or systematic character lies in the degrees or levels of knowledge. We might say that, in contrast to the world view of the Andamanese or the Siriono, the world view of the Dogon has perspective. But—and I stress this—it seems to have a coherent perspective, an integration in depth, one might say. Each level is an outgrowth of the others, a further development of the others.

To push this inquiry any distance into the world views of civilized peoples is beyond my powers. I do not believe we know very much about the world views of people in our own society and civilization. I have the impression that, taking any one member of our society, and thinking of what may be his world view in comparison with that of others also in our society and civilization, his world view is probably not well integrated, is composed of parts or alternatives very different from one another, and is not closely consistent with the world view of many of those others. It may be that for a rapidly changing and heterogeneous civilized people the notion of world view is quite unmanageable.

I retreat to peoples within civilizations of whom the anthropologist begins to have some understanding. I think of tribal peoples much influenced by civilizations, or of peasantry, who constitute a component—one might almost say an estate—within a civilization. If one thinks of such peoples, I imagine that one is prepared to find with them also, as with such peoples as the Dogon, a world view with perspective. Many a tribesman incorporated within a civilization and many a peasant has to take account of priests, teachers, gentry, administrative and other elites whose views of things make connection with his own; he knows they know and believe things that affect him and that are in some relation—either in further development or perhaps in conflict with what he knows and believes. But in introducing in this sentence the word "conflict," I have begun to entertain a possibility as to the nature of world views within civilizations which I now offer.

Years ago, in looking into the world views of Yucatecan Mexicans living in tribal, peasant, or town communities, I thought I saw differences as among the world views of one community and another as to the presence or absence of inconsistency or conflict within the parts composing the world view of any one individual or within the world view characteristic of one community as compared with another.[14] In looking, from the outside, as a student of a system of native ideas, at a view of the universe entertained by a people in a fairly isolated and peasant-like village, Chan Kom, I saw what I called "a seam running down the fabric of ideas": the mind of the native moved within one system of religious and cosmogonic and moral ideas which I knew to be of Spanish origin and another system which I knew to be of aboriginal origin. But it seemed to me that the native moved from one to the other without tension, distress. Both were his local tradition; both parts he knew and carried on—no outsider had much to do with it. But in the railroad town, where many more and more recent ideas had entered, I did find this tension, ambivalence, doubt and difficulty in the minds of the people themselves. So the possibility I entertain appears again: that, in civilizations or in simpler societies within civilizations, the structure of world view becomes divided, at least to the outside student and, in certain conditions of civilization, also in the thoughts and feelings of the member of the civilized community himself: it is a structure in both confusion and tension.

Recently, in studying the Andalusian town of Alcalá, Pitt-Rivers[15] saw a certain opposition between the institutions and ways of thought of the common people and those impressed on them by formal authority—priest administrator, teacher—and in part lived by that superior local class called *señoritas*, who lived their lives partly in the mountain town and partly in the thought and activities of the city. Toward the ruling group Pitt-Rivers detected in ordinary people an ambivalence, and ambivalence too toward their *own* whole traditional way of life. The *plebs*, he says respect and trust the knowledge of the herbal curer but also listen to the condemnation of the Church on that practitioner. They admire the bandit as a hero but also respect the voice of authority that tells them that the bandit is a traitor. Pitt-Rivers sums up his impressions thus: "The two systems (local and formal) are at the same time interdependent and in opposition. They are both parts of the same structure." And he adds that this is a system in tension because of this opposition. Translating these observations into questions, as to the structure of world view, one may ask if, in civilizations, there do not come about world views structured in tension, in ambivalence, in parts felt to be in opposition. I do not think one can say so of the Dogon.

There is a difference in the situations of these two peoples, the Yucatecan villager and the Andalusian isolated townsman, to which I call attention. In Alcalá the conflict and tension are presently renewed and maintained by the coexistence within the community of two kinds of people, *plebs* and señoritos, peasant-like townsmen and educated elite. The world view is divided between, or is in tension because of, a view of things that is local and traditional and a view of things that is centered outside the local community but is constantly impressed on the local people. In Chan Kom, on the other hand, the separation, the "seam" that I thought I saw, was not, so far as I could tell, experienced by the native as a current conflict. It was for him a separation between doing this and then also or alternatively, but not inconsistently, doing that. And the cause of this separation or seam, if there was one, lay, as the outsider knew, in the fact of Conquest of Indians by missionizing Europeans four hundred years before; though, certainly, the intruding world view had continued to be communicated during the intervening centuries by way of priests and others to the ancestors of the natives I knew. But in this village I saw no tension experienced by the people themselves. I did see it, very plainly, in the railway town of Dzitas, where the situation as to conflict of traditions or world views was much like that in Alcalá.

Very recently Michael Mendelson has written an unpublished account and analysis of the world view of the people of Santiago Atitlán,[16] that large village on the shores of the lake of that name in western Guatemala. His interpretation of facts there brings us further to consider the possibility of conflict and tension in world view. He centered his attention on the religious rituals and symbols. The short conclusion to which he came was this: he saw a world view divided and in tension as experienced by the natives and attributed this division and tension to the imperfect reconciliation of pagan and Christian teaching, of local traditional views of the nature of man and the universe and the corresponding imported view. Mendelson felt that he was able to identify the two symbols central to these imperfectly combined world views: San Martin and Jesucristo. His interviews and texts do seem to show that the native assumes at one moment a view of the universe, of time, and of ethics, corresponding to an unseen world headed by San Martin, and at another a view of these matters headed by Jesucristo. In the pagan view custom is ritual and ritual is custom; *costumbre* sums up all time in one natural, cyclical Time: that of nature and its yearly waning and rebirth. Jesucristo states the solution of the Christian world, stressing Man's salvation through the dying and rebirth of a God of love, through "folk Catholicism." This interpretation Mendelson develops in a series of contrasts and demonstrations of the evidence of conflict, with respect to such matters as the morality of sex and the relation of the self to others.

But there is more than this in his analysis. In Santiago the striking figure and symbol is a being called Maximon, about whom Samuel Lothrop[17] told us a little something years ago. Maximon is the immediately, supremely potent supernatural, embodied in a grotesque scarecrow-like figure, cigar in mouth, resurrected, with gestures of extreme solemnity, every spring in Holy Week. This figure is conflict and ambiguity incarnate: he or it is treated with awe and respect, and he or it is also derided, mocked. During the times of emphasis on the Christian world when the Passion is in part enacted, Maximon becomes Judas. At other times he is propitiated and appealed to for exercises of his extraordinary power for both good and evil. Mendelson's thesis is that in Maximon the two worlds, pagan and Christian, meet and that in this figure conflict and ambivalence are ritualized, institutionalized. During his stay in Atitlán, Maximon was the center of many kinds of disputes and differences, religious, as introduced by Protestant missionaries, political and factional too. Mendelson writes of the Atitecos' concern with Maximon as "obsessive." If his analysis is substantially correct, there is here a world view in marked tension, a tension so old and unreconciled that the tradition itself has come to embrace it and to provide forms for its persisting expression.

For me this case helps to continue a progression, a progression in the development of world views as structures or systems more or less simple or complex, shallow or provided with perspective, coherent or incoherent, separated or unified, held in unconflicting integrity or split and held in tension. One might almost speak of the world view of Atitecos, a local people within a civilization alien to their local tradition, as a "fractured" world view. When, in the histories of civilizations, do world views take on a wider integration? When do they incur a kind of breakage, a division that becomes, for that people then, their characteristic experience?

Notes

1. Robert Redfield, *The Papers of Robert Redfield: Human Nature and the Study of Society,* vol. 1. Edited by Margaret Park Redfield (Chicago: University of Chicago Press, 1962), 364-391.
2. M. N. Srinivas, *Religion and Society among the Coorgs of India* (Oxford: Clarendon Press, 1952).
3. Milton Singer, "The Cultural Pattern of Indian Civilization: A Preliminary Report of a Methodological Field Study," *The Far Eastern Quarterly,* XV, No. 1 (1955), 23-36.
4. Robert Redfield, *Peasant Society and Culture* (Chicago: University of Chicago Press, 1956).

5. George Foster, "What Is Folk Culture?" *American Anthropologist,* LV, No. 2 (1953), Pt. 1, 159-73.
6. Redfield, *Peasant Society and Culture.*
7. Ibid.
8. McKim Marriott and Bernard S. Cohn, "Networks and Centers in the Integration of Indian Civilization," *Journal of Social Research* (Ranchi, Bihar, India), I, No. 1 (1958), 1-9.
9. Milton Singer, "Cultural Pattern of Indian Civilization" and "Introduction" and "The Great Tradition in a Metropolitan Center: Madras," in *Traditional India: Structure and Change,* ed. Milton Singer (Philadelphia: American Folklore Society, 1958, 1959).
10. McKim Marriott, "Little Communities in an Indigenous Civilization," in *Village India,* ed. McKim Marriott (Chicago: University of Chicago Press, 1955).
11. Allan R. Holmberg, *Nomads of the Long Bow: The Siriono of Eastern Bolivia* (Washington, D.C.: Smithsonian Institution, Institute of Social Anthropology, Publication No. 10,1950).
12. Marcel Griaule, *Dieu d'Eau* (Paris: Les Éditions du Chêne, 1958).
13. Marcel Griaule, "Le Savoir des Dogon," *Journal de la Société des Africanistes,* XXII, Nos. 1 and 2 (1952); "L'Enquête orale en ethnologie," *Revue Philosophique de la France et de l'Étranger,* CXLII (1952). Marcel Griaule and Germaine Dieterlen, "La Harpeluth des Dogon," *Journal de la Société des Africanistes,* XX (1950), 209-28; "Un Systeme soudanais de Sirius," ibid., 273-94; "Signes graphiques soudanais," *L'Homme, cahiers d'ethnologie, de géographie, et de Ie linguistique,* III (1951).
14. Robert Redfield, *The Folk Culture of Yucatan* (Chicago: University of Chicago Press, 1941).
15. .J. A. Pitt-Rivers, *The People of the Sierra* (New York: Criterion Books, 1954).
16. E. Michael Mendelson, "Religion and World-View in Santiago Atitlán" (Ph.D. diss., University of Chicago, 1956); "Religion and World-View in a Guatemalan Village" ("Microfilm Collection of Manuscripts on Middle American Cultural Anthropology," No. 52 [Chicago: University of Chicago Library, 1957]); "The King, the Traitor, and the Cross: An Interpretation of a Highland Maya Religious Conflict," *Diogenes,* No. 21 (Spring, 1958).
17. Samuel Lothrop, "Further Notes on Indian Ceremonies in Guatemala," *Indian Notes* (New York: Heye Foundation), VI, No. 1 (1929).

Selected Bibliography

Primary Sources

Redfield, Robert. "War Sketches." *Poetry* 12 (August 1918): 242-243.

———. "Anthropology, A Natural Science?" *Social Forces* 4 (June 1926): 715-721.

———. "A Plan for the Study of Tepoztlán, Morelos." Ph.D. diss., University of Chicago, 1928.

———. "Among the Middle Americans." *University of Chicago Magazine* 20 (March 1928): 242-247.

———. *Tepoztlán, A Mexican Village: A Study of Folk Life*. Chicago: University of Chicago Press, 1930.

———. "The Regional Aspect of Culture." *Publications of the American Sociological Society* 24, no. 2 (1930): 33-41.

———. "Sociological Investigation in Yucatan." In *Carnegie Institution of Washington, Year Book 30*, 122-124. Washington, D.C.: Carnegie Institution of Washington, 1931.

———. "Ethnological Research." In *Carnegie Institution of Washington Year Book 31*, 111-114. Washington, D.C.: Carnegie Institution of Washington, 1932.

———. "Sociological Study." In *Carnegie Institution of Washington Year Book 32*, 100-104. Washington, D.C.: Carnegie Institution of Washington, 1933.

———. "Culture Changes in Yucatan." *American Anthropologist* 36 (January-March 1934): 57-69.

———. "The Long Road Back." *University of Chicago Magazine* 27 (February 1935): 131-134.

———. "The Second Epilogue to Maya History." *Hispanic American Historical Review* 17 (May 1937): 170-181.

———. Review of *Man and Culture*, 6th ed., by Clark Wissler. *American Journal of Sociology* 44 (November 1938): 477.

———. Introduction to *St. Denis: A French Canadian Parish*, by Horace Miner. Chicago: University of Chicago Press, 1939.

———. "Primitive Merchants of Guatemala." *Quarterly Journal of Inter-American Relations* 1 (October 1939): 42-56.

———. "The Folk Society and Culture." *American Journal of Sociology* 45 (March 1940): 731-742.

———. *The Folk Culture of Yucatan*. Chicago: University of Chicago Press, 1941.

____. "The Folk Society." *American Journal of Sociology* 52 (January 1947): 293-308.
____. *A Village That Chose Progress: Chan Kom Revisited*. Chicago: University of Chicago Press, 1950.
____. Interview by Anne Roe, 1950, Anne Roe Papers, American Philosophical Library, Philadelphia.
____. "The Frontier of Underdeveloped Areas." In *Frontiers for Freedom*, edited by R. Gordon Hoxie. Denver: University of Denver Press, 1952.
____. "Social-Science Research in General Education." *Journal of General Education* 6 (January 1952): 81-91.
____. "The Primitive World View." *Proceedings of the American Philosophical Society* 96 (February 1952): 30-36.
____. *The Primitive World and Its Transformations*. Ithaca, N.Y.: Cornell University Press, 1953.
____. "Relations of Anthropology to the Social Sciences and to the Humanities." In *Anthropology Today: An Encyclopedic Inventory*, edited by A. L. Kroeber, 728-738. Chicago: University of Chicago Press, 1953.
____. "The Natural History of the Folk Society." *Social Forces* 31 (March 1953): 224-229.
____. "Community Studies in Japan and China: A Symposium." *Far Eastern Quarterly* 14 (November 1954): 3-10.
____. *The Little Community: Viewpoints for the Study of a Human Whole*. Chicago: University of Chicago Press, 1955.
____. "The Social Organization of Tradition." *Far Eastern Quarterly* 15 (November 1955): 13-21.
____. "Societies and Cultures as Natural Systems." *Journal of the Royal Anthropological Institute of Great Britain and Ireland* 85 (January-December 1955): 19-32.
____. *Peasant Society and Culture: An Anthropological Approach to Civilization*. Chicago: University of Chicago Press, 1956.
____. "The Relations between Indians and Ladinos in Agua Escondida, Guatemala." *America Indigena* 16 (October 1956): 253-276.
____. *The Papers of Robert Redfield: Human Nature and the Study of Society*, vol. 1. Edited by Margaret Park Redfield. Chicago: University of Chicago, 1962.
____. *The Papers of Robert Redfield: The Social Uses of Social Science*, vol. 2. Edited by Margaret Park Redfield. Chicago: University of Chicago Press, 1963.
Redfield, Robert, Ralph Linton, and Melville J. Herskovits. "Memorandum for the Study of Acculturation." *American Anthropologist* 38 (January-March 1936): 149-152.
Redfield, Robert, and Milton Singer. Foreword to *Studies in Chinese Thought*, edited by Arthur F. Wright, v-viii. Chicago: University of Chicago Press, 1953.
____. "The Cultural Role of Cities." *Economic Development and Cultural Change* 3 (October 1954): 53-73.

_____. Foreword to *Village India: Studies in the Little Community*, edited by McKim Marriott. Chicago: University of Chicago Press, 1955.

Redfield, Robert, and Alfonso Villa Rojas. *Chan Kom: A Maya Village*. Washington, D.C.: Carnegie Institution of Washington, 1934; reprint, Chicago: University of Chicago Press, 1962.

Secondary Sources

Arensberg, Conrad M., and Solon T. Kimball. *Culture and Community*. New York: Harcourt, Brace & World, 1963.

Beeman, Richard R. "The New Social History and the Search for 'Community' in Colonial America." *American Quarterly* 29 (Fall 1977): 422-443.

Bell, Colin, and Howard Newby. *Community Studies: An Introduction to the Sociology of the Local Community*. New York: Praeger, 1972.

Bender, Thomas. *Community and Social Change in America*. New Brunswick, N.J.: Rutgers University Press, 1978; reprint, Baltimore: Johns Hopkins University Press, 1982.

Bock, Philip K. "Tepoztlán Reconsidered." *Journal of Latin American Lore* 6 (Summer 1980): 129-150.

Brick, Howard. *Age of Contradiction: American Thought and Culture in the 1960s*. New York: Twayne Publishers, 1998; reprint, Ithaca, N.Y.: Cornell University Press, 2000.

Cappetti, Carla. *Writing Chicago: Modernism, Ethnography, and the Novel*. New York: Columbia University Press, 1993.

Cole, Fay-Cooper, and Fred Eggan. "Robert Redfield, 1897-1958." *American Anthropologist* 61 (August 1959): 652-662.

Collins, June, Everett C. Hughes, James B. Griffin, and Margaret Mead, discussants. "American Ethnology: The Role of Redfield." In *American Anthropology: The Early Years, 1974 Proceedings of the American Ethnological Society*, edited by John V. Murra, 139-145. St. Paul, Minn.: West Publishing, 1974.

Davis, Richard H. *South Asia at Chicago: A History*. Chicago: Committee on Southern Asian Studies, University of Chicago, 1985.

Delpar, Helen. *The Enormous Vogue of Things Mexican: Cultural Relations between the United States and Mexico, 1920-1935*. Tuscaloosa: University of Alabama Press, 1992.

De Waal Malefijt, Annemarie. *Images of Man: A History of Anthropological Thought*. New York: Alfred A. Knopf, 1974.

Dumond, D. E. "Competition, Cooperation, and the Folk Society." *Southwestern Journal of Anthropology* 26 (Autumn 1970): 261-286.

Fisher, Berenice M., and Anselm L. Strauss. "The Chicago Tradition and Social Change: Thomas, Park, and Their Successors." *Symbolic Interaction* 1 (Spring 1978): 5-23.

Fox, Richard G. *Urban Anthropology: Cities in Their Cultural Settings*. Englewood Cliffs, N.J.: Prentice Hall, 1977.

French, Robert Mills, ed. *The Community in Perspective*. Itasca, Ill.: F. E. Peacock, 1969.

Godoy, Ricardo. "The Background and Context of Redfield's *Tepoztlán*." *Journal of the Steward Anthropological Society* 10 (Fall 1978): 47-79.

Goldkind, Victor. "Social Stratification in the Peasant Community: Redfield's Chan Kom Reinterpreted." *American Anthropologist* 67 (August 1965): 863-884.

———. "Class Conflict and Cacique in Chan Kom." *Southwestern Journal of Anthropology* 22 (Winter 1966): 325-345.

Hansen, Asael T. "Robert Redfield, the Yucatan Project, and I." In *American Anthropology: The Early Years, 1974 Proceedings of the American Ethnological Society*, edited by John V. Murra, 167-186. St. Paul, Minn.: West Publishing, 1976.

Hauser, Philip M., and Leo F. Schnore, eds. *The Study of Urbanization*. New York: John Wiley & Sons, 1965.

Hewitt de Alcántara, Cynthia. *Anthropological Perspectives on Rural Mexico*. London: Routledge & Kegan Paul, 1984.

Hoover, Dwight. "The Long Ordeal of Modernization Theory." *Prospects* 11 (1986): 407-451.

Kadel, Kathryn Jean. "Little Community to the World: The Social Vision of Robert Redfield, 1897-1958." Ph.D. diss., Northern Illinois University, DeKalb, Ill., 2000.

Kleiman, Jordan. "Modernization." In *A Companion to American Thought*, edited by Richard W. Fox and James T. Kloppenberg. Cambridge, Mass.: Blackwell, 1995.

König, René. *The Community*. Translated by Edward Fitzgerald. London: Routledge & Kegan Paul, 1968.

Leslie, Charles M. "Redfield, Robert." In *International Encyclopedia of the Social Sciences*, edited by David L. Sills. New York: Macmillan and Free Press, 1968.

———. "The Hedgehog and the Fox in Robert Redfield's Work and Career." In *American Anthropology: The Early Years, 1974 Proceedings of the American Ethnological Society*, edited by John V. Murra, 146-166. St. Paul, Minn.: West Publishing, 1976.

Lessa, W. A. "Folk Culture." In *A Dictionary of the Social Sciences*, edited by Julius Gould and William L. Kolb. New York: Free Press of Glencoe, 1964.

Lewis, Oscar. *Life in a Mexican Village: Tepoztlán Restudied*. Urbana: University of Illinois Press, 1951.

Paine, Robert. "A Critique of the Methodology of Robert Redfield: 'Folk Culture' and Other Concepts." *Ethnos* 31, no. 1 (1966): 161-172.

Pells, Richard H. *Radical Visions and American Dreams: Culture and Social Thought in the Depression Years*. New York: Harper & Row, 1973; reprint, Middletown, Conn.: Wesleyan University Press, 1984.

Potter, Jack, May N. Diaz, and George M. Foster, eds. *Peasant Society: A Reader*. Boston: Little, Brown & Company, 1967.

Redfield, James. "Redfield, Robert." In *Thinkers of the Twentieth Century*, edited by Roland Turner. 2d ed. Chicago: St. James Press, 1987.

Rees, David A., ed. *The Ethnographic Moment: Correspondence of Robert Redfield and F.G. Friedmann* (New Brunswick, N.J.: Transaction Publishers, 2006.
Reissman, Leonard. *The Urban Process: Cities in Industrial Societies.* New York: Free Press, 1964.
Rubinstein, Robert A., ed. *Fieldwork: The Correspondence of Robert Redfield and Sol Tax.* Boulder, Colo.: Westview Press, 1991.
Sartori, Andrew. "Robert Redfield's Comparative Civilizations Project and the Political Imagination of Postwar America." *Positions* 6, no. 1 (1998): 33-65.
Singer, Milton. "Robert Redfield: Anthropologist." *Man in India* 39 (April-June 1959): 81-91.
_____. "Robert Redfield's Development of a Social Anthropology of Civilizations." In *American Anthropology: The Early Years,* 1974 Proceedings of the American Ethnological Society, edited by John V. Murra, 187-260. St. Paul, Minn.: West Publishing, 1976.
_____. "Robert Redfield." In *Remembering the University of Chicago,* edited by Edward Shils, 413-429. Chicago: University of Chicago Press, 1991.
_____. "Redfield, Robert." In *International Dictionary of Anthropologists,* edited by Christopher Winters. New York: Garland, 1991.
Sollors, Werner. "Anthropological and Sociological Tendencies in American Literature of the 1930s and 1940s: Richard Wright, Zora Neale Hurston, and American Culture." In *Looking Inward, Looking Outward: From the 1930s through the 1940s.* European Contributions to American Studies 18, edited by Steve Ickringill, 22-75. Amsterdam: VU University Press, 1990.
Stocking, George W., Jr. "Pedants and Potentates: Robert Redfield at the 1930 Hanover Conference." *History of Anthropology Newsletter* 5, no. 2 (1978): 10-13.
_____. *Anthropology at Chicago: Tradition, Discipline, Department.* Chicago: Joseph Regenstein Library of the University of Chicago, 1979.
_____. "Redfield, Robert." In *Dictionary of American Biography,* supplement 6. Edited by John A. Garraty. New York: Charles Scribner's Sons, 1980.
_____. "Ideal Types and Aging Glands: Robert Redfield's Response to Oscar Lewis's Critique of Tepoztlán." *History of Anthropology Newsletter* 16 (June 1989): 3-10.
_____. *The Ethnographer's Magic and Other Essays in the History of Anthropology.* Madison: University of Wisconsin Press, 1992.
Strickon, Arnold. "Hacienda and Plantation in Yucatan: An Historical-Ecological Consideration of the Folk-Urban Continuum in Yucatan." *America Indigena* 25 (January 1965): 35-63.
Sullivan, Paul. *Unfinished Conversations: Mayas and Foreigners between Two Wars.* New York: Alfred A. Knopf, 1989.
Susman, Warren I. *Culture as History: The Transformation of American Society in the Twentieth Century.* New York: Pantheon, 1984.
Tarn, Nathaniel. "The Literate and the Literary: Notes on the Anthropological Discourse of Robert Redfield." In *Views from the Weaving Mountain:*

Selected Essays in Poetics and Anthropology. Albuquerque: University of New Mexico Press, 1991.
Vincent, Joan. *Anthropology and Politics: Visions, Traditions, and Trends*. Tucson: University of Arizona Press, 1990.
Weaver, Thomas. "From Primitive to Urban Anthropology," in *Crisis in Anthropology: View from Spring Hill, 1980*. eds. E. Adamson Hoebel, Richard Currier, and Susan Kaiser. New York: Garland, 1982.
Wilcox, Clifford. "Encounters with Modernity: Robert Redfield and the Problem of Social Change." Ph.D. diss., University of Michigan, 1997.
____. *Robert Redfield and the Development of American Anthropology* (Lanham, Md.: Lexington Books, 2004).
Wolf, Eric R. *Anthropology*. Englewood Cliffs, N.J.: Prentice Hall; reprint, New York: W. W. Norton, 1973.
____. *Peasants*. Englewood Cliffs, N.J.: Prentice Hall, 1966.

Note

For a much fuller listing of Redfield's writings and secondary sources related to Redfield's work, see the bibliography in Wilcox, *Robert Redfield and the Development of American Anthropology*, 189-225.

Index

acculturation, 20, 31, 48, 87, 228
Alcalá, 170, 261
Altekar, A. S., 142
"Alternatives," 64-65,178; associated with interdependence of elements of a culture, 66-67
American Journal of Sociology, 85, 97
Andaman islanders, 102-103, 163, 207-210, 255, 260
anomie, xix
anthropology, comparative method, 35; cultural, 31; functional, 19; social, xiii, xvi, xxv, 30, 33n7, 124; and sociology, 85-87; urban, xxix, 157, 227; and Western civilization, 137
Aranda, 207
Arapesh, 199-202, 205
Arensberg, Conrad, 164
Armillas, Pedro, 211
Aztecs, 44

Barnes, J. A., 160-162, 164-166, 168-169
Benedict, Ruth, xiii, 87, 91, 195; *Patterns of Culture*, 157-158
Bharat Mata (Mother India), 243-244
Boas, Franz, xiii, xvii, xxv, xxxn1, 3-5, 17-18, 25; community studies, use of, xvii; *see also* Redfield, Robert, challenge to Franz Boas; *Anthropology: A Lecture Delivered at Columbia University, December 18, 1907*, 17; "The Limitations of the Comparative Method of Anthropology," 18
Boeke, J. H., 148
Boorstin, Daniel, 199, 202
Braidwood, Robert, xxi, 138, 144
Bremnes, 160-162, 165
Buck, Peter, 40
Buddhism, 214
Bunzel, Ruth, 201

Burgess, Ernest, xvi; *Introduction to the Science of Sociology*, 4-5

Case, C. M. *Outlines of Sociology*, 4
Carnegie Institution of Washington, xviii, 35, 43; *Year Book*, xxvi
cenote, 181-185
Chan Kom, xviii, 36-37, 58, 64-66, 69, 73, 76, 177, 179-181, 261-262
Chicago, xvi
"Chicago School" of sociology, xv-xvii, xxxin6, 13; as defined by Robert E. Park, 40
Chichen Itzá, 36, 213
Chichicastenango, 101, 163
Childe, V. Gordon, 135, 146
China, 212, 214
city (cities), as center of innovation, 246; and civilization, 137-138, 227-249; and folk society, 233-235; and Great Tradition, 233; heterogenetic, xxix, 234; orthogenetic, xxix, 234, 238, 240; orthogenetic versus heterogenetic, 232, 238, 240; symbolism of, 229
civilization, 1920s critique of, xiv-xv, xxx-xxxin3; centers of, 228-229; as compound, 216-217; and culture, 131; defined, 254; Maya, 211-212; in Mesoamerica, 211-212; modern industrial, 20-21, 30, 36-37, 91; origins of, 136; and peasants, 135, 207-225; primary and secondary, 212-213; process of, 20-21, 36, 48, 66, 88, 137, 148, 207-225; as a "complex," 20, 30; as a structure, 254, 256, 257; Western, xv, 20, 22, 26, 30, 50, 137
civilizations, comparative study of, xiv, xxi, xxiii-xxv, xxviii-xxx, 177, 207, 253; "clash of," xiv

272 Social Anthropology

Code of Hammurabi, 146
Cold War, xiv
Cohn, Bernard, 256
community studies, xxviii, 35; methodology, xx
Conde, Jesus, 15-16
Confucianism, 214
Confucius, 210
Copan, 212
Coorgs, 219
Cornell University, 135
correctos, xviii, 124-127; *see also tontos*
corrido, 29-30
culture (cultures), areas, 124; as autonomous system, 208; and civilization, 56, 131, 209-210; core, 236; folk, 65, 209; hierarchic and lay, 209-211; 214-217; high and low, 209; intermediate, 123; of Maya, 211; as "organized body of conventional understandings," 63-64, 67-68, 103, 131; peasant, 208; sacred, 235; transformation to civilization, xvi, 236; and world view, 195
cultural change, xx, 231, 246-247

Dahomey, 169, 210, 255
Dewey, John, xv
diffusion, 18-21, 30, 32, 54, 147, 246; changes in Yucatan conceived as, 73, 76; in Tepoztlán, 124-127
disorganization, cultural, xx, 32, 60; causes of, 62, 67, 76-78; correlation with lessening isolation and homogeneity, 58, 60, 116; in relation to increase of subcultures, 66; and secularization, 77-78; *see also* disorganization, social
disorganization, social, xix-xx; as defined by Thomas and Znaniecki, 71
Dogon, 259-261
Dopsch, Alfons, 230
Durkheim, Emile, xvi, xix, 57, 61, 72, 89, 99, 131; and definition of sacred, 68-70
Dzitas, xviii, 58, 64, 66, 71, 73, 74, 76, 177-178, 262

Eberhard, Wolfram, 235
Economic Development and Cultural Change, 227

Eliot, T. S., xv
Embree, John, *Suye Mura: A Japanese Village*, 88
ethnographic present, xvii
ethos, xxiii, 152, 195, 240
evolution, *see* social evolution
existentialism, 199

Faris, Ellsworth, 86
Fei, Hsaio-Tung, 139
Firth, Raymond, 223
Fitzgerald, F. Scott, xv
folk, xviii, xxvii; culture, characterized, 66; culture, transformation, 211, 241; defined, 25-27; mentioned by Linton, 65; Mexican, 25-27, 31; as peasant society, 88, 123; versus primitive society, 208; society, 85, 92, 97-118, 233-248; transformation into civilization, 22, 31, 37, 56, 65-66, 124, 133, 135-153, 235-238, 247; as type, 97-99, 140, 144; versus urban society, 98; *see also* culture, folk
folk-urban continuum, xx, xxvi-xxvii, xxxin13, 39, 57, 85
folkways, 106
Ford Foundation, xxii, 253
Foster, George, 208-209, 212
Francis, E. K. L., 143-144
Frankfort, Henri, xxi, 203
functionalism, 157

Galen, 209
Gamio, Manuel, 14
Gemeinschaft and Gesellschaft, xx, 89, 98
Goldenweiser, A. A., 98
Great Tradition(s), 233, 237, 239, 240, 241, 244; and folk culture, 241; Hindu, 220; and Little Tradition(s), xxii-xxiv, xxviii-xxix, 207, 209, 227, 229, 238, 242, 243, 246, 253
Griaule, Marcel, 210, 259
Gruening, Ernest, 25
Grunebaum, G. von, 215-216, 222
Guatemalan highlands, impersonal character of societies in, 79-80; individualistic character of, 71, 78-81; secular character of, 78-81; villages in as folk societies, 101

Hansen, Asael T., 37, 43, 54, 60, 178

Hanssen, Börje, 164
Harper, William Rainey, 146
Harris, Chauncey, 235
Harvard University, xv
Herskovits, Melville J., xiii; *Dahomey, An Ancient West African Kingdom*, 158
Hesiod, *Works and Days*, 143-144
Heterogenetic, *see* cities, heterogenetic
Hippocrates, 209
Holmberg, Allen R., 198, 258
Hopi, 163
Hoselitz, Bert, 227, 230
Hutchins, Robert Maynard, xxi

ideal type, *see* type, ideal
idiographic, *see* social science, idiographic
immigrants, Mexican, 14, 20
India, 167-168, 177, 212-217, 219, 222, 254
individualization, xix-xx, 58; causes of, 74, 76-78, correlation with lessening isolation and homogeneity, 58, 60, 116
Introduction to the Science of Sociology, 4; see also Park, Robert E.
Ireland, 164

Jacobsen, Thorkild, xxi, 200, 202
James, William, xv
Jefferson, Thomas, 202

Kidder, A. V., 213
Kimball, Solon T., 164
Kishan Garhi, 167, 220-221
Koran, 210, 216
Kroeber, A. L., xxi, 7, 19, 31; *Anthropology*, 6; review of *Primitive Society* by Robert Lowie, 10n12
Kwakiutl, 146

Laksmi, 220
de Landa, Diego, 44, 47, 50
Latin America, peasant societies in, 208
Lewis, Oscar, 166, 177
LeTourneau, Roger, 222
Linton, Ralph, 64-66 (*The Study of Man*)
literati, 146-147, 230, 231, 236, 241-243

Little Tradition(s), transformation into Great Tradition(s), 229; *see also* Great Tradition
Longyear, John, 212
Lothrop, Samuel, 263
Lowie, Robert, 108; *Primitive Religion*, 19; *Primitive Society*, 10
Lynd, Robert S. and Helen, *Middletown*, 87

Madras, 223
magic, 112; black, 54, 58
Mahabharata, 223, 244
Maine, Henry Sumner, 57, 61, 72, 89, 98, 108, 139
Malinowski, Bronislaw, 19, 31, 157; "functional anthropology," 19
Maori, 210, 255, 259
marginality, marginal man, 147, 236
Marrett, R. R., 203
Marriott, McKim, 167, 220-222, 256
Matthews, Fred H., xxxin4
Maya, xxii, 36-37, 44-50, 80, 140-141, 163, 211
Maximon, 263
McBryde, Webster, 164
Mead, George Herbert, xxiii, 196
Mead, Margaret, xiii, 158, 159, 198-201
Mendelson, Michael, 262-263
Mérida, xviii-xix, 37, 41-42, 49, 54, 58, 60, 65-67, 71, 74, 76-77, 116, 178
Merton, Robert, xviii
Mesoamerica, 211-212, 249n4
Mesopotamia, xxi
Mexico, post-revolutionary, xvii; villages, xvii, 25
Mexico City, xvii, 14-15
milpa, 53, 69, 181, 183-186, 191-192
Miner, Horace, 170, *St. Denis: A French Canadian Parish,* xxvii, 88, 129-133
modernity, xviii, 25
modernization, xviii, xxv-xxvi, 20, 27, 30, 37, 227, 249
moral order, 144, 148, 149, 150, 151, 205, 232, 234-235, 240; of Maya, 211; *see also* technical order
Morelos, Mexico, 16
Morgan, Lewis Henry, *League of the Iroquois*, 87

Morocco, 216, 222

Nahuatl, 16
Narayan, 221
national character, xxiii, 195
Navajo, 111, 139, 152
Nehru, Jawaharlal, (*Discovery of India*), 243-244
Nigeria, 165, 210
nomothetic, *see* social science, nomothetic
Northrop, F. S. C., xxi, 195, 251-252n32
Norway, 160, 161, 170

Oikumenê, universal, 231
Orthogenetic, *see* cities, orthogenetic

Papago, 104, 105, 111
Park, Robert E., 3, 14; education, xv; influence on Redfield, xiv-xvi, xxvi, xxxin4; *Introduction to the Science of Sociology*, 4-5; on "Chicago School" of sociology, *see* "Chicago School" of sociology
"parochialization," 221
Parsons, Talcott, xxv
peasant(s), 26, 207; culture, 208; defined, 123, 129; as folk society, 88, 123; Indian villages, 220; Latin American, 208-209; as part society, 208; relationship to cities, 130-131, 138-139, 141; relationship to civilization, 135, 142, 235; societies, 157, 160; society as hinge, 161; studies, xxiv-xxv, xxvii-xxviii, xxx, 123, 129, 157; as synchronic system, 208; as type, 138, 144; and writing, 142-143
Perry, W. J., 9
Persia, 216
Pierson, Donald, 170
Pirenne, Henri, 230
Pitt-Rivers, J. A., 170, 261
"primitive," definition as used in *Folk Culture of Yucatan* study, 62
Proceedings of the American Philosophical Association, xxix
Puerto Rico, 159
Purana(s), 214, 220-221, 223, 243

Quebec, 131

Quintana Roo, 37, 49-50, 76-77, 79-80, 141-142, 149, 178, 180

racism, xiii
Radcliffe-Brown, A. R., 102, 124, 140, 157, 210; *The Andaman Islanders*, 102-103
Radin, Paul, 106
Raghavan, V., 214, 216, 218, 222
Ramayana, 214, 218, 223
Redfield, Margaret Park, "Greta," 14-16, 37, 43
Redfield, Robert, and ambulance corps (WWI), xv; anthropology, conception of, xiii-xiv; challenge to Franz Boas, xiii, xvii, xxv-xxvi, 17-18, 25; "Chicago School" of sociology, influence of, xv-xvii; civilization, 1920s critique of, xiv-xv; collaboration with Milton Singer, xxix; community studies, use of, xvii; comparative civilizations studies, xiv, xxi-xxiv, xxviii-xxx; education, xiv-xv; ethnographic method of, 20-21; Park, Robert E., influence of, xiv-xvii, xxvi, 39; University of Chicago, career, xviii, xx-xxi, xxvii, 39; curricular reform of 1930s to 1940s, xxi; "The Folk Society" course, 39; Mexico, travels in, xvi-xvii; Tepoztlán, dissertation research, xvii, xxv, 13-16, 17, 25, 88, 123-127; Yucatan studies, xviii-xix, xxii, xxxin10, 43, 48, 50, 57; World War I, experience in, xv
Works: "Among the Middle Americans," xxv; "Anthropology, A Natural Science?," xxv; *Chan Kom: A Maya Village*, xxii; "Civilizations as Societal Structures? The Development of Community Studies," xxix, 253; "Civilizations as Things Thought About," xxix, 253; "The Cultural Role of Cities," xxix; "Culture Changes in Yucatan," xxvi; *The Folk Culture of Yucatan*, xix-xx, xxii, xxvii, xxviii, xxxin13, 57, 177; "The Folk Society," xxvii; "The Folk Society and Culture," xxvii, 97; "A Plan for the Study of Tepoztlán, Morelos," xxv; *Peasant Society and Culture: An Anthropological Approach to Civilization*, xxiii, xxviii; "The Primitive

World View," xxviii, 253; *The Primitive World and Its Transformations*, xxii, xxix, 195, 253; "Sociological Investigation in Yucatan," xxvi, 39; *Tepoztlán, A Mexican Village: A Study of Folk Life*, xvii-xviii, xxvi-xxvii, 35, 123, 129

Revista Mexicana de Sociología, 97

revolution, food-producing, 135; urban, 135

Rig-Veda, 243

Rivers, W. H. R., 9, 87; *Social Organization*, 9; *Medicine, Magic, and Religion*, 9

sacred, 90; center, 244, 249; culture, 235; as defined by Durkheim, 68; definition of, 68-69; geography, 244; and Great Tradition, 238; and orthogenetic cities, 242; scriptures, 242, 244; sacred versus secular, 68-70

Saladin, 215

Sanders, Irwin T., 170

Sankarcharya, 214

Sanskritization, 254

Sapir, Edward, xv; "Time Perspective in Aboriginal American Culture: A Study in Method," 8

Sartre, Jean Paul, 199

secular versus sacred; *see* sacred versus secular

secularization, xix-xx, 54; causes of, 62, 76-78; correlation with lessening isolation and homogeneity, 58, 60, 74, 116; and disorganization, 77-78; in connection with religion, 68-70; *see also* disorganization, cultural

Shaivism, 217

Simmel, Georg, xv, 90

Singer, Milton, xxix, 222-223, 227, 253-254, 256; "The Cultural Role of Cities," ; see also Redfield, Robert, Works

Siriono, 198, 258, 260

Sjoberg, Gideon, 172

Smith, Adam, 245

Smith, Elliott, 9

Smith, Marian, 167

social change, study of, xvi-xvii, xx, xxiv-xxv, 17-21, 30-31, 35-36, 39, 43, 123-127, 133, 135

social evolution, xiii, 17-18

"social fields," 160-165

Social Forces, 13

social organization, 41, 223

social processes, *see* social change

social science, idiographic, xv; nomothetic, xv, xvii

Social Science Research Council, 14

society, modern, 25, 61, 99; *see also* civilization, modern industrial

Sombart, Werner, 90

Sorokin, Pitirim, xxi, 136, 143

Spencer, Herbert, xvi

Spengler, Oswald, xv, 136; *Decline of the West*, xxi

Srinivas, M. N., 219, 254

Steward, Julian, 100, 158-160

Stocking, George W., Jr., xxxn1

Sumner, William Graham, 89, 100

Susman, Warren, xxxin3

Swarthmore College, 157

syncretization, 220

"taman" (piety), 192, 193

Taoism, 214, 217

Tax, Sol, 43, 64, 72-73, 81, 90

technical order, 148-151, 232, 235, 239-240

Teggart, F. J., *The Processes of History*, 4, 41

Tepoztlán, Mexico, xvii, 13-16, 31, 207; methodology of study, 123-127; periphery of change within, 124-125

Thomas, W. I., xvi; *The Polish Peasant in Europe and America*, 86

Tiv, 165, 210

Tönnies, Ferdinand, xvi, xix, 57, 61, 72, 89, 99; *see also* Gemeinschaft and Gesellschaft

tontos, xviii, 124-127; *see also* correctos

Toynbee, Arnold J., xxi, 135-136, 146-148, 150-152, 245, 248, 251-252n32

tradition, 25

Trilling, Lionel, 152

Trobriand islanders, 207, 209

Troyat, Henri, 144

Tusik, xviii, xix, 58, 66, 71, 73, 76, 177-178

Tylor, Edward B., 4-5, 18, 203

type, ideal, 59, 61; folk society as, 97-99, 114, 144; primitive society as, 89, 91
typical personality, 240

"Universal," 65
universals, human, 196
"universalization," 242
University of Berlin, xv
University of Chicago, anthropologists, 13; College, 97; Comparative Civilizations Program, 253; Oriental Institute, xxi; Social Science Research Building, 85
University of Chicago Magazine, 13
University of Hawaii, xxvi, 39
University of Heidelberg, xv
University of Michigan, xv
urbanization, 228; primary, 235-241; secondary 236-241

Vaishnavism, 217
values, 152, 195
variables, defined for *Folk Culture of Yucatan* study, 62
"Variants," 64-65
Vedas, 214, 216-217
Villa Rojas, Alfonso, xxii, 36-37, 43, 49-50, 141-142

War of the Castes, the, 76
Warner, W. Lloyd, 87, 92, 158-159
Washington, D.C., 40; *see also* Carnegie Institution of Washington
Weber, Max, xxv, 118, 146, 162
Westermarck, Edward, 216; *History of Human Marriage*, 5

Westernization, 228, 248
Wilson, John, xxi
Windelband, Wilhelm, xv
Wirth, Louis, xxvii; "Urbanism as a Way of Life," 82n5, 85, 97
Wissler, Clark, 18, 30, 31, 87; *Man and Culture*, 9, 19
Wittfogel, Karl, 136
world view, xxii-xxiii, 195-196, 240; and civilization, 205; Arapesh versus Zuñi, 200; defined, 177, 196; existentialism as, 199; and God, xxiii, 197; Hebrew versus Greek, 200, 204; Maya, 200; Mesopotamian, 200; and moral order, 204-205; and nature, xxiii, 197; "primitive," 202-204; of Santiago Atitlán, Guatemala, 117, 262-263; self as axis, xxiii, 196; structure of, 257-258; studies, xxiv, xxviii, 177, 195; as "system of ideas," 179; universal categories within, 197-199; Yucatecan, 260; *see also* national character

X-Cacal, 69, 180

Yucatan, xviii, xix, xxvi, 35, 39-40, 42-81, 90, 115-116, 149, 212; history of, how analyzed in *Folk Culture of Yucatan* study, 58-59

Zapata, Emiliano, 16
Znaniecki, Florian, 71; *The Polish Peasant in Europe and America*, 86
Zuñi, 114, 163, 166, 200-202, 205, 207-208, 224